Photoshop Elements 3

for Windows

one-on-one™

D1714526

Advance Praise for *Photoshop Elements 3 for Windows One-on-One*

"With Photoshop Elements for Windows One-on-One, Deke has woven text and video to create a whole new approach to hands-on learning. No showing off, no dumb pet tricks, just plenty of useful information that you can apply to your own images and make them look better. Whether you're a student or a teacher, you won't be able to stop turning the pages to see what pearls of wisdom lie ahead!"

—Katrin Eismann
Author, *Photoshop Masking & Compositing* and
Photoshop Restoration & Retouching
www.photoshopdiva.com

"It's obvious to see why Deke is one of the most popular teachers of Photoshop Elements. Stepping through the exercises in this book, you feel like he's right there with you. It's really one-on-one!"

—Julieanne Kost
Photoshop Evangelist, Adobe Systems
www.adobeevangelists.com

Also from Deke Press

Adobe Photoshop CS One-on-One
Adobe InDesign CS One-on-One

Photoshop Elements 3

for Windows

one-on-one™

DEKE McCLELLAND

WITH GALEN FOTT

deke™
PRESS
O'REILLY®

BEIJING • CAMBRIDGE • FARNHAM • KÖLN • PARIS • SEBASTOPOL • TAIPEI • TOKYO

Photoshop Elements 3 for Windows One-on-One

by Deke McClelland with Galen Fott

This title is published by Deke Press in association with O'Reilly Media, Inc., 1005 Gravenstein Highway North, Sebastopol, CA 95472.

O'Reilly Media books may be purchased for educational, business, or sales promotional use. Online editions are also available for most titles (*safari.oreilly.com*). For more information, contact O'Reilly's corporate/institutional sales department: 800-998-9938 or *corporate@oreilly.com*.

Managing Editor:	Carol Person	**Video Directors:**	Denise Maffitt
Associate Editor:	Deb Cameron	**CD Producer:**	Barbara Ross
Copyeditor:	Susan Pink, Techright	**Video Editors:**	Denis Logan and Barbara Stillwell
Indexer:	Julie Hawks	**CD Graphic Designer:**	Barbara Driscoll
Technical Editors:	Jason S. Woliner	**Video Compression:**	Carey Matthew Brady
Production Manager:	Claire Cloutier	**Video Interface Programmers:**	Melissa Symolon and Marc Johnson
Cover Designer:	Emma Colby	**CD Quality Assurance:**	Anthony Packes
Interior Designer:	David Futato		

Print History:

April 2005:   First edition.

Special thanks to John Bell, Brian Maffitt, Jerry Yen, Dave Murcott, Steve Johnson, J. Scott Klossner, Jodi Richter, Richard Lainhart, Dena Forster, Uncle Zeke, Mikkel Aaland, David Rogelberg, Sherry Rogelberg, Stacey Barone, Katrina Bevan, Sue Willing, Bill Takacs, Glenn Bisignani, Laurie Petrycki, Mark Brokering, Steve Weiss, and Tim O'Reilly as well as Patrick Lor, Val Gelineau, and the gangs at iStockPhoto.com, PhotoSpin, NAPP, Peachpit Press, and Adobe Systems. Extra special thanks to Amy Thomas Buscaglia and our relentlessly supportive families, without whom this series and this book would not be possible.

This book was typeset using Adobe InDesign CS and the Adobe Futura, Adobe Rotis, and Linotype Birka typefaces.

0-596-00844-9
[C]

RepKover™ This book uses RepKover™, a durable and flexible lay-flat binding.

For our
little elements,
Sam and Max.

CONTENTS

PREFACE

HOW ONE-ON-ONE WORKS

Welcome to *Photoshop Elements 3 for Windows One-on-One*, the third in a series of highly visual, full-color titles that combine step-by-step lessons with two hours of video instruction. As the name *One-on-One* implies, I walk you through Photoshop Elements 3 just as if I were teaching you in a classroom environment. Except that instead of getting lost in a crowd of students, you receive my individualized attention. It's just you and me.

I created *One-on-One* with three audiences in mind. If you're a digital photographer or graphic artist—professional or amateur—you'll appreciate the hands-on approach and the ability to set your own pace. If you're a student working in a classroom or vocational setting, you'll enjoy the personalized attention, structured exercises, and end-of-lesson quizzes. If you're an instructor in a college or vocational setting, you'll find the topic-driven lessons helpful in building curricula and creating homework assignments. *Photoshop Elements 3 for Windows One-on-One* is designed to suit the needs of beginners and intermediate users. But I've seen to it that each lesson contains a few techniques that even experienced users don't know.

Read, Watch, Do

Photoshop Elements 3 for Windows One-on-One is your chance to learn and have fun with Photoshop Elements under the direction of a professional trainer with 20 years of computer design and imaging experience. Read the book, watch the videos, do the exercises. Proceed at your own pace and experiment as you see fit. It's the best way to learn.

Figure 1.

Photoshop Elements 3 for Windows One-on-One contains twelve lessons, each made up of three to six step-by-step exercises. Every book-based lesson includes a corresponding video lesson (see Figure 1), in which I introduce the key concepts you'll need to know to complete the exercises. Best of all, every exercise is project-based, culminating in an actual finished document worthy of your labors (see Figure 2). The exercises include insights and context throughout, so you'll know not only what to do but, just as important, why you're doing it. My sincere hope is that you'll find the experience entertaining, informative, and empowering.

All the sample files required to perform the exercises are included on the CD-ROM at the back of this book. The CD also contains the video lessons. (This is a data CD, not a music CD or DVD. It won't work in a set-top device; it works only with a computer.) Don't lose or destroy this CD. It is as integral a part of your learning experience as the pages in this book. Together, the book, sample files, and videos form a single comprehensive training experience.

Start with a file...

follow the steps...

and end with an effect you're proud of.

Figure 2.

One-on-One Requirements

The main prerequisite to using *Photoshop Elements 3 for Windows One-on-One* is having Photoshop Elements 3 (see Figure 3) installed on your Microsoft Windows-based PC. If you're a Macintosh user, you may be wondering why this book excludes Apple's Mac OS X. After all, Adobe sells a Mac version of Photoshop Elements 3 as well. The problem is, Adobe chose to make the PC version of Photoshop Elements 3 so much more powerful. Only Elements for Windows includes the Organizer, an independent program that consumes most of Lessons 1, 11, and 12 of this book. If you prefer the Mac—and who can blame you?—you should be able to follow along with most of Lessons 2 through 10 without much problem. But that still leaves 25 percent of the book inaccessible to you. And frankly, I can't justify that. So I reckon, better to be honest and include the word *Windows* in the title of this book.

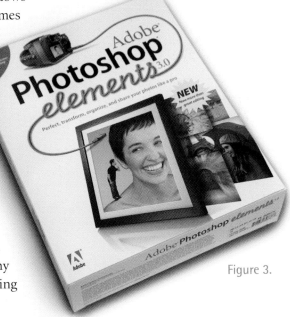

Figure 3.

Any computer that meets the minimum requirements for Photoshop Elements 3 also meets the requirements for using *Photoshop Elements 3 for Windows One-on-One*. Assuming you own a PC, you'll need an Intel Pentium III or 4 processor running Windows XP or Windows 2000 with Service Pack 4. If you own a Mac and you elect to take on this book despite my warnings, you need a PowerPC G3 processor or faster running Mac OS X version 10.2.8 or higher.

Regardless of platform, your computer must meet the following minimum requirements:

- 256MB of RAM
- 750MB of free hard disk space (600MB for Elements and 150MB for the *One-on-One* project and video application files)
- Color monitor with 16-bit color video card
- 1,024-by-768-pixel monitor resolution
- CD-ROM drive

To play the videos, you will need Apple's QuickTime Player software version 5.0.2 or later. Many computers come equipped with QuickTime; if yours does not, you will need to install QuickTime using the link provided on the CD included with this book.

Finally, you'll need to install the *One-on-One* project files and video software from the CD that accompanies this book, as explained in the next section.

One-on-One Installation and Setup

Photoshop Elements 3 for Windows One-on-One is designed to function as an integrated training environment. Therefore, before embarking on the lessons and exercises, you must first install a handful of files onto your computer's hard drive. These are:

- QuickTime Player software (if it is not already installed)
- All sample files used in the exercises (120MB in all)
- Total Training video training software
- Nearly 100 custom layer styles, which you'll be using throughout the exercises in this book

All of these files are provided on the CD that accompanies this book. To install the files, follow these steps:

1. *Quit the Organizer and Editor workspaces.* If Photoshop Elements is running on your computer, you must exit the program before you install the *One-on-One* files. Choose the **Exit** command from the **File** menu or press Ctrl+Q or Alt+F4.

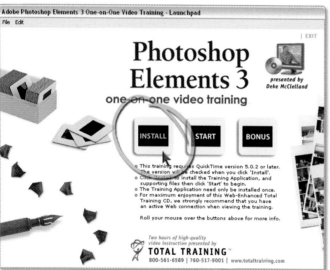

2. *Insert the One-on-One CD.* Remove the CD from the book and place it in your computer's CD or DVD drive.

3. *Open the Photoshop Elements 3 One-on-One Launchpad.* With any luck, the Launchpad window pictured in Figure 4 opens automatically. If it doesn't, choose **My Computer** from the **Start** menu. Then double-click the *PSE1ON1* CD icon in the ensuing window.

The Launchpad includes everything you need to install the files and play the videos to complete this training experience. You perform these operations by clicking one of the three slides, just below the words *one-on-one video training.*

Figure 4.

4. *If necessary, get QuickTime.* Click the **Install** slide to copy to your hard drive all the files required to complete the exercises in this book. The installer software starts by performing a compatibility test, to see whether QuickTime is running. If you see some clouds float by and hear some watery music, click the **Continue** button. If not, click **Get QuickTime** and follow the on-screen instructions. When you finish installing the Quick-Time software, proceed to the next step.

5. *Install all support and training files.* The installer software next displays a plain gray but highly informative **Installation** screen, which tells you that you have three steps ahead of you, two of which you can skip if you like (see Figure 5). Don't believe it—I want you to perform *all* of them. Here's a quick walk-through:

Figure 5.

- Click the **Continue** button to advance to the first step.

- Next comes the **Step 1** screen. By default, the installer wants to create a folder called *Lesson Files-PE3 1on1* on your computer's desktop. You'll need this folder to complete the exercises in this book. The desktop is the most convenient location for the lesson files, but if you'd like to put them elsewhere, click the **Browse** button and specify a location.

- Click the **Install** button. A progress bar tells you that the installer is writing a total of 116 files. A few moments later, a message tells you that the lesson files have been successfully copied, as in Figure 6. Click the **OK** button.

- At the **Step 2** screen, click the **Install** button once again. The installer copies the custom layer styles to Photoshop Elements' Presets folder. Click **OK** when this brief process completes. The styles will load the next time you start Elements' Editor workspace.

Figure 6.

- At the **Step 3** screen, click the **Install** button one last time. This installs the software required to run the video training, produced by Total Training and hosted by me. You see a progress bar for a few seconds and then another message tells you about another successful installation. Click **OK**.

- At the final screen, click the **Finish** button to return to the Launchpad (shown in Figure 4).

You should see a new folder called *Lesson Files-PE3 1on1* on your computer's desktop. You'll be referencing this folder a lot during the lessons in this book.

6. *Close the Launchpad (or don't).* We're finished with the Launchpad for the moment. If you like to keep your on-screen world tidy, close the Launchpad by clicking the **Exit** button in the top-right corner. But bear in mind, the Launchpad is your gateway to the videos. If you plan on watching them in the near future (as explained in the upcoming "Playing the Videos" section on page xvii), leave the Launchpad open.

7. *Check your screen resolution.* To use Elements effectively, your monitor should be set to display 1024 by 768 or more pixels. If it isn't, or you aren't quite sure, right-click an empty portion of your on-screen desktop. Then choose **Properties** from the shortcut menu. Click the **Settings** tab in the top-right corner of the **Display Properties** dialog box. Then increase the **Screen Resolution** setting to at least **1024 by 768 pixels** or as high as you can take it and still comfortably read type on-screen. Click the **OK** button. Your screen may flicker on and off. That's perfectly normal. Follow the instructions you see on-screen and you should be fine.

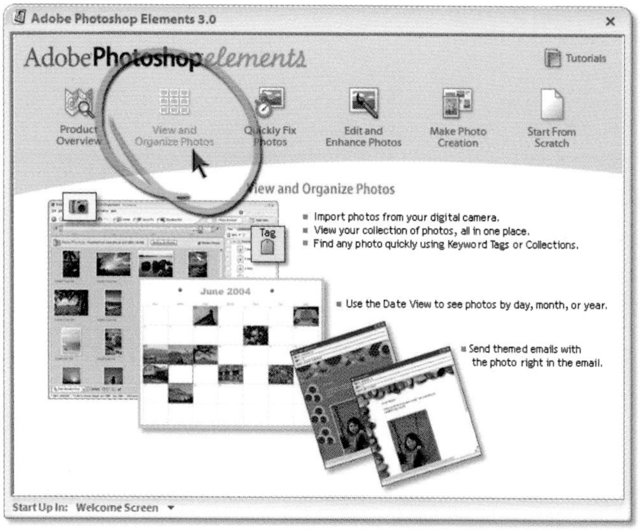

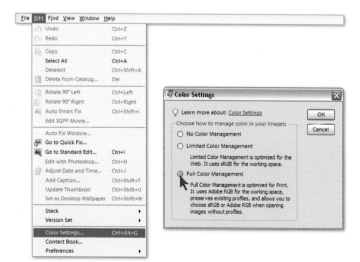

Figure 7.

8. *Start Photoshop Elements.* Double-click the **Adobe Photoshop Elements 3** program icon on your desktop or, if there isn't an icon, click the **Start** button and choose **Adobe Photoshop Elements 3**. (If you don't see the program listed on the left-hand side of the Start menu, you'll have to dig for it. It may be located in the **Programs** or **All Programs** submenu, possibly inside an **Adobe** submenu.)

9. *Launch the Organizer.* Unless you've specifically asked it to do otherwise, Elements starts you off on the Welcome screen. Click the **View and Organize Photos** button, which I've circled in Figure 7. This launches the Organizer workspace, which lets you organize images.

10. *Turn on color management.* Photoshop Elements ships with a killer color management engine that helps ensure that your colors remain consistent from one computer to another, as well as from your monitor to your printer. The problem is, it's turned off by default. Let's remedy that. Choose **Edit→Color Settings**. Inside the **Color Settings** dialog box, select the **Full Color Management** option (see Figure 8). To accept your changes, click the **OK** button. Now the colors of your images will match (or at least more closely match) those shown in the pages of this book.

Figure 8.

11. *Maximize the Organizer workspace.* Does the Organizer workspace take up your entire screen? If so, skip to the next step. If not, maximize the interface by clicking the ☐ icon in the upper-right corner of the window.

12. *Quit the Organizer.* You've come full circle. Choose **File→ Exit** or press Ctrl+Q. Quitting the Organizer not only closes the program but also saves the changes you made to the color settings and window size.

Congratulations, you and I are now in sync, and you're ready to begin following along with the exercises in this book.

Playing the Videos

At the outset of each book-based lesson, I ask you to play the companion video lesson from the CD. Ranging from 7 to 12 minutes apiece, these video lessons introduce key concepts that make more sense when first seen in action.

The fact that I provide these videos on CD may lead you to question their playback quality. If so, you're in for a surprise. Produced by the computer training pioneers at Total Training, each video is rendered at a resolution of 640 by 480 pixels, roughly the equivalent of broadcast television. (If the video looks smaller on your computer monitor, bear in mind that your monitor packs in way more pixels than a TV.) Total Training employs state-of-the-art capture technology and gold-standard Sorenson compression to pack these vivid, legible videos onto the relatively small space available on a CD. This is video training at its finest.

To watch a video, do the following:

1. *Insert the One-on-One CD.* You must have the CD in your computer's CD drive to watch a video.

2. *Open the Photoshop Elements 3 One-on-One Launchpad.* Again, the Launchpad window should open automatically on your PC. But if it doesn't, choose **My Computer** from the **Start** menu. Then double-click the *PSE1ON1* CD icon in the ensuing window.

3. *Click the Start button.* Click the button in the middle of the Launchpad, which is circled in Figure 9. Assuming that you installed the Total

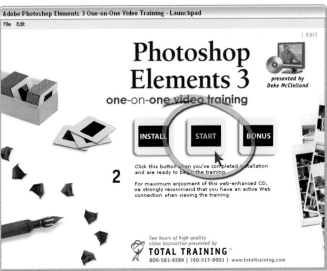

Figure 9.

Figure 10.

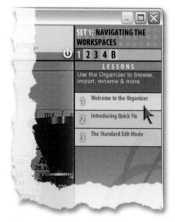

Figure 11.

Figure 12.

Training video training software as directed in Step 5 on page xv, you'll be treated to a startup screen (see Figure 10) followed by a welcoming message from your genial host, me.

4. *Switch to the video lesson you want to watch.* The thirteen videos are divided into four sets of three to four lessons each. To switch between sets, click one of the numbered buttons above the word Lessons in the upper-right corner of the player window: **1**, **2**, **3**, or **4**. (A fifth set, **B**, offers access to two bonus videos. I'll explain that button in just a moment.) To switch between lessons in a set, click a lesson name in the list below the set buttons, as in Figure 11. Set 1 contains Lessons 1 through 3; Set 2 contains Lessons 4 through 6; and so on. You can watch any video lesson in any order you like. However, the video lessons make the most sense and provide the most benefit when watched at the outset of the corresponding book-based lesson.

The video is surrounded by an interface of navigational buttons and play controls. To hide the interface and view only the video, move your cursor inside the video image; when the cursor changes into a magnifying glass, click. If you prefer to magnify the video so it fills your entire screen, press the Alt key and click. To restore the video to its normal state, with interface and all, click anywhere inside the video.

Use the play controls in the lower-left corner of the screen (see Figure 12) to play, pause, and fast-forward the video. You can also take advantage of the following keyboard shortcuts:

- To pause the video, press the spacebar. Press the spacebar again to resume playing.

- To skip to the next lesson, press the → key. This is also a great way to play the next lesson after the current one ends. For example, after viewing my initial and enthusiastic personal introduction, press the → key to play Video Lesson 1.

- To return to the preceding lesson, press ←. For example, you might revisit one of my personal introductions after watching a lesson.

- Adjust the volume by pressing the ⊞ and ⊟ (plus and minus) keys.

5. *Check out the bonus videos.* Also included on the CD are more than 20 minutes of bonus videos, excerpted from my full video series *Total Training Presents: Adobe Photoshop Elements 3 Unleashed.* Compatible with both Windows and the Mac (!), this six-hour series provides detailed information on the more advanced capabilities of Photoshop Elements 3's Editor workspace, including features that most professionals don't know about.

To watch the bonus videos, you'll need an unlock code. Here's how to get it:

- Click the yellow **B** button to display the promotional page pictured in Figure 13.

- Click the red link (*http://www.totaltraining.com/pse/ 1on1/bonus*) to visit the Total Training Web site and register. The process is simple and requires just a name and an email address. In return, you'll be presented with an unlock code.

- Select the unlock code in your browser window and copy it by choosing **Edit→Copy**. Then return to the Total Training software, click in the big blue box, and choose **Edit→Paste**.

- Click the yellow **Unlock»** button. A red message lets you know that you have successfully unlocked the bonus content.

To watch the videos, click the no-longer-yellow **B** button. You should see the welcome screen pictured in Figure 14. Click B1 in the Lessons list to find out how to create one of those silhouette effects that they use in iPod advertisements (see Figure 15). Or click B2 to learn about rendering photorealistic distortions.

Notice that the welcome screen in Figure 14 explains that the bonus lessons do not include lesson files. This happens to be the case for all the *One-on-One* video lessons. You work along with me inside the book; you sit back and relax during the videos.

Click to here register Paste the unlock code

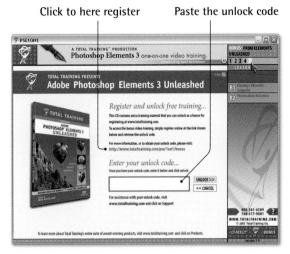

Figure 13.

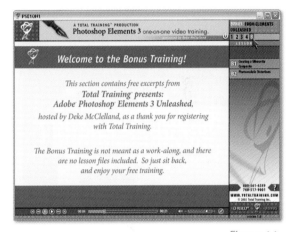

Figure 14.

Figure 15.

Finally, for help on any element of the interface, click the yellow-on-blue ❓ icon in the lower-right portion of the screen.

Structure and Organization

Each of the dozen lessons conforms to a consistent structure designed to impart skills and understanding through a regimen of practice and dialog. As you build your projects, I explain why you're performing the steps and why Photoshop Elements works the way it does.

Each lesson begins with a broad topic overview. Turn the first page of each lesson, and you'll find a section called "About This Lesson," which lists the skills you'll learn and directs you to the video-based introduction.

Next come the step-by-step exercises, in which I walk you through some of Elements' most powerful and essential image editing features. A CD icon, like the one on the right, appears whenever I ask you to open a file from the *Lesson Files-PE3 1on1* folder that you installed on your computer's hard drive. To make my directions crystal clear, command and option names appear in bold type (as in, "choose the **Open** command"). Figure references appear in colored type. More than 600 full-color, generously sized images diagram key steps in your journey so you're never left scratching your head, puzzling over what to do next. And when I refer you to another step or section, I tell you the exact page number to go to. (Shouldn't every book?)

PEARL OF ⬤ WISDOM

Along the way, you'll encounter the occasional "Pearl of Wisdom," which provides insights into how Photoshop Elements and the larger world of digital imaging work. Although this information is not essential to performing a given step or completing an exercise, it may help you understand how a function works or provide you with valuable context.

More detailed background discussions appear in independent sidebars. These sidebars shed light on the inner workings of the Quick Fix mode's Auto buttons, the mysteries of the visible-color spectrum, the mechanics of print resolution, and other high-level topics that are key to understanding Photoshop Elements.

A colored paragraph of text with a rule above and below it calls attention to a special tip or technique that will help you make Photoshop Elements work faster and more smoothly.

Each lesson ends with a "What Did You Learn?" section, which features a multiple-choice quiz. Your job is to choose the best description for each of 12 key concepts outlined in the lesson. Answers are printed upside-down at the bottom of the page.

The Scope of This Book

No one book can teach you everything there is to know about Photoshop Elements, and this one is no exception. If you're looking for information on a specific aspect of Elements, here's a quick list of the topics and features discussed in this book:

- Lesson 1: An overview of the Organizer workspace, including getting photos into a catalog, zooming and rotating images, creating and applying tags, finding photos by date, and comparing similar photos

- Lesson 2: The Quick Fix mode, including automatic color corrections and lighting and focus adjustments, as well as ways to save your edited images as independent files or in sets

- Lesson 3: Color and brightness adjustments, including the Remove Color Cast and Color Variations commands, Hue/Saturation and Levels, the Shadows/Highlights command, and the Camera Raw dialog box

- Lesson 4: Selection tools, including the magic wand, marquee, and lasso tools, as well as the selection brush and the commands in the Select menu

- Lesson 5: Ways to crop and transform an image, including the crop tool, as well as the Divide Scanned Photos, Image Size, and Canvas Size commands

- Lesson 6: Painting and retouching, including the paintbrush, dodge, burn, and red-eye removal tools, as well as the healing brushes and the various brush settings in the options bar

- Lesson 7: The Editor's extensive collection of filters, including the Unsharp Mask, High Pass, the many effects in the Filter Gallery, and the powerful Liquify function

- Lesson 8: Layer functions, including the Layers palette, stacking order, blend modes, transformations, and the eraser tools

- Lesson 9: Text and shape layers, including the type and shape tools, formatting attributes, scalable vector objects, and the Warp Text dialog box

- Lesson 10: Layer styles and adjustment layers, including the Styles and Effects palette, the Style Settings dialog box, the Gradient Map command, and layer masks

- Lesson 11: Ways to share your digital images, including printing single images and multiple photos, as well as emailing image files and posting them online

- Lesson 12: The wide world of Creations, including Video CDs, photo albums, greeting cards, wall calendars, Web galleries, and panoramas that comprise several photos stitched together

To find out where I discuss a specific feature, please consult the Index, which begins on page 383.

While I touch on almost every aspect of Photoshop Elements in some degree of detail, a few specialized topics fall outside the scope of this book. In the Organizer, I don't cover how to use File→Backup to make duplicates of your photos for safekeeping, nor do I explain how to use File→Burn to copy images to a CD. And although I provide a general and, I think, very educational lesson on filters (Lesson 7, "Filters and Distortions"), I don't cover all of the Editor's filter commands. It's a pretty small list of missing functions, but I like to be clear on this stuff up front, don't you know.

I now invite you to turn your attention to Lesson 1, "Getting and Organizing Photos." I hope you'll agree with me that *Photoshop Elements 3 for Windows One-on-One*'s combination of step-by-step lessons and video introductions provides the best learning experience of any Photoshop Elements training resource on the market.

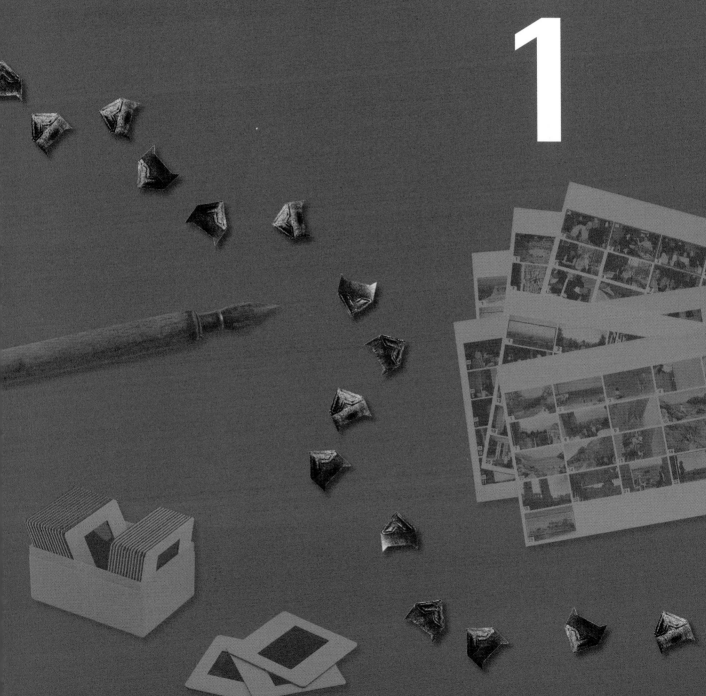

LESSON

1

PHOTOSHOP ELEMENTS 3 for Windows may be the best bargain in the history of digital imaging. Modeled after the professional-grade, industry-standard Adobe Photoshop CS2, Photoshop Elements delivers far and away more capabilities than any other image-editing program under $100.

From the tadpole that was Photoshop LE (short for Light Edition)—a freebie version of Photoshop in which many of the program's most powerful functions were merely turned off—Photoshop Elements 3 for Windows has matured into a unique piece of software that incorporates many of Photoshop's best features and tosses in a few dozen tricks of its own. It's an easy matter to chart the top capabilities of the two Photoshops and make Elements come out the winner. Admittedly, such a table is unfair, which is why it appears barely rescued from the dust heap in Figure 1-1. Elements provides only rudimentary support for some features, and most of Photoshop CS2's strengths are so rich and deep that they put the program in a class by itself. Still, the table makes a point. For a fraction of the price of the full-blown Photoshop CS2, Elements provides more features than most digital photographers will ever use. This is a consumer-level program for folks with professional-quality aspirations.

	Adobe Photoshop CS2	Photoshop Elements 3
File browser	X	X
Graphical image tags		X
Date view with calendar		X
Stack related photographs		X
Quick Fix mode		X
Smart Fix image correction		X
Histogram palette	X	X
Correct flash and backlighting	X	X
Auto-crop scanned images	X	X
Cookie-cutter cropping		X
Healing brush	X	X
Red-eye correction	X	X
Multiple undos	X	X
Special effects filters	X	X
Free-form distortions	X	X
Perspective cloning	X	
Independent layers	X	X
Smart objects	X	
Image extraction tools	X	X
Alpha channels	X	
Transparency control	X	X
Layer styles	X	X
High-resolution text	X	X
Text warp	X	X
Vector-based shapes	X	X
Output to email		X
Color-managed printing	X	X
Convert to CMYK	X	
Print multiple images		X
Online picture sharing		X
Create albums and cards		X
Print wall calendars		X
Web photo gallery	X	X
Stitch photos into panorama	X	X

Figure 1-1.

What Is Photoshop Elements?

Photoshop Elements 3 for Windows is really a combination of three programs running in tandem. Adobe calls these programs *workspaces*. The first is the Welcome screen, which invites you to the

ABOUT THIS LESSON

Project Files

Before beginning the exercises, make sure that you've installed the lesson files from the CD, as explained in Step 5 on page xv of the Preface. This should result in a folder called *Lesson Files-PE3 1on1* on your desktop. We'll be working with the files inside the *Lesson 01* subfolder.

Before you can set about correcting and modifying your digital photographs, you must know how to import and organize image files. In the following exercises, you'll learn how to:

Video Lesson 1: Welcome to the Organizer

When you first run Elements 3 for Windows, the program greets you with an interactive Welcome screen, which walks you through the various operations you can perform. Click the ▦ icon (labeled View and Organize Photos) to launch the Organizer, which allows you to create catalogs of images and view the images as thumbnails.

The Organizer is so useful that I've made it the subject of the first video lesson on the CD. To view this video, insert the CD, click the **Start** button, and then select **1, Welcome to the Organizer** from the Lessons list on the right side of the screen. The movie lasts 8 minutes and 47 seconds, during which time you'll learn about the keyboard equivalents and shortcuts listed below:

Operation	Keyboard equivalent or shortcut
Create a new catalog	Ctrl+Shift+C, Enter
Get images from a digital camera or card reader	Ctrl+G
Go back to all photos after importing images	Alt+← (or Backspace)
Rotate image clockwise or counterclockwise	Ctrl+→ or Ctrl+←
Zoom in or out of thumbnails	⊞ (plus) or ⊟ (minus)
Hide or show detail below thumbnails	Ctrl+D

software and explains some of the tasks you can accomplish. The second workspace, the Organizer, is a *file browser*. It lets you import images from a digital camera or scanner, preview many images at a glance, name and otherwise label them, and decide which (if any) you want to edit and print. The final workspace, the Editor, is an *image editor*. It lets you open a photograph and change it. You can adjust the brightness and contrast, adjust the colors, move things around, sharpen the focus, retouch a few details, and even combine two photographs. When you're finished, you can save your changes, print the result, attach it to an email, or post it online.

But it doesn't end there. You can also use Photoshop Elements to enhance artwork that you've scanned from a hand drawing or created with another graphics program. If you're artistically inclined, you can start with a blank document and create a piece of artwork from scratch. If that's not enough, Elements offers a wide variety of illustration tools, special effects, and text-formatting options.

In this lesson, you'll take your first look at the Organizer. Specifically, you'll look at how you acquire images, collect them into libraries, review and evaluate them, keep them organized so you can quickly find an image in the future, and compare one photo to another.

PEARL OF WISDOM

As I mentioned in the preface, Photoshop Elements 3 for the Macintosh computer is limited to the Editor workspace. In other words, there is no Organizer. If you use Photoshop Elements 3 on the Mac, skip to Lesson 2, "Quick Fix and Save" (page 48), to find out what you can do.

Getting Photos into Elements

After you've successfully opened the Organizer workspace (as explained in Video Lesson 1, "Welcome to the Organizer"), the next step is to tell the Organizer where your photos are. Happily, the Organizer gives you a number of easy ways to do this. You can direct the program to scour your hard drive for any image files it can find. From that point on, you can rely on Elements to transfer new photos from your camera to your hard drive automatically. Just insert your camera's memory card into a card reader or connect the camera directly to your computer via a USB or FireWire connection, and Elements automatically sets about importing the photos.

Elements keeps track of imported images in a *catalog*, which remembers the links to the images on your hard drive and stores any information that you might want to associate with the images. By default, Elements creates a catalog for you, giving it the apt but generic name *My Catalog*. A single catalog can manage hundreds or even thousands of photos, even if the images are scattered in multiple folders on different hard drives or even on backup CDs.

To see the Organizer import images from a digital camera media card, watch Video Lesson 1, "Welcome to the Organizer," included on the CD (see page 4). In this exercise, however, you won't be working with your photos. So that I can be sure that what happens on your screen exactly matches the steps and figures shown in this book, I want you to import a select group of images that I've provided—sort of a "control group," as the scientists say. And if you've been experimenting on your own and have already imported some photos into Elements, don't worry. We'll begin this exercise by creating a fresh new catalog file just for this lesson. The *My Catalog* file you've been using will be saved exactly as you left it, and I'll tell you how to open it again at the end of the exercise.

1. ***Launch Elements.*** You'll start this exercise in the Organizer workspace. Start up Photoshop Elements 3 for Windows. In the Welcome screen, click the **View and Organize Photos** button. If this is the first time you've launched the Organizer, it'll ask you whether you want to import photos into your default *My Catalog* file. For the present, click **No**. (You can always do this later by choosing File→Get Photos→By Searching and clicking the Search button.)

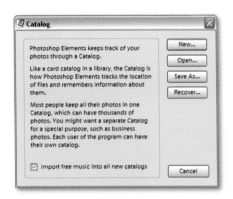

Figure 1-2.

2. ***Create a new catalog.*** Choose the **Catalog** command from the **File** menu or press Ctrl+Shift+C. As pictured in Figure 1-2, the resulting **Catalog** dialog box provides a few helpful instructions on the left and a column of buttons on the right. The buttons work as follows:

   - Click the New button or press the Enter key to make a new catalog file, which will initially appear empty.

   - Click Open to open a catalog you created in the past.

   - Use Save As to change the name of your catalog file.

   - If your catalog becomes damaged by a power failure or computer glitch, try clicking the Recover button to relocate the original images and rebuild the catalog file.

   Leave the check box at the bottom of the dialog box turned on to import 13 music files into your catalog, which you can use to accompany slide shows and the like. Next click the **New** button to display the **New Catalog** dialog box.

3. *Name the new catalog and confirm a few settings.* Enter "PE3 1on1" in the **File name** option box. Leave all other options unchanged and click the **Save** button. The Organizer workspace should appear as pictured in Figure 1-3. Notice that the Organizer window is empty and the title bar at the top of the window sports the new catalog name, *PE3 1on1*.

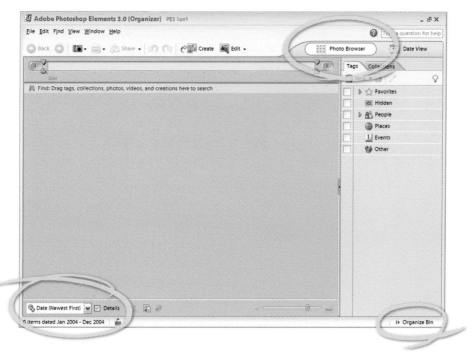

Figure 1-3.

Just to make sure that you and I are in perfect agreement—and thus avoid the possibility of confusion later—check the settings of the following options (all circled in Figure 1-3):

- Select **Photo Browser** in the shortcuts bar in the top-right portion of the workspace. This tells Elements to display multiple thumbnails at a time. Or you can press Ctrl+Alt+O.

- Set the pop-up menu in the lower-left corner of the screen to **Date (Newest First)**.

- Make sure the next-door **Details** check box is turned on.

- Do you see a couple of palettes along the right side of the window. If so, good. If not, click the ◄I **Organize Bin** text in the lower-right corner of the workspace.

- If you see big blue icons for the 13 music files (most likely you won't, but just in case), choose **View→Media Types**, turn off the **Audio** check box, and click **OK**. (Leave the **Photos**, **Video**, and **Creations** check boxes on.)

4. *Add photos to the catalog.* Click the camera button in the shortcuts bar in the top-left corner of the Organizer. Choose **From Files and Folders** from the pop-up menu to display the **Get Photos from Files and Folders** dialog box, as in Figure 1-4. (For the record, you can also choose File→Get Photos→from Files and Folders or press Ctrl+Shift+G.)

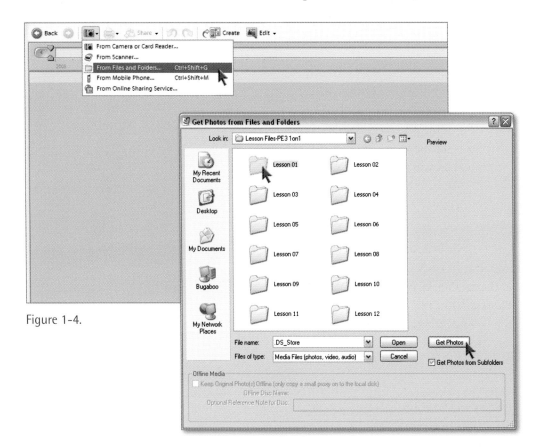

Figure 1-4.

5. *Navigate to the Lesson 01 folder.* Click the **Desktop** button on the left side of the dialog box to navigate to your computer's desktop. Locate and double-click the *Lesson Files-PE3 1on1* folder that you installed in the preface (see Step 5, page xv) to open this folder. Inside you will see folders for each of the twelve lessons in this book. Click the *Lesson 01* folder to select it.

6. *Get the photos.* Turn on the **Get Photos from Subfolders** check box. This tells Elements to import all photos inside any and all folders that may reside in the *Lesson 01* folder. Then click the **Get Photos** button. Elements displays a fleeting window titled

Getting Photos while it imports each of the 30 photos contained inside the *Lesson 01* folder (see Figure 1-5).

Figure 1-5.

7. **Dismiss the message.** After Photoshop Elements imports the photos, the Organizer presents you with the image thumbnails as well as the message shown in Figure 1-6. Turns out, this message is irrelevant. Here's the gist: Elements is telling you that if you already had any photos in this new catalog, the older images would now be hidden. But you didn't, so there it is. Turn on the **Don't Show Again** check box so you're not hounded by this rather tedious reminder every time you import photos and click **OK**.

8. **Click the Back to All Photos button.** Or press the Backspace key. The newly imported photos are the only images in the catalog, so clicking **Back to All Photos** doesn't really change things. But you might as well get in the habit for when it does, right?

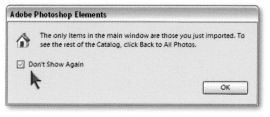

Figure 1-6.

9. **Make the thumbnails their absolute smallest.** Click the little ▢ button (the one that appears circled in red in Figure 1-7) to shrink the thumbnails to their smallest possible size. You should now be able to take in all 30 thumbnails at once—even though, it must be said, the thumbnails are very tiny. Incidentally, you might be tempted to play with the slider to the right of this icon. But I'd be much obliged if you would save at least some playing for the next exercise, during which I'll introduce you to the wonders of this seemingly innocuous slider.

Figure 1-7.

Organizing Your Photos

The Organizer is obviously great at showing you a "big picture" overview of the photos in your catalog. But when you want to examine one of those photos in closer detail, the Organizer can also show you—quite literally—the *big picture*. This flexibility makes the workspace ideal for sorting through a large, thousand-photo catalog of images. You can zoom in to inspect the most minute details of a particular photo and then zoom back out to view the thumbnail in the context of its mates.

However, the Organizer is much more than a means to view your photos. It also lets you make important changes to images, including correcting rotation problems and changing filenames, precisely what we'll be doing in this exercise. But first we'll learn how to use the Organizer's flexible controls to examine image thumbnails—which is, after all, one of the workspace's most fun functions.

1. *Open the catalog.* If the *PE3 1on1* catalog remains open from the preceding exercise, skip to Step 2. Otherwise, choose **File→Catalog** or press Ctrl+Shift+C. Then click the **Open** button and double-click the file *PE3 1on1.psa* to open it.

   If necessary, click the ▣ icon to again zoom all the way out, as you did at the end of the previous exercise (see Figure 1-7 on the preceding page). Notice that the month and year in which each image was taken appears beneath its thumbnail. If this information does not appear on your screen, turn on the Details check box at the bottom of the Organizer workspace.

2. *Enlarge the photos.* Slowly slide the thumbnail scale slider in the lower-right corner of the photo browser all the way to the right. Don't release the mouse button until you've reached the end of the slider. If you've a keen eye, you'll notice several things as you move the slider:

   • The thumbnails grow bigger, and therefore you see fewer of them on screen at a time.

- At a certain point, Elements adds the date to the details displayed below each thumbnail. Then it adds the time of day when each photo was taken.

- Once you've moved the slider as far as it will go to the right (see Figure 1-8), you've entered what the Organizer calls *single-photo view.* Elements also displays any caption information that you may have entered for the image. In our case, the Olympus-brand camera used to take these photos has automatically captioned each image Olympus Digital Camera. (Yes, I know the captions appear in capital letters, but all caps would ruin the flow of my pristine text.) This information doesn't exactly help differentiate one photo from the next, but you can always click the caption below the large thumbnail, press Ctrl+A to select it, and enter a new caption.

Figure 1-8.

3. *Display filenames.* Turns out, I've already given these files something every bit as good as captions—distinctive filenames. So let's show these names. Choose **Edit→Preferences→General** or press Ctrl+K to open the **Preferences** dialog box. Then turn on the **Show File Names in Details** check box and click **OK.** (Depending on your default email client, Elements might request that you take a moment to enter an email address into the E-mail preferences. You can either do so or just set the E-mail Client option to something other than Adobe E-mail Service.) With any luck, the Organizer will display the filename *Leaves Max & Sam-1.jpg* beneath the date and time.

The Organizer Interface

Your journey with Photoshop Elements 3 for Windows begins with the Organizer, which is where you acquire and manage your digital photographs. To make sure that you and I are speaking the same language as we venture through the exercises in this lesson, I'd like to take a moment to introduce you to this essential workspace. Labeled in the figure below, the key elements of the Organizer interface are as follows, in alphabetical order. (Red labels indicate terms that are discussed in the context of other interface elements.)

- **Catalog title:** The Organizer uses catalogs to keep track of the images on your hard drive, CDs, and other media. You can create a catalog using File→Catalog, or just accept the one the Organizer creates for you by default.

- **Cursor:** The cursor (sometimes called the *pointer*) is your mouse's on-screen representative, moving to keep pace with your mouse. Use the cursor to select items, choose commands, and adjust settings.

- **Details:** In the photo browser mode, the Organizer lists information about a photograph below its thumbnail. You should at least see the date when the image was captured. To see the filename as well, press Ctrl+K and turn on Show File Names in Details. If the time or date is wrong, just click the date to change it.

To show or hide details, turn on or off the Details check box at the bottom of the workspace or press Ctrl+D.

- **Image thumbnail:** In the digital realm, the word *image* is a general term for any photograph or piece of scanned artwork. The Organizer previews images by displaying them as reduced *thumbnails*, varying in size from postage-stamp tiny to dollar-bill big. Clicking on a thumbnail selects it and gives it a heavy blue outline. Press Shift while clicking to select a range of thumbnails; press Ctrl and click to select multiple nonadjacent thumbnails.

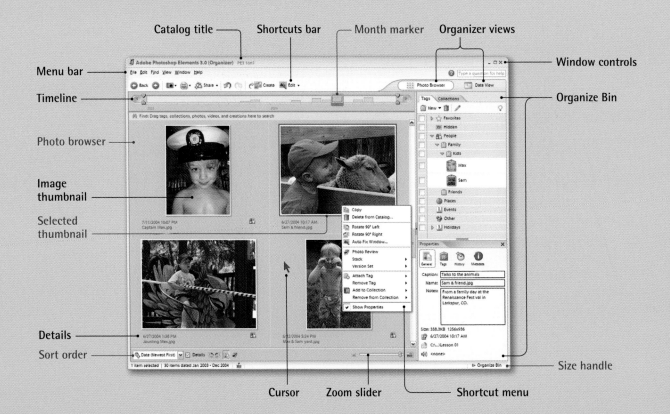

- **Menu bar:** Click a name in the menu bar to display a list of commands. Choose a command by clicking on it. A command followed by three dots (such as Catalog...) displays a window of options called a *dialog box*. Otherwise, the command works right away.

- **Organize Bin:** Aligned to the right-hand edge of the workspace, the Organize Bin contains the Tags, Collections, and Properties *palettes*, which are windows of options that can remain visible on the screen even when performing other tasks. Move a palette by dragging the title bar at the top of the palette. Many palettes contain multiple panels. Display a palette by choosing it from the Window menu or by clicking the tab that contains the palette's name.

Of the three palettes, I judge Properties to be the most critical for day-to-day work. The Properties palette lets you change filenames, add captions, and examine the EXIF metadata captured by a digital camera. To hide and show the Properties palette, press Alt+Enter. To free the Properties palette from the Organize Bin so it appears *free-floating*, choose the command Window→Dock Properties in Organize Bin to turn it off.

- **Organizer views:** Click one of the two buttons in the top-right corner of the workspace to switch between the photo browser and date view modes. The *photo browser* shows a collection of thumbnails in the order defined by the sort order pop-up menu in the bottom-left corner of the workspace. Not shown in the figure, the *date view* organizes thumbnails into calendars, either by year, month, or day.

- **Shortcuts bar:** Located below the menu bar, the *shortcuts bar* offers quick access to some of the Organizer's most common functions. Icons with tiny down-pointing triangles next to them (as in ▼) display menus of commands. Others produce immediate effects.

- **Shortcut menu:** Click the right mouse button (or *right-click*) to display a shortcut menu related to the item on which you clicked. The Organizer provides shortcut menus in the photo browser and date view, as well as inside some portions of the Tags, Collections, and Properties palettes.

- **Timeline:** Perched atop the photo browser window, the *timeline* charts the number of images that you captured on a month-by-month basis in the form of a standard-issue column graph. Each vertical bar is a month; a taller bar means more photos were shot in that month. Drag the blue month marker or click in the timeline to view a different month of thumbnails in the photo browser.

- **Window controls:** The top-right corner of the Organizer window sports three controls that let you hide, resize, and close the workspace, respectively. Except when the Organizer is maximized (as when you click the ☐ icon), you can drag the size handle in the bottom-right corner of the workspace to make the window bigger or smaller.

- **Zoom slider:** Click or drag along the slider bar in the lower-right corner of the workspace to change the size of the scalable, always-smooth thumbnails. Or press the ⊞ or ⊟ keys to zoom incrementally. To zoom all the way in or out, click one of the icons on either side of the slider. You can also zoom all the way in—so that you see just one big thumbnail at a time—by pressing the Enter key.

As long as we're on the topic of preferences, I've another bit of info for those of you who may be curious. Because the Photo Browser Arrangement menu is set to Date (Newest First), the images at the top of the browser are the most recent. But strangely, within a given day's grouping, the photos are displayed from oldest to newest. For instance, the photos taken on 10/18/2004 appear before the one snapped on 9/19/04, but the image shot at 5:16 P.M. appears before the one taken three minutes later. After you've finished this book, if you would rather the photos appear in *absolute* reverse chronological order, choose Edit→Preferences→General and select the option called Show Newest First within Each Day.

4. *Return to the small thumbnail size.* Previous to this, you've clicked the 🖾 icon to switch to the small thumbnail view. This time, I want you to try something different: Click the green **Back** arrow (⬤) in the upper-left corner of the Organizer workspace or press the Backspace key (or Alt+←). This option works like the Back button in a Web browser, taking you back to the most recent view.

5. *Switch to the largest thumbnail size.* Take your pick and do any one of the following:

   • Click the right-pointing arrow icon (the one that looks like ⬤) to the right of **Back**.

   • Press the equivalent keyboard shortcut, Alt+→.

   • Click the large 🖾 icon at the right side of the thumbnail size slider bar.

   Whichever method you choose, you will once again maximize the *Leaves Max & Sam-1.jpg* image in the photo browser.

9/19/2004 10:58 AM
King Max.jpg

Figure 1-9.

You can also make the thumbnail size shrink and grow by pressing the ⊟ and ⊞ keys, respectively. (That's the minus and plus keys, in case you can't quite identify them without reading glasses. And I say that as one who quite unfortunately identifies.)

6. *View the first several photos.* To cycle through the images in single-photo view, press the → and ← keys. Press → to advance through the photos of me and my boys playing in the leaves. (I'm the big kid with the facial hair.) Feel free to press ← to back up. Stop when you get to the *King Max.jpg* photo shown in Figure 1-9. As you can see, this photo is in need of some rotation.

7. *Rotate the photo.* You can use the icons at the bottom of the screen to rotate images 90 degrees counterclockwise or clockwise. Max needs a clockwise rotation, so click the ⬆ icon (circled in red in Figure 1-10) or press Ctrl+→. Figure 1-10 shows the result.

8. *Shrink the thumbnail view size.* Several other images need rotation, so we might as well correct them all at once. Drag the thumbnail slider triangle to the left or press the ⊟ key until you can see all 30 thumbnails clearly. You'll notice that the newly rotated *King Max.jpg* thumbnail now has a blue border, indicating that it is selected. This happens anytime you inspect a thumbnail in the single-photo view.

9. *Select the other thumbnails that need rotating.* Select the thumbnail for the next photo that needs rotating (dated 9/14/2004). Then press the Ctrl key and click the other photos that appear on their sides. As Figure 1-11 shows, you should end up with 15 selected thumbnails.

9/19/2004 10:58 AM
King Max.jpg

OLYMPUS DIGITAL CAMERA

Figure 1-10.

10. *Rotate the selected thumbnails.* Press Ctrl+→ or click the ⬆ icon. A moment later, the Organizer rotates the selected thumbnails upright.

Figure 1-11.

11. *View the last photo in single-photo view.* Now there's only one other problem to correct. All the images have descriptive filenames except for the last photo in the photo browser. We need to fix that. This time, just double-click the last thumbnail. The selected image fills the photo browser window, as shown in

Figure 1-12.

Figure 1-12. I used a slow sync flash—that is, a flash that fired after a long exposure—to create the ghostly visage of my younger son Sammy. Chills the bone, doesn't it? As witnessed below the thumbnail, the photo still subscribes to the nondescript name assigned by the digital camera, *P7230025.jpg*. Chills the marrow.

12. **View the Properties palette.** Click the ⬒ button to the right of the rotation icons at the bottom of the workspace, or press the keyboard shortcut Alt+Enter to display the **Properties** palette. If the Properties palette even slightly blocks your view of Sammy, choose **Window→ Dock Properties in Organize Bin**. This takes what is otherwise a *free-floating palette* and anchors it to the Organize Bin. The Properties palette displays an abundance of information about the selected image. You can even use it to edit the image information.

13. **Rename the selected photo.** Let's change both the caption and the filename assigned to this photo:

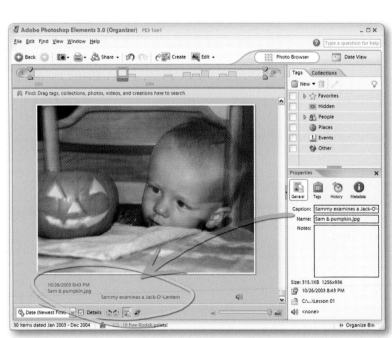

Figure 1-13.

- Click the **General** icon in the top-left corner of the Properties palette. This displays the Caption and Name fields.

- Click in the **Caption** field. Press Ctrl+A to select the existing Olympus advertisement and replace it with "Sammy examines a Jack-O'-Lantern," or words to that effect.

- Press the Tab key to advance to the **Name** option and replace it with "Sam & pumpkin.jpg." Then press the Enter key to accept the change.

Figure 1-13 shows the new caption and filename as they appear both in the Properties palette and under the magnified image preview.

When you rotate thumbnails, add captions, or change filenames in the Organizer, Elements updates the original image files on your hard drive. And this brings up a very important point: The images you manage with the Organizer are the *original images on your hard drive*. This means you should take care when deleting photographs from a catalog. The saving grace: A catalog file shows low-resolution *proxies* of imported images, not the full-resolution originals. So when you remove a proxy from a catalog by pressing the Delete key, you are presented with an alert message with a check box that gives you the option of deleting the original image as well. Do *not* turn this check box on unless 1) you hate the photo and you want to delete it forever and always, or 2) you have backed up the photos to a CD or DVD using File→Backup.

Creating and Using Tags

Computers and digital cameras have transformed the way we capture photographs. But although the trappings are different, the methods are often familiar. Consider storage and organization, for example. Where once we had shoeboxes, now we have hard drives. More often than not, our pictures reside in those digital shoeboxes just as pell-mell as in their physical counterparts. But what the traditional shoebox doesn't have is the Organizer. Assuming that you're willing to invest the time—a big *if*, to be sure—you can document photos in minute detail, which permits you to later search through them in a matter of seconds. This feature is so fantastic that many seasoned Photoshop CS2 users rely on the Organizer for its unique image management capabilities.

Photoshop Elements lets you assign labels to images using tags. Strictly speaking, a *tag* is a descriptive keyword that you can associate with a photo. The tag also includes a tiny graphic, giving it some visual presence and making it easier to identify. You can apply a tag to many photos at once, and a single photo may include multiple tags. For instance, if you and your brother take a vacation to Guatemala, you might create a Guatemala tag and apply it to all those vacation photos. You might also want to create a tag for your brother, which you would naturally apply to all the photos you shot of your brother, including those taken in Guatemala (as symbolically illustrated in Figure 1-14). You can create tags for virtually anything—people, pets, places, events, you name it—and share them between images as much as you like.

Figure 1-14.

All this tagging pays off when you're searching through thousands of digital photos for a specific shot. Double-click the Guatemala tag, for example, and the Organizer displays only the photos with that tag attached. Add the tag for your brother to the mix, and the Organizer displays only those photos that show your brother in Guatemala. Or, you could *exclude* your brother's tag from the Guatemala shots, displaying only brotherless vacation photos. The virtual nature of tags makes it possible to group, sort, and arrange photos in multiple ways. If you've ever been frustrated trying to organize a large number of physical objects—should your *Tommy* CD be filed under Opera or The Who?—you'll love the infinite flexibility of tags.

In this exercise, we're going to create and apply tags to some of the 30 imported photos in the *PE3 1on1* catalog. Because tags are so flat-out amazing, this exercise is a little longer than some. But trust me, your time will be well spent. Just imagine the payoff when you apply tags to not just 30 photos but to your own vast and ever-growing library of photographs.

You create and manage tags in the Tags palette. (If you don't see the Tags palette at the top of the Organize Bin, click the Tags tab to bring it forward.) Every catalog starts out with a few starter tags as well as some categories and subcategories to keep the tags organized. (Turns out, you can also assign categories directly to thumbnails, too.) As you tag your own images, you'll likely want to create a hierarchical system of tag categories and subcategories. Just remember that the tags you create are saved in a particular catalog file, not with the associated images. If you start a fresh catalog, the Organizer makes only its default tags available to you.

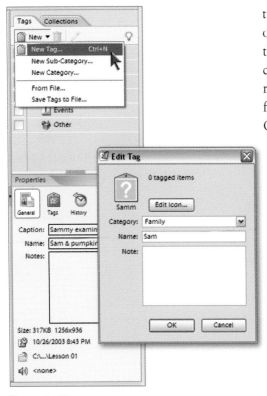

Figure 1-15.

1. *Open the lesson catalog.* This exercise starts exactly where the last one left off. If you're not already there, open the *PE3 1on1* catalog using the File→Catalog command. Then scroll to the last thumbnail, *Sam & pumpkin.jpg*, and double-click it so that you see it in the single photo view.

2. *Create a new tag.* Choose **New Tag** from the **New** pop-up menu or press Ctrl+N to display the **Create Tag** dialog box. Then enter the information shown in Figure 1-15, like so:

   • This tag will be applied to pictures of my pumpkin-curious son Sammy, so type "Sam" in the **Name** field.

   • As is often the case, our new tag fits handily in an existing category. Go to the **Category** pop-up menu and select **Family**, which is a subcategory of People.

- Click the **OK** button to create the new tag. The ▼'s next to the People and Family categories automatically twirl open to reveal the Sam tag.

Choose View→Collapse All Tags or press Ctrl+Alt+T to twirl closed all the categories in the Tags palette. Choose View→Expand All Tags or press Ctrl+Alt+X to twirl them all open.

Graphical creatures that they are, tags display little thumbnails to tie a visual reference to the tag. The Sam tag sports a question mark because we haven't yet applied it to an image. We'll remedy that in the next step.

Incidentally, don't double-click the tag. I mention this because it's such a natural operation—seemed logical to me, anyway—but it runs a search, one that comes up empty. If I didn't catch you in time and you have accidentally double-clicked, just click the 🔍 icon in front of the Sam tag to turn the search results off. Then press the End key to advance to the final image in the catalog, the one of Sam.

---

3. *Apply the Sam tag.* Instead of double-clicking, drag and drop the Sam tag onto the picture of Sam and the pumpkin. You'll notice that several things happen:

   - The tag appears momentarily in the lower-left corner of the thumbnail, and then disappears.

   - The details area below the thumbnail shows the Sam tag and the People category icon, circled in Figure 1-16.

   - Also circled in the figure, Elements replaces the question mark on the tag with an itty-bitty Sammy.

As it so happens, this particular photo of Sam doesn't make a good tag graphic because we can't see all of his face and he's lost in the tiny 22-by-22-pixel icon. We'll fix that in Step 10 (see page 22). In the meantime, let's add an event tag to tell us that this is a Halloween photo.

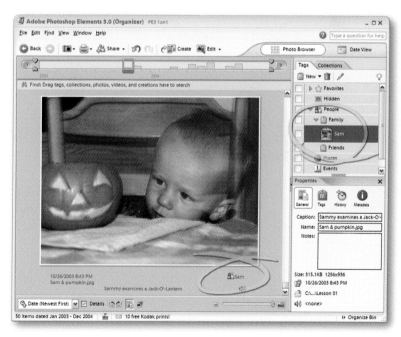

Figure 1-16.

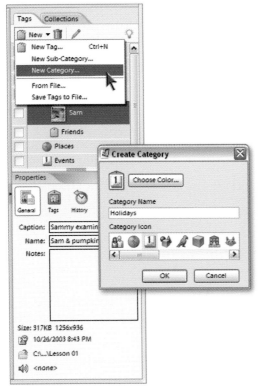

Figure 1-17.

4. *Create a Holidays tag category.* We could place the Halloween tag in the predefined Events category, but I reckon holidays are sufficiently special to deserve their own category. That's the great thing about tags; you can organize them any way you like. Here's how (as documented in Figure 1-17):

- Click the **New** button at the top of the Tags palette and choose **New Category** from the resulting pop-up menu to display the Create Category dialog box.

- Click the **Choose Color** button to select a color to represent this category. This color is then used to color the tops and edges of all subcategories and tags, just as the current Family and Friends sub-categories and the Sam tag use the orange color of the People category. Turquoise is the default color; click **OK** to accept it.

- Type "Holidays" in the **Category Name** field.

- Select a representative category icon. My suggestion: click the third option, the desk calendar. Click **OK** and the Holidays category appears at the bottom of the Tags palette.

PEARL OF WISDOM

By default, you can move categories up or down in the Tags palette in any order you want, but tags are alphabetized within their categories. If you don't like this behavior, choose Edit→Preferences→Tags and Collections. Then click the options to switch categories, sub-categories, and tags between Manual and Alphabetical modes.

5. *Create a Halloween tag.* Instead of going back up to the New button at the top of the Tags palette, just right-click the **Holidays** category and choose **Create new tag in Holidays category**. The Holidays category is already selected in the Create Tag dialog box. Simply type "Halloween" in the **Name** field and click **OK**. The new tag appears complete with question mark and sporting the Holidays category's turquoise color.

6. *Apply the Halloween tag.* This time, drag and drop the image of Sammy and his orange friend onto the **Halloween** tag in the Tags palette. As you can see, tagging images works both ways. The Holidays icon and Halloween tag appear alongside the People icon and Sam tag below the image preview.

7. *Edit the Halloween tag icon.* If you ask me, the jack-o'-lantern actually makes a good icon for the Halloween tag, but we need to edit the icon to make it more legible. With the Halloween tag still selected, do the following:

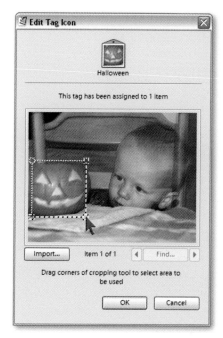

Figure 1-18.

- Click the pencil icon (✎) at the top of the Tags palette to display the **Edit Tag** dialog box.

- Next click the **Edit Icon** button to display the **Edit Tag Icon** dialog box. The animated square marquee on the big image thumbnail shows the cropping area for the tag icon.

- Resize and reposition the marquee so that it frames the pumpkin's face, as in Figure 1-18. Drag a square corner handle of the marquee to shrink it; drag inside the marquee to move it. Notice that the preview at the top of the dialog box updates to show you what the tag icon will look like. When you're happy with the preview, click **OK**.

- Click **OK** again in the Edit Tag Icon dialog box to change the Halloween tag in the Tags palette.

8. *Apply the Halloween tag.* One more image needs the Halloween tag. To locate it, drag the thumbnail size slider or press the ⊡ key until you can see all 30 thumbnails. Most likely, the tag details will disappear from below the final thumbnail. Instead, you'll see a blue tag icon, which tells you that at least one tag is applied.

Locate the photo of Max in a Batman costume. It's the eighth image in the list, dated 9/14/2004. (Max was trying on his costume a bit early.) Then do like so:

- Double-click the thumbnail to zoom in on it.

- In the name of discovering yet another way to apply tags, right-click the *Maxman.jpg* image preview. Then choose **Attach Tag→Holidays→Halloween**. Sort of cumbersome, but it's a technique. The Halloween icon appears momentarily, shortly replaced by the Holiday icon and Halloween tag below and to the right of the preview.

Whether your images appear large or small, you can still inspect the tags that are applied to a thumbnail. Just select the thumbnail in the Organizer and click the Tags icon at the top of the Properties palette.

9. *Apply the Sam tag to other photos.* Press ⊟ to zoom out from the thumbnails. Then click and Ctrl-click to select the other photos of Sammy, which appear highlighted in Figure 1-19. (If you can see the filenames, note that all files with Sam in them feature his name.) You should end up with at total of 16 photos selected. And don't bother selecting the final thumbnail; we already applied the Sam tag to it.

Having selected all the Sam images, drag the **Sam** tag from the **Tags** palette onto any one of the selected thumbnails. This tags all the thumbnails at once, making it the fastest way to tag a group of images.

Figure 1-19.

10. *Select and edit a new tag icon for Sammy.* Now it's time to add a more legible icon to Sam's tag.

   - With the **Sam** tag selected, click the ✐ icon at the top of the Tags palette to display the **Edit Tag** dialog box, which tells you that you have assigned this tag to 17 items.

   - Click the **Edit Icon** button to open the **Edit Tag Icon** dialog box, which still features Sammy and his pumpkin.

   - Notice that the Find button at the bottom of the dialog box is flanked by two arrowheads, which allows you to scroll through the 17 tagged images. That's great, but it's even easier to just click the **Find** button itself, which displays a scrolling list of all the tagged images.

- See that photo of Sammy with the juice that I've selected in Figure 1-20? Sammy has a bit of a trail running out of his nose. (If you're grossed out by baby goop, do yourself a favor and don't inspect the picture too closely.) But it is a good full-on face shot, so select the image and click **OK**.

- Back in the Edit Tag Icon dialog box, adjust the marquee until it focuses on Sam's face as in Figure 1-21. Then click the **OK** button.

- Click **OK** once more to escape the maze of dialog boxes and update the Sam tag in the Tags palette.

Figure 1-20.

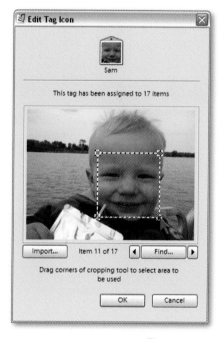

Figure 1-21.

11. *Create a tag for Max.* Right-click the **Family** subcategory in the **Tags** palette and choose **Create new tag in Family sub-category**. Enter "Max" in the **Name** field. Even though you haven't applied this tag to a thumbnail—heck, you haven't even officially created the darn thing yet—you can click the Edit Icon button and hunt for a picture of Max on your hard drive. But it's much easier to choose a tag icon after the tag has been applied to an image or two. So click **OK** to add the Max tag with question mark to the Family subcategory.

12. *Select the photos of Max.* Click the first thumbnail in the catalog and then Shift-click the seventh, all of which feature Max. Then Ctrl-click to select the others, some 19 in all, as highlighted in Figure 1-22. Some of the selected images already include the Sam tag, but that's okay. In fact, the more tags the merrier.

Figure 1-22.

Because all the Max images have *Max* in their filenames, you can round them up automatically. Choose Find→By Filename or press Ctrl+Shift+K. Then enter "Max" and click OK or press the Enter key. Just like that, Elements limits the thumbnails in the photo browser to the 19 photographs of Max. Press Ctrl+A to select them all and you're ready for Step 13. Note that this technique works only for properly named files, and digital cameras *never* generate properly named files. In other words, only if you've named the files yourself will this command work. So when editing your own photos, you'll most likely have to select them manually, as Step 12 and a few of the others describe.

13. *Apply the Max tag to the selected photos.* Drag the Max tag onto the *Captain Max.jpg* thumbnail that I circled in yellow in Figure 1-22. Not only does Elements apply the Max tag to all the selected thumbnails, it assigns the *Captain Max.jpg* image as the tag's icon. If you drag a question mark tag onto a selected thumbnail, that thumbnail becomes the tag icon. The icon could probably use a little cropping, so feel free to click the ✐ icon and adjust the marquee at your discretion.

14. *Create a subcategory.* If you have a large family, you might want a category for each branch of the family tree. Luckily, the Organizer lets you create an unlimited number of categories. Right-click the **Family** item to display a shortcut menu and choose **Create new sub-category in Family sub-category**. Then type "Kids" in the **Sub-Category Name** option and click **OK**.

15. *Place the tags inside the sub-category.* Click and Shift-click the Max and Sam tags to select them. Then drag and drop the two tags onto the **Kids** icon to place them in that subcategory.

By now, you've done a lot of work. You've created tags and categories, you've assigned the tags to images, and you've edited tag icons. Plus, you've spent a fair amount of time meticulously selecting thumbnails, which is great practice for working in the Organizer. But truth be told, applying tags is only half the battle. The big payoff comes when you want to quickly find certain kinds of pictures. If you want to take a break, now's a good time. Otherwise, stick with me as we exploit the true power of tags, searching.

16. *Search for thumbnails with the Sam tag.* Notice in the Tags palette that there's an empty square to the left of each tag and category name. Click inside the box to the left of the **Sam** tag to display only thumbnails associated with the tag, as indicated by the 🔍 icon. As Figure 1-23 shows, the tag that governs (or *filters*) the search appears at the top of the Organizer window. The Matching information on the right shows that the 17 images of Sammy best fit the search while 13 others do not fit the search at all.

Figure 1-23.

17. *Add the Halloween tag to the search filter.* Scroll down the Tags list and click in the square to the left of the **Halloween** tag. This displays another 🔍 icon and refines the search to only those images that contain both the Sam and Halloween tags (not one or the other, as you might expect). Thus, only one image appears in the Organizer, the one of Sam and his pumpkin.

You can also refine a search by dragging a tag from the Tags palette directly into the Find area above the thumbnails.

18. *View the closely matching search results.* Notice that the check box labeled 1 Best is selected above the thumbnails, which indicates that the one thumbnail that best matches the search is being displayed. Turn on the 17 **Close** check box and deselect the **1 Best** check box. As Figure 1-24 shows, the Organizer now reveals the images that fit the search filter closely, but not the one that matches exactly. In other words, the 17 images visible in the photo browser include either the Sam tag or the Halloween tag, but not both. If you were to view the 12 Not results, the Organizer would show you the dozen images that have neither tag (either in addition to the current thumbnails or instead of them, depending on whether you turn off 17 Close).

Figure 1-24.

19. *View all the images.* Click the **Back to All Photos** button above the photo browser window. The Organizer cancels the search filter—both 🏛 icons disappear from the Tags palette—and the photo browser once again displays all 30 thumbnails.

20. *Search for all images with the Max tag.* To search for images linked to a single tag, double-click the appropriate tag. For example, double-click the **Max** tag in the Tags palette and the Organizer displays the 19 images with the Max tag.

21. *Filter out the Sam tag images.* Right-click the **Sam** tag in the Tags palette and choose **Exclude photos with Sam tag from search results**. A red ◕ icon appears next to the Sam tag, showing that any image featuring Sammy is excluded from the search (poor guy). In other words, as pictured in Figure 1-25, the Organizer shows the 8 images that feature Max but not Sam.

Incidentally, just in case you're wondering whether you can search for thumbnails that have *no* tags, the answer is, why certainly. Just choose Find→Untagged Items or press Ctrl+Shift+Q.

Figure 1-25.

Now that you know how to create tags—and just how powerful they can be—a few quick words about getting rid of them: To remove a tag from a thumbnail, right-click the thumbnail and choose Remove Tag. You'll be presented with a submenu showing all applied tags. Select the tag you want to remove and the job is done. If you want to completely delete a tag from the Tags palette, either select the tag and click the trashcan icon at the top of the palette or right-click the tag and choose the Delete command. You can delete any of the Organizer's default tags except the Favorites and Hidden tags (the latter of which lets you hide thumbnails without removing them from a catalog). Deleting a tag removes it from any photos to which it has been applied; the photos themselves stay put.

Making Collections

If tags are virtual Post-it notes that you affix to your images, then *collections* are virtual paper trays that permit you to sort your photos. Simply put, they let you assemble mini-catalogs of images, related by whatever topics you might dream up. Photoshop Elements 3 for Windows implements collections very much like it implements tags. You create and modify collections in a palette, and then drag and drop them from the Collections palette onto thumbnails in the photo browser window.

The one big advantage collections have over the search results produced by tags is that you can change the order of your photos in the browser window and save that sort order with the collection. So if you need to arrange a sequence of images in a specific order inside a group, collections are the way to go.

Nephew! Where in thunder is my slide show?

Figure 1-26.

You might also think of tags and collections this way: Generally speaking, tags are designed to organize images that share a common subject; collections are for images that share a common destination. In this brief exercise, we'll create a collection of images and turn them into a slide show to send to my Uncle Zeke. (The fact that I don't really have such an uncle, and if I did, he wouldn't look anything like the guy in Figure 1-26, is of no consequence.) We'll add a few photos to the collection and then arrange them in a specific order. Having just completed the preceding exercise on tags, a lot of this exercise will seem familiar, but never fear; I'll point out many subtle but important distinctions as we go along.

1. *Open the Organizer.* If you have the Organizer open from the last exercise, skip to Step 2. If not, choose **File→Catalog**, click the **Open** button, and open the *PE3 1on1.psa* file. I'm assuming that you've completed the three previous exercises. If you haven't, you'll have the most luck if you perform them in order.

2. *Display the Collections palette.* Click the **Back to All Photos** button at the top of the photo browser to see all 30 thumbnails. Then click the **Collections** tab to the right of Tags.

3. *Create a new collection.* Click the **New** button at the top of the Collections palette to bring up a pop-up menu that lets you create a new collection or a new collection group. Like tag categories, *collection groups* let you organize collections into, well, groups. If you're feeling fussy, you can even nest one collection group inside another. But unlike tags, Elements doesn't require

collections to be organized. Whereas a tag must belong to a category, a collection can roam free. So there's no need to create a collection group unless you really want to.

That said, here's what I want you to do:

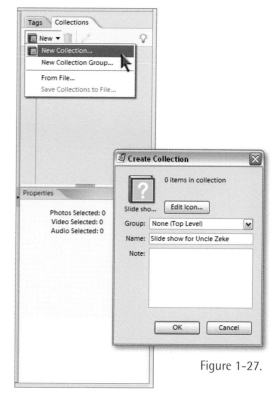

- Choose **New Collection**. If you already created one or more collection groups, they would be listed in the Group pop-up menu. As it is, your only choice is None (Top Level).

- Type "Slide show for Uncle Zeke" in the **Name** option, as in Figure 1-27. (If you can't bring yourself to enter that, name the collection whatever you want.)

- Click **OK** to add the new collection to the Collections palette, complete with a question mark to show it's empty.

4. *Select a few photos.* Now to add some photos to the collection. Scroll to the bottom of the photo browser. Select the five sculpted busts by clicking the first one and then Shift-clicking the last. Shot in the Victoria and Albert Museum in London, these heads hail from the famous Fakes and Forgeries gallery. Being an art forger by trade, Uncle Zeke should be interested. But since he's also a family guy, we need to add a picture of my kids and me. So press Ctrl+Home to move to the top of the catalog without deselecting the statues. Then Ctrl-click the first thumbnail—the one of my boys and me in the leaves—to add it to the selection.

Figure 1-27.

5. *Add the images to the collection.* As with tags, you can right-click one of the selected thumbnails and choose Add Selected Items to Collection from the shortcut menu. But better to drag the question mark icon from the Collections palette onto the first sculpture thumbnail. This way, the bearded fellow becomes the icon for the collection, as illustrated in Figure 1-28. If you don't like the way the icon is cropped or centered, click the 🖉 icon at the top of the Collections palette and then click the Edit Icon button, as directed in the preceding exercise (see Step 7, page 21). Personally, I figure that dignified old phoney looks pretty swell as he is.

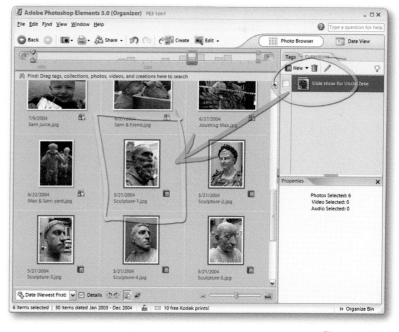

Figure 1-28.

Depending on your zoom level, you may notice that the sculpture thumbnails sport blue tags; they have in essence been "tagged" with a collection. (As I implied earlier, the distinction between tags and collections can be a little cloudy.) Larger thumbnails sport little book icons when they're part of a collection.

6. *View the photos in the collection.* Click the box to the left of the Uncle Zeke collection in the Collections palette to place the 📖 icon. As in Figure 1-29, the photo browser displays the six images in your collection. Although this might seem identical to filtering images with tags, there is a difference: You can't combine multiple collections to filter thumbnails as we did with the Sam and Halloween tags in the preceding exercise. One collection search cancels the other.

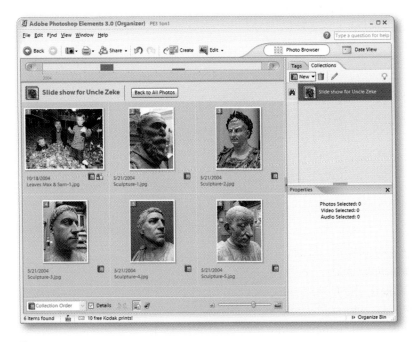

Figure 1-29.

Notice that each thumbnail presents a number in its upper-left corner. Because you added the thumbnails at the same time, they remain in date order, as in the Organizer. If you had added thumbnails to a collection one at a time, they would appear in the order in which they were added. But regardless of their initial order, you can re-sort the thumbnails any time you like.

7. *Reorder the images.* Let's save the image of me and the lads for the end of the slide show. Drag the first thumbnail to the end of the collection. As you drag, notice that a vertical yellow line shows you where the photo will land. When the yellow line appears after the sixth thumbnail, release your mouse button.

Because I'm particularly fond of the expression that adorns the last of the sculpted busts—he has this sort of "What, me awake?" thing going on—drag it to the front of the collection. Make sure your thumbnails are arranged as they appear in Figure 1-30.

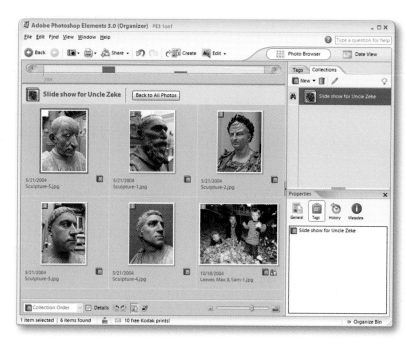

Much to my delight, the images now appear in the order that I want to show them to my dear Uncle Zeke. To preview this collection of images as a slide show, choose View→Photo Review or press the F11 key. For this specific collection, I recommend you turn off the Include Captions check box and set the Background Music option to None. Then click the OK button to enter the full-screen photo review mode. Click the green play button (◉) in the top-left corner of the screen to set the slide show playing. When you've had enough, click the stop button (◉) or press the Esc key. For complete information on the photo review mode, read the last exercise in this lesson, "Comparing Similar Photos," which begins on page 40.

Figure 1-30.

Finding Photos by Date

Often, a photo's most distinguishing feature isn't the who, the what, or the where—it's the *when*. And if you need to search for photos by when they were taken, the Organizer gives you the *how*. I'm speaking of the *date view*, which fills your screen with a calendar and shows thumbnails of your images in the date cells. It's a great way to view your photos in the context of time, giving you an illustrated calendar of your very own special events.

The Organizer draws a photo's date from its *EXIF metadata*. Although this sounds technical, EXIF (pronounced *ek-sif*) is actually a common standard that imparts such basic information as the time the photo was taken, the make and model of camera, the aperture setting, the focal length, and whether the flash fired. Most digital cameras save EXIF metadata when the shot is taken. If no EXIF info exists, as in the case of a scanned image, the Organizer uses the date the image was last modified.

This system works extremely well—except when the Organizer assigns a date that's just plain wrong. And it's pretty easy for that to happen. For example, if you don't set your camera's clock, the EXIF metadata will be inaccurate. And if you scan in an ancient photo, you'll probably want the Organizer to manage the image according to when it was originally taken, not when you last edited it. Luckily, the Organizer gives you the power to override the recorded info and assign new dates and times.

In this exercise, we'll do just that, adjusting the time for a few photographs to account for shifting time zones. Then we'll move on to explore the timeline and see how it lets you limit searches to a specific period of time. Finally, we'll take a look at the date view's various calendar settings and see how to change the display of thumbnails and important events.

1. *View all imported thumbnails.* As in previous exercises, take a moment to make sure the *PE3 1on1* catalog is open inside the Organizer. Also, if necessary, click the **Back to All Photos** button at the top of the workspace to make sure all 30 images are available in the photo browser.

2. *Examine the recorded date and time for the first piece of sculpture.* Check that the **Properties** palette is open. (If it isn't, press Alt+Enter to bring it up.) Then double-click the thumbnail for the *Sculpture-1.jpg* photo—the one of the fellow with the great beard—to magnify the image so it fills the screen. Now view the **General** settings in the Properties palette. As shown in Figure 1-31, Elements seems to be under the impression that I shot the photo on Friday, May 21, 2004 at 7:27 A.M. Strange, that, since I distinctly remember still being in bed at that time, dreaming about things that thankfully had nothing to do with Photoshop Elements or digital photography. Meanwhile, the V&A museum doesn't even open until 10 A.M.

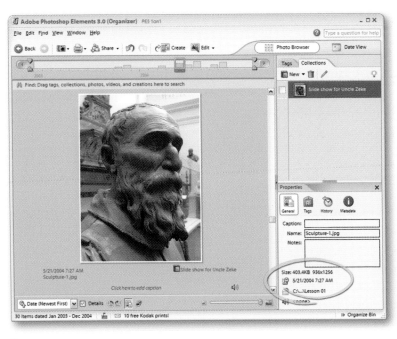

Figure 1-31.

I shot these photos in London. But my camera, an Olympus C-5060, was still on Colorado time, seven hours earlier. And so the otherwise spiffy C-5060 embedded Colorado's time of day into the metadata of all the London photos.

3. *Adjust the time of day for the V&A pics.* Zoom out and select all five of the sculpture photos by clicking the first one
and Shift-clicking the last. Then click the date under any one
of the selected thumbnails to display the winsome dialog box
shown in Figure 1-32. (You can also choose Edit→Adjust Date
and Time of Selected Items or press Ctrl+J, but only if you like
doing things the hard way.) This dialog box presents you with
four options:

Figure 1-32.

- The first allows you to set all selected photos to a single
date and time, according to your specifications.

- The second option tells the Organizer to ignore the EXIF
metadata and instead sets all files' dates and times to the
last time they were modified.

- The third option allows you to enter a new date and time
for the earliest of the selected photos and then shifts the
others relative to the first. If your camera's clock was set
incorrectly—as was mine—the relative increments from
one wrong time to the next are accurate. In other words,
fix the earliest photo in the sequence and the others will
be updated correctly.

- The fourth option lets you shift photos by a set number of
hours, just what we need to fix the time zone problem.

Select the final option, **Shift by set number of hours (time zone
adjust)**, and then click **OK**. Elements displays another dialog
box (also shown in Figure 1-32) that lets you move the time
forward or backward a prescribed number of hours. Select the
Ahead option and set **Hours** to 7. Then click the **OK** button.
Once again, click the first thumbnail bust and note the new
time: 2:27 P.M. The Organizer now records the time just as if
I had had the wherewithal to advance my camera's clock when
I was in London.

PEARL OF ⬤ WISDOM

It's worth noting that the new times are recorded within the context of the
catalog file only. Photoshop Elements scrupulously avoids changing the EXIF
metadata embedded in the files because Adobe's lawyers regard EXIF as legal
data, potentially admissible in a court of law. Although I personally consider
this notion ridiculous—it's an easy matter to fake EXIF information with no
one the wiser—the cogs of the great legislative wheel turn slowly. For now,
EXIF is (supposedly) off-limits.

4. *Take a look at the timeline.* That long strip between the short-cuts bar and the photo browser is the Organizer's *timeline*. Pictured in Figure 1-33, the timeline contains a series of pale blue bars—like those in a standard bar graph—with each bar representing a month in which the photos in the catalog were originally captured by a digital camera. The taller the blue bar, the more photos there are for that month. You can drag the dark blue marker (the one with the green bar inside it) along the timeline to focus on a particular month. Or just click a bar to reposition the marker.

Figure 1-33.

5. *Change the thumbnail size and view.* To appreciate how helpful the timeline can be, we need to adjust our view of the photo browser a bit. First, click the ▶ **Organize Bin** item in the bottom-right corner of the workspace to hide the palettes along the right side of the screen. Then drag the thumbnail size slider to the right or press the ⊡ key until three or four thumbnails fit on the screen horizontally. Finally, press Ctrl+End so you're viewing the final images in the catalog. As you may recall, these are the earliest images in the catalog, with the last photo captured October 2003.

6. *Focus on the tallest bar.* To switch to a different point in time, click the third bar from the right in the timeline, which represents the seven photos from July, 2004. As Figure 1-34 shows, the photo browser jumps to the first thumbnail for that month, which shows Max on a four-wheeler. Just to make sure you don't miss the thumbnail, Elements temporarily outlines it in green and flashes the time marker. No need to wonder what photos you shot in a specific month; Elements couldn't make it more crystal clear.

Figure 1-34.

7. *Narrow the timeline's date range to 2003.* In addition to the vertical bars, the timeline features *range markers*—the blue down-and-up pointers on either side of the timeline—that you can use to narrow in on a specific period of time. Drag the right-hand range marker to **2004** under the timeline. As witnessed in Figure 1-35, this limits the photo browser photos so we are only seeing photos shot after 2003.

Dragging the range markers lets you limit the time range in one-month increments. If you need to set specific start and end dates for your range, choose Find→Set Date Range or press Ctrl+Alt+F, and then specify the start and end dates for your search. To clear a date range, choose Find→ Clear Date Range or press Ctrl+Shift+F.

---

8. *View images that have the Max tag.* The timeline interacts with tag filters to help you find exactly the photos you're looking for. Bring back the Organize Bin and display the **Tags** palette. Then double-click the **Max** tag. Despite the fact that the catalog includes 19 images tagged to Max, only the 2 from 2003 appear on the screen. If you look closely, you may also notice that the timeline changes to reflect the influence of the tag. Of the 3 images for November 2003, 2 feature Max, so the bar for that month is two-thirds green and one-third empty. The preceding month, October 2003, includes a single photo and Max isn't in it; therefore, that bar is empty.

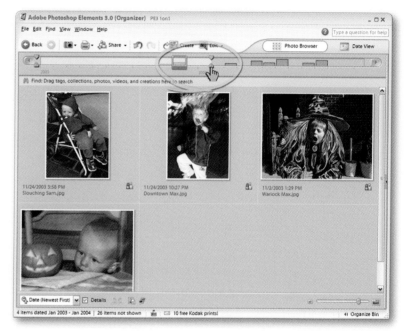

Figure 1-35.

9. *Switch to date view.* Now let's check out the date view. Click the large **Date View** button in the upper-right corner of the workspace. In the date view, the **Properties** palette becomes a free-floating window that interferes with your view of the calendar. So click the ✕ button in the upper-right corner of the palette to close it. You should now see a month calendar; if not, click the Month button at the bottom of the screen.

Click the ◐ and ◑ buttons on either side of the month name at the top of the calendar to switch from one month to another. Or you can press the bracket keys, ⎡ and ⎤.

---

10. *Navigate to October 2004.* Whether by button or by bracket key, make your way to October 2004. As pictured in Figure 1-36, the calendar displays the holidays of Thanksgiving (Canada) and Halloween in lavender. Even more significantly, an image thumbnail appears in the cell for October 18, which happens to be the very day that my wife shot the photos of the boys and me playing in the leaves. That's the beauty of Month view—the photos you take on a given day are automatically assigned to the corresponding cell in the calendar.

The right side of the workspace includes information about the selected day, October 18:

- Click the big green ◉ button to the right of the calendar to play an instant slide show of all the images for the selected day. Click the gray ◉ or ◉ buttons to move through the images one at a time. Click the icon to the right of ◉ to display the featured image in the photo browser.

- The tiny desk calendar icon below the right side of the inset slide show window lets you add special events to the calendar. You'll learn more about this shortly.

- Directly below the slide show is the Daily Note area, where you can enter any information that occurs to you about the selected day. I very much recommend it. Just a few notes can spark a lot of memories later.

Figure 1-36.

Since the timeline, tags, and collections aren't features of the date view, the various limits and filters of the photo browser have no effect here. All photos for a specific month are available from the date cells and inset slide show window.

11. *Navigate to May 2004.* This time, click the word **October** at the top of the calendar to display a pop-up menu that lists the other months of the year. A photo icon indicates that the month includes pictures. Choose **May** from the menu.

May has four holidays, and I'd like to add a special event, Uncle Zeke's birthday. I could accomplish this by clicking the cell for his birthday, which is May 23, and then clicking the desk calendar icon on the far right side of the workspace. But for holidays and events, I prefer to go to command central: the Calendar preferences.

12. *Customize the Calendar preferences.* Choose **Edit→Preferences→Calendar** to display the dialog box shown in Figure 1-37. The first category of calendar preferences is Options, of which there is only one: Whether to use Monday as the first day of the week or keep it as Sunday. Leave this check box turned off.

Take a scroll through the Holidays list, and you'll see that Adobe has perversely decided to deactivate only one holiday from their long list: April Fools' Day. Someone at Adobe probably figures it inspires too much inner-office ruckus. But it's such fun ruckus! So by golly, turn on the **April Fools' Day** check box. If you want to eliminate the bad ruckus, I say turn off **Valentine's Day**. (Gents, back me up here.)

Finally, here's the category of options we're looking for: Events. Figure 1-38 on the next page shows what I want you to do. This list tells you:

- Click the **New** button to display the **Create New Event** dialog box.

- Enter "Uncle Zeke's Birthday" in the **Event Name** field.

- Set the **Month** to **May** and the **Day** to 23.

- Keep the **Repeating Event** and **Every Year** check boxes turned on, since Uncle Zeke has a birthday practically every year. (Let's do the old guy a favor and leave the Until option turned off.)

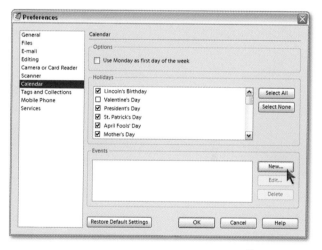

Figure 1-37.

Figure 1-38.

- Click **OK**, and you'll see Uncle Zeke's Birthday (May 23) in the Events window.

- Click **OK** to close the Calendar preferences. The May 23 cell now lists Uncle Zeke's Birthday in green, as I've circled in Figure 1-38.

13. *Change the cell icon for May 21.* Now let's turn our attention to May 21. By default, the cell for that date shows the first photo I shot. But you can change that. First, I need you to leave Month view and enter Day view. Click the **May 21** cell to select it, and then click the **Day** button at the bottom of the screen. Or just double-click the May 21 cell. This enters the Day view, which is essentially an expanded version of the right side of Month view (see Figure 1-39). The Daily Note section appears larger

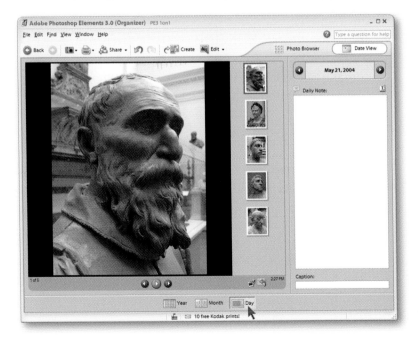

Figure 1-39.

and the slide show expands to fill the window. Click the big green ● button to watch the slide show, or click one of the flanking buttons to step through the images manually. You can also click a thumbnail in the column to see the image in the large preview.

To change which photograph serves as the date icon in the Month view, right-click the last of the five thumbnails—the one of the sleepy guy—and choose the only option, **Set as Top of Day**. The drowsy fellow immediately appears both in the preview and at the top of the thumbnail column, as in Figure 1-40. Now click the **Month** button at the bottom of the screen, and you'll see the new thumbnail in the calendar cell.

14. *Switch to Year view.* Finally, let's take a step back and look at the year in review. Click the **Year** button at the bottom of the screen to reveal the Year view, pictured in Figure 1-41. Although this view lacks thumbnails, it has everything else. Holiday dates are lavender, custom events are turquoise. Dates containing photos are shaded blue. The active date gets a thick outline, and you have access to the slide show and Daily Note field. From here you can click a date cell to select it, double-click a date cell to open it in Day view, or double-click a month name to open that month in Month view. The Organizer makes time-traveling so easy, H. G. Wells would be jealous.

Figure 1-40.

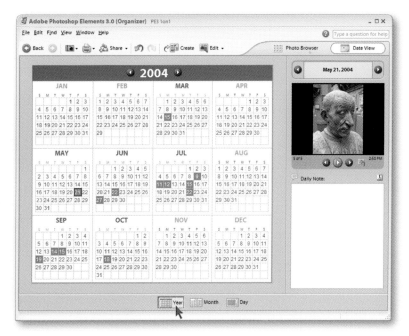

Figure 1-41.

Comparing Similar Photos

Digital photography encourages you to take a lot of pictures. After you finish paying for the camera, the memory card, and other equipment, snapping a digital photo is as close to free as anything the material world has to offer. But as you attempt to capture the perfect photo, you're liable to end up with piles of similar shots. It's possible to have so many shots, in fact, that you might want to see only the best one in the photo browser. But how do you choose which photograph is the best?

In this exercise, we'll look at two methods for studying and comparing photos, Photo Review and Photo Compare. You'll then learn how to create a *stack*, so that one shining image can serve as the representative for other similar photos in the photo browser.

1. *Go to October 18, 2004 in the Day view.* Assuming that you're picking up this exercise from the point at which we left the last one, make sure the **Date View** icon is active at the top-right corner of the screen. Click the **Year** button at the bottom of the workspace and navigate to that bygone year, 2004. Then double-click the cell for **October 18** in the calendar. Your screen should look like the one in Figure 1-42.

Figure 1-42.

2. *Enter photo review mode.* Notice the  icon below the thumbnail column (which I've circled in the figure). This icon launches the *photo review mode*, which is the Organizer's instant, full-screen slide show function. Photoshop Elements is big on slide shows, allowing you to create everything from inset slide shows in the date view to full-blown multimedia creations, deliverable in a PDF file or on a Video CD (as I examine in Lesson 12, "Slide Shows and Other Creations"). The photo review function falls somewhere in between, making it a great way to create an impromptu slide show without a lick of advanced preparation.

Click the icon or press the F11 key to display the **Photo Review** dialog box. Here I want you to make two changes:

- You're about to hear one of those hidden audio files that we imported into the catalog way at the beginning of the lesson. I'm not a big fan of the default choice. It's upbeat and cheerful to be sure, but it doesn't hold up well to repeated listenings. In other words, it will drive you nuts before this exercise is over. Set the **Background Music** option to something that wears better, namely **Light_Jazz.mp3**.

- Turn off the **Include Captions** check box. Unless you have specifically taken the time to add your own captions in the Properties palette, this option is more likely than not to display a statement from the camera vendor that does nothing but obscure your view of your images.

Figure 1-43.

When your Photo Review dialog box looks like the one in Figure 1-43, click the **OK** button. The workspace switches to the one pictured in Figure 1-44 on the next page. Problem is, nothing happens. The first image just sits there on the screen. Where the heck is the slide show?

3. *Start the slide show.* To get things rolling, click the green ⏵ button in the toolbar at the top of the screen. Or you can press the spacebar or the F5 key. The mellow piano music plays as the six images fade gracefully from one to the next. After Elements displays the final image, the slide show stops. But the piano plays on. For a moment there, it seems like it's going to stop. But after a brief lull, it starts up again. Nice music and everything, but enough is enough. How in the world do you get it to stop?

4. *Make the music stop.* Click the icon to the right of the trash-can in the toolbar to display a menu of options. Then choose the final one, **Photo Review Preferences**. Change the **Background Music** option to **None** and click **OK**. Ah, much better. Now I can hear myself type.

A few words about that toolbar, as labeled in Figure 1-44:

- Use the play controls to start and stop the slide show. Or better yet, press the spacebar to play and pause; use the ←·· and ··→ keys to advance from one slide to the next.

- The edit controls let you rotate and delete photos. The final edit control displays a pop-up menu of commands for tagging photos and adding them to collections.

- The next pair of icons let you switch between the photo review mode and the related-yet-altogether-different photo compare mode, which I explain in Step 5.

Figure 1-44.

- The zoom controls let you define how the images appear on the screen. By default, Elements scales an image to fit the screen size. If the image looks jagged, click the second zoom icon or press Ctrl+Alt+⓪ (that's the zero key) to view them at their smoothest size. You can also monkey around with the zoom slider (or press Ctrl+☐ or Ctrl+☐) to make the image shrink and grow.

In addition to playing slide shows, the photo review mode invites you to view single images at a time with its great zoom capabilities. For example, suppose that you're trying to inspect an image in the photo browser, but you just can't get in close enough, even at the highest level of magnification. Select the photo and choose View→Photo Review or press the F11 key. Then press Ctrl+☐ to zoom in as close as you want.

---

5. *Enter Photo Compare mode.* In addition to the photo review mode, Photoshop Elements provides a close companion known as *photo compare*, which splits the screen so that you can view two photos side by side (good for vertical, portrait-style shots) or top and bottom (better for horizontal photos like these). To enter the photo compare mode, do like so:

   - Click the first photo at the top of the right column of thumbnails. Once again, you should see me with my boys and my mouth wide open in an expression of manic joy.

   - Click the light blue ▤ icon in the toolbar (labeled *Photo compare* in Figure 1-44). Then choose the **Above and Below** command.

Elements divides the screen into two horizontal sections, with the first image at the top and the second at the bottom, as in Figure 1-45. Notice that Elements has numbered the corresponding thumbnails on the right side of the screen 1 and 2.

As you might guess, the photo compare mode is great for comparing photos. So let's compare the images of me and my kids, choose the best one, and stack the other five under our favorite in the photo browser.

Figure 1-45.

6. *Swap the second image for the third.* The top half of the screen is currently selected; you can tell because it's outlined in blue. I like this photo, so let's leave it up on screen. But that second photo can go. To select it, click in the bottom half of the screen so the blue outline surrounds it.

   Now click the third thumbnail in the right column or press the ↓ key. The image loads into the bottom half of the screen, and the third thumbnail receives the number 2.

7. *Examine the two images.* To examine the two images and choose the best, we need to increase their magnification.

   - In the toolbar, click ⊕ or press Ctrl+⊡. Elements zooms in on the lower image because it's selected.

   - Now click the 🔗 button on the far right side of the toolbar. This links the upper image to the lower one, so that the two zoom and pan together.

   - Continue clicking ⊕ or pressing Ctrl+⊡ until you reach 200 percent zoom level (as identified in the toolbar).

   - Drag inside either image with the hand-shaped cursor until my face is visible in both images, as in Figure 1-46.

   At this magnification level, it's clear that the focus is much sharper in the bottom image. Furthermore, the bottom image features the endearing sight of my little Sammy shoving a handful of leaves

Figure 1-46.

and twigs into my eye. How can you top that? Clearly, the bottom image is superior. Let's mark it as such by right-clicking the image and choosing **Attach Tag**→**5 Stars**. Or you can press Ctrl+5. As rated by me, this is now a five-star photograph.

8. *View the first six thumbnails in the photo browser.* Now that we know which photo is the best (okay, we didn't look at all six photos, but we saw enough), it's time to return to the photo browser.

   - Click the ⊗ button in the toolbar or press the Esc key to exit the photo compare mode.

   - With the top thumbnail selected in Day view, click the Byzantine little 🖻 button at the bottom of the thumbnail column. The Organizer cancels all filters left over from the preceding exercise and displays the image of me with the gaping maw in the photo browser.

9. *Stack the six leaves photos.* Adjust the zoom setting in the photo browser so you can see all six leaves images. Then select all six by clicking the first photo and Shift-clicking the last, as in Figure 1-47. Next, choose **Edit**→**Stack**→**Stack Selected Photos** or press Ctrl+Alt+S. All but the newest of the six photographs disappear. As shown in the magnified Figure 1-48, the remaining photo appears to be stacked in front of some other photos and bears a special icon, circled in yellow in the figure. This thumbnail indicates the existence of a *stack*.

Figure 1-48.

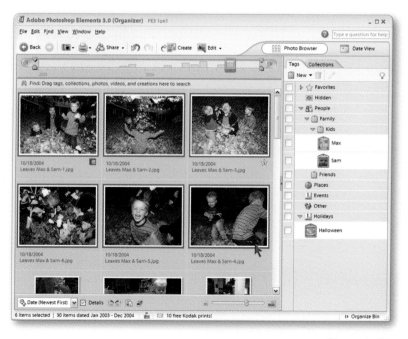

Figure 1-47.

Figure 1-49.

10. *View all six photos in the stack.* Although the stacked photos are currently invisible, they're still in the catalog. Let's view them: Choose **Edit→Stack** to display a submenu of commands. Notice that you can choose Unstack Photos to undo the stacking, or Flatten Stack to delete all stacked images from the catalog except the one that's visible. I want you to choose **Reveal Photos in Stack** or press the keyboard shortcut Ctrl+Alt+R. As shown in Figure 1-49, the Organizer hides all photos except the six inside the selected stack.

11. *Place the fourth thumbnail at the top of the stack.* Right-click the leaves-in-the-eye thumbnail—the one marked with the yellow ☆ that we assigned in Step 7—and choose **Stack→Set as Top Photo**. The 5-star image becomes the first thumbnail in the browser window.

12. *View all photos.* Click the **Back to All Photos** button. As shown in the magnified Figure 1-50, the new thumbnail assumes its place of honor as the representative photo in the stack.

Figure 1-50.

Now you have an idea of what the Organizer can do, and what you can do with it. In the next lesson, we move on to the Editor. But never fear, we will revisit the Organizer on a regular basis in the forthcoming lessons, and eventually settle back inside it in Lessons 11 and 12. By any measure, this is an extraordinary and highly practical workspace.

WHAT DID YOU LEARN?

Match the key concept in the numbered list below with the letter of the phrase that best describes it. Answers appear upside-down at the bottom of the page.

Key Concepts

1. Welcome screen
2. The Editor
3. The Organizer
4. Catalog
5. Photo browser
6. Timeline
7. Tags
8. Collections
9. Date view
10. EXIF metadata
11. Stack
12. Photo review

Descriptions

A. These minicatalogs let you group images that share a common destination, such as a slide show; you also have the option to manually sort the order of images inside these groups.

B. Embedded in digital photographs, this special information explains the time the photo was taken and the make and model of the camera.

C. This Organizer view shows a collection of thumbnails in the order defined by the sort order pop-up menu.

D. This exceptional workspace serves as a file browser and lets you import images from a digital camera as well as a hard drive or CD.

E. When you assemble thumbnails into one of these, a single thumbnail serves as the representative for the other photos in the group.

F. This Organizer view sorts thumbnails into calendars, either by year, month, or day.

G. Photoshop Elements' main workspace (and the only one included on the Mac), this program lets you open and make changes to photos, such as adjusting brightness and contrast and retouching details.

H. A method for studying images in slide show format, with accompanying music (to drive you insane).

I. This introductory workspace explains some of the tasks the program can accomplish and provides direct links to the most essential features.

J. Strictly speaking, these are descriptive keywords that you can associate with one or more images.

K. The Organizer houses image thumbnails inside this kind of file, which remembers the links to the images on your hard drive and stores any information that you might want to associate with those images.

L. A feature of the photo browser, this charts the number of images that you captured on a month-by-month basis in the form of a column graph.

Answers

1I, 2G, 3D, 4K, 5C, 6L, 7J, 8A, 9F, 10B, 11E, 12H

QUICK FIX AND SAVE

WHILE THE ORGANIZER workspace is great for acquiring, managing, and comparing your photographs, its ability to change an image file is very limited. You can rotate a digital photo that was captured on its side. You can add keywords in the form of tags. You can even experiment with a few automatic correction functions by choosing Edit→Auto Fix Window (which just so happens to contain several options that we examine in this lesson). But when it comes time to really roll up your sleeves and improve the appearance of an image—whether to correct its brightness, sharpen its focus, or apply a few cool effects—you need the other great workspace included with Photoshop Elements 3, the Editor.

Available on both the PC and the Mac, the Editor workspace comes in two flavors. The first, the Standard Edit mode, is so capable and complex that I devote more than half of this book to it (see Lessons 3 through 10). The second, the Quick Fix mode, lets you apply a variety of corrections quickly and with little effort. As illustrated in Figure 2-1, Quick Fix relies on a series of buttons and slider bars along with original and corrected previews of the image. Happily, Quick Fix is simple enough to cover in a single lesson, and this lesson is it.

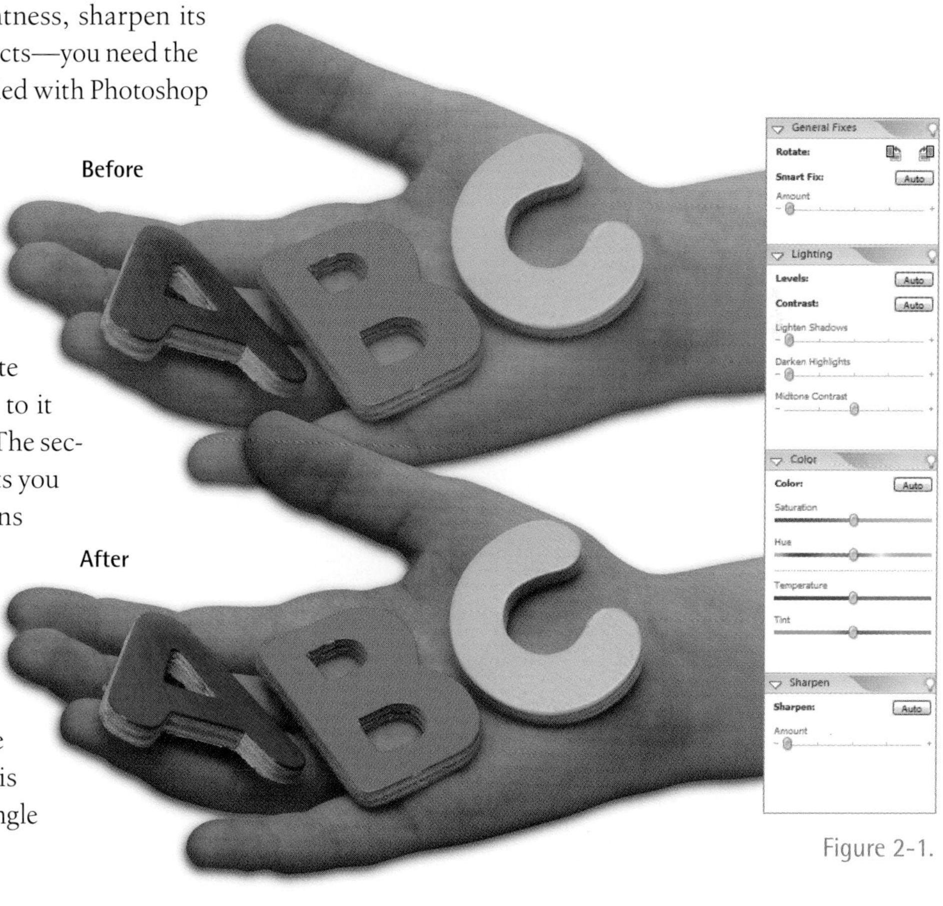

Before

After

Figure 2-1.

ABOUT THIS LESSON

Project Files

Before beginning the exercises, make sure that you've installed the lesson files from the CD, as explained in Step 5 on page xv of the Preface. This should result in a folder called *Lesson Files-PE3 1on1* on your desktop. We'll be working with the files inside the *Lesson 02* subfolder.

This lesson examines the Quick Fix mode, which lets you correct the colors in an image by clicking buttons and adjusting slider bars. Over the course of the lesson, you'll learn how to:

Video Lesson 2: Introducing Quick Fix

The Organizer is a great tool for acquiring and managing photographs. But if you want to modify an image, whether to correct its colors or apply a special effect, you need to turn to Photoshop Elements' more powerful workspace, the Editor. The Editor provides two modes, Quick Fix and Standard Edit. Although Quick Fix is far and away the simpler of the two, a treasure trove of hidden features slumber within.

To get an early glimpse at the Quick Fix mode, as well as learn how to navigate inside the Editor workspace, watch the second video lesson on the CD. To view this lesson, insert the CD, click the Start button, and then select 2, Introducing Quick Fix from the Lessons list. In just 6 minutes and 58 seconds, I explain the following operations and shortcuts:

Operation	Keyboard equivalent or shortcut
Apply the slider bar edits	Enter
Magnify the image preview	Click with the zoom tool
Zoom out from the image preview	Alt-click with the zoom tool
Fit the image on screen	Ctrl+⊡ (zero)
Zoom in to the Actual Pixels view	Ctrl+Alt+⊡ (zero)
Scroll with the hand tool	spacebar-drag inside image
Scroll up or down	Page Up or Page Down
Scroll to the right or left	Ctrl+Page Up or Ctrl+Page Down

Quick Fix Pros and Cons

To get to the Quick Fix mode, select one or more pictures that you want to edit inside the Organizer, and then choose Edit→Go to Quick Fix. (Alternatively, you can click the button labeled Quickly Fix Photos in the Welcome screen.) If the Editor workspace is not yet running, you'll have to wait a few moments for Photoshop Elements to start this independent program. You'll know that the Quick Fix mode is ready to go when you see a column of palettes headed by General Fixes (see Figure 2-2) on the right side of the screen. You should also see one or two large previews of your image; if not, open an image file from your hard drive by choosing File→Open.

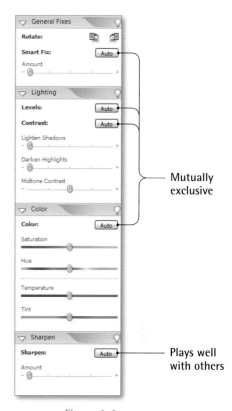

Figure 2-2.

The purpose of the Quick Fix mode is to address the most common problems that might face an image, as simply and efficiently as possible. To its credit, the program does an admirable job of matching a quick solution with a common problem. But I wouldn't go so far as to call the Quick Fix interface easy to use. The order in which options are presented is confusing and suggests relationships that don't exist. Among the Lighting controls, for example, the three slider bars have nothing to do with the Levels and Contrast options above them. Meanwhile, four of the five Auto buttons are mutually exclusive. If you don't like the results of clicking one, choose Edit→Undo before trying another. Of the five Auto buttons, only Sharpen should be combined with the others (see Figure 2-2).

If I'm starting to sound a bit critical, I beg your pardon, for I have one more cautionary note to share: Don't place much faith in the Auto buttons. Like all automated functions, these buttons trade control and predictability for ease of use. Given the current state of artificial intelligence—which is to say, pretty rudimentary—an Auto button is every bit as likely to produce a bad result as a good one.

All I'm saying is, the Quick Fix mode is no image magician. Like most computer software, it's a collection of useful controls that respond well to the reasoned input of an educated user. Fortunately, that's all right with you, because an educated user is precisely what you'll be when you finish this lesson. In the next several pages, I'll explain how the various palette settings work, what kind of color problems they're designed to fix, and when you can expect the best results. I'll also show you how to save your changes to disk, and how to use version sets to track the changes you've made to an image. By the end of this lesson, you'll not only have a sense of how the Quick Fix mode works, but also be ready to take on the more capable color adjustments that I cover in Lesson 3.

This lesson covers the color and focus options in the right column of palettes. Other options provided by the Quick Fix mode—namely, the tools in the upper-left corner of the screen—are duplicates of those included in the Standard Edit mode. For complete information on the crop and red-eye removal tools, see Lessons 5 and 6, respectively. To learn how to navigate inside the Quick Fix mode using the zoom and hand tools, watch Video Lesson 2, "Introducing Quick Fix" (see page 50).

Automatic Color Correction

The Auto buttons couldn't be easier to use. Click a button and watch it do its thing. You don't need my help to figure that out. The problem is, what "thing" is the Auto button doing? And is that thing going to benefit your image or make it worse? To answer these questions, we have to dig a bit deeper, which is the purpose of this first exercise.

The following steps examine the behavior of the first four Auto buttons, which let you modify the brightness and contrast of the colors in your image. (To learn about the other palette options, read "Lighting, Color, and Focus," which begins on page 65.) One of the buttons, Smart Fix, comes with a slider bar that lets you specify the amount of correction you want to apply. The rest are one-shot wonders. Each button is meant to be used independently of the others. Click a button. If you like the result, great. If not, undo and try another. Here's an example:

1. *Start the Quick Fix mode.* To start things off, I want you to enter the Quick Fix mode without opening an image. You can do this in one of two ways:

   • Click the **Quickly Fix Photos** button along the top of the Welcome screen.

   • In the Organizer, choose **Edit→Deselect** to turn off all the thumbnails. Then choose **Edit→Go to Quick Fix** (also available from the shortcuts bar).

   Photoshop Elements launches the Editor workspace and displays the Quick Fix interface. To confirm, check the upper-right corner of the screen and make sure that the Quick Fix icon is active, as labeled in Figure 2-3 on the facing page.

2. *Open an image.* Click the yellow folder icon, labeled on the left side of Figure 2-3. Alternately, you can choose **File→Open** or press the keyboard shortcut Ctrl+O. However you go about it, the **Open** dialog box is sure to appear on the screen. Make your way to the *Lesson 02* folder inside the *Lesson Files-PE3 1on1* folder that you installed from the CD. Then select the file called *Low contrast skull.jpg* and click the **Open** button.

Quick Fix mode is active

Open an image file

Figure 2-3.

3. *Assign the Adobe RGB profile to the image.* If you followed my advice in the preface and activated Full Color Management from the Color Settings dialog box (see page xvi), you'll be greeted by the alert message pictured in Figure 2-4, which tells you that the image lacks a *color profile*. Therefore, we can't be sure where the image came from or how its colors should really look. In this case, that's okay because the image requires such an enormous amount of correction that its source is ultimately irrelevant. Click the second option (as in the figure) to bring *Low contrast skull.jpg* into the current Adobe RGB color space, and then click **OK**. The dull and lifeless photo of a saber-toothed tiger skull appears on screen.

Figure 2-4.

The Editor Interface

The Editor workspace divides into two parts: the Quick Fix mode, shown on this page, and the Standard Edit mode, pictured on the next. Labeled in the figures in the bottom half of this two-page spread, the key elements of the Editor interface are as follows, in alphabetical order. (The orange labels indicate items that I discuss in the context of other interface elements; for a discussion of the small italic items, see pages 12 and 13 of the previous lesson.)

- **Editor modes:** Click a button in the top-right corner of the workspace to switch between the Quick Fix and Standard Edit modes. Pictured below, the Quick Fix mode lets you correct the colors in an image with relatively little effort. All other edits—from selections to filters, from layers to effects—are the domain of the Standard Edit mode, pictured on the facing page.

- **Image previews:** The Quick Fix mode presents you with one or two image previews. To determine how many previews appear, as well as their orientation, select an option from the View pop-up menu in the lower-left corner of the interface.

- **Image window:** In the Standard Edit mode, each open image appears inside a separate window, thus permitting you to open multiple images at once. The figure on the facing page shows five images open. But I've minimized all but one to keep the screen moderately tidy.

- **Options bar:** Available only in the Standard Edit mode, the settings here modify the behavior of the active tool. The options bar is *context sensitive*, so you see a different set of options each time you switch to a different tool.

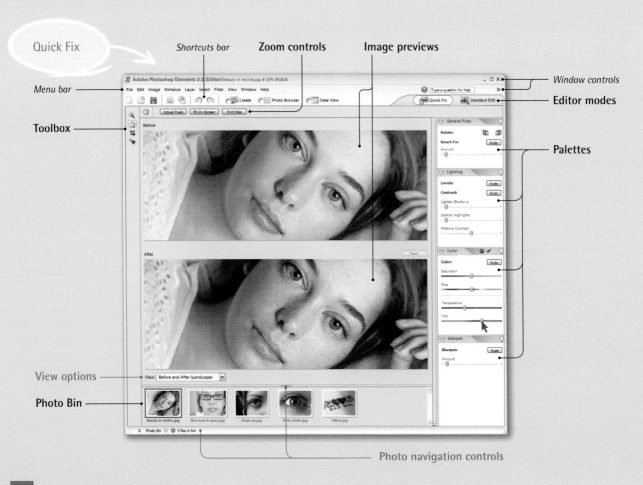

- **Palettes:** A *palette* is a window of options that remains on screen regardless of what you're doing. Most palettes reside in the Palette Bin, permanently affixed to the right side of the interface. But in the Standard Edit mode, palettes can "float" in front of the image window. To move a floating palette, drag the gray title bar at the top of the palette. To add a floating palette to the Palette Bin, click the More button and choose Place in Palette Bin, then click the ⊠ button in the palette's title bar.

- **Photo Bin:** One of the best additions to Photoshop Elements 3, the Photo Bin lets you browse through all images that are open in the Editor. In the figure below, I have a total of five images open, all provided by the good people at iStockPhoto.com. Click ◐ or ◑ to cycle from one image to the next. You can show or hide the Photo

Bin by clicking either of the buttons labeled *Photo navigation controls* below.

- **Toolbox:** The toolbox provides access to the Editor's drawing, editing, and selection tools. Click an icon to select a tool, then use the tool in the image preview or window. A small wedge (as in ◢) shows that multiple tools share a single box, or *slot*. Click and hold a slot to display a flyout menu of alternate tools. Or press the Alt key and click a slot to cycle between tools.

- **Zoom controls:** Use the zoom controls at the top of the Quick Fix window (see the facing page) to change the magnification of the image previews. You can also press the keyboard shortcuts Ctrl+⊡ or Ctrl+⊟ to zoom in or out, regardless of the mode.

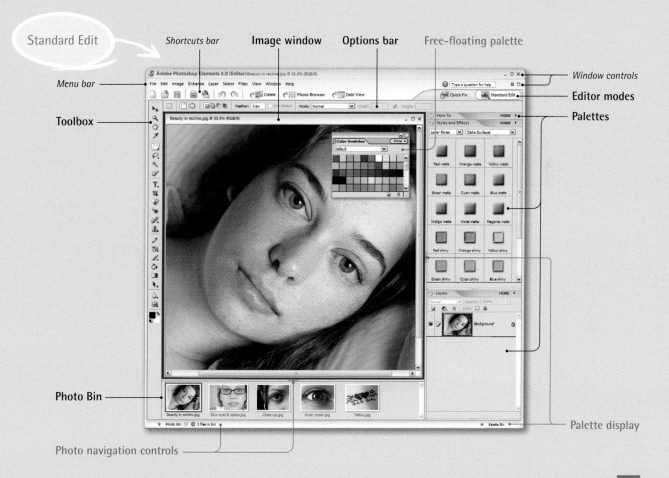

Standard Edit

Shortcuts bar · Image window · Options bar · Free-floating palette

Menu bar · Window controls · Editor modes · Palettes

Toolbox

Photo Bin

Photo navigation controls

Palette display

If you see the message pictured in Figure 2-4 when dealing with your own images, I recommend you likewise follow the advice on page 53. By bringing the image into the Adobe RGB color space, you ensure that your image will display and print correctly, even on a different computer. Getting consistent color from one device to the next is one of the most vexing parts of dealing with digital images, and color profiles help enormously.

If you don't get the error message, and you want to get in sync with the rest of the book, here's how: Click the lower of the two ✕ buttons in the upper-right corner of the screen to close the skull image. Next, choose Edit→Color Settings, select the Full Color Management option, and click OK. Now reopen the skull image and change its color space, as directed on page 53.

4. *Switch to a before-and-after view.* Given that you're not sure how best to go about correcting this image, you may find it helpful to compare the altered image to its original state. Go to the **View** menu in the lower-left corner of the window and choose **Before and After (Portrait)**. The view shifts so that the portrait-oriented (that is to say, vertical) photo is displayed in two side-by-side previews, as in Figure 2-5. The Before view shows the image as it looked when you first entered the Quick Fix mode; the After view shows the results of your edits.

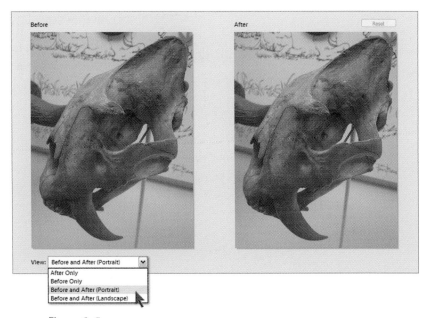

Figure 2-5.

5. *Apply Auto Contrast.* The skull image suffers from both low contrast and a slightly purple cast. Because the word contrast figures into the title of the image, let's try to fix that problem first. Go to the **Lighting** palette and click the **Auto** button to the right of the word **Contrast**. True to its name, the Quick Fix mode quickly fixes the image. As witnessed in Figure 2-6, the contrast improves dramatically, but the purplish cast lives on. It's okay, but I have a sneaking suspicion that a different Auto button might serve us better.

6. *Undo the last adjustment.* Before you can apply a new color adjustment, you need to "unapply" the preceding one in one of the following ways:

   - Click the blue ↩ icon in the shortcuts bar.

   - Choose **Edit→Undo Auto Contrast**.

   - Press Ctrl+Z.

   However you undo, Elements restores the right-hand preview to the original version of the image.

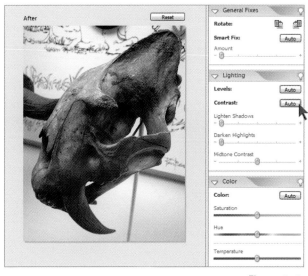

Figure 2-6.

7. *Apply Auto Levels.* Click the **Auto** button to the right of the word **Levels**. This time, Elements produces the effect shown in Figure 2-7. It's a better correction than the last one, almost entirely removing the purple cast. But is it the best the Quick Fix options can do? After all, the skull now looks a bit too brown, and other Auto color-correction functions remain untested.

The only way to know whether the other Auto buttons can do better is to try them out, which means undoing Auto Levels. At the same time, I want to reserve the right to come back to this edit. The next step explains a hidden method for doing just that.

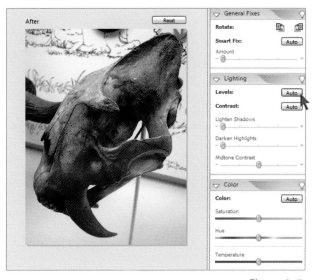

Figure 2-7.

8. *Switch to Standard Edit, then back to Quick Fix.* Without undoing or resetting the image, click the **Standard Edit** button in the upper-right corner of the screen. Photoshop Elements displays the corrected skull in an independent image window. Then click the **Quick Fix** button to return to the Quick Fix mode. Now both the Before and After views show the results of the Auto Levels adjustment.

9. *Undo the last adjustment.* Now here's the remarkable part: Click the blue ↺ icon in the shortcuts bar or press Ctrl+Z. Elements undoes the effects of the Auto Levels function and restores the original, low-contrast image to the After view. Thus in two easy steps, we've managed to swap the Before and After views, as in Figure 2-8. This permits us to keep the Auto Levels adjustment while trying out new ones.

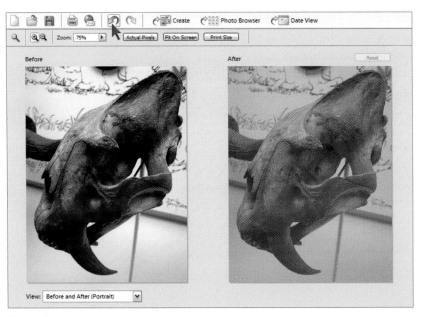

Figure 2-8.

10. *Apply Auto Color.* Click the **Auto** button at the top of the **Color** palette. Shown in Figure 2-9 on the facing page, the result comes close to accurately representing the original scene. But the real question is, do I like it the best? The greenish cast gives it a hospital flavor that I'm not too crazy about—and not just because this particular animal is beyond the help of modern medicine.

11. *Undo the correction.* Click the ↶ icon at the top of the screen or press Ctrl+Z to undo the operation.

Normally, you also have the option of clicking the Reset button to restore the image as it first appeared when you entered the Quick Fix mode. But in our case, this would reset the After view so it matches the present Before view (the post-Auto Levels state), and we don't want that. To step backward a single operation, undo is the way to go.

---

12. *Apply Auto Smart Fix.* Click the very first **Auto** button, the one to the right of the words **Smart Fix**. Photoshop Elements applies the most complex of its automatic adjustments. Pictured in Figure 2-10, the result bears a strong resemblance to the Auto Levels adjustment that you applied in Step 7. But if you look closely, you'll notice two important differences: First, the contrast of the Smart Fix image is more subtle, with lighter, more detailed shadows. Second, the Smart Fix image hangs on to some residual purple, in contrast to the strong orange cast of the Auto Levels correction. (If you're having problems seeing the differences on your screen, try flipping between Figure 2-10 on the right and Figure 2-7 on page 57. The figures are located in the same positions on their respective pages, so you can move back and forth between them like frames in a flip book.)

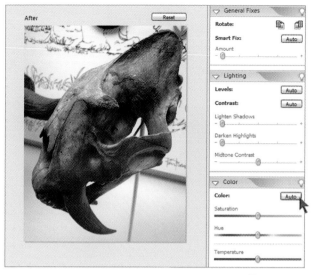

Figure 2-9.

EXTRA ⭐ CREDIT

The Smart Fix adjustment happens to be my favorite of the bunch, but it's still slightly more purple than I'd like. If it's good enough for you, feel free to skip to the next exercise, "Saving Your Changes," which begins on page 62. Or stick with me here and in a few brief steps, learn how you can adjust the performance of the Smart Fix function using a slider bar. It's subtle stuff, but worthy of a quick look.

---

13. *Undo the Smart Fix adjustment.* To see the results of the Smart Fix slider bar, you need to first cancel the effects of the previous adjustment. So as you've done so often in the past, click the blue ↶ icon in the shortcuts bar or press Ctrl+Z.

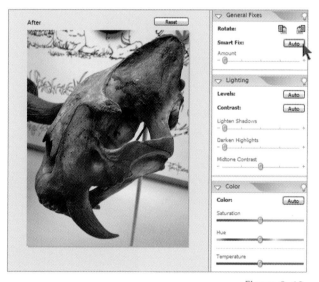

Figure 2-10.

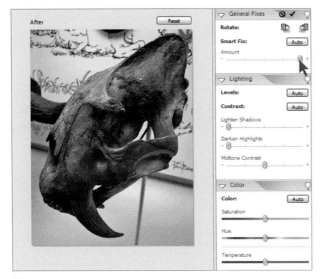

Figure 2-11.

14. *Adjust the Smart Fix Amount slider.* The Amount slider bar in the top palette permits you to vary the intensity of the Smart Fix operation. The middle setting is equivalent to clicking the Auto button. Experiment with moving the slider tab back and forth. Cranking the Smart Fix slider all the way to the left still has a profound effect on the image, but it leaves behind more purple than Auto. Moving the slider to the right trends the image toward yellow. Yellow is just what this photo needs. So drag the slider option all the way to the right, as in Figure 2-11.

15. *Commit the Smart Fix adjustment.* Elements doesn't apply the slider setting until you request it to do so in one of the following ways:

- Click the ✔ icon to the right of the General Fixes tab (just left of the light bulb).

- Press the Enter key.

- Apply a different color adjustment.

For now, just press the Enter key. For the sake of comparison, the final image appears beside the original in Figure 2-12. Keep this image open; we'll save it in the very next exercise.

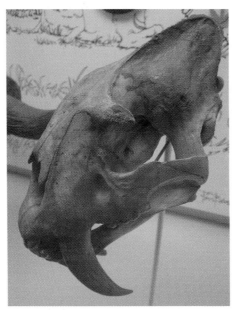

Uncorrected skull

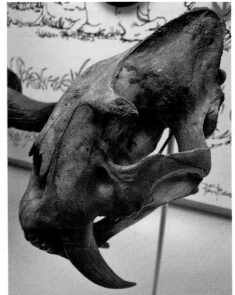

Smart Fix, cranked up to full volume

Figure 2-12.

By definition, an Auto button adjusts an image without troubling you with the details. But that doesn't mean it applies the same level of correction to one photograph as it does to another. Quite the contrary—each Auto button analyzes an image and corrects it accordingly. A dark image receives different correction than a light one, a yellowish image receives different correction than a bluish one, and so on.

Although every image gets individualized attention, the Auto button modifies it according to a consistent set of rules. The following list explains how each function works:

- **Auto Contrast** locates the darkest color in an image and makes it as dark as it can be without changing its color. It then makes the lightest color as light as possible. For example, if the darkest color is blue and the lightest color yellow, the blue becomes a darker blue and the yellow a lighter yellow. The color balance remains unchanged—just what you want when an image is properly colored but not at all what you want when it's not.

- **Auto Levels** makes no attempt to preserve colors. Instead, it makes the darkest color a neutral black and the lightest color a neutral white. The result is more often than not a shift in color balance. This can be a good thing if the color balance needs fixing. But Auto Levels may go too far, replacing one color cast with another. In the example below, the color cast shifts from pink to blue.

- **Auto Color** can be a bit slower because it tries to do more. Like Auto Levels, it deepens shadows and lightens highlights with the intention of creating neutral blacks and whites. But where Auto Levels may shift the shades in between from one color to another, Auto Color tries to pinpoint brightness ranges and keep them neutral as well. Among these are the middle colors in an image, known as the *midtones*. Auto Color finds the midtones that are closest to gray and then leeches away the color. By sheer coincidence, this happens to be the best method for automatically correcting the colors in the image below.

- Unique to Photoshop Elements, **Auto Smart Fix** is the most complex of the automatic color correction functions. Like Auto Contrast, it expands the contrast of an image without changing the lightest and darkest colors. It then brings out details by lightening the shadows and darkening the highlights. And finally, it evaluates the color cast and shifts the colors in the opposite direction. For the photo below, the result is a shift toward green.

Because it attempts to balance shadows, highlights, and colors, the Smart Fix function frequently outperforms the rest of the Auto pack. But it's by no means foolproof, as illustrated below. That's why I recommend that you test each of the Quick Fix mode's Auto functions and decide for yourself which one delivers the most desirable results.

| Original image | Auto Contrast | Auto Levels | Auto Color | Auto Smart Fix |

Saving Your Changes

Permit me to relate a rather sad but illustrative story. Back in March of 1994, I got my hands on my first digital camera, a QuickTake 100 from Apple. By modern standards, the images were tiny, measuring a scant 640 by 480 pixels. But at the time, the QuickTake was the height of cool technology. I knew Photoshop quite well by then, so I didn't hesitate to edit the photos and save the changes. In other words, I saved over the originals.

To understand the significance of this rash act, consider the photo in Figure 2-13. After shooting this image, I increased the brightness and contrast, rotated it, exaggerated the sharpness, and cropped it to a heartbreaking 409 by 634 pixels (reproduced here at a mere 140 pixels per inch). Today, I regard this image with a combination of horror and dismay. Garish, and noisy, it leans slightly to the left and drunkenly into the pinks. If I had the original, I could reapply my edits with the subtlety and savvy born of another decade of experience, not to mention the accuracy afforded by a more sophisticated screen display. But alas, I was so confident of my abilities and conservative with disk space that the edited file is all that remains.

Fortunately, Photoshop Elements prevents you from making such mistakes. The first time you choose File→Save, Elements asks you to save the image under a new name or in a different location so that the original file—the one captured by the digital camera or scanner—will remain intact. And it's a good thing too. As your image-editing acumen grows, you'll probably grow dissatisfied with your early efforts, just as I have. With the original images at hand, you can take a fresh crack at improving those old photos.

This exercise explains how to save your changes to an image with the future in mind.

Figure 2-13.

1. *Start with the corrected skull.* If you closed this photo, take heart; it's quick work to replay the last exercise. Open the file *Low contrast skull.jpg* in the *Lesson 02* folder. Then crank the Smart Fix slider all the way to the right and press the Enter key. Who knew I could summarize seven pages in a single paragraph?

2. *Choose the Save command.* Choose **File→Save** or press Ctrl+S to display the **Save As** dialog box. Most likely, Elements automatically takes you to the *Lesson 02* folder that contains the original skull photo. If not, make your way to the *Lesson Files-PE3 1on1* folder and then enter the *Lesson 02* folder.

To see thumbnail previews of your saved images, click the ▦ icon in the upper-right corner of the Save As dialog box and choose the thumbnails option, as illustrated in **Figure 2-14**.

---

3. *Rename the edited image.* The existing occupant of the **File name** option box hardly fits your newly edited image, does it? So change the name to "STT skull.jpg" or something similar. (STT stands for saber-toothed tiger, in case you're wondering.)

4. *Leave the other settings unchanged.* Pictured in Figure 2-14, these settings include the following:

   - The Format option determines how a file is saved and how it can be used in the future. The most common format for digital images is JPEG (pronounced *jay-peg*), which makes files small and portable. For higher quality images, you can choose TIFF, the format used to print all the images in this book. Or you can select Elements' native PSD (Photoshop Document), which lets you save your images with all the program's advanced features intact, including selections, layers, and editable text. For this exercise, leave the **Format** option set to **JPEG (*.JPG; *.JPEG; *.JPE)**.

   - Turn on the **Include in the Organizer** check box to automatically list the saved image inside the catalog that you last opened in the Organizer workspace. Assuming you haven't switched catalogs since you completed the last lesson (if you did, please take a moment now to switch it back), Photoshop Elements will add the corrected skull to the *PE3 1on1* catalog.

   - Turn on the **ICC Profile: Adobe RGB (1998)** check box to embed a color profile into your image, which identifies how Elements last displayed the colors. If you later open the image on another computer using an application that recognizes color profiles (such as Photoshop Elements,

Figure 2-14.

Photoshop CS2, and most other Adobe applications), there's a good chance the image will look approximately the same as it does on your computer.

- For compatibility with all varieties of computer systems—Windows, Macintosh, or otherwise—leave the **Use Lower Case Extension** check box turned on. This way, the filename will end in *.jpg* and not *.JPG*.

5. *Click the Save button.* Click **Save** to accept your filename and other settings and exit the Save As dialog box. Elements next displays the **JPEG Options** dialog box, which asks you to specify how you want the JPEG file to be saved.

6. *Confirm the JPEG settings.* The JPEG file format reduces the size of a file by compromising the quality of the image using what's know as *lossy compression*. Less quality means a smaller file on disk; more quality means a larger file. For the best balance, I recommend you adjust the settings in the JPEG Options dialog box as follows:

- Use the Quality setting to define the amount of compression applied to an image. You can adjust this value from as high as 12 to as low as 0. To see the effect of the Quality setting on the image, leave the Preview check box turned on and watch the After image in the Quick Fix mode. Elements also estimates the resulting file size at the bottom of the dialog box. For instance, a Quality setting of 12 results in a file size of about 750K, but a Quality of 0 takes it down to a mere 50K. For a decent looking image that's light on your hard drive, set the **Quality** option to 10.

- The remaining options controls how your JPEG image loads in a Web page. To ensure compatibility with other software, select the first option, **Baseline ("Standard")**.

7. *Save the image.* Click the **OK** button to save the image to disk. A second or two later, Photoshop Elements displays the new name of the image, *STT skull.jpg,* in the top-left corner of the Quick Fix mode window.

Congratulations, you've managed to save your corrected image and maintain the original digital photograph for posterity. Click the second ✕ in the upper-right corner of the screen or choose **File→Close** to close the skull image. (The first ✕ quits the program.)

Lighting, Color, and Focus

There's more to Quick Fix than a bunch of one-shot Auto buttons. You can achieve more control—and make dramatic improvements to an image—using the slider bars. In this exercise we'll explore the sliders in the Lighting, Color, and Sharpen palettes. And rather than opening an image directly into the Editor as we did at the beginning of the lesson, we'll try out a different scenario by importing an image into the Organizer and then handing it off to the Quick Fix mode. These steps will also set the foundation for the final exercise in this lesson, in which you'll learn about the Organizer's unique version sets.

1. *Open the Organizer.* Assuming you're still in the Quick Fix mode from the previous exercise, click the **Photo Browser** button in the shortcuts bar, as in Figure 2-15. (Depending on the size of your screen, you may see just the ⟲▦ icon without the text. That's the Photo Browser button, so go ahead and click it.) A few moments later, Elements loads the Organizer workspace and displays the photo browser.

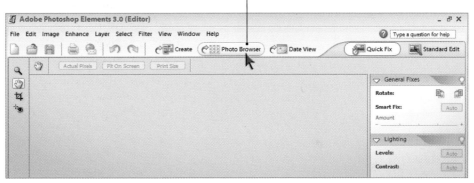

— Photo Browser button

Figure 2-15.

2. *View all the thumbnails.* If necessary, open the *PE3 1on1.psa* catalog using File→Catalog. Scroll to the bottom of the file browser and you'll find the corrected version of the saber-toothed tiger photograph, which Elements loaded into the Organizer per our instructions in the Save As dialog box (see Step 4, page 63). I shot the photo during a visit to the La Brea Tar Pits on February 22, 2003, making this the earliest image in the catalog. So it appears last in the sort order, as highlighted in Figure 2-16 on the next page.

3. *Import an image into the catalog.* Click the camera icon in the shortcuts bar and choose **From Files and Folders**, or just press Ctrl+Shift+G. Use the **Look in** pop-up menu at the top of the dialog box to switch to the *Lesson 02* folder inside *Lesson Files-PE3 1on1*. Select the file named *London Elle.jpg* and then click the **Get Photos** button. After the Organizer displays the imported image in the photo browser window, click the **Back to All Photos** button or click the Backspace key to see the image in context with the other photos in the catalog. I captured this photo of my wife drinking tea on May 19, 2004, just a couple of days before I shot the V&A busts. (As usual with these London photos, the time is off by several hours.)

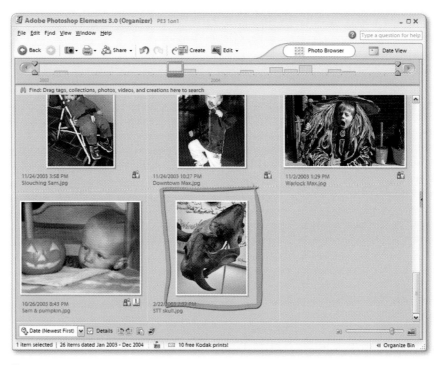

Figure 2-16.

4. *Open the image in Quick Fix mode.* Scroll to the imported image, the eighth from the end in the Organizer. Click to select it. Then click the **Edit** button in the shortcuts bar and choose the **Go to Quick Fix** command. A few moments later, Elements switches to the Quick Fix mode and inserts the photo in the Before and After previews.

If you want to see something interesting, press Alt+Tab or go to your Windows task bar and switch back to the Organizer for a moment. The thumbnail for *London Elle.jpg* now sports a red band and a lock icon (see **Figure 2-17**), signifying that it's open inside the Editor. The result: You can't tinker with it inside the Organizer. Who says the left hand doesn't know what the right hand is doing? Press Alt+Tab to switch back to the Editor and continue.

Figure 2-17.

5. *Experiment with the Smart Fix option.* While Elle is brightly lit, her background is the fabulous, formless darkness of a dimly lit pub during the morning rush hour. Much is hidden in the shadows. As a lark, click the **Auto** button to the right of **Smart Fix** in the top-right corner of the screen. In a flash, Elements exposes a world of detail in the shadows. But it also creates a weird bluish-green haloing, most evident in and around the right side of the image. Plus, it makes the light areas of the image pink. Nice try, Elements, but no cigar. Press Ctrl+Z to undo the operation and restore the original image.

Figure 2-18.

Figure 2-19.

6. *Lighten the shadows.* Now suppose you try a hand at drawing out the details in the shadows. Drag the **Lighten Shadows** slider until it's just a little to the right of the second tick mark (or more precisely, under the *d* in *Shadows*), as in Figure 2-18. This pulls a lot of detail from the background, but it doesn't have the same detrimental effect on the foreground as the Smart Fix option. Sure enough, you also draw out some of those nasty green edges, but don't fret; we'll take care of those in a few steps.

7. *Darken the highlights.* To offset the overly light areas in the foreground, drag the **Darken Highlights** slider to the right until it's under the letter *n* in the word *Darken*. Elements darkens the areas around the mug and the white objects on the table.

8. *Adjust the contrast in the midtones.* This helps to balance the extreme difference between the lighting of the foreground and the background objects. But to my way of thinking, the contrast remains a bit too hot, so a little more balancing is in order. Drag the **Midtone Contrast** slider a smidgen to the left, so it's under the *a* in *Contrast*, as in Figure 2-19. The image is a bit softer, a bit more subtle, a bit more representative of what I meant to shoot in the first place.

PEARL OF   WISDOM

At this point, you could accept the changes you made in the Lighting palette (Steps 6 through 8) by clicking the ✔ at the top of the palette or by pressing the Enter key. But no need. The moment you begin fooling around with the Color sliders in the next step, Elements will accept the Lighting adjustments automatically. The program then stores those adjustments as a single operation and restores the sliders to their original positions, allowing you to apply new adjustments as you so desire. If you were to later decide that you didn't like your Lighting adjustments, you would click ↶ or press Ctrl+Z to undo the operation and then reassign all three sliders.

---

9. *Experiment with the Hue control.* We need to somehow offset the olive-green cast of the image. The **Color** palette gives us several ways to accomplish this, so let's turn our collective attention to it. If you're working

on a small screen, click the ▽'s in front of General Fixes and Lighting to twirl those palettes closed.

We'll start with the Hue option, which lets you spin colors around the rainbow. Drag the **Hue** slider tab back and forth and see what happens. You can make my wife lime green, blueberry blue, and a host of other fruity flavors. But never better. A slight tweak left of center eliminates the green of the background, but it also makes Elle a hot pink. (That tea she's drinking can't be *that* hot.) As we'll see in Lesson 3, there are lots of uses for Hue adjustments, but this isn't one of them. Click the ⊘ at the top of the palette or press Esc to return the Hue slider to its default position.

10. *Adjust the Temperature and Tint setting.* Having witnessed the results of the Hue slider, it's obvious we don't really want to rotate *all* the colors in the image around the rainbow. We just want to peel away some of the greens. The Quick Fix mode offers two ways to remove a predominant color:

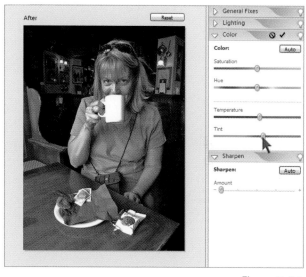

Figure 2-20.

- The job of the Temperature slider bar is to make colors cooler (that is, more blue) or warmer (more red). This image could use a little warming up, so drag the **Temperature** slider tab *very* slightly to the right, to the point just before you reveal the seam between blue and red in the slider bar.

- The Tint slider moves colors along a different axis, namely green to magenta. In our case, we want to do whatever it takes to move away from green. So drag the **Tint** slider a tab width to the right to urge those greens into remission without adding too much magenta, as in Figure 2-20.

11. *Boost the saturation.* Now that we have some good colors to work with, let's intensify them. Drag the **Saturation** slider a couple of tab widths to the right until Elle's T-shirt is a vivid orange, as in Figure 2-21. The effect is a bit much, but it serves to demonstrate the big difference a few tiny adjustments to a few slider bars can make.

Figure 2-21.

These steps provide a very basic introduction to color correction. We'll deal with all these issues—and many more—at greater length in Lesson 3, "Correcting Colors." But before we leave the Quick Fix mode, there's one more aspect to this photograph that I want to improve: the focus.

12. *Zoom the image to 100 percent.* Look closely at the Before and After previews. Notice how jagged the transitions are, especially around the edges of my wife's shirt and in her hair. Because we're zoomed out from the image, Elements is having to perform some very rough approximations. This jaggedness isn't a big deal when you're trying to adjust a photograph's colors, but if you want to concentrate on the focus, you need a smoother, more accurate view of the image.

    Click the **Actual Pixels** button in the top-left portion of the screen. This enlarges the image to the 100-percent view, so that every pixel in the image is matched to a pixel on your monitor's display. Get the hand tool from the toolbox on the left side of the screen (the one that looks like 🖐) and drag inside one of the image previews so that you can see Elle's face. The strands of her hair are now smoothly rendered. The 100 percent view is better for gauging the focus of an image, but you can't see as much of the image on-screen at any one time.

13. *Maximize your view of the image.* If you want to see more of the photograph, expand the amount of room devoted to the image previews:

    - First make sure the Editor workspace is taking up the entire screen. If it isn't, click the maximize button (▫) in the upper-right corner of the interface.

    - Second, hide the thumbnails at the bottom of the screen by clicking the ▼ **Photo Bin** button in the bottom-left corner of the screen.

    Figure 2-22 atop the facing page shows a detail from my expanded preview area, complete with larger and more magnified Before and After images.

14. *Try out Auto Sharpen.* If you need still more room, twirl closed the Color palette by clicking its ▽. Then click the **Auto** button in the **Sharpen** palette. Elements applies what it considers to be an ideal amount of image sharpening, but in my opinion, it's too much. Assuming you agree with me, click the ↺ icon in the shortcuts bar or press Ctrl+Z to remove the effects of the Auto button. Let's try the slider instead.

Figure 2-22.

15. *Sharpen the image manually.* In the Sharpen palette, drag the **Amount** slider tab so the tab appears under the *n* in the word *Amount.* As Figure 2-23 shows, this provides us with a more subtle sharpening effect that better outlines the important details in the image. Go ahead and click the ✔ or press the Enter key to accept this final adjustment.

Now that you've corrected the image, keep it open and continue directly into the next brief exercise, in which I show you how to save the edited image along with the original in the Organizer.

Saving in a Version Set

Now that you have this wonderfully improved version of *London Elle.jpg*, you'll naturally want to save and manage it in the Organizer just like the *STT skull.jpg* image. The difference this time is that the original version of *London Elle.jpg* is already in the Organizer. One solution is to change the name of the edited version to keep it from overwriting the original. But then you'd end up with two versions of the same photo in the Organizer. And is that what you really want?

Figure 2-23.

For example, suppose that while you want access to all incarnations of an image, you want to see just one thumbnail preview. And you want that one thumbnail to show the image at its best. As luck would have it, Elements provides the answer. You can save both the edited and original versions of the image in a version set. Generally speaking, a *version set* behaves like the stack of playing-in-the-leaves photographs that you created at the end of the last lesson (see Step 9, page 45). However, stacks are useful for manually consolidating similar photos in the Organizer, but version sets are created by the Editor workspace to consolidate photos that are *identical* except for color adjustments and other modifications. In the next steps, you'll save the edited version of my wife drinking tea in a version set along with the original image. You'll then see how the version set looks in the Organizer's photo browser.

Figure 2-24.

1. *Open the Save As dialog box.* Make sure the edited version of *London Elle.jpg* remains open inside the Quick Fix mode. (If the image is not open, follow the steps in the preceding exercise, "Lighting, Color, and Focus," which begins on page 65.) Then choose **File→Save** or press Ctrl+S to display the **Save As** dialog box.

2. *Turn on the Version Set option.* Turn on the **Save in Version Set with Original** check box, highlighted with an orange arrow in Figure 2-24. The Editor automatically suggests a new name for the file, *London Elle_edited-1.jpg.* This keeps the edited file from overwriting the original; plus, it initiates a numbering scheme, in the event you decide to save other edited versions of the image.

3. *Save and close the edited image.* Make sure the Save As dialog box is trained on the *Lesson 02* folder. Then confirm that all check boxes except As a Copy are turned on (as you can review in Figure 2-24) and click the **Save** button.

4. *Dismiss the Version Set message.* Elements greets you with a long but helpful message that explains the nature and purpose of version sets. After you've read and thoroughly digested the information, turn on the **Don't show again** check box and then click **OK**.

5. *Confirm the JPEG settings.* Next comes the familiar **JPEG Options** dialog box. Set the **Quality** value to 10, keep **Baseline ("Standard")** selected, and click **OK**.

6. *Close the image.* To best view the image in the Organizer, close it and free it from the Editor workspace. Choose **File→Close** or click the second ✕ in the upper-right corner of the interface.

7. *View the version set in the Organizer.* After closing the photograph in the Editor, Elements should automatically switch you to the Organizer workspace. If not, press Alt+Tab or click the **Organizer** button down in the Windows task bar to activate it. If necessary, scroll to the eighth image from the bottom, where you'll find the new *London Elle_edited-1.jpg* thumbnail, which appears highlighted in Figure 2-25. The version set icon appears in the upper-right corner of the thumbnail.

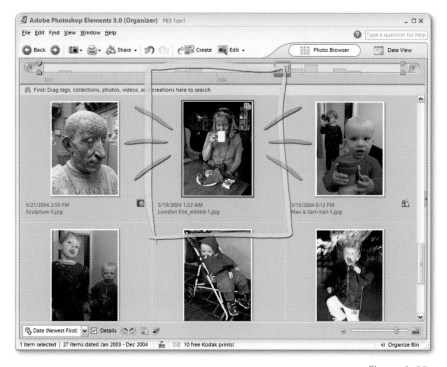

Figure 2-25.

8. *View the two photos in the version set.* Right-click the version set thumbnail and choose **Version Set** to display a submenu that makes available three commands:

   • Choose Reveal Photos in Version Set to display just those images contained in the version set.

   • The Flatten Version Set command disbands the version set and deletes all photos except the top thumbnail photo (by default, the edited version) from the catalog.

   • The third command, Revert to Original, disbands the version set and deletes all photos except the original.

Choose **Reveal Photos in Version Set** to view just two images in the photo browser, as in Figure 2-26. In case you don't recognize them, that's the edited version on the left and the original on the right.

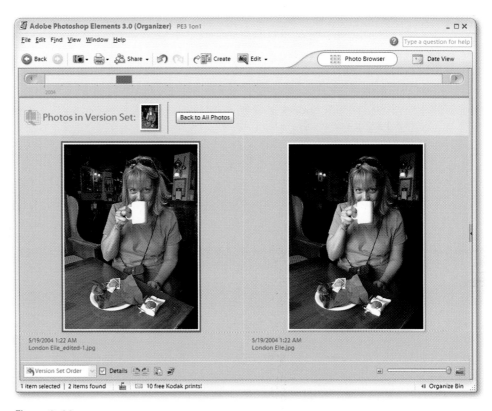

Figure 2-26.

Version sets let you have your cake and eat it too. You can manage all edited iterations of an image within the Organizer without the burden of having them take up space inside the photo browser. To return to the standard thumbnail view, click the **Back to All Photos** button or press the Backspace key.

WHAT DID YOU LEARN?

Match the key concept in the numbered list below with the letter of the phrase that best describes it. Answers appear upside-down at the bottom of the page.

Key Concepts

1. Quick Fix
2. Standard Edit
3. Color profile
4. Photo Bin
5. Auto Contrast
6. Auto Levels
7. Auto Color
8. Auto Smart Fix
9. JPEG
10. Temperature
11. Tint
12. Version set

Descriptions

A. The most powerful of the Auto functions, this button expands an image's contrast, lightens the shadows, darkens the highlights, and attempts to correct the color cast—all with varying degrees of success.

B. Makes the darkest color in an image as dark as possible and the lightest color as light as possible, without actually changing the colors.

C. This Editor mode offers the most capable and complex image editing tools in Photoshop Elements.

D. Similar to a stack, the Editor creates this type of image group to pair all edited versions of a photo with the untouched original.

E. Makes the darkest color in an image neutral black and the lightest color neutral white, usually creating a shift in color balance.

F. Makes colors cooler (more blue) or warmer (more red).

G. Embedded in an image file, this information helps maintain the image's consistent appearance from one computer screen to another, or from the computer screen to a printer or other device.

H. Adjusts colors along a strictly green-to-magenta axis.

I. This Editor mode lets you apply a variety of corrections to an image with only small investments of time and effort.

J. Deepens shadows and lightens highlights in an image, while at the same time changing them to neutral grays. It also leeches away the color from the midtones that are closest to gray.

K. This component of the Editor interface features clickable thumbnails that allow you to browse through all the images you have open.

L. This file format reduces the size of a file by compromising the quality of the image to the extent that you specify.

Answers

1I, 2C, 3G, 4K, 5B, 6E, 7J, 8A, 9L, 10F, 11H, 12D

LESSON

3

CORRECTING COLORS

I ADMIRE the Quick Fix mode. It really does try like crazy to automatically address some of the most common problems that afflict digital images. But it is not what I would call predictable. Even if you know exactly what a specific Auto button is supposed to do, clicking it is as likely to mess up an image as make it better. Photoshop Elements' brand of artificial intelligence is no substitution for the real thing.

Which brings us to the more complex but likewise more powerful Standard Edit mode. Once upon a time, Standard Edit was all there was to Photoshop Elements, and it remains the program's nucleus. As you'll experience in this and the next seven lessons, Standard Edit is far and away Elements' most capable, versatile, and practical workspace.

At heart, the Standard Edit mode is nothing more or less than an image cobbler. Its primary mission is to take a worn photograph, with the pixel-based equivalent of sagging arches and holes in its heels, and make it better. As with shoes, not all images can be repaired; some are hopelessly defective from the moment they leave the factory. But most images have more life left in them than you might suspect. And if anyone can fix them, you and the Standard Edit mode can (see Figure 3-1).

Over the next several lessons, I'll show you many different ways to correct a photograph—and the order in which these corrections are best applied. In addition to explaining how to use Photoshop Elements' tools and commands to their utmost ability,

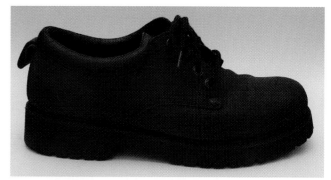
Uncorrected shoe

Corrected automatically (with Smart Fix) in the Quick Fix mode

Corrected in the Standard Edit mode
(could still use a real cobbler)

Figure 3-1.

ABOUT THIS LESSON

This lesson introduces you to Photoshop Elements' most capable color adjustment commands. We'll also explore such concepts as white balance and color temperature when we look at Elements' integrated support for Camera Raw. You'll learn how to:

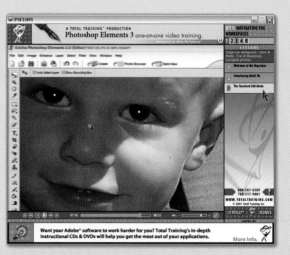

Project Files

Before beginning the exercises, make sure that you've installed the lesson files from the CD, as explained in Step 5 on page xv of the Preface. This should result in a folder called *Lesson Files-PE3 1on1* on your desktop. We'll be working with the files inside the *Lesson 03* subfolder.

- Neutralize a pronounced color cast . . . .
- Correct an image with a widespread color imbalance . . . .
- Increase the saturation of a drab photo . . . .
- Correct highlights, shadows, and midtones using the Levels command . . . .
- Reduce backlighting and boost shadow detail . . .
- Import and edit a high-color photograph shot with a digital camera . . . .

Video Lesson 3: The Standard Edit Mode

The Quick Fix mode is great at performing simple color manipulations. But when it comes time to roll up your sleeves and do some real work, there's no substitute for the Standard Edit mode. This is where the real power of Photoshop Elements resides, so much so that it fully occupies our attention for eight of the twelve lessons in this book.

To acquaint yourself with the Standard Edit mode, watch the third video lesson on the CD. To view the video, insert the CD, click **Start**, and then select **3, The Standard Edit Mode** from the Lessons list on the right side of the screen. This 8-minute 35-second movie tells you everything you need to know to get around inside the Standard Edit mode, and includes the following navigational shortcuts:

Tool or operation	Keyboard equivalent or shortcut
Open an image from the Organizer in the Standard Edit mode	Ctrl+I
Undo or redo an operation	Ctrl+Z or Ctrl+Y
Hide or show any free-floating palettes	Tab
Advance from one open image to the next	Ctrl+Tab
Zoom in or out	Ctrl+= (plus), Ctrl+- (minus)
Scroll with the hand tool	spacebar-drag in image window
Zoom in or out with the magnifying glass	Ctrl+spacebar-click or Alt+spacebar-click

I'll answer a rarely addressed question: When should you do what? Because every change you make to an image builds on the previous adjustment, sequence makes a difference.

In this lesson, you'll learn how to correct the colors in an image. In the next lesson, you'll use selections to isolate your corrections. And after that, we'll move on to cropping, sharpening, and so on. Amend each attribute of your troubled photograph in the order suggested by these lessons and you can rest assured that the results will look as good as they possibly can. This is how the pros do it.

Figure 3-2.

Hue, Saturation, and Brightness

Before we set about correcting the colors in an image, it may help to know what the term color means. As it just so happens, it means a lot. Color is too complex to define with a single set of names or numerical values. For example, if I describe a color as orange, you don't know if it's yellowish or reddish; vivid or drab; dark, light, or somewhere in between. To give you a better sense of what a color looks like, Photoshop Elements divides it into three properties called *hue*, *saturation*, and *brightness*:

- Sometimes called the *tint*, the hue is the core color—red, yellow, green, and so on. When you see a rainbow, you're looking at pure, unmitigated hue.

- Known variously as *chroma* and *purity*, saturation measures the intensity of a color. By way of example, compare Figure 3-2, which shows a sampling of hues at their highest possible saturation values, to Figure 3-3, which shows the same hues at reduced saturations.

Figure 3-3.

- Also known as *luminosity*, the brightness of a color describes how light or dark it is.

The contrast between Figures 3-2 and 3-3 may lead you to conclude that bright, vivid hues make for better colors. But while this may be true for fruit and candy, most of the real world is painted in more muted hues, including many of the colors we know by name. Pink is a light, low-saturation variation of red; brown encompasses a range of dark, low-saturation reds and oranges. Figure 3-4 shows a collection of browns at normal and elevated saturation levels. Which would you prefer to eat: the yummy low-saturation morsel on the left or the vivid science experiment on the right?

Figure 3-4.

Photoshop Elements provides a wealth of commands for correcting the colors in an image. The best of these—that is to say, the ones we'll be looking at—provide you with *selective control*, meaning that the commands let you adjust one color property independently of another. For example, you might change the brightness without affecting the hue or saturation. Armed with these amazingly capable commands, you have all the tools you need to get the color just right. Be it red or blue, night or day, the sky's the limit.

Eliminating a Color Cast

One of the most common color problems associated with digital images and photographs in general is color cast, a malady in which one color permeates an image to an unrealistic or undesirable degree. For example, an old photograph that has yellowed over the years has a yellow cast. A snapshot captured outdoors using the wrong light setting may suffer from a blue cast.

Naturally, Photoshop Elements offers a solution. Designed to restore a photograph's natural color balance, Enhance→Adjust Color→Remove Color Cast is superb at combining ease of use with great results. In fact, I might go so far as to call Remove Color Cast Elements' most successful consumer-level color correction function. As it just so happens, the command is available from both the Quick Fix and Standard Edit modes. We'll invoke the command from the Standard Edit mode, if for no other reason than Standard Edit is where we'll be spending the next eight lessons of the book.

1. *Open an image.* Make sure you're inside the Editor workspace. Then open the image called *Museum of the dead.jpg*, included in the *Lesson 03* folder inside *Lesson Files-PE3 1on1*. I captured this photograph of a deceased bighorn sheep through a plate of glass in the superb Denver Museum of Nature and Science. Thanks to the creature's willingness to remain still, the image is perfectly composed and focused. But my failure to account for the warm lighting of the diorama makes for an unnaturally yellow image. As a result, the saturation's okay but the ewe is all wrong.

2. *Switch to the Standard Edit mode.* Click the **Standard Edit** button in the upper-right corner of the application window, labeled in Figure 3-5 on the facing page. Elements populates the toolbox, switches out the palettes along the right side of the screen, and relegates the image to a free-floating window.

Click the
Standard Edit
button...

to see new
palettes...

not to mention,
a free-floating
image window

Figure 3-5.

If you prefer that the image fill the interface the way it does in the Quick Fix mode, choose Window→Images→Maximize Mode or click the ☐ icon in the upper-right corner of the image window. To reinstate the free-floating image window, choose the Maximize Mode command again or click the ⧉ icon immediately above the Standard Edit button, in the upper-right corner of the screen.

3. *Choose the Remove Color Cast command.* Choose **Enhance→Adjust Color→Remove Color Cast** to display the wordy dialog box pictured in Figure 3-6, which serves little purpose except to explain how the command works. No sense in reading Adobe's prose; you'll experience the feature for yourself a few short steps from now. But do leave the dialog box on screen until I tell you to dismiss it.

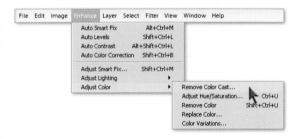

Unlike other color correction commands, Remove Color Cast does not list a shortcut. But if you like being able to access commands from the keyboard, there is a way. Press the Alt key and type the letters N-C-T (as in No Color casT). Alt+N displays the Enhance menu, C opens the Color submenu, and T selects Remove Color Cast. I must admit, it's not the most memorable keyboard trick, but I reckon I'd be remiss if I didn't pass it along.

Figure 3-6.

Figure 3-7.

4. *Magnify the image.* To see more detail and better evaluate the image, choose **View→Actual Pixels** or press Ctrl+Alt+⓪ (zero). This magnifies the image to the 100-percent zoom ratio. Amazingly, Elements lets you navigate inside the image window even when a color correction dialog box is on screen.

5. *Click inside the image.* Move the cursor out of the dialog box and into the photograph. Notice that the cursor changes to an eyedropper, which is Elements' way of showing you that you're about to read, or *sample,* a color. Now click. Assuming that the Preview check box is on, the image updates immediately.

   What's happening? When you click a color in the image, Photoshop Elements leeches away its saturation, making it *neutral.* This neutral color creates a kind of vacuum, one that Remove Color Cast fills by shifting neighboring colors. The trick, then, is to click on a color that ought to be colorless—black, white, or gray—so that other colors can emerge in its place.

   Feel free to click at different points inside the image. The changes are not cumulative—each click references the original image—so you can click as many times as you like. Figure 3-7 shows the results of clicking at four points inside the photo. (I added the yellow circles for emphasis.) Note that the lower-left corner of the cursor is the "hot spot," meaning that it defines the color that Elements neutralizes.

6. *Click the OK button to accept your changes.* Once you arrive at a group of colors you like—for my part, I like the final image in Figure 3-7—click the **OK** button in the dialog box.

7. *Apply the Auto Levels command.* The corrected image is a tremendous improvement over the original, but it's not perfect. My biggest complaint: there remains a slight lilac color cast. To get rid of it, choose **Enhance→Auto Levels** or press Ctrl+Shift+L. Yes, the Auto Levels function is available inside the Standard Edit mode, and yes, it helps. The final image appears below the original in Figure 3-8.

You are now finished with this image. Close the file by choosing File→Close, pressing Ctrl+W, or clicking the × icon in the upper-right corner of the image window. When Elements asks you if you would like to save the image, click the No button. The image has served its purpose; you won't be needing the saved changes. From this point on, I'll instruct you to save changes only when a subsequent technique or exercise demands it. Otherwise, when you arrive at the end of an exercise, feel free to close any images you may have open, abandon the changes, and move on.

Balancing the Colors

The Remove Color Cast command is swell so long as your image contains a color that should be gray. But what if no neutral color candidate exists? For those times, Photoshop Elements provides another command, Enhance→Adjust Color→Color Variations.

Like Remove Color Cast, the Color Variations command takes a straightforward approach to color restoration. But rather than previewing your corrections in the main image window, Color Variations presents you with a collection of tiny thumbnail previews. Your job is to click the one thumbnail that looks better than the others. You can click as many thumbnails as you like and in any order. The following exercise walks you through a typical use for the Color Variations command:

1. *Open an image.* Open the file named *Color science.jpg*, included in the *Lesson 03* folder inside *Lesson Files-PE3 1on1*. Captured without a flash under colored lights on the set of my Photoshop Elements video series for Total Training—in which I played one of those kooky chemists whose specialty is dry ice—this image suffers from what I like to call "A Nutty Preponderance of Red" (see Figure 3-9).

   To look at it, you might assume that this image would be well suited to the Remove Color Cast command. After all, the lab coat and bottled smoke contain gobs of what ought to be neutral colors. The problem is, Remove Color Cast applies wholesale changes, thus affecting all colors in an image by roughly equal amounts. (Try it for yourself and you'll see what I mean.) This photo requires a more nuanced approach.

2. *Choose the Variations command.* Choose **Enhance→Adjust Color→Color Variations** to display the **Color Variations** dialog box, as shown in the first figure on the next page, Figure 3-10.

   Again, Photoshop Elements does not provide a shortcut for Color Variations. But you can choose the command using Windows-imposed hot keys. To do so, press the Alt key and type N-C-N.

Before

After Remove Color Cast and Auto Levels

Figure 3-8.

Figure 3-9.

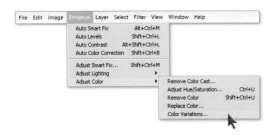

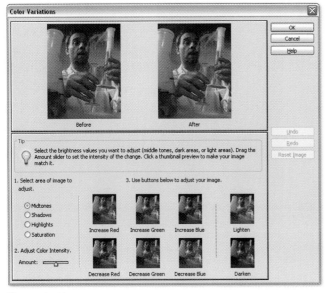

Figure 3-10.

Figure 3-11.

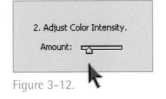

Figure 3-12.

3. *Select the Midtones option.* The Color Variations command lets you modify certain color ranges independently of others. It does so by subdividing the brightness of an image into three tiers—shadows, highlights, and midtones, or what the uninitiated might call dark colors, light colors, and everything in between. To specify the desired range, select one of the first three items in the lower-left portion of the Color Variations dialog box. Of the three, Shadows is sometimes useful, Highlights almost never. That leaves Midtones the option of choice. (As for Saturation, we'll come to it in a moment.) If it isn't already selected, give **Midtones** a click.

4. *Set the intensity slider to the middle.* The slider bar labeled **Adjust Color Intensity** lets you modify the intensity of your edits. Set the triangle to the exact middle of the slider, as it is by default.

5. *Click the Decrease Red thumbnail twice.* When Shadows, Midtones, or Highlights is active, the bottom portion of the dialog box contains a total of eight thumbnails: six hue variations and two brightness. Click any hue variation thumbnail to nudge the colors in the image toward or away from a range of hues. For example, Increase Blue represents not only blue, but a whole range of hues—violet, cobalt, and so on—that have blue at their center. (For more information about these and other hues, refer to the sidebar "The Visible-Color Spectrum Wheel," which appears on the facing page.)

Our problem color is red, so click the **Decrease Red** thumbnail twice in a row. (Be sure you get both clicks in; if you click too fast, Elements has a tendency to ignore one.) All hue thumbnails update to reflect the change, as illustrated in Figure 3-11.

6. *Decrease the intensity setting.* The remaining problems with the image are more subtle. To prepare for the subtle solutions, move the **Adjust Color Intensity** slider triangle two notches to the left. The triangle should now appear just slightly to the right of the far left side of the slider, as in the diminutive Figure 3-12. This setting will reduce the intensity of the next steps.

To feel comfortable working in the Color Variations dialog box, you have to understand the composition of a little thing called the *visible-color spectrum wheel*. Pictured below, the wheel contains a continuous sequence of hues in the visible spectrum, the saturation of which ranges from vivid along the perimeter to drab gray at the center.

The colors along the outside of the circle match those that appear in a rainbow. But as the labels in the circle imply, the colors don't really fit the childhood mnemonic Roy G. Biv, short for red, orange, yellow, green, blue, indigo, and violet. An absolutely equal division of colors in the rainbow tosses out orange, indigo, and violet and recruits cyan and magenta, producing Ry G. Cbm (with the last name, I suppose, pronounced *see-bim*). Printed in large colorful type, these six even divisions just so happen to correspond to the three primary colors of light—red, green, and blue—alternating with the three primary pigments of print—cyan, magenta, and yellow.

In theory, cyan ink absorbs red light and reflects the remaining primaries, which is why cyan appears a bluish green. Cyan and red represent *complementary colors*, meaning that they form neutral gray when mixed together. The Color Variations dialog box treats complementary colors as opposites. In other words, clicking the Decrease Red thumbnail not only reduces the amount of red in the image but also adds cyan. Similarly, Decrease Green adds magenta and Decrease Blue adds yellow.

Of course, Ry G. Cbm is just a small part of the story. The color spectrum is continuous, with countless nameable (and unnameable) colors in between. I've taken the liberty of naming secondary and tertiary colors in the wheel. Since there are no industry standards for these colors, I took my names from other sources, including art supply houses and consumer paint vendors. I offer them merely for reference, so you have a name to go with the color.

The practical benefit is that you can use this wheel to better predict a required adjustment in the Color Variations dialog box. For example, the color orange is located midway between red and yellow. Therefore, if you recognize that an image has an orange cast, you can remove it by clicking red's opposite, Decrease Red, and then clicking yellow's opposite, Increase Blue.

The other color-wheel-savvy command, Adjust Hue/Saturation (see the "Tint and Color" exercise on page 86), tracks colors numerically. A circle measures 360 degrees, so the Hue value places each of the six primary colors 60 degrees from its neighbors. Secondary colors appear at every other multiple of 30 degrees, with tertiary colors at odd multiples of 15 degrees. To track the difference a Hue adjustment will make, just follow along the wheel. Positive adjustments run counterclockwise; negative adjustments run clockwise. So if you enter a Hue value of 60 degrees, yellow becomes green, ultramarine becomes purple, indigo becomes lavender, and so on. It may take a little time to make complete sense of the wheel, but once it sinks it, you'll want to rip it out of the book and paste it to your wall. Trust me, it's that useful.

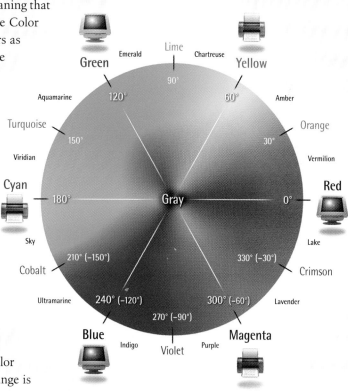

7. *Click the Lighten thumbnail.* At this point, the photo strikes me as a wee bit dark. So click the **Lighten** thumbnail to make the image lighter. Because the Midtones button is active (Step 3), clicking the Lighten thumbnail affects only the medium colors in the image. The darkest and lightest colors remain untouched.

8. *Click the Increase Green thumbnail.* After all these wonderful changes, the image remains a bit too purple. There is no Decrease Purple thumbnail. But by referring to "The Visible-Color Spectrum Wheel" chart on the preceding page, we find that purple's closest complement is green. So click the **Increase Green** thumbnail to infuse the image with green and reduce the amount of purple.

9. *Select the Saturation option.* So much for the brightness and hue, now on to saturation. To display the saturation controls, select **Saturation** in the lower-left portion of the dialog box. Color Variations swaps in two new thumbnails, which let you add or delete saturation.

10. *Click the Less Saturation thumbnail.* The colors in the photograph are a bit too vivid. Click **Less Saturation** to leech away colors and make them more neutral.

11. *Click the OK button.* It's hard to judge for sure from a bunch of dinky thumbnails, but the After image in the upper-right portion of the dialog box appears more or less on target. Click **OK** or press the Enter key to exit the Color Variations dialog box and apply your changes.

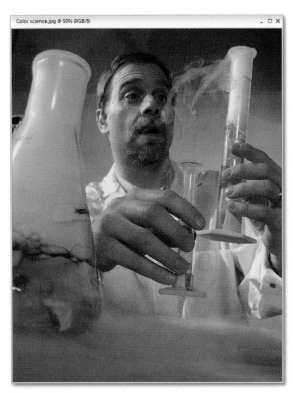

Figure 3-13.

Figure 3-13 shows the finished image, unencumbered by color cast, with my natural pale skin tone restored to all its pasty glory. We dry-ice chemists don't get out much.

Tint and Color

Like the Color Variations command, Enhance→Adjust Colors→ Adjust Hue/Saturation lets you edit a range of colors independently from or in combination with luminosity values. But where Color Variations permits you to limit your adjustments to brightness ranges (highlights, shadows, and midtones), Adjust Hue/Saturation lets you modify specific hues. This means you can adjust the hue, saturation, and luminosity of an entire photograph or constrain your changes to, say, just the blue areas. The following exercise provides an example.

1. *Open an image.* Open the *Helicopter & hotel.jpg* file in the *Lesson 03* folder inside *Lesson Files-PE3 1on1*. Having awoken one downtown Los Angeles morning to the unrelenting thrashing of a circling helicopter, I snapped this photo from the window of my hotel room. As shown in Figure 3-14, I was pointed into the sun, so reflected light obscures the view and washes out the image.

2. *Apply the Auto Smart Fix command.* The photo obviously suffers from low contrast and pale shadows. To right these wrongs, choose **Enhance→Auto Smart Fix** (yet another function available in both the Quick Fix and Standard Edit modes) or press Ctrl+Alt+M. The result appears in Figure 3-15.

3. *Choose the Hue/Saturation command.* Choose **Enhance→ Adjust Colors→Adjust Hue/Saturation** or press the keyboard shortcut Ctrl+U to display the **Hue/Saturation** dialog box, as shown in Figure 3-16.

4. *Raise the Saturation value.* Click the word **Saturation** to select the numerical value and change it to +60 percent. This radically increases the intensity of colors throughout the image. (Unlike the Color Range dialog box, Hue/Saturation updates the appearance of the image dynamically.)

Figure 3-14.

Figure 3-15.

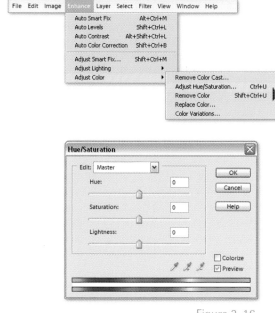

Figure 3-16.

Figure 3-17.

You can change the Saturation value by entering 60 into the option box (the + sign is not necessary) or by dragging the corresponding slider triangle. Alternatively, you can press Shift+↑ to raise the value in increments of 10. Or, weirdest of all, you can *scrub* the value by dragging directly on the word **Saturation**. Press Shift while scrubbing to adjust the value in increments of 10.

5. *Lower the Hue value.* The sky and mirrored windows of the building are trending distinctly toward purple. My sense is that they would look better if they trended toward blue. According to the color wheel ("The Visible-Color Spectrum Wheel," page 85), shifting the hues from purple to blue is a clockwise rotation, which means a negative value. Press Shift+Tab to select the **Hue** value. Then press Shift+↓ to reduce the value to –10 degrees, which removes the slight purple tint, as in Figure 3-17.

Generally speaking, the dramatic boost to the Saturation value holds up nicely. The red brick of the building looks terrific, as do the yellow reflections and some of the other touches. But the blue sky is just too much. In a lesser piece of software, we'd have to split the difference—that is, come up with a Saturation value high enough to boost the brick but low enough to avoid overemphasizing the sky. Fortunately, Elements lets us work on the sky and brick independently.

6. *Isolate the blues.* The Edit pop-up menu at the top of the Hue/Saturation dialog box is set to Master. This setting tells Elements to transform all colors in an image by an equal amount. To limit your changes to just the sky colors, select **Blues** from the **Edit** menu instead. This appears to wipe out your previous values. But don't worry, they remain in force; they're just hidden so we can work on new values.

Now just because you select Blues doesn't mean you've isolated the *right* blues. The blues in this particular photograph could exactly match Elements' definition of blue, but just as likely they could lean toward ultramarine, indigo, cobalt, or sky (again, see page 85). Although the Edit pop-up menu doesn't provide access to these colors, it does permit you to nail a range of hues by moving your cursor into the image window and clicking on the precise color you want to identify. The following step explains how.

7. *Confirm the colors in the image window.* The numerical values at the bottom of the dialog box read 195°/225° and 255°\285°. According to the color wheel chart, this tells

you Elements is prepared to modify the colors between ultramarine (225°) and indigo (255°), centered at blue. The change will taper off as the colors decline to sky (195°) and purple (285°).

Change your cursor to an eyedropper by moving it outside the Hue/Saturation dialog box. Then click near the moon in the upper-left region of the image. The numbers at the bottom of the dialog box should shift to something in the neighborhood of 180°/210° and 240°\270°, as in Figure 3-18. (If your numbers differ by more than 5 degrees, move your cursor slightly and click again.) These values describe a range of cobalt (210°) to blue (240°), with a softening as far away as cyan (180°) and violet (270°). In other words, Elements has shifted the focus of the adjustment by –15 degrees; so instead of changing the blues in the image, you're all set to change the slightly greener ultramarines.

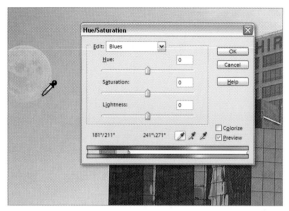

Figure 3-18.

Admittedly, the theory is dense, but one click is all it takes to translate the theory into action. Having isolated the colors in the sky, you're ready to make your changes.

8. *Lower the Saturation value.* Reduce the **Saturation** value to –40 percent to take some of the intensity out of the sky. This large Saturation shift may seem to make only a modest difference. But the sky no longer overwhelms other elements of the image, so all is well.

9. *Click OK.* Or press the Enter key to accept your changes and exit the Hue/Saturation dialog box.

The final image (Figure 3-19) is both more accurate and more dramatic than the original. One might argue that, of the two attributes, drama is given the edge. Well for crying out loud, the photograph has a helicopter in it. If that doesn't call for drama, I don't know what does.

Figure 3-19.

PEARL OF WISDOM

You may have noticed that throughout the entire exercise, I never once touched the Lightness value. And for good reason—it's rarely useful. The Lightness value changes the brightness of highlights, shadows, and midtones by compressing the luminosity range. Raising the value makes black lighter while fixing white in place; lowering it affects white without harming black. It's not the worst luminosity modifier I've ever seen, but other commands—most notably Levels and Shadows/Highlights—provide much better control. Happily, these very commands are the topics of the next exercises.

Adjusting Brightness Levels

Thus far, we've looked at three commands that permit you to adjust colors inside Photoshop Elements. But what happens if your image problems have less to do with color and more to do with luminosity? You most often hear such problems characterized as issues of brightness and contrast, where *brightness* indicates the prevailing lightness or darkness of an image and *contrast* denotes the degree of difference between light and dark colors.

Photoshop Elements pays lip service to this colloquialism with a little ditty known as Enhance→Adjust Lighting→Brightness/Contrast. Although exceedingly easy to use, this command lacks what I would describe as a reasonable degree of predictability and control. Simply put, Brightness/Contrast leaves you shooting in the dark; it is every bit as likely to damage an image as it is to make it better.

Figure 3-20.

Which is why we turn our collective attention to a better command, Enhance→Adjust Lighting→Levels. Although relatively difficult to use—this command isn't shy about asking you to roll up your shirtsleeves and smear on the elbow grease—Levels provides a perfect marriage of form and function. It lets you tweak highlights, midtones, and shadows predictably and with absolute authority while maintaining smooth transitions between the three. In other words, it makes an image looks its absolute best.

PEARL OF WISDOM

The Levels command is better at increasing contrast than decreasing it. To decrease the contrast of an image—particularly one with overly harsh shadows and highlights—see the exercise "Compensating for Flash and Backlighting," which begins on page 96.

The following exercise explains how to correct the brightness and contrast of an image with the Levels command:

1. *Open an image.* Open *End of rail.jpg*, found in the *Lesson 03* folder inside *Lesson Files-PE3 1on1*. Captured with an Olympus C-5050 at the top of Pikes Peak—right at the point where the cog railway drops into the abyss—this image features some atrocious light metering (see Figure 3-20). But don't blame the camera; I dropped it and broke off an important dial hours before I shot the photo. Fortunately, even though the camera was damaged, it captured enough color information to repair the photo in Photoshop Elements.

2. *Choose the Levels command.* Choose **Enhance→Adjust Lighting→Levels** or press Ctrl+L. Pictured in Figure 3-21, the stark and technical dialog box that follows may seem like something of a cold slap in the face, especially when compared with its user-friendly counterparts from preceding exercises. And so I feel it incumbent to provide an option-by-option introduction. If you don't care to be introduced, skip to the next step—it won't affect your ability to follow along with the steps one iota. Then again, you may find that you understand what you're doing a little better if you take a few moments to read the following:

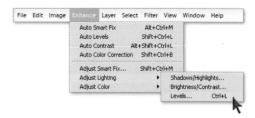

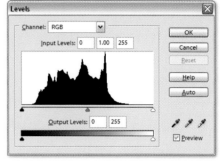

Figure 3-21.

- In the word of digital photography, an image is expressed as a combination of three primary colors: red, green, and blue. Each of the three primary colors resides in an independent reservoir called a *channel*. Located at the top of the Levels dialog box, the Channel pop-up menu lets you edit the contents of each primary channel independently. To edit the entire image at once, choose RGB, which just so happens to be the default setting.

- The three Input Levels values list the amount of adjustment applied to the shadows, midtones, and highlights, respectively. The default values—0, 1.00, and 255—indicate no change. More about these in a moment.

- The black blob in the middle is the *histogram*, which is a graph of the brightness values in your image. For more information on this item, read the sidebar, "How to Read and Respond to a Histogram," which begins on page 94.)

- The two Output Levels values let you lighten the darkest color in the image and darken the lightest color. In other words, they let you reduce the contrast. Although useful for dimming and fading, they rarely come into play when correcting an image.

- The Auto button applies the equivalent of the Auto Levels command, which you can then modify as needed.

- See the three eyedropper tools above the Preview check box? Select an eyedropper and then click in the image window to modify the clicked color. The black eyedropper makes the clicked color black; the white one makes it white; and the gray one robs it of color, leaving it a shade of gray.

- Turn on the Preview check box to see your changes applied dynamically to the active image.

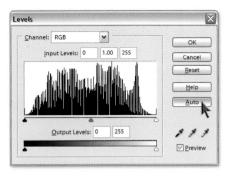

Figure 3-22.

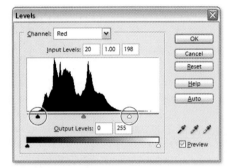

Figure 3-23.

Turn off the Preview check box to see what the image looked like before you chose the Levels command. Obvious as this may sound, the Preview option is great for before-and-after comparisons.

3. *Click the Auto button.* Click the **Auto** button to apply the Auto Levels function. The histogram stretches to fill the center portion of the dialog box, but the numerical Input Levels values stay the same, as in Figure 3-22. (You'll see why in the next step.) As in the previous lesson, Photoshop Elements' automated adjustment isn't perfect, but it's a good place to start. Now, however, we can use Levels to tweak the adjustment.

4. *Switch to the Red channel.* Choose **Red** from the **Channel** pop-up menu or press Ctrl+1. You now see the histogram for the Red channel, complete with adjusted Input Levels values, as shown in Figure 3-23.

PEARL OF WISDOM

Clicking Auto in Step 3 changed the Input Levels settings on a channel-by-channel basis. So even though you see an altered histogram in the composite view (as in Figure 3-22), you have to visit the individual channels to see the numerical changes.

5. *Nudge the shadows and highlights.* Notice the black and white slider triangles directly below the histogram (highlighted red in Figure 3-23). They correspond to the first and last Input Levels values, respectively. In my case, the black slider tells me that any pixel with a brightness of 20 or less will be made black in the Red channel; the white slider says any pixel 198 or brighter will be made white. (Your values may differ slightly. Remember, 0 is absolute black and 255 is absolute white.) Those values are okay, but I recommend you tighten them up a little—that is, send a few more colors to black or white. Nudge the black value from 20 to 30; nudge the white value from 198 to 168.

By *nudge*, I mean use the arrow keys on the keyboard. Highlight the 20 and press Shift+↑ to raise it to 30. Highlight 198 and press Shift+↓ three times to lower the value to 168. Together, these adjustments make the image slightly redder.

6. *Raise the midtones value.* Increase the middle **Input Levels** value to 1.23, thus increasing the brightness of the midtones in the Red channel. The result appears in Figure 3-24.

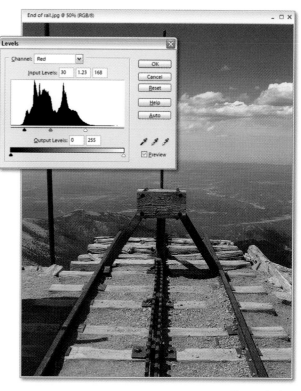

Figure 3-24.

7. *Switch to the Green channel.* Choose **Green** from the **Channel** pop-up menu or press Ctrl+2.

8. *Adjust the shadows, midtones, and highlights.* Change the three **Input Levels** values to 36, 1.25, and 205. This brightens the green values, as in Figure 3-25.

9. *Switch to the Blue channel.* Choose **Blue** from the **Channel** pop-up menu or press Ctrl+3.

10. *Adjust the shadows, midtones, and highlights.* This time, change the three **Input Levels** values to 50, 1.26, and 187. The changes to the black and white values darken the Blue channel, while the change to the gamma value lightens the midtones. The result is a slight shift in colors in the evergreens in the background and the dirt beneath the track.

11. *Switch to the RGB composite image.* Choose **RGB** from the **Channel** pop-up menu or press Ctrl+⊡. The ⊡ key is the ~ to the left of the 1.

12. *Raise the gamma value.* Advance to the second **Input Levels** value. (If this value was last active in the Blue channel, it remains active in the composite image.) Then press Shift+↑ twice to raise the value to 1.2. This lightens the midtones across all color channels, as shown in Figure 3-26 on page 96.

13. *Click OK.* Or press the Enter key to accept your changes and exit the Levels dialog box.

The resulting image is significantly brighter than the original photograph, especially where the midtones are concerned. One of the downsides of lightening midtones is that it tends to bleed some of the color out of an image. Fortunately, you can restore color using Adjust Hue/Saturation, as explained in the next step.

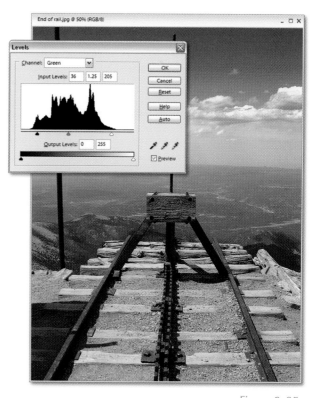

Figure 3-25.

How to Read and Respond to a Histogram

In the world of statistics, a *histogram* is a kind of bar graph in which the bars vary in both height and width to show the distribution of data. In the Levels dialog box, it's a bit simpler. The central histogram contains exactly 256 vertical bars. Each bar represents one brightness value, from black (on the far left) to white (on the far right). The height of each bar indicates how many pixels correspond to that particular brightness value. The result is an alternative view of your image, one that focuses exclusively on the distribution of colors.

Consider the annotated histogram below. I've taken the liberty of dividing it into four quadrants. If you think of the histogram as a series of steep sand dunes, a scant 5 percent of that sand spills over into the far left quadrant; thus, only 5 percent of the pixels in the image are dark. Meanwhile, fully 25 percent of the sand resides in the big peak in the right quadrant, so 25 percent of the pixels are light. The image represented by this histogram contains more highlights than shadows.

One glance at the image itself (opposite page, top) confirms that the histogram is accurate. The photo so obviously contains more highlights than shadows that the histogram may

seem downright redundant. But the truth is, it provides another and very helpful glimpse into the image. Namely, we see where the darkest colors start, where the lightest colors drop off, and how the rest of the image is weighted.

With that in mind, here are a few ways to work with the histogram in the Levels dialog box:

- **Black and white points:** Bearing in mind the sand dune analogy, move the black slider triangle below the histogram to the point at which the dunes begin on the left. Then move the white triangle to the point at which the dunes end on the right. (See the green graph below.) These adjustments make the darkest colors in the image black and the lightest colors white, which maximizes contrast without harming shadow and highlight detail.

- **Clipping:** Take care not to make too many colors black or white. If you do, you'll get *clipping*, an effect in which Photoshop Elements renders entire regions of your image flat black or white. Clipping is fine for graphic art but bad for photography, where you need continuous color transitions to convey depth and realism.

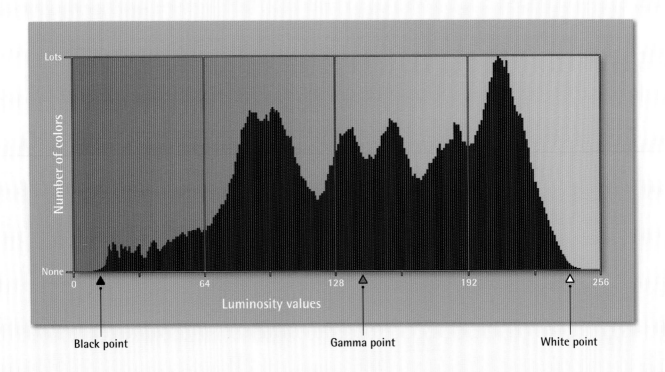

To preview exactly which pixels will go to black or white, press the Alt key as you drag a slider triangle. When dragging the black triangle, any pixels that appear black or any color *except* white (as in the example at the bottom of this page) will be clipped. When dragging the white triangle, Photoshop Elements clips the non-black pixels.

- **Balance the histogram on the gamma:** When positioning the gray gamma triangle, think "center of gravity." Imagine that you have to balance all that sand in the histogram

on a teetering board poised on this single gray triangle. If you position the gamma properly, you can distribute the luminosity values evenly across the brightness spectrum, which generally produces the most natural results.

Bear in mind that these are suggestions, not rules. For example, clipped colors can result in interesting effects. Meanwhile, an overly dark image may look great set behind white type. These suggestons are meant to guide your experimentation so you can work more quickly and effectively inside the Levels dialog box.

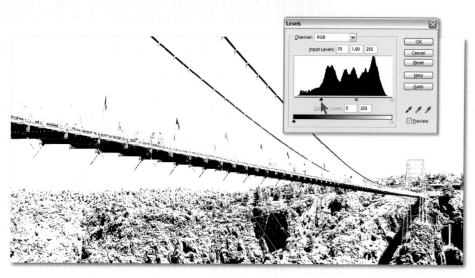

Figure 3-26.

Figure 3-27.

14. *Choose the Hue/Saturation command.* Choose **Enhance→Adjust Color→Adjust Hue/Saturation** or press Ctrl+U. As we saw in the "Tint and Color" exercise that began on page 86, the Hue/Saturation dialog box is especially adept at modifying the intensity of colors in an image.

15. *Raise the Saturation value.* Press Tab to advance to the **Saturation** value. Press Shift+↑ three times to raise the value to +30 percent. Then click **OK** or press the Enter key. The once drab image is now brimming with color, as shown in Figure 3-27.

The final image is a resounding success. But you may wonder how in the world I arrived at the specific values that you entered into the various Input Levels option boxes. The answer, of course, is trial and error. I spent a bit more time flitting back and forth between the channels and nudging values than the exercise implies, just as you will when correcting your own images. But as long as you keep the Preview check box turned on, you can see the effect of each and every modification as you apply it.

That said, my approach wasn't entirely random. Back in Step 8, I didn't know that 36 was the magic shadow value, but I suspected it was somewhere in that neighborhood. The trick is knowing how to read and respond to a histogram, as I explain in the aptly named sidebar "How to Read and Respond to a Histogram" on page 94.

Compensating for Flash and Backlighting

Photography is all about lighting—specifically, how light reflects off a surface and into the camera lens. So things tend to turn ugly when the lighting is all wrong. One classic example of bad lighting is *backlighting*, where the background is bright and the foreground subject is in shadow. Experienced photographers know that you adjust for backlighting by adding a fill flash, but even the best of us forget. An opposite problem occurs when shooting photos at night or in a dimly lit room using a consumer-grade flash. You end up with unnaturally bright foreground subjects set against dark backgrounds.

Whether your image is underexposed or overexposed, the solution is Enhance→Adjust Lighting→Shadows/Highlights. New to Photoshop Elements 3, this marvelous function lets you radically transform shadows and highlights while maintaining reasonably smooth transitions between the two. Here's how it works:

Figure 3-28.

1. *Open an image.* Open *Sammy in snow.jpg* from the *Lesson 03* folder inside *Lesson Files-PE3 1on1*. Having set my youngest against such a bright background (see Figure 3-28), I should have known better than to shoot a picture without a flash. But if, indeed, even the best of us forget, it's a wonder I remember anything at all. The result of my inattention is a photograph that casts Sammy in deep gloom, quite out of keeping with his sunny personality. Fortunately, Elements let me fix that.

2. *Open the Histogram palette.* Shadows/Highlights lets you modify the contrast of an image in ways that the Levels command simply can't match. But as we'll see, it lacks the Levels command's most prominent feature, the histogram. Fortunately, Photoshop Elements 3 lets you display the histogram any time you need it as a separate palette. Choose **Window→ Histogram** to display the **Histogram** palette, which shows you the very same histogram you see in the Levels dialog box. As you might expect, the histogram includes peaks on the left and right sides with a valley in the center, indicating lots of shadows and highlights separated by scarce midtones.

3. *Refresh the histogram.* Most likely, you'll see a tiny caution icon (⚠) in the upper-right corner of the histogram, which means you're viewing a cached (that is, old and inaccurate) version of the histogram. Caching saves Elements some computational effort, but it proves a hindrance when you're trying to gauge the colors in an image. To update the histogram based on the latest and greatest information, click the circular ↻ arrows or the yellow ⚠ icon, as in Figure 3-29. And incidentally, go ahead and leave the Histogram palette open. You may find it helpful to keep an eye on it in future steps.

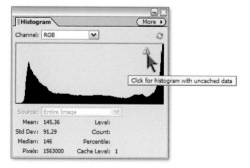

Figure 3-29.

Figure 3-30.

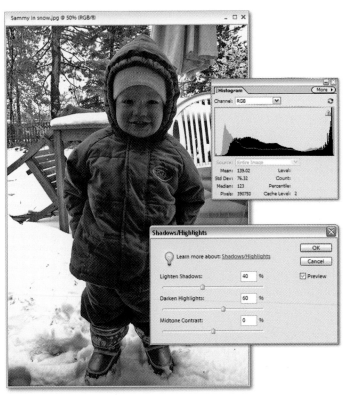

Figure 3-31.

4. *Choose the Shadows/Highlights command.* Choose **Enhance→ Adjust Lighting→Shadows/Highlights**. The resulting **Shadows/Highlights** dialog box (see Figure 3-30) contains just three slider bars:

  - The Lighten Shadows option lets you lighten the darkest colors in the photo—i.e., Sammy.

  - The Darken Highlights option darkens the lightest colors, which would be the snowy background.

  - The Midtone Contrast expands or contracts the midtones in the image to increase or reduce the amount of contrast between light and dark pixels.

No Ctrl-key shortcut exists for Shadows/Highlights. To choose the command using Windows-imposed hot keys, press the Alt key and type N-L-W. Again, it isn't memorable, but it's an option.

5. *Adjust the shadows and highlights.* By default, Elements is a little bit too enthusiastic about lightening the shadows and not enthusiastic enough about darkening the highlights. To temper the dark colors, reduce the **Lighten Shadows** value to 40 percent. Then raise the **Darken Highlights** value to 60 percent. Assuming the Preview check box is on (as by default), Elements updates both the image and the histogram. As Figure 3-31 shows, the black portion of the histogram is the updated view; the gray portion is the original.

6. *Reduce the contrast.* In lightening the shadows and darkening the highlights, the Shadows/Highlights command effectively reduces the contrast of the image. Elements provides the Midtone Contrast option so you can restore the contrast. But we have the opposite problem. This photograph exhibited such radical contrast in the first place that, if anything, we need to remove more. So press the Tab key to advance to the **Midtone Contrast** value and reduce the value to −40 percent.

7. *Apply your changes.* Click **OK** or press the Enter key to accept your changes and exit the Shadows/Highlights dialog box.

The result, which appears in Figure 3-32, is an improvement over the original, but it still needs some help. The shadows are now a bit too light; the midtones are a bit too dark. There's little I can do about this with the Shadows/Highlights command—not without compromising the integrity of the image, anyway. But I can easily fix both problems with Levels.

8. *Choose the Levels command.* Go to the **Enhance** menu and choose **Adjust Lighting→Levels** or press Ctrl+L. The **Levels** dialog box appears on screen.

9. *Change the shadows and midtones values.* Darken the shadows by changing the first **Input Values** option to 20. Then lighten the midtones by tabbing to the gamma value and changing it to 1.3. When you arrive at the effect pictured in Figure 3-33, click the **OK** button.

Shadows/Highlights is an amazing command, capable of reconstructing image detail captured under some of the worst lighting conditions imaginable. But it may produce some undesirable effects. Witness the almost greenish glow of Sammy's face and the shiny, color-shifting pattern of his coat and pants. In the course of exacting its radical brightness adjustments, the Shadows/Highlights command tends to flatten or exaggerate color transitions in ways that may compromise the credibility of surfaces and textures. The upshot is that even an inexperienced viewer might look at the photo and wonder, "Did you do something to this?"

Still, I regard these issues as acceptable casualties of correction. The lighting is now significantly more balanced than it was in the original photograph. Sammy no longer appears shrouded in silhouette. Heck, if you look closely, you can make out that he has brown eyes, compared with nearly solid black in the original. Despite its occasional compromises, Shadows/Highlights is Photoshop Elements' best tool for correcting extremely high-contrast images.

Figure 3-32.

Figure 3-33.

Correcting Camera Raw

The final method for correcting colors with Photoshop Elements 3 applies to photographs captured by a midrange or professional-level digital camera and saved in the camera's so-called *raw* format. This raw file represents the unprocessed data captured by the camera's image sensor. Such a file is typically several times larger than the equivalent JPEG file that digital cameras normally use for saving images, but it also contains more information. This means you can shoot fewer pictures at a time, but you capture a wider range of colors and more accurate image detail. Plus, in Photoshop Elements, you can open a raw image and correct its colors and luminosity values in a single operation.

PEARL OF WISDOM

At present, Photoshop Elements supports raw files from a select group of digital cameras sold by Canon, Minolta, Nikon, Olympus, and a few others. If you purchased a new camera for under $500, chances are it does not qualify (that is to say, it shoots only JPEG images, which you can open and modify using the techniques outlined in all the exercises *except* this one). Note: TIFF files are not considered raw files. If your camera supports both raw and TIFF, raw is the better choice; it offers all the advantages of TIFF and the file sizes are smaller. Check your camera's documentation for more information.

1. *Open a raw image.* Open the file *Daniel balloons.dng* in the *Lesson 03* folder inside *Lesson Files-PE3 1on1*. I captured this photo with an Olympus E-1 and saved it as an ORF (Olympus Raw Format) file. Then I converted the image to the more universal DNG (Digital Negative) format using Adobe's Digital Negative Converter software, which you can download for free from *www.adobe.com/dng*.

   Rather than opening the photograph in a new image window, Elements displays the Camera Raw window pictured in Figure 3-34. The window includes a high-resolution preview of the image and a full-color histogram, both of which update as you adjust the color settings. Use the zoom and hand tools in the upper-left corner of the window to magnify and scroll the preview, respectively.

   The title bar lists the model of camera used to shoot the photo as well as the light sensitivity (ISO), shutter speed, aperture, and focal length in use when the photo was captured. Elements uses this information to automatically process the image in the event that you decide to skip manual adjustments and go straight for the OK button.

Olympus E-1: Daniel balloons.dng (ISO 100, 1/200, f/7.1, 14.0 mm)

Figure 3-34.

2. *Rotate the image upright.* Click the second rotate icon (↻) in the lower-right corner of the image preview to rotate the photo 90 degrees clockwise. Or you can press the R key (short for rotate right).

3. *Set the White Balance controls.* The color cast of highlights in a photograph is commonly known as the *white balance*. Because of the trickle-down nature of white balance, you can neutralize a color cast throughout an image using the White Balance controls. Here's how:

- By default, the **White Balance** option is set to As Shot, which refers to the default calibration settings for this specific model of camera. To override this setting, select a lighting condition from the White Balance pop-up menu or dial in your own Temperature and Tint values, as follows.

- The **Temperature** value compensates for the color of the lighting source, as measured in degrees Kelvin. Low-temperature lighting produces a yellowish cast, so Elements "cools down" the image by making it more blue. Higher temperature lighting such as shaded daylight produces bluish casts, so Elements "warms up" the image by tilting it toward yellow. The closest thing to neutral is direct sunlight, which hovers around 5500 degrees.

- **Tint** compensates for Temperature by letting you further adjust the colors in your image along a different color axis. Positive values introduce a magenta cast (or remove a green one); negative values do just the opposite.

This particular image was shot outdoors with moderate cloud cover and no flash. So set the **White Balance** to **Shade**, which results in a **Temperature** of 7500 degrees and a **Tint** of 0, as shown in Figure 3-35. This setting makes the photograph a little warmer than it probably ought to be, but I like it that way.

Another way to set the white balance is to use the eyedropper tool in the upper-left corner of the Camera Raw window. Select the eyedropper and click a color in the image that should be white or neutral gray. Elements sets the Temperature and Tint values as needed. If you don't like the results, try again. Double-click the eyedropper icon to restore the As Shot values.

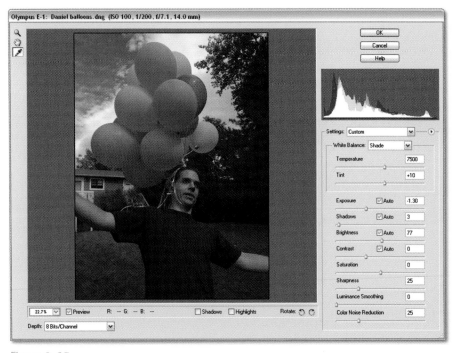

Figure 3-35.

4. *Adjust the highlights and shadows.* The Exposure and Shadows values are analogous to the white and black slider triangles, respectively, inside the Levels dialog box (see "Adjusting Brightness Levels," Step 5, page 92). The main difference is that Exposure is computed in f-stops. For example, raising the Exposure to +0.50 simulates opening the lens aperture of the camera a half stop wider.

I recommend raising the **Exposure** value to –1.10, a slight adjustment from the automatic setting but sufficient to help elevate the whites. Because the image contains plenty of black pixels, lower the **Shadows** value to 0.

Press the Alt key and drag the Exposure or Shadows slider triangle to preview clipped pixels. When you adjust the Exposure, non-black pixels indicate clipped highlights; for Shadows, non-white pixels represent clipped shadows.

---

5. *Lower the Brightness setting.* The closest thing to a gamma control in the Camera Raw window is the Brightness setting. It's not an exact match, but it does let you adjust midtones using a rough percentage system. Values below 50 compress shadows and expand highlights, thereby lightening an image; values above 50 do just the opposite. In this example, change the **Brightness** value to 125 to lighten what was previously an overly dark photograph.

6. *Adjust the Contrast and Saturation values.* The rest of the slider bars have no equivalents in the Levels dialog box, but I wish they did. The Contrast slider expands or compresses the histogram to increase or decrease the contrast between pixels, respectively. As always, the Saturation value increases or decreases color purity. Enter a **Contrast** value of –10 and a **Saturation** value of +20.

7. *Zoom in on the image.* The three remaining options let you sharpen the focus of a photo and smooth away noise artifacts. To best judge the details in your image, double-click the zoom tool icon in the upper-left corner to zoom in to 100 percent. Then press the spacebar and drag the image so you can see the look of abject terror in my brother's face, so very evident in Figure 3-36 on the next page.

8. *Set the Sharpness, Smoothing, and Noise values.* Here's how the three final slider bars work:

   - Raise the **Sharpness** value to increase the amount of contrast between neighboring pixels. Unlike Contrast, Sharpness doesn't affect the overall histogram; rather, it compares adjacent pixels and increases their difference from one another. (Lesson 7, "Filters and Distortions," contains lots more information.) The result is increased edge definition, which gives the appearance of sharper focus.

- If you increase the Sharpness value too much, you'll increase the contrast between pixels that should be smooth. The result is randomly colored pixels, or *noise*. To soften areas of noise that are the result of variations in lightness and darkness, increase the **Luminance Smoothing** value.

- To soften noise that results from variations in hue or saturation, increase the **Color Noise Reduction** value.

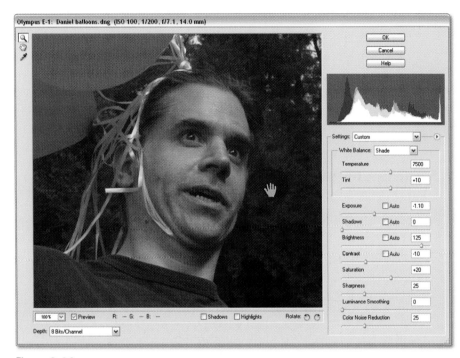

Figure 3-36.

PEARL OF WISDOM

If you plan to make significant changes to an image—particularly changes involving filters or layers (see Lessons 7 and 8, respectively)—you should leave all three values set to 0 to avoid overly harsh edges and increased noise down the road.

If you don't anticipate any major edits to a photograph, I advise that you crank the Sharpness up to 100 so you can see the image noise at full volume. Then use Luminance Smoothing and Color Noise Reduction to smooth out the rough patches. And finally, revisit the Sharpness option and adjust it to taste.

For this image, my preferred settings are **Sharpness**: 50, **Luminance Smoothing**: 20, and **Color Noise Reduction**: 50.

9. *Leave the Depth setting unchanged.* I now ask you to turn your attention to the bottom-left corner of the Camera Raw window, where you'll find an option called Depth. At the risk of overloading your brain—trust me, I wouldn't do it if I didn't have to—Photoshop Elements supports two varieties of full-color images. One contains 8 bits of data per channel, which works out to a maximum of 16.8 million potential colors. The other contains 16 bits of data per channel, which works out to as many as 281.5 *trillion* colors.

This particular raw image contains slightly more than a billion possible colors. In other words, Elements needs to convert it. You have two options for this conversion: reduce the colors by a factor of 64 to the 16.8 million-color space, or preserve all billion colors inside the gargantuan 281.5 trillion-color space.

The latter option might sound more logical, but it comes at an enormous price: 16-bit images are extremely demanding, so much so that most of Elements' editing functions don't work in the 16-bit color mode. Furthermore, no monitor or printer supports the 16-bit space, so all but a fraction of those trillions of colors are wasted.

My advice: Make sure **Depth** is set to **8 Bits/Channel**, as by default. Otherwise, you'll slow down the performance of the software, sacrifice much of the program's functionality, and gain almost nothing in return.

10. *Click OK.* Confirm that your values match those pictured in Figure 3-37. Then click the **OK** button. After you do, Photoshop Elements imports the image from the raw DNG format and applies the color and focus corrections that you specified in the previous steps. Note that the program does not save the zoom information; the image will appear zoomed out, so that it fits on the screen.

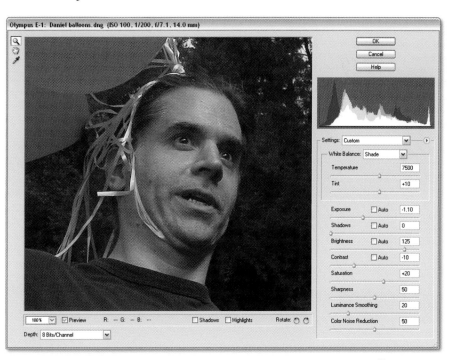

Figure 3-37.

The corrected photograph appears on the left side of Figure 3-38. For the sake of comparison, I include, on the right, the same photo subject to the default settings defined by the camera. (To see the image on your screen in this same condition, open the file again and choose Camera Default from the Settings pop-up menu in the Camera Raw window.) Quite obviously, the camera's default suggestions were off, as were the automatic guesses made by Elements' Camera Raw function. It just goes to show you, taking the time to assign your own deliberate and carefully considered color corrections makes all the difference in the world.

Final color-corrected raw photograph

Same photo according to the camera's default settings

Figure 3-38.

WHAT DID YOU LEARN?

Match the key concept in the numbered list below with the letter of the phrase that best describes it. Answers appear upside-down at the bottom of the page.

Key Concepts

1. Hue
2. Saturation
3. Brightness
4. Shadows
5. Highlights
6. Midtones
7. Complementary colors
8. Contrast
9. Channels
10. Histogram
11. Gamma value
12. Camera Raw

Descriptions

A. This file format preserves the unprocessed data captured by a camera's image sensor.

B. Sometimes referred to as *tint*, this property defines a color's core value—red, yellow, green, and so on.

C. Located on opposite sides of the visible-color spectrum wheel, these form neutral gray when mixed together.

D. The darkest range of colors in an image.

E. In the constitution of a digital photo, there are three of these independent reservoirs, one for each of the primary colors (red, green, and blue).

F. Also known as *luminosity*, this color property describes how light or dark the color is.

G. This is generally the most useful range of colors to adjust with the Color Variations command.

H. The degree of difference between an image's light and dark colors.

I. Known variously as *chroma* and *purity*, this property measures the intensity of a color.

J. A bar graph in which each bar represents one brightness value in an image, from black (on the far left) to white (on the far right).

K. The lightest range of colors in an image.

L. Known as the Levels command's "center of gravity," adjusting this setting modifies the midtones in an image independently of the shadows or highlights.

Answers

1B, 2I, 3F, 4D, 5K, 6G, 7C, 8H, 9E, 10J, 11L, 12A

MAKING SELECTIONS

MANY COMPUTER PROGRAMS let you ma-
nipulate elements on a page as objects. That is to say, you click or
double-click an object to select it, and then you modify the object
in any of several ways permitted by the program. For example, if
you go to the Windows desktop and double-click the Recycle Bin
icon, your PC shows you a window full of files that you've thrown
away. To make a word bold in Microsoft Word, you double-click
the word and then click the Bold button. Every object is a unique,
selectable thing.

The real world harbors a similar affinity
for objects. Consider the three sunflowers pictured in Figure 4-1. In life, those
flowers are objects. You can reach out
and touch them. You can even cut them
and put them in a vase.

But while Photoshop Elements lets you
modify snapshots taken from the world
around you, it doesn't behave like that
world. And it bears only a passing resemblance to other computer programs.
You can't select a sunflower by clicking
it because Elements doesn't perceive the
flower as an independent object. Instead, the program sees pixels. And as
the magnified view in Figure 4-1 shows,
every pixel looks a lot like its neighbor.
In other words, where you and I see three
sunflowers, Photoshop Elements sees a
blur of subtle transitions, without form
or substance.

Where you
see flowers...

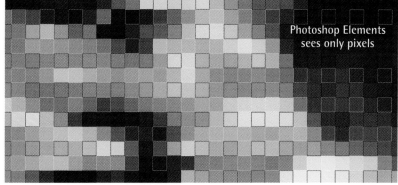

Photoshop Elements
sees only pixels

Figure 4-1.

ABOUT THIS LESSON

Project Files

Before beginning the exercises, make sure that you've installed the lesson files from the CD, as explained in Step 5 on page xv of the Preface. This should result in a folder called *Lesson Files-PE3 1on1* on your desktop. We'll be working with the files inside the *Lesson 04* subfolder.

This lesson examines ways to select a region of an image and edit it independently of another region using the magic wand, marquee, lasso, and selection brush tools as well as a few commands under the Select menu. You'll learn how to:

- Select a region that shares a common and continuous color . . . . page 112

- Define and use geometric selection outlines . . . . . page 119

- Select free-form portions of an image with the lasso and polygonal lasso tools . . . . page 125

- Create a selection outline by painting with the selection brush . . . . page 132

Video Lesson 4: Selection Tools

The selection tools in Photoshop Elements rank among the program's most fundamental capabilities. Simply put, unless you want to apply an operation to an entire image or layer, you have to first define the area that you want to affect by dragging or clicking with a selection tool.

To see an overview of the program's four selection tools, as well as some of the most common commands from the

Select menu, watch the fourth video lesson on the CD. To view this video, insert the CD, click the Start button, click the Set 2 button in the top-right corner of your screen, and then select 4, Selection Tools from the Lessons list. The movie lasts 10 minutes and 32 seconds, during which you'll learn about the following tools and shortcuts in the order listed below:

Tool or operation	Keyboard equivalent or shortcut
Rectangular or elliptical marquee tool	M (or Shift+M)
Move marquee as you draw it	press and hold the spacebar
Feather selection	Ctrl+Alt+D
Inverse (reverse selection)	Ctrl+Shift+I
Fill selection with background color	Backspace
Lasso or polygonal lasso tool	L (or Shift+L)
Subtract from a selection	Alt-click or drag with selection tool
Scroll image while drawing with polygonal lasso tool	spacebar-drag in image window
Hide selection outline	Ctrl+H
Magic wand tool	W
Add to a selection	Shift-click or drag with selection tool
Selection brush tool	A
Draw straight lines with the selection brush	Click, and then Shift-click

So rather than approaching an image in terms of its sunflowers or other objects, you have to approach its pixels. This means specifying which pixels you want to affect and which you do not using *selections*.

Isolating an Image Element

For example, let's say you want to change the color of the umbrella shown in Figure 4-2. The umbrella is so obviously an independent object that even an infant could pick it out. But Photoshop Elements is no infant. If you want to select the umbrella, you must tell the program exactly which group of pixels you want to modify.

Fortunately, Elements provides a wealth of selection functions to help you do just that. Some functions select regions of colors automatically, others require you to painstakingly define the selection by hand. Still others, like the tools I used to describe the bluish regions in Figure 4-3, select geometric regions. All the tools can be used together to forge the perfect outline, one that exactly describes the perimeter of the element or area that you want to select.

As if to make up for its inability to immediately perceive image elements such as umbrellas and sunflowers, Photoshop Elements treats *selection outlines*—those dotted lines that mark the borders of a selection—as independent objects. You can move selection outlines independently of an image. You can combine them or subtract from them. You can undo and redo selection modifications. You can even save selection outlines for later use.

Selected umbrella

Colorized using Gradient Map

Figure 4-2.

Figure 4-3.

Figure 4-4.

Furthermore, a selection can be every bit as incremental and precise as the image that houses it. Not only can you select each and every pixel inside an image—as a group or independently—you can also specify the degree to which you want to select a pixel—all the way, not at all, or in any of a couple of hundred levels of translucency in between.

This means you can match the subtle transitions between neighboring pixels by creating smooth, soft, or fuzzy selection outlines. In Figure 4-4, I selected the umbrella and the man holding it and transferred the two to an entirely different backdrop. Not only was I able to maintain the subtle edges between the man and his environment, I was also able to make the darkest portions of his coat translucent so they would blend with the backdrop. Selections take work, but they also deliver the goods.

Selecting Colored Areas with the Magic Wand

We'll start things off with one of the most automated tools in all of Photoshop Elements, the magic wand. A fixture of the program since way back when it was called Photoshop LE, the magic wand lets you select an area of color with a single click. It works especially well for removing skies and other relatively solid backgrounds, as the following exercise explains.

1. *Open two images.* Make sure the Editor workspace is running. Then open the *PhotoSpin giraffe.jpg* and *Bolivian backdrop.jpg* files, located in the *Lesson 04* folder inside *Lesson Files-PE3 1on1*. Press Ctrl+⊡ a couple of times to zoom out from both images, and then move the image windows onscreen so you can see most of both of them. Click the title bar for *PhotoSpin giraffe.jpg* to bring it to the front, as illustrated in Figure 4-5 on the facing page. Our goal during this exercise will be to select the giraffe with the magic wand tool and bring it into the *Bolivian backdrop.jpg* image. The fact that the two images come from different continents doesn't bother Photoshop Elements one bit.

PhotoSpin giraffe.jpg @ 50% (RGB/8)

Figure 4-5.

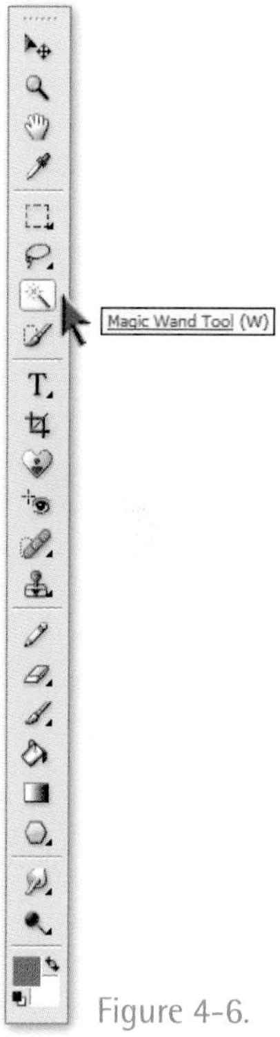

Magic Wand Tool (W)

Figure 4-6.

2. *Select the magic wand tool in the toolbox.* Click the magic wand tool in the toolbox along the left side of the Editor screen (see Figure 4-6) or press the W key.

3. *Confirm the options bar settings.* Pictured in Figure 4-7, the options bar displays a series of settings for the magic wand. Confirm that they are set as follows:

- The **Tolerance** value defines how many pixels the wand selects at a time. I discuss this very important option in Step 5. In the meantime, leave it set to its default, 32.

- Turn on the **Anti-aliased** check box to soften the selection outline just enough to make it look like an organic, photographic boundary. I talk more about this option in Step 13 on page 117.

- Turn on **Contiguous** to make sure that the magic wand selects uninterrupted regions of color. We'll get a sense of how contiguous selections work in Step 6.

Because this image does not include layers, the Use All Layers check box has no effect.

Tolerance: 32 ☑ Anti-aliased ☑ Contiguous ☐ Use All Layers

Figure 4-7.

Selecting Colored Areas with the Magic Wand   113

4. *Click anywhere in the sky.* For the record, I happened to click at the location illustrated by the cursor in Figure 4-8. But if my experimentations are any indication, you can click just about anywhere and you won't select the entire sky. Which may seem like an odd thing. Here's this tool that selects regions of color, and it can't select what may be the most consistently colored cloudless sky ever photographed. What good is it?

PhotoSpin giraffe.jpg @ 50% (RGB/8)

Figure 4-8.

5. *Raise the Tolerance value.* The Tolerance setting determines how many colors are selected at a time, as measured in luminosity values. By default, Photoshop Elements selects those colors that are 32 luminosity values lighter and darker than the click point. After that, the selection drops off. Given that Elements did not select the entire sky, the Tolerance must be too low.

   I suggest raising the value to 50. The easiest way is to click the word **Tolerance** in the options bar to highlight the value, enter 50, and press the Enter key. Note that this has no immediate effect on the selection. Tolerance is a *static* setting, meaning that it affects the next operation you apply, as Step 6 explains.

6. *Expand the selection using the Similar command.* The Select menu provides two commands that let you expand the range of a selection based on the Tolerance setting. They both affect any kind of selection, but they were created with the wand tool in mind:

   • Select→Grow reapplies the magic wand, as if we had clicked on all the pixels at once inside the selection with the magic wand tool. In other words, it uses the selection as a base for a larger selection. Grow selects only contiguous pixels—pixels adjacent to the selected pixels.

- Select→Similar is almost identical to Grow, except that it selects both adjacent and non-adjacent pixels. So where Grow would select blue sky pixels up to the point where it encounters non-blue pixels, such as the giraffe's mane, Similar selects all blue pixels within the Tolerance range regardless of where they lie, including those deep inside the mane.

Figure 4-9.

For our purposes, we want to get all the blue pixels, wherever they may reside, so choose **Select→Similar** as shown in Figure 4-9.

7. *Fill out the selection.* With a modicum of luck, you should have selected the entire sky. But if you miss a spot, press the Shift key and click on that spot in the image window. Shift-clicking with the magic wand adds to a selection.

8. *Reverse the selection.* You may wonder if this approach makes sense. You want to select the giraffe, and yet you've gone and selected the sky. As it turns out, this is by design. It's easier to select a solid-colored sky than a spotty-colored giraffe, and you can always reverse the selection. Choose **Select→Inverse** or press Ctrl+Shift+I to select those pixels that are not selected and deselect those that are. In this case, the giraffe is selected and the sky is not (see Figure 4-10).

Figure 4-10.

Figure 4-11.

9. *Select the move tool in the toolbox.* Click the move tool in the toolbox (see Figure 4-11) or press the V key (as in mooV). The move tool lets you move selected pixels within an image or from one image to another.

10. *Drag the giraffe into the Bolivian backdrop.* This operation is a little tricky, so make sure you read the following paragraph before you begin.

Position your move tool cursor inside the giraffe so the cursor appears as a plain arrowhead. Then drag the giraffe from the *PhotoSpin giraffe.jpg* image window into the *Bolivian backdrop.jpg* image window. Before you release the mouse button, press and hold the Shift key. Finally, release the mouse button and then release the Shift key.

What you just did is called a "drag with a Shift-drop." By pressing Shift, you instructed Photoshop Elements to center the giraffe inside its new background, as shown in Figure 4-12. Had you not pressed Shift, the giraffe would have landed wherever you dropped it. (If you didn't get it quite right, press Ctrl+Z to undo the operation and try again.)

Figure 4-12.

At this point, you have successfully used the magic wand tool to transfer the giraffe into a new habitat. The only problem is, it doesn't look particularly realistic. In fact, it looks like what it is—a digital montage. If that's good enough for you, skip ahead to the next exercise, "Using the Marquee Tools," which begins on page 119. But if you want to make this giraffe look like it's really at home, we have a few steps to go.

11. *Select the Background layer in the Layers palette.* The **Layers** palette most likely appears in the bottom-right corner of your screen, in the Palette Bin. If not, choose **Window→Layers** or press the F11 key to open it. You should see two layers, one for the giraffe—an imported selection always appears on a new layer—and another for the background. Click the **Background** layer to make it active, as shown in Figure 4-13.

Figure 4-13.

12. *Apply the Gaussian Blur filter.* To create a more realistic depth-of-field effect, blur the background. The best command for this purpose is **Filter→Blur→Gaussian Blur**. Choose this command, change the **Radius** value to 12 pixels, and click the **OK** button, as demonstrated in Figure 4-14.

13. *Zoom in on a few details.* Use the zoom tool at the top of the toolbox to zero in on the giraffe's horns and mane to gauge how well Elements selected the image. As you can see in Figure 4-15 on the next page, the selection has some slight problems:

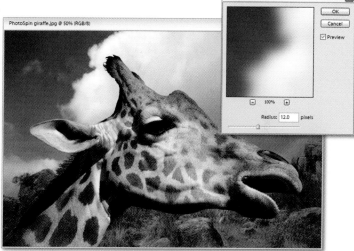

Figure 4-14.

- The horns look a little jagged. More careful inspection reveals that the jagged edges are mitigated by a slight softening effect. Known in technical circles as *antialiasing*, this softening is a function of the Anti-aliased check box that you turned on back in Step 3. The check box instructed the magic wand to partially select a thin line of pixels around the perimeter of the selection, thus creating a slight fade between the giraffe and its new background. Had you turned Anti-aliased off, the edges of the horns would appear even more jagged.

Selecting Colored Areas with the Magic Wand

- Pictured in the right half of Figure 4-15, the mane exhibits a problem called *haloing*, where a foreground image is outlined with a fringe of background color, in this case blue.

The jagged edges aren't perfect, but they look fine when we're zoomed out and are likely to print fine as well. The haloing is another matter. That you should fix. And fix it you shall with the help of a predefined layer style.

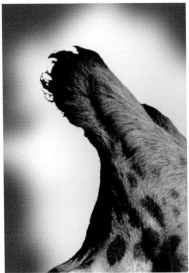

Figure 4-15.

14. *Select the giraffe layer in the Layers palette.* Click the **Layer 1** item to make it active.

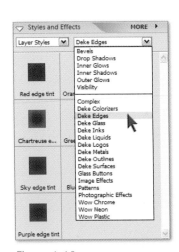

Figure 4-16.

15. *Bring up the Deke Edges styles.* Directly above the Layers palette, you should see a palette called **Styles and Effects**. If not, choose **Window→Styles and Effects** or press the F7 key to open it. The palette begins with two side-by-side pop-up menus:

   - Choose **Layer Styles** from the first pop-up menu to gain access to a series of drop shadows, glows, and other methods for tracing the perimeter of a layer.

   - Click the second pop-up menu to unfurl it. In the second half, you should see a collection of options that begin with the word Deke (see Figure 4-16). Choose Deke Edges to trace the inside edge of a layer with any of 10 colors.

16. *Apply the Orange Edge Tint style.* Of all the hues represented by the Deke Edges styles, orange is the one that best matches the yellowish brown of the animal's mane, spots, and horns. So click the thumbnail named **Orange Edge Tint** in the Styles

and Effects palette. Elements traces a subtle corona of orange around the inside perimeter of the giraffe.

17. *Adjust the layer style settings.* Currently, the inner glow effect is too thick, meaning that it doesn't merely tint the edges; it seeps into the giraffe's face as well. Fortunately, you can change this. Notice the ❷ to the far right of Layer 1 in the Layers palette? This symbol indicates that a style has been applied to the layer. Double-click the ❷ to display the **Style Settings** dialog box, and reduce the **Inner Glow Size** value to 40 pixels (see Figure 4-17) so the glow just covers the mane. Then click **OK**.

The Orange Edge Tint style ably corrects the blue haloing, as demonstrated in Figure 4-18. To learn more about layer styles and their many practical and creative uses, read Lesson 10, "Styles and Adjustment Layers."

Using the Marquee Tools

After seeing the magic wand and its ability to select irregular regions of color, you may question the usefulness of a geometric selection tool like the rectangular or elliptical marquee. After all, how many image elements are precisely rectangular or elliptical? The answer is: plenty. Every image begins life as a rectangle, and ellipses are as common as, well, our own Mother Earth.

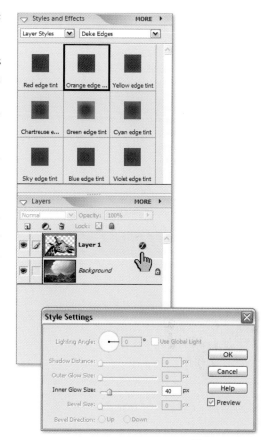

Figure 4-17.

Figure 4-18.

But it goes beyond that. Both are great for selecting general regions that you want to use for any of a wide variety of purposes, as the following exercise makes clear:

1. *Open three images.* Open the *PhotoSpin red sky.jpg*, *PhotoSpin road.jpg*, and *PhotoSpin moon.jpg* files, all of which appear in Figure 4-19. These files are located in the *Lesson 04* folder inside *Lesson Files-PE3 1on1*. In the following steps, we'll combine these images into a relatively complex composition using the undeniably simple rectangular and elliptical marquee tools. We'll also add a dynamic fill layer to make the colors of the road and moon conform to those of the vivid red sky.

2. *Select the rectangular marquee tool in the toolbox.* Bring the *PhotoSpin road.jpg* image to the front and click the rectangular marquee tool in the toolbox (see Figure 4-20) or press the M key. (If you accidentally select the elliptical marquee tool, press the M key again.) The rectangular marquee tool lets you select rectangular portions of an image.

Figure 4-19.

Figure 4-20.

3. *Confirm the options bar settings.* In the options bar, make sure that the **Feather** value is set to 0 and the **Mode** is set to **Normal**. These default settings ensure that the marquee tool draws hard-edged rectangles of unconstrained height and width. In other words, they cause the tool to behave normally.

4. *Select the bottom portion of the image.* Drag with the rectangular marquee tool to select the bottom portion of the *PhotoSpin road.jpg* image shown in Figure 4-21. Make sure you select all the way to the edges.

If you miss a bit of an edge, press the spacebar (while keeping the mouse button down) to temporarily stop drawing the marquee and instead adjust its position. When the spacebar is down, the marquee moves; release the spacebar to continue drawing.

---

5. *Choose the Feather command.* Choose **Select→Feather** or press Ctrl+Alt+D to display the **Feather Selection** dialog box, which allows you to blur the boundaries of a selection outline. Enter a relatively enormous **Feather Radius** value such as 120 pixels, and click **OK** (see Figure 4-22). Although the selection outline does not appear to change, have faith: This creates a gradual transition between selected and deselected pixels, as we'll see in the next step.

Figure 4-21.

PEARL OF WISDOM

If Feather is so deft at creating gradual transitions, why didn't we use it to fix the edges of the giraffe? The purpose of the Feather command is to blur the edges of a selection so that it has an indistinct boundary. A blurry boundary around a sharply focused giraffe would have looked all wrong. But a road that declines gradually into its background will look great.

---

6. *Drag the selected road and drop it into the red sky image.* You could use the move tool at the top of the toolbox, as in Steps 9 and 10 of the preceding exercise (see page 116), but this time I'd like you to try something different.

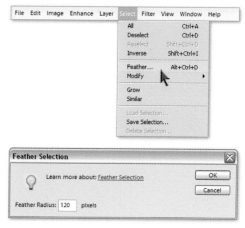

Figure 4-22.

Press and hold the Ctrl key to get the move tool on the fly. With Ctrl down, drag the selected portion of the road from *PhotoSpin road.jpg* into the *PhotoSpin red sky.jpg* image window. Before you drop the selection, press and hold the Shift key to center the selection inside its new home. Release the mouse button, and then release both keys. You should get the result shown in **Figure 4-23** on the next page.

---

7. *Bring the moon image to the front.* Click the title bar for *PhotoSpin moon.jpg* to bring it to the front.

8. *Select the elliptical marquee tool.* Go to the toolbox and choose the elliptical marquee tool from the marquee tool flyout menu. Or press the M key (or Shift+M, depending on your preferences).

9. *Select the moon (and then some).* Drag with the elliptical marquee tool to select an area well outside the moon, as illustrated in Figure 4-24.

Here are three keyboard tricks that can help you define your selection: Press the Alt key while dragging with the elliptical marquee tool to draw from the center of the image out. Holding Alt helps you align the selection outline evenly around the moon. Press the Shift key to constrain the ellipse to a circle. (The moon is not quite circular, but you still may find Shift helpful.) Press the spacebar to move the ellipse on-the-fly.

Figure 4-23.

Figure 4-24.

10. *Feather the edges of the selection.* Choose **Select→Feather** or press Ctrl+Alt+D. Enter a **Feather Radius** value of 12 pixels and click **OK**. Although you can't tell yet, this value blurs the outline around the moon. Granted, it's not as blurry as the super-gradual transition we assigned to the road, but it's blurry nonetheless.

11. *Drag the moon into the red sky image.* Press Ctrl and drag the moon into the *PhotoSpin red sky.jpg* image window. This time, instead of pressing the Shift key to center the moon, just drop it in front of the sun over the road, as pictured in Figure 4-25.

To move an image element after you drop it, press the Ctrl key and drag it to the desired location. You can also press the Ctrl key and nudge the image using the four arrow keys (↑, ↓, ←, →).

---

12. *Invert the colors in the moon.* Choose **Filter→Adjustments→ Invert** or press Ctrl+I to invert the light and dark colors in the moon. The moon turns a deep blue, as in Figure 4-26. I like the luminosity values, but I want the colors to match the rest of the image.

Figure 4-25.   Figure 4-26.

13. *Add a layer of vermilion.* We'll colorize the image in an unusual but highly effective way. Go to the **Layers** palette and click the ◕ symbol in the top row of icons. This displays a pop-up menu of specialty layers. Choose **Solid Color**, which creates a layer filled with a single color. To find out what color you'd like, Elements displays the **Color Picker** dialog box. The first three values—**H**, **S**, and **B**—stand for Hue, Saturation, and Brightness. Change them to 20, 100, and 100, respectively, as in Figure 4-27. Then click **OK**. Elements creates a new layer, completely filled with vermilion. This probably seems like a weird step—after all, you just blotted out your entire image! But suspend your disbelief for a moment and trust me, your devoted trainer: it'll look great.

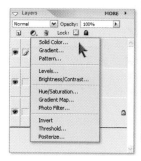

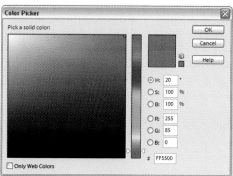

Figure 4-27.

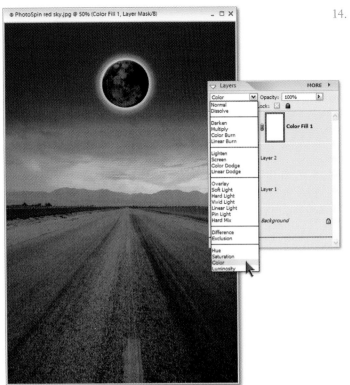

Figure 4-28.

Figure 4-29.

14. *Change the blend mode to Color.* Now to mix the vermilion with the layers below it. Click the word **Normal** at the top of the **Layers** palette and choose **Color** from the pop-up menu that appears. This retains the hue and saturation of the vermilion layer and mixes them with the luminosity values of the moon, road, and sky below it. See? All better. The colorized result appears in Figure 4-28.

15. *Create a new layer in front of the road.* Click the **Layer 1** item in the Layers palette. If you accurately followed the steps, Layer 1 contains the image of the road. Click the ▣ icon at the top of the palette to create a new layer in front of the road.

16. *Draw a new marquee.* Get the rectangular marquee tool by pressing M, pressing Shift+M, or selecting it from the toolbox. Then draw a marquee that connects the moon to the road. It should be slightly narrower than the moon and descend slightly into the road, as shown in Figure 4-29.

17. *Feather the selection.* When you choose **Select→Feather**, notice the Feather Radius value is still set to 12 pixels, as you specified back in Step 10. This continues to be a wonderful setting. To accept it and move on, click **OK**. The corners of the rectangular marquee appear to round off slightly.

18. *Hide the selection outline.* The selection outline is a bit intrusive for my taste, so let's hide it. Choose **View→Selection** or press Ctrl+H to hide the animated dotted outline—AKA, "marching ants"—around the marquee.

Note that the selection outline is still there; the animated outline is merely hidden so you better see the results of your changes. To redisplay the marching ants, press Ctrl+H again.

19. *Fill the selection with white.* Press the D key to restore the default foreground and background colors, black and white. Then press Ctrl+Backspace to fill the selection with the background color. Even though the selection is invisible, Elements goes ahead and colors it white.

20. *Reduce the Opacity setting.* The white rectangle is too opaque. I suggest we make it more translucent. Select the **Opacity** value in the Layers palette and change it to 40 percent. Or forget about selecting the value and just press the 4 key. So long as the marquee tool is still active, the column of white turns translucent, as in Figure 4-30.

Figure 4-30.

The Opacity value acts as an ingredient mixer. If you think of the white rectangle as one ingredient and the road below it as another, Opacity determines how much of each image is used to create the final blend. A value of 100 percent favors the rectangle. So 40 percent makes the rectangle quite translucent, with 60 percent of the road showing through.

The most amazing aspect of this other worldly composition is that we managed to pull it off using Elements' simplest selection tools, the rectangular and elliptical marquees. Of course, it didn't hurt to soften the transitions with the Feather command. I sincerely hope that the exercise leaves you with a sense of the many and varied applications for geometric selection outlines in Photoshop Elements.

Lassoing an Irregular Image

The lasso tools let you select irregular portions of an image. The primary lasso tool invites you to drag around an image to trace it freehand. But like freehand tools in all graphics programs, the lasso is haphazard and hard to control. That's why Photoshop Elements also includes a polygonal lasso, which allows you to select straight-edged areas inside an image. Admittedly, the polygonal lasso tool doesn't suit all images, particularly those that contain rounded or curving objects. But as you'll see, the tool is easy to control and precise to boot.

Figure 4-31.

Figure 4-32.

In the following exercise, you'll experiment with both the standard and polygonal lasso tools, and get a feel for why the latter is typically more useful. You'll also get the opportunity to play with a couple of special-effects commands from Elements' Filter menu.

1. *Open an image.* Open the *Denver Public Library.jpg* file located in the *Lesson 04* folder inside *Lesson Files-PE3 1on1.* This image captures an amazing work of architecture with a terribly dull backdrop, as shown in Figure 4-31. It seems to me that a structure like this should always be paired with a dramatic sky. Fortunately, Photoshop Elements excels at dark and stormy nights.

2. *Click the lasso tool in the toolbox.* It's the one that looks like a Wild-West-style lariat. Alternatively, you can press the L key. As I say, the lasso tool can be difficult to control. But I'd like you to experience the tool for yourself so you can decide what you think of it firsthand.

3. *Try dragging around the library building.* The portion of the building I'd like you to select appears highlighted in Figure 4-32. Trace along the red line to select the area inside the building. (The green area represents the region outside the selection.)

   The lasso is flexible, scrolling the image window to keep up with your movements and permitting you to drag outside the image to select the extreme edges. But if you're anything like me, you'll have a heck of a time getting halfway decent results out of it.

4. *Deselect the image.* Assuming your selection looks like complete and utter garbage, choose **Select→Deselect** or press Ctrl+D to throw it away and start over. If, on the other hand, your selection outline looks great, give yourself a gold star and skip to Step 7.

5. *Select the polygonal lasso tool in the toolbox.* Click and hold the lasso icon to display a flyout menu of additional tools and then choose the polygonal lasso (see Figure 4-33). Or just press L or Shift+L a couple of times. Either way, the polygonal lasso lets you select straight-sided areas inside an image.

6. *Click around the roof of the library.* I added the yellow arrowheads in Figure 4-34 to point to the eight corners at which you need to click. Start by clicking at the corner labeled ❶. (There's no special reason to start at this particular corner; it just seems as good a point of reference as any of the others.) Then move the cursor down to corner ❷. As you do so, a straight line connects the cursor to ❶. Make sure this line follows the line of the roof, and then click to set the corner in place. Keep clicking the corners in the order indicated in the figure.

Figure 4-33.

If you have problems, some words of advice. First, take your time. Click slowly and take care not to double-click, because that completes the selection. Second, if you make a mistake, press Ctrl+D to abandon the selection and try again. Third, hang in there; you'll get it.

After you click at corner ❽, you have two options for completing the selection:

- Click corner ❶ to come full circle and close the selection outline.

- Double-click at point ❽ to end the selection and connect points ❶ and ❽ with a straight segment. Or click at ❽ and press Enter.

7. *Select the elliptical marquee tool.* The central tower of the building is a cylinder, and the top of a cylinder is elliptical. You could try to select the rounded edges using the lasso. Or you could use a tool better suited to ellipses. Press M (or Shift+M) a couple of times or select the elliptical marquee from the toolbox flyout menu.

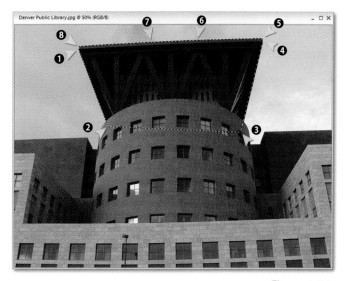

Figure 4-34.

8. *Select the cylindrical top of the building.* This is another tricky step, so read the following paragraph before you begin.

Press and hold the Shift key. Then drag with the elliptical marquee tool to add the new ellipse to the existing straight-sided selection. (Shift always adds; Alt subtracts.) After you begin your drag, you can release the Shift key.

Figure 4-35.

Figure 4-36.

As you drag, remember that you can press the spacebar to move the ellipse on-the-fly. When you get it into position, release the spacebar and continue dragging. When the ellipse is properly sized (as in **Figure 4-35**), release the mouse button.

9. *Select the polygonal lasso.* Click the lasso icon in the toolbox and select the polygonal lasso tool from the flyout menu. Or press the L key or Shift+L to return to the tool.

10. *Select the lower portion of the cylinder.* Press the Shift key and click the perimeter of the central building. It should take you just four clicks (see Figure 4-36). Remember to double-click or press Enter to close the selection.

So far, everything we've drawn has been a crisp-edged selection. The only softening is due to antialiasing, which minimizes jagged transitions. But let's say you want all future edges to be fuzzy. For example, in this image, we have yet to select the portion of the building at the bottom of the photo. For purely aesthetic reasons, I think it'd be terrific if this area sported a blurry selection outline. This requires adjusting the lasso tool's Feather value, as follows.

11. *Raise the Feather value in the options bar.* Click the **Feather** item in the options bar to highlight the value. Then enter 6 and press Enter. Like most of the values in the options bar, this one has no influence over the existing selection; instead, it affects the next selection outline you create.

12. *Increase the size of the image window.* Size the window so that you can see a generous amount of light gray pasteboard around all sides of the image. (The dark gray background of the application window doesn't count.) The easiest way to see the pasteboard is to maximize the image window by clicking the ☐ icon in the top-right corner of the window. If necessary, you can also press Ctrl+⊟ to zoom out.

13. *Select the main building with the polygonal lasso tool.* Press the Shift key and click around the lowest elements of the building. To make sure you select everything, click outside the image in the light gray pasteboard, as illustrated in Figure 4-37.

Figure 4-37.

14. *Send the selection to its own layer.* Now let's set about transforming the background into the dark and stormy night that I promised at the outset of the exercise. With the entire building now selected, choose **Layer→New→Layer via Copy**, or press Ctrl+J to send it to its own layer.

15. *Select the Background layer in the Layers palette.* Make sure the **Layers** palette is visible on the right side of the screen. (If it isn't, press the F11 key.) Then click the **Background** layer in the palette to make the lowest layer active.

16. *Lift some dark blue from the windows.* To make the dark and stormy night, we'll be using a filter that relies on the active foreground color. This means changing the foreground color to something dark and stormy, such as deep blue. Begin by selecting the eyedropper tool in the toolbox or pressing the I key. Then click a dark blue pixel in one of the front and center windows in the cylindrical portion of the library. Elements updates the foreground color at the bottom of the toolbox; for now, nothing else changes.

Figure 4-38.

17. *Apply the Fibers filter.* Choose **Filter→Render→ Fibers** to open the **Fibers** dialog box. New to Photoshop Elements 3, this filter draws rough vertical lines of color in the foreground and background colors. In our case, the dark blue and white create an effect similar to rain. The default values shown in Figure 4-38 are fine, so click **OK** to accept.

18. *Apply the Difference Clouds filter.* Choose **Filter→Render→Difference Clouds** to merge a cloud pattern into the Fibers rain and create a dark, nasty storm.

19. *Repeat Difference Clouds a few times.* Pressing Ctrl+F repeats the most recently applied filter. Each additional application of Difference Clouds inverts the background and applies more clouds. To achieve the effect pictured in Figure 4-39, I pressed Ctrl+F five times in a row.

Given that rain rarely falls strictly in back of a building, you could add a layer of Fibers rain in front of the structure as well. But frankly, I prefer the look of the stormy sky when isolated to the background. It makes the library seem safer—more like a cozy, kooky, mad-scientist's hangout—the kind of place where you can curl up and read a really scary book.

Figure 4-39.

The final lasso tool, the magnetic lasso, is one of the most amazing selection tools in Photoshop Elements' arsenal. No kidding, this tool can actually sense the edge of an object and trace it automatically, even when the contrast is low and the background colors vary. But as miraculous as this sounds, the magnetic lasso has never won the hearts and minds of Photoshop Elements users the way, say, the magic wand has. Why? Part of the reason is that it requires you to work too hard for your automation. Perhaps worse, the tool makes a lot of irritating mistakes, thereby requiring you to work *even harder* for your automation. Even so, the magnetic lasso can work wonders, especially when tracing highly complex edges set against evenly colored backgrounds.

Select the magnetic lasso from the lasso tool flyout menu. As when using the polygonal lasso, click along the edge of the image element that you want to select to set a point. Next, move the cursor—no need to drag, the mouse button does not have to be pressed—around the image element. As you move, Elements automatically traces what it determines is the best edge and lays down square *anchor points*, which lock the line in place. In the figure below, I clicked the bottom-left corner of the library's trapezoidal roof and then moved the cursor up and around to the right.

Some other techniques:

- If the magnetic lasso traces an area incorrectly, trace back over the offending portion of the line to erase it. Again, just move your mouse; no need to press any buttons.

- Anchor points remain locked down even if you trace back over them. To remove the last anchor point, press the Backspace key.

- Elements continuously updates the magnetic lasso line until it lays down a point. To lock down the line manually, just click to create your own anchor point.

- Of the various options bar settings, the most useful is Width, which adjusts how close your cursor has to be to an edge to "see" it. Large values allow you to be sloppy; small values are great for working inside tight, highly detailed areas.

The best thing about this setting is you can change it on the fly by pressing one of the bracket keys. While working with the magnetic lasso, press [to make the Width value smaller; press] to make it larger.

- Double-click or press Enter to complete the selection. You can also click the first point in the shape. Press the Esc key to cancel the selection.

Photoshop Elements' smartest lasso tool is clearly the most challenging to use. But it's usually worth the effort. And remember, you can always combine it with other tools.

Painting a Free-Form Selection

The final selection tool, the selection brush, offers two advantages over the others. First, for many of us, painting with a brush is easier than dragging with, say, a lasso. Particularly if you're using a drawing tablet from Wacom or some other manufacturer, painting gives you the utmost control over your selection outline.

The second advantage of the selection brush is that it simulates the more sophisticated *masking* functions of the senior Photoshop CS2. Remember when we feathered the selection outline around the moon back in the "Using the Marquee Tools" exercise (see Step 10, page 122)? As you may recall, the marching ants were incapable of accurately representing the soft-edged selection. Masking eschews marching ants for a translucent overlay; the overlay shows you varying degrees of selection by equating them to levels of transparency. If a pixel is completely selected, the overlay is transparent. Otherwise, the overlay becomes murkier and murkier as the selection fades away.

In this exercise you'll use the selection brush both in the standard marching ants selection mode and in the mask mode to select a couple of objects in a layered image. You'll also see how Elements lets you save and load selection outlines, a tremendous timesaver should you ever need to select a complex object more than once.

Figure 4-40.

1. *Open a layered image.* Open the file named *My someday prince.psd*, which is located in the *Lesson 04* folder inside *Lesson Files-PE3 1on1*. Figure 4-40 shows a lovely, blue poison arrow frog captured by Terry McGleish for iStockPhoto.com. An inspection of the Layers palette reveals that this is a layered document. We'll begin with the image of the frog set against white on the top layer. As you might guess, you'll be selecting this frog with the selection brush.

2. *Load a selection outline.* I've already selected part of the frog to get you started. To load this selection, choose **Select→Load Selection** to display the dialog box in Figure 4-41 on the opposite page. Make sure that **Frog** is active in the **Selection** pop-up menu. Also confirm that the **Invert** check box (which reverses the selection) is turned off, and then click **OK**. Elements draws marching ants around one front leg and one rear leg. Your task is to complete the job.

3. *Choose the selection brush from the toolbox.* Click the selection brush in the toolbox (see Figure 4-42) or press the A key.

4. *Adjust the brush size.* You'll begin your frog selection by roughing in the frog's body. But you need a nice big brush. As Figure 4-43 shows, the selection brush offers its share of unique options in the options bar:

- Click ▼ on the left side of the options bar to display a pop-up menu that lets you choose from a vast library of brush shapes and sizes. These options can be quite useful when painting (as you will in Lesson 6, "Paint, Edit, and Heal"), but basic is better when creating selections. Look at the menu if you like, but leave the default setting as is.

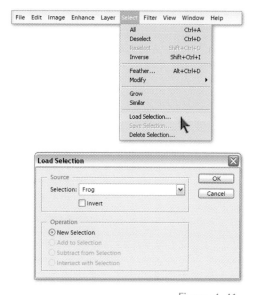

Figure 4-41.

Figure 4-42.

- The Size option changes the diameter of the brush. Increase the **Size** to 40 pixels to get that nice big brush I alluded to a moment ago.

- The Mode pop-up menu offers two options, Selection and Mask. Make sure it's set to **Selection**.

Figure 4-43.

- The Hardness value sets the sharpness of the brush. Make sure **Hardness** is set to 100 percent, which results in an antialiased brush. Like a roll of cheap toilet paper, it retains only the barest hint of softness.

You can resize the selection brush using the bracket keys. Press ⬚ to shrink the brush or ⬚ to make it bigger. Press Shift+⬚ to make the brush softer; press Shift+⬚ to make it harder. These shortcuts might seem odd, but they can be big time-savers.

---

5. *Rough in the middle of the frog.* Press Ctrl+Alt+⬚ to zoom in to the 100 percent view size. Spacebar-drag to center the frog in the image window. Then paint a selection well inside the central portion of the frog's body, as in Figure 4-44. Right away, the selection brush behaves differently from the other selection tools. Even though you already have an active selection (the one you loaded in Step 2), there's no need to press the Shift key to add to it. The brush automatically operates in add mode.

Figure 4-44.

If you accidentally paint outside the edges of the frog, you have two options for getting back inside the lines:

- Click the ⟲ button in the shortcuts bar or press Ctrl+Z to undo the last brush stroke.

- Press the Alt key and paint over the mistake. Alt puts the selection brush in subtract mode. So rather than painting over the area you want to select, Alt-drag to paint over the area you want to deselect.

6. *Paint around the edges of the amphibian's body.* Now to hone in and select those pesky edges. For that, you'll want to be closer. Press Ctrl+⊡ to magnify the image to 200 percent. Then press the ⊡ key twice to reduce the brush diameter to 20 pixels. Because the edges of the frog aren't razor-sharp, we need to soften the brush. Pressing Shift+⊡ lowers the Hardness value in 25 percent increments, which would take it down to 75 percent. That's too soft for these edges, so I recommend you click **Hardness** in the options bar and change the value to 90 percent.

Paint around the perimeter of the frog. Don't leave any gaps between the already selected middle of the animal and its meandering edges. Leave the front leg deselected for now. And don't obsess about getting the outline super-smooth. He's a frog, after all; what do a few warts matter? When you finish, your selection should look something like the one pictured in Figure 4-45.

Figure 4-45.

7. *Select the frog's leg.* Because the sides of the frog's foreleg—oh heck, let's call it a *forearm*—are reasonably straight, I'll teach you a trick for selecting them. First, press the ⎡ key to reduce the diameter of the brush to 10 pixels. Then position your cursor as shown in the top window in Figure 4-46, making sure the edge of the cursor is along the upper edge of the frog's forearm. Click once to create a small circle of selection. Next, move your cursor to the location indicated by the bottom window in the figure and Shift-click. Photoshop Elements paints a straight stripe of selection. Shift-clicking always connects the last click point to the next one, so it's an easy way to create straight-edged selections throughout a selection. Repeat this trick along the lower edge of the frog's forearm.

To paint the details of the frog's fingers, shrink the brush size to 6 pixels or so. Then continue painting until the entire outline of the frog is filled in. And don't forget to Shift-click like crazy. This guy's fingers are rife with straight segments.

8. *Save the selection.* After all the time you spent painting the frog selection, you owe it to yourself to save it. Choose **Select→Save Selection**. In the **Save Selection** dialog box, set the **Selection** option to **Frog**. Leave the **Replace Selection** option turned on and click **OK**. Elements replaces the partial selection that I drew for you with the full frog outline.

9. *Delete the frog's background.* The frog is selected. So to get rid of the background, we need to reverse the selection. Choose **Select→Inverse** or press Ctrl+Shift+I. If you're zoomed in on a detail of the frog, you'll swear nothing happened. But press Ctrl+⎡ to zoom all the way out and you'll see those ants marching around the entire perimeter of the image. The frog outline now represents a hole in the selection.

Press the Backspace key to reveal the background beneath the Frog layer. Wishing and hoping below the blue critter is a dreamy-looking little girl photographed by Gisele Wright, once again available from iStockPhoto.com.

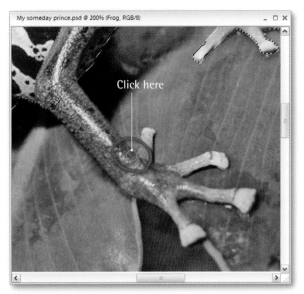

Figure 4-46.

10. *Give the frog a shadow.* Let's add a layer style to the frog to help it stand out from its brand-new off-white background. Choose **Select→Deselect** or press Ctrl+D to deselect the animal's empty background. Next, do the following:

- Go to the **Styles and Effects** palette on the right side of the screen. (If it's missing, press the F7 key.)

- Choose **Layer Styles** from the upper-left pop-up menu and **Drop Shadows** from the right menu.

- Finally, click the third thumbnail, **Noisy**.

The result appears in Figure 4-47.

11. *Switch to the Mask mode.* Now let's shift to the Background layer and complete the design. Click the **Background** layer in the **Layers** palette or press Alt+⌊. Next, change the **Mode** setting in the options bar to **Mask**. Although there's no immediate change to the image, the options bar gets two new options.

- The Overlay Opacity setting determines the translucency of the masked areas. Unless you have some reason for changing it, I'd leave this option set to 50 percent.

- The next option, Overlay Color, defines the color of the mask. The default color is red, harkening back to the old pre-computer days of publishing, when you masked photographs and other artwork by cutting red plastic sheets called *rubylith*. Thing is, if you're trying to select a maraschino cherry sitting on top of a red-frosted cake, a ruby red overlay isn't going to do you much good. To change the overlay color, click the color swatch and select another color. For our purposes, however, red will do just fine.

12. *Paint inside the girl's outline.* Change the **Size** of the selection brush to 150 pixels. Then paint inside the girl's face and body, taking care to stay well within the lines. As you do so, you lay down a translucent coating of red. Fair enough, but what the heck is going on?

Figure 4-47.

In the Selection mode, you paint to select; in the Mask mode, you paint to deselect. So the red coating indicates an area that is not selected. The area outside the coating—where the rubylith is transparent—is selected. True to its name, a mask protects an image from harm and leaves the rest of the image vulnerable to edits.

As in the Selection mode, holding down the Alt key reverses the tool. Therefore, if you find yourself painting outside the boundary of the girl, you can Alt-drag with the brush to erase the mask.

13. *Paint around the perimeter of the girl.* Now to get in and brush those edges. I won't lie to you, this takes some skill and determination. So your mask may come out looking a little different than mine. But I can offer some pointers:

- When filling in the girl's arms and shoulders, I recommend shifting to a smaller, softer brush. Press the ⬚ key several times to reduce the diameter of the brush to 50 pixels or so. The focus on the girl is pretty soft, so press Shift+⬚ once to lower the **Hardness** value to 75 percent.

- Before tracing her ears, decrease the **Size** value even further, to about 20 pixels.

- We want a nice soft outline around the girl's scalp. So for her hair, decrease the **Hardness** value another notch to 50 percent.

As you'll no doubt be happy to hear, you can skip the tendrils of hair sticking up from the top of her head because the next step eliminates any need to accurately select them. So when you finish your mask, it should look vaguely similar to the one in Figure 4-48.

Figure 4-48.

14. *Paint a thought balloon.* The next step is to use the Mask mode's unique selection-display ability to paint a dreamy thought balloon behind the girl's head. In the options bar, take the **Hardness** value all the way down to 0 and increase the brush **Size** to 300 pixels.

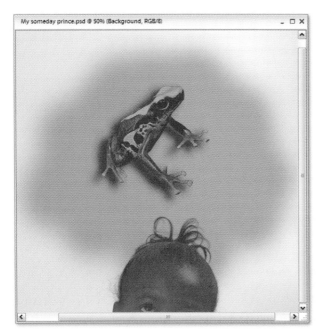

Figure 4-49.

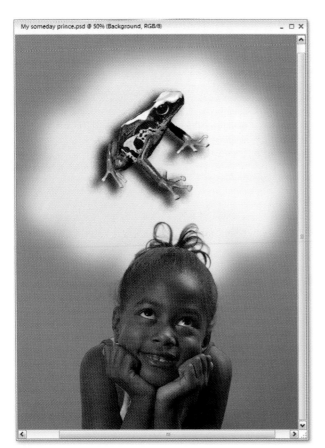

Figure 4-50.

Scrub over the frog and the protruding strands of the girl's hair to mask those areas completely. Then paint a cloud-like balloon over and behind the girl's head, as in Figure 4-49. Yours doesn't have to look exactly like mine; let your artistic muse be your guide.

15. *Hide the overlay.* Choose **View→Selection** or press Ctrl+H to hide the red overlay so you can better see the results of the next step.

16. *Fill the selection with blue.* Choose **Edit→Fill** or press Shift+Backspace to display the **Fill** dialog box. Then do the following:

   • Choose **Color** from the **Use** pop-up menu. Change the **H**, **S**, and **B** values to 220, 50, and 90, respectively. Then click **OK**.

   • Set the **Mode** option to **Multiply**. Then click **OK**. The blue merges with the background inside the selected portions of the Background layer, as in Figure 4-50.

17. *Save your newest selection.* Now that you've spent all that time working on this wonderful mask, you might as well save it. Choose **Select→Save Selection**, which lets you save a selection, regardless of what form it's in. Leave the **Selection** option set to **New**, enter "Girl and balloon" in the **Name** field, and click **OK**. This image now has two saved selection outlines, which you can load and use again at any time simply by choosing **Select→Load Selection**.

WHAT DID YOU LEARN?

Match the key concept in the numbered list below with the letter of the phrase that best describes it. Answers appear upside-down at the bottom of the page.

Key Concepts

1. Magic wand
2. Tolerance
3. Grow
4. Similar
5. Move tool
6. Antialiasing
7. Inverse
8. Feather
9. Polygonal lasso
10. Anchor points
11. Mask
12. Rubylith

Descriptions

A. This selection brush mode uses a translucent overlay to show you varying degrees of selection by equating them to levels of transparency.

B. Click with this tool to select regions of color inside an image.

C. This command selects currently deselected pixels and deselects currently selected pixels.

D. Use this tool to select free-form, straight-sided areas in an image.

E. A setting in the options bar that determines how many colors the magic wand selects at a time, as measured in luminosity values.

F. The magnetic lasso automatically lays these down to lock the selection outline in place.

G. Accessible by pressing and holding the Ctrl key, this tool permits you to move selected pixels, even between images.

H. This command expands the range of a selection to include additional adjacent pixels.

I. A slight softening effect applied most commonly to selection outlines to simulate smooth transitions.

J. This command blurs the edges of a selection outline to create fuzzy transitions.

K. Named after a red sheet of plastic used for masking photographs back in the old days, Elements uses this term to refer to the selection brush's default red masking overlay.

L. This command expands the range of a selection to include additional nonadjacent pixels.

Answers

1B, 2E, 3H, 4L, 5G, 6I, 7C, 8J, 9D, 10F, 11A, 12K

CROP, STRAIGHTEN, AND SIZE

I SUPPOSE IT'S possible that on some planet, there are those who believe that the perfect photograph is one that needs no editing. On this far-flung world, programs like Photoshop Elements are tools of last resort. The very act of opening a photograph in an image editor is a tacit declaration that the photo is a failure. Every command, tool, or option applied is regarded as a mark of flimflam or forgery.

But that's hardly the case here on Earth. Despite oft-voiced (and occasionally reasonable) concerns that modern image editing is distorting our perception of places and events, image manipulation has always been part and parcel of the photographic process. And there's no better example of this than cropping.

Since long before computers were widely available and eons before Elements and its older sibling Photoshop hit the market, it has been common practice among professional photographers to frame a shot and then back up a step or two before snapping the picture. This way, they have more options when it comes time to crop. Of course, nothing says you have to crop the image the way you first framed it; as illustrated in Figure 5-1, you can crop it any way you want to. And that's just the point. Even back in the old days, photographers shot their pictures with editing in mind because doing so ensured a wider range of post-photography options.

Whole–Image Transformations

If image editing is the norm, the norm for image editing is whole-image transformations. This includes operations such as scale and rotate applied to an entire image all at a time. While whole-image transformations may sound like a dry topic, they can produce dramatic and surprising effects.

Figure 5-1.

ABOUT THIS LESSON

Project Files

Before beginning the exercises, make sure that you've installed the lesson files from the CD, as explained in Step 5 on page xv of the Preface. This should result in a folder called *Lesson Files-PE3 1on1* on your desktop. We'll be working with the files inside the *Lesson 05* subfolder.

In this lesson, we explore ways to crop, straighten, and resize digital photographs using a small but essential collection of tools and commands. You'll learn how to:

- Automatically crop and straighten one or more images scanned to a single file . . . . page 144

- Use the crop tool to straighten an image and crop extraneous background information . . . . . page 148

- Cut an image into a custom shape and set it against a new background . . . . page 153

- Adjust the resolution of an image and select the best interpolation setting . . . . page 159

Video Lesson 5: Image and Canvas Size

The exercises in this lesson deal with one of the most fundamental topics in Photoshop Elements: changing and managing the number of pixels in an image. To fully understand this topic, you must come to terms with the concepts of *image size* and *canvas size*. Both describe the number of pixels in an image, but in different ways.

For an introduction to these key concepts—as well as the commands named for them—watch the fifth video lesson on the CD. To view this video, insert the CD, click the **Start** button, click the **Set 2** button in the top-right corner of your screen, and then select **5, Image & Canvas Size** from the Lessons list. The movie lasts 10 minutes and 43 seconds, during which time you'll learn about the following tools, commands, and shortcuts:

Tool, command, or operation	Keyboard equivalent or shortcut
Show or hide Info palette	F8
Change unit of measurement from Info palette	Click ┿ icon, next to X, Y coordinates
Image Size	Alt+I, R, I
Scrub a numerical value	Drag back and forth on option name
Scrub in 10× increments	Shift-drag on option name
Canvas Size	Alt+I, R, ↓, Enter
Advance from one numerical option to the next	Tab

More important, whole-image transformation forces you to think about basic image composition and ponder some important questions:

- The photo in Figure 5-2 is clearly at an angle, but just what angle is it? Photoshop Elements not only gives you ways to discover that angle (47.7 degrees), but automates the process to boot.

- After you rotate the image, you have to crop it. Never content to limit you to a single approach, Elements dedicates no fewer than two tools, five commands, and a score of options to the task (symbolically illustrated in Figure 5-3). Variety is the spice of life, but which one do you use when?

- After the crop is complete, there's the problem of scale. Should you reduce or increase the number of pixels? Or should you merely reduce the resolution to print the image larger, as in Figure 5-4?

I provide these questions merely to whet your appetite for the morsels of knowledge that follow. If they seem like a lot to ponder, never fear; the forthcoming lesson makes the answers perfectly clear.

Figure 5-2.

Figure 5-3.

Figure 5-4.

The Order in Which We Work

At this point, you may wonder why I've waited until Lesson 5 to talk about such a fundamental topic as cropping. Bearing in mind that I'm addressing topics in the order you actually apply them, wouldn't it make more sense to first crop an image and then correct its colors, as discussed in Lesson 3? The answer is in some cases yes, but in more cases no.

PEARL OF WISDOM

Scaling an image changes the number of pixels. Straightening an image changes the orientation of pixels. Both operations throw away pixels and make up new ones—a process called *interpolation*—which is best performed after you get the colors in line. In fact, interpolation can actually help a color correction by smoothing out the rough transitions sometimes produced by commands such as Shadows/Highlights and Adjust Hue/Saturation.

On its own, cropping does not require interpolation, and may therefore be applied in advance of color adjustments. However, Elements offers a few functions that crop and interpolate an image all at once, in which case, you're better off correcting the colors first.

So by way of general advice, fix the colors to the best of your ability up front, and then set about cropping and straightening the image.

Auto Crop and Straighten

The best straightening and cropping commands are designed to accommodate scanned images, particularly those captured by a flatbed scanner. Photoshop Elements can open a crooked image, rotate it upright, and crop away the area outside the image—all automatically, without so much as batting an eye. Better yet, the program can work this magic on multiple images at the same time.

We'll begin by investigating the way Adobe recommends rotating and cropping a scanned photograph. Then we'll look at a better way, one that is not only more accurate, but also offers the benefit of rotating and cropping several pictures at a time. Prepare to be amazed.

1. *Open the scanned image.* Open *Me at 21.jpg* in the *Lesson 05* folder inside *Lesson Files-PE3 1on1*. It features a photo of me in a Paris subway back when I was a twig of a lad (see Figure 5-5). Diet secret: split a loaf of bread with your travelling buddy every day for two weeks and save the rest for beer. Forget Atkins; a pure carb diet works wonders.

2. *Choose the Straighten and Crop Image command.* Conventional wisdom (not to mention, Adobe's documentation) holds that the best way to fix a crooked scan is to choose a command called Straighten and Crop Image. But there's one tiny problem: it works only occasionally. The command performs well when a photo is set against a squeaky clean white background. But any amount of dust, hair, or color variation throws it off. To see what I mean, choose **Image→ Rotate→Straighten and Crop Image** and watch what happens. Thanks to the deep blue color of the background and a smattering of dust, Elements incorrectly evaluates the image and rotates it nearly 45 degrees clockwise, or about six times as far as it should. Worse, the program chops off the corners of the photo, leaving us with less information than we started with. Just for laughs, the astonishingly wrong result appears in Figure 5-6.

Figure 5-5.

3. *Undo the last operation.* Clearly, we can't leave the image the way it is. So choose **Edit→Undo Straighten and Crop Image** or press Ctrl+Z to restore the image file to its previous canvas size and orientation.

   So fair enough. At least where this image is concerned, Straighten and Crop Image is an unqualified failure. Fortunately, a much better solution is close at hand.

4. *Choose the Divide Scanned Photos command.* To straighten and crop a scanned photo set against even a dusty, colored background, choose **Image→Divide Scanned Photos**. Then sit back and watch. As if on autopilot, Photoshop Elements duplicates the image and then runs a sequence of operations that culminate with the expertly corrected photograph shown in Figure 5-7 on the next page. And because the revised photo appears in its own image window, the original scan remains unscathed, just in case you want to take another swing at it later.

Figure 5-6.

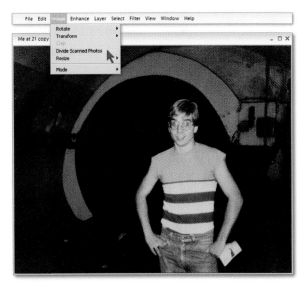

Figure 5-7.

Figure 5-8.

Wonderful feature, right? But what's with the name? Why in the world is a command that straightens and crops snapshots called Divide Scanned Photos? Divide them from *what*, exactly? Well, from each other, as it turns out. Although Divide Scanned Photos is just the ticket for straightening and cropping a single photo, it's even better at addressing multiple photos at a time, as the next steps explain.

5. *Open another scan.* Close the *Me at 21.jpg* image without saving it. Then open the file called *The gang.jpg*, also included in the *Lesson 05* folder. Therein, you'll find a collection of seven images of various shapes and sizes—some photographs, some printed artwork, all witnessed in Figure 5-8. I created this file by taking the seven pictures and throwing them down on a flatbed scanner. Then, rather than using the scanner's software to assign each image to a separate file, I captured them all to one file. Called *gang scanning*, this previously ill-advised technique works wonders in Photoshop Elements 3.

6. *Choose the Divide Scanned Photos command.* Amazingly, that's all there is to it. The moment you choose **Image→Divide Scanned Photos** (or press Alt+I-D), the windows start flying as Photoshop Elements duplicates, rotates, and crops each image. Honestly, if all of Elements was this easy, I'd be out of a job.

7. *Review the cropped images.* In less than a minute on most systems, the Divide Scanned Photos command makes order from chaos. In all, the command generates seven separate image windows, each named *The gang copy* followed by a number, in the order shown in Figure 5-9. (To create the figure, I chose Window→Images→Cascade and then dragged each image window to a separate location.) Note that Elements analyzes the pictures from top to bottom. This is why the photo of my son Sammy—which is slightly higher than that of my late, lamented, much-beloved tabby—comes up first.

The Divide Scanned Photos command does a swell job of straightening the images, even managing to accurately evaluate pictures with irregular edges, such as the perforated special delivery stamp and the clipped magazine photo of the hard drive. But it doesn't know when an image is on its side. That means the snapshot of the late, lamented tabby still needs our assistance.

Figure 5-9.

8. *Rotate the cat photo.* Click the title bar for the cat photo, which Elements has named *The gang copy 3*. (Oh, heartless program!) Then choose **Image→Rotate→90° Right**, which rotates the image window one-quarter turn clockwise. Alternatively, you can hold down the Alt key and type I-E-0. (That last character is the zero key, ⓪.) This rotates the entire image, changing it from vertical to horizontal, as in Figure 5-10.

9. *Save the images.* Elements does not automatically save the images it generates; you have to do that manually. So if you want to keep any of these images, you have to save it. (Where this book is concerned, we're through with these files, so trash them at will. But for the sake of background, I'll continue.) When saving a photograph, the JPEG format with a high Quality setting is your best bet. But because JPEG modifies image details in its attempt to minimize the file size, it is not well suited to high-contrast artwork, such as the stamps. You may prefer to save these images as TIFF files. Then again, you may prefer not to save the images at all. I leave that decision up to you.

If an image (such as the hard drive) requires further cropping, or you simply aren't happy with the Divide Scanned Photos command's choices, you can take advantage of the crop tool, as I discuss in the next exercise.

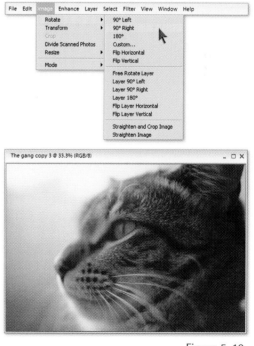

Figure 5-10.

Using the Crop Tool

The Divide Scanned Photos command works wonders on crooked images captured with a scanner, but it doesn't work worth a hill of beans on crooked images shot with a digital camera. Consider the landscape in Figure 5-11. The photo admirably captures the unfettered beauty of the magestic Colorado foothills, even if I do say so myself. But the beauty came at a price. Despite appearances, I shot the photo under cloud cover by a waning twilight. The relatively low light required me to use a long exposure ($^1/_{15}$ second), too long for a hand-held shot. With the kids in tow, I had decided against a tripod. And so I was forced to work with what I had, the uneven top of a signpost. Naturally, the post leaned slightly, so the photograph leans with it.

Figure 5-11.

Without an obvious rectangle to work with, neither of the commands we've seen so far does any good. (In fact, each leaves the image very nearly unchanged.) This means you have to resort to a manual solution. The aptly named crop tool lets you draw and scale the canvas boundary directly in the image window. You can also rotate the boundary to accommodate a crooked image. Granted, you have to do the work yourself, but you're guaranteed good results—assuming of course that you follow my advice.

1. *Open an image.* Open the file *Northern foothills.jpg* located in the *Lesson 05* folder inside *Lesson Files-PE3 1on1*. In addition to being crooked, the snapshot is too tall for my tastes. Our goal is to crop away large chunks of the grass and sky to create a more focused—not to mention level—panorama.

2. *Select the crop tool in the toolbox.* Click the crop tool in the toolbox (see Figure 5-12) or press C for *crop*, not to mention *clip*, *cut*, and *curtail*.

3. *Draw the crop boundary.* Drag inside the image window to draw a rectangle around the portion of the image you want to keep, as demonstrated in Figure 5-13. As you do so, you enter the *crop mode*. From this point until you press Enter or Esc, most of Elements' commands and palettes are unavailable. You have now made a commitment—albeit a very short-term one—to cropping.

As with the marquee tools, you can adjust the position of the crop boundary on-the-fly by pressing and holding the spacebar. But don't get too hung up on getting things exactly right. You can easily move and resize the crop boundary after you draw it, as demonstrated in Step 5.

Figure 5-12.

Figure 5-13.

4. *Change the shield attributes in the options bar.* Elements indicates the area that will be cropped away by covering it with a translucent *shield*. Black by default, the shield is too dark to suit this particular image. Go to the options bar and click the ▾ arrow to the right of the **Color** swatch to display a list of alternate colors. Select the white swatch, as in Figure 5-14, and then click the options bar to hide the list. (Don't press the Enter or Esc key or you'll exit the crop mode.) I also recommend lowering the **Opacity** value to 35 percent.

Figure 5-14.

5. *Move and scale the crop boundary.* Drag inside the crop boundary to move it. Drag the dotted outline or one of the eight square handles surrounding the crop boundary to scale it (that is, change its size). Also worth noting:

   - Press the Shift key while dragging a corner handle to scale the crop boundary proportionally.

   - Press the Alt key while dragging to scale with respect to the center of the boundary. In other words, the corners move but the center stays in place.

6. *Rotate the crop boundary.* To rotate the crop boundary, move your cursor outside the boundary and drag. Bear in mind that you need to rotate the boundary in the opposite direction that you want to rotate the image. Rotating the crop boundary counterclockwise, for example, ultimately rotates the image the other way, clockwise.

To straighten the image, you'll need a frame of reference. I suggest that you drag the top edge of the crop boundary down so that it intersects the purple and blue areas of the mountain range. Then rotate the boundary to match the angle of the horizon, as in **Figure 5-15**. (Don't worry that the top edge is now in the wrong place; you can fix that in a moment.)

Origin point

Rotate cursor

Figure 5-15.

Note that Elements rotates the boundary around a central origin point, labeled in Figure 5-15. This origin point is located smack dab in the center of the crop boundary.

To monitor the angle of the rotation, choose **Window→Info** to display the **Info** palette. Then note the angle value (**A**) in the upper-right corner of the palette. I finally settled on an angle of –3.2 degrees.

7. *Make any last-minute tweaks.* You'll at least need to move the top edge of the boundary above the mountains to incorporate some of the cloudy sky. But feel free to move, scale, and rotate the crop boundary as much as you like until you get it exactly the way you want it. My final boundary appears in Figure 5-16.

Figure 5-16.

8. *Apply your changes.* Click the check mark (✔) in the options bar or press the Enter key to accept your changes. Elements crops away the pixels outside the boundary and rotates the image upright. The result is the more compelling landscape featured in Figure 5-17.

Figure 5-17.

Cropping with the Cookie Cutter

Photoshop Elements 3 provides a second cropping tool, the cookie cutter tool, which looks like a Valentine with a simplified person in it. But although the cookie cutter icon immediately follows the crop tool in the toolbox and features a cropping mode that works a lot like the crop tool, that's not really its main purpose. Just as a real-world cookie cutter stamps shapes from rolled-out cookie dough, the cookie cutter tool stamps shapes out of images, discarding the excess pixels that lie outside the shape. (Unfortunately, you can't lump the excess pixels into a ball and roll them out again.) Cookie cutting is ideal for scrapbooking—say, when you want to crop a wedding photo into the shape of a heart and place it against another background. But there are other practical and creative uses for the tool, as you'll discover in this exercise.

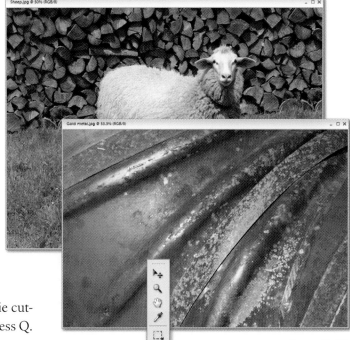

1. *Open two images.* Go to the *Lesson 05 folder* inside *Lesson Files-PE3 1on1* and open *Gold metal.jpg* and *Sheep.jpg.* Arrange the image windows in the Editor workspace so that *Gold metal.jpg* is in front, as in Figure 5-18. Because both are JPEG images, they are flat files that contain one Background layer apiece and nothing more.

Figure 5-18.

2. *Select the cookie cutter tool.* Click the cookie cutter tool in the toolbox, as in Figure 5-19, or press Q.

3. *Select a frame shape.* But first, let's take a moment to review the settings available in the options bar at the top of the screen:

   - Click Shape to see a pop-up palette of shapes that you can draw with the cookie cutter tool. It's a lot of shapes, but it ain't all of them. Click the ⊙ arrow to display several libraries of additional shapes. Choose the first option, All Elements Shapes, to gain instant access to a jaw-dropping 569 predefined shapes.

   - The Shape Options pop-up menu features options for constraining the cookie cutter to a specific aspect or size.

   - The Feather option gives the shape a fuzzy outline.

   - By default, the cookie cutter crops a shape out of an image, but leaves the canvas size unchanged. If you turn on the Crop check box, the tool crops the canvas to fit the shape.

Figure 5-19.

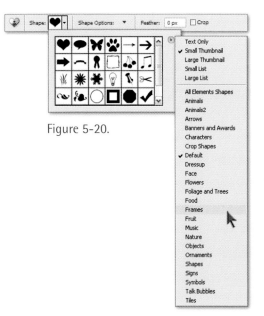

Figure 5-20.

Click the ▾ arrow to open the **Shape** pop-up palette. Then click the ⊙ on the right. Choose **Frames** (see Figure 5-20) to load a library of predrawn frame outlines. If you hover the cursor over a shape, a tool tip reveals the name of the shape. But to expedite things, click the ⊙ again and choose **Large List** from the top of the submenu. The palette now displays a thumbnail along with the name of the shape. Scroll down to **Frame 14** and double-click on it.

4. *Crop the frame.* Armed with the cookie cutter tool, drag from the upper-left region of photographer Yohan Juliardi's *Gold metal.jpg* image to the lower-right region, as in Figure 5-21. Several things happen. Most obviously, a frame appears in the image, surrounded by a cropping marquee. Behind the frame you see a gray-and-white checkerboard pattern; this is how Elements represents transparency, which is what the cookie cutter leaves outside the cropped shape. Meanwhile, if you take a peek at the Layers palette, you'll see that the Background layer has turned into a full-fledged layer called Layer 0.

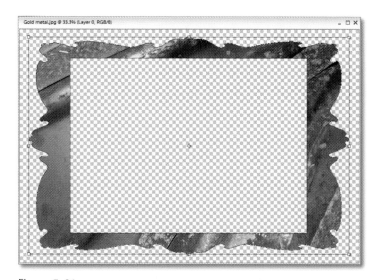

Figure 5-21.

PEARL OF WISDOM

The cookie cutter stamps shapes out of layers and makes any pixels that fall outside the shape transparent. Background layers can't contain transparency, so if you use the image on a Background layer, the tool has no choice but to promote the Background to a full-fledged layer. If you're concerned about losing the rest of the image, duplicate the Background layer by pressing Ctrl+J and then use the cookie cutter on the duplicate.

Just as with the crop tool, the cookie cutter tool lets you tweak your cropping before making it final. Drag the corners of the crop marquee to the corners of the image window. Assuming that View→Snap to Grid is turned on, the marquee will snap to the perimeter of the canvas size. Click the ✔ icon in the options bar or press the Enter key, and you have a new frame shape.

5. *Restore the Background layer.* We're going to try our hands at building a layered composition inside this image. And for the best results, we need a Background layer. Click the ▣ icon in the upper-left corner of the **Layers** palette to create a transparent Layer 1 on top of Layer 0. Then choose **Layer→New→Background From Layer**. Assuming the background color is white, Elements converts Layer 1 into a white Background layer.

6. *Crop a shape.* Now bring the *Sheep.jpg* image forward. Captured by Tobias Ott, this photo (like the others in this exercise) comes to us from iStockPhoto.com. Click the ▾ in the options bar to open the **Shape** pop-up palette. Then click the ⊙ and choose the **Crop Shapes** library. Finally, double-click the shape called **Crop Shape 12** to select it. Drag from one corner to the opposite corner in the photo to frame it, more or less as you see in Figure 5-22. For compositional reasons, we don't want the marquee to align with the extreme edges of the image. Remember, as you draw the shape, you can adjust its position by pressing and holding the spacebar. Click ✔ or press Enter to accept the shape. The sheep appears cropped inside an artful, brush stroke shape.

Figure 5-22.

7. *Drag and drop the sheep.* Press the V key to get the move tool. Then drag the sheep, hold down the Shift key, and drop the shape into the *Gold metal.jpg* window. Shift centers the shape.

Note that you *have* to use the move tool; when using the cookie cutter, you can't move images by Ctrl-dragging them, the way you can when using the selection tools (see Step 6, page 121). So I'll give you a new tip instead: If your screen is too crowded to get to the *Gold metal.jpg* image, no problem. Just drag the sheep from its image window into the thumbnail of the gold metal image in the Photo Bin along the bottom of the screen, as illustrated in **Figure 5-23**. Elements automatically centers the sheep shape, without the help of the Shift key.

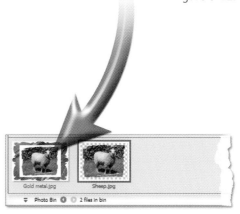

Figure 5-23.

8. *Add some dimension to the shapes.* Make sure that the *Gold metal.jpg* image window is in front. Now that we have this wonderful sheep-in-a-frame composition, let's add a couple of layer styles to the mix:

Figure 5-24.

- Go to the **Styles and Effects** palette and choose **Layer Styles** from the left pop-up menu and **Drop Shadows** from the right. With the sheep layer (Layer 1) selected in the **Layers** palette, click the **Low** drop shadow thumbnail in the **Styles and Effects** palette to add a subtle drop shadow behind the wool-bearing animal.

- Next, click **Layer 0** in the Layers palette or press Alt+⬚ (assuming that Layer 0 is at the top of the stack). Then click the **High** item in the Styles and Effects palette.

- Finally, switch the pop-up menu in the top-right corner of the Styles and Effects palette to **Bevels**, and then click the **Inner Ridge** thumbnail. Your image should now look like Figure 5-24.

One problem: the High drop shadow that you added to the frame extends beyond the boundaries of the image. Easily remedied. Choose **Image→Resize→Reveal All** and the canvas grows to the minimum size needed to fully accommodate the shadow.

EXTRA ★ CREDIT

You've managed to clip a couple of cookie cutter shapes and imbue them with layer styles to create a distinctive photo frame. So you might very well consider the image complete, and bask in the glow of the sheep's gentle majesty. Or you can follow along with the remaining steps and turn the whole thing into a cheap visual joke, totally robbing the animal of its last vestige of dignity. And who knows? Along the way, you might even learn a few more things about the cookie cutter tool.

9. *Open a few more images.* Close *Sheep.jpg* if you like but leave the layered *Gold metal.jpg* composition open. Then open three more photos from iStockPhoto.com, also found in the *Lesson 05* folder. These are *Fairgrounds.jpg*, *Shell.jpg*, and *Text.jpg*. Make sure *Fairgrounds.jpg* is in the front.

10. *Select a wig shape.* Press Q to get the cookie cutter tool. Display the **Shape** pop-up menu, click the ⊙ arrow, and select the **Dressup** library. Then double-click the first shape, **Wig 1**.

11. **Cut a shape out of the cotton candy.** Photographer Ginger Garvey might have had something different in mind when she shot this image. But my take is this: That cotton candy would make a great sheep's wig. And for the optimal effect, I reckon the edges should be a bit fuzzy. Click the word **Feather** in the options bar, change the value to 4 pixels, and press the Enter key. Then constrain the proportions of the wig by Shift-dragging with the cookie cutter tool.

While Shift-dragging, you can also press the spacebar to reposition the shape on-the-fly. When you're happy with the location of the wig relative to the cotton candy, release the spacebar. But keep the Shift key down until you've finished drawing.

Figure 5-25.

Encircle as much cotton candy as the wig shape will hold. When the shape looks like the one in Figure 5-25, release the mouse button, release Shift, and press the Enter key.

12. **Put the wig on the sheep.** Press V for the move tool and drag the wig shape into *Gold metal.jpg*. (If your screen is a jumble, drop the wig onto the *Gold metal.jpg* thumbnail in the Photo Bin.) Then position the wig on the sheep's head, as in Figure 5-26. The humiliation has only begun.

13. **Cut out some glasses.** Our farmyard friend could use some stylish glasses, and what better substance for eyeglass than tortoise shell? Bring the *Shell.jpg* image (care of Angelika Stern) to front and press Q for the cookie cutter tool. Click the **Shape** pop-up palette, scroll to the bottom of the list, and double-click **Glasses 2**. You don't want fuzzy glasses, so reduce the **Feather** value to 0 pixels.

Figure 5-26.

Try to position your cursor as close to the center of the tortoise shell image as possible and begin dragging. While pressing the mouse button, hold down both the Shift and Alt keys. Shift constrains the proportions; Alt draws the shape from the center out. When you've drawn the shape about as large as the image accommodates (see the tiny but powerful Figure 5-27), release the mouse and then release the keys. Press Enter to accept the new shape.

14. **Put the glasses on the sheep.** Press the V key to slip back into the move tool. Drag the glasses by whatever means necessary into the increasingly elaborate *Gold metal.jpg* composition, and move the glasses over the sheep's eyes.

Figure 5-27.

15. **Put words in the sheep's mouth.** To give the sheep something to say, switch to the *Text.jpg* image. Press Q for the cookie cutter. And do the following:

- Display the **Shape** pop-up palette, click the ⊙, and load the **Talk Bubbles** library. Then double-click **Talk 1**.

- Draw the talk balloon shape inside *Text.jpg* (photographed by Marcie Cheatham). For now, keep the shape small; we need some wiggle room for our edits.

- The balloon's tail should point in the other direction. After you release the mouse button, notice that you get transformation handles. So drag the left side handle all the way to the other side of the shape to flip it. (If it's easier to drag the right handle, or both the left and right, fine.)

- Then drag the corner handles and stretch the bubble until it nicely frames the text. You should end up with a talk balloon like the one in Figure 5-28.

- Press Enter to accept the shape.

Figure 5-28.

16. **Move the balloon.** For the last time, press the V key for the move tool. Then drag the talk bubble into *Gold metal.jpg*. Inside the multilayer composition, move the talk balloon so that it overlaps the top of the frame. (If your talk balloon is behind the frame, choose Layer→Arrange→Bring to Front or press Ctrl+Shift+⬚ to move it to the front.) Match the location pictured in Figure 5-29, bearing in mind that your balloon will actually extend beyond the top of the image. Don't worry; we'll fix that problem in a jiffy.

17. **Apply the finishing touches.** Set the right pop-up menu in the **Styles and Effects** palette to **Drop Shadows** and click the **High** style. Then choose **Image→Resize→Reveal All** to display the final masterpiece, As Figure 5-29 shows, this is one piece of cookie cutter art that's anything but.

Figure 5-29.

Resizing an Image

Now we leave the world of rotations and canvas manipulations in favor of what may be the single most essential command in all of Photoshop Elements: Image→Image Size. Designed to resize an entire image all at once—canvas, pixels, the whole shebang—Image Size lets you scale your artwork in two very different ways. First, you can change the physical dimensions of an image by adding or deleting pixels, a process called *resampling*. Second, you can leave the quantity of pixels unchanged and instead focus on the *print resolution*, which is the number of pixels that print within an inch or a millimeter of page space.

PEARL OF WISDOM

Contrary to what you might reasonably think, print resolution is measured in *linear* units, not square units. For example, if you print an image with a resolution of 300 pixels per inch (*ppi* for short), then 300 pixels fit in a row, side-by-side, an inch wide. In contrast, a square inch of this printed image would contain 300 × 300 = 90,000 pixels.

Whether you resample an image or change its resolution depends on the setting of a check box called Resample Image. As we'll see, this one option has such a profound effect on Image Size that it effectively divides the command into two separate functions. In the following steps, we explore how and why you might resample an image. To learn about print resolution, read the "Changing the Print Size" sidebar on page 162.

1. ***Open the image you want to resize.*** Open the file named *Enormous chair.jpg*, included in the *Lesson 05* folder inside *Lesson Files-PE3 1on1*. Shown in Figure 5-30, this 21-foot tall rocking chair is not only enormous in real life but also contains the most pixels of any file we've seen so far (not including layers).

2. ***Display the Info palette.*** Choose **Window→Info** or press the F8 key to display the **Info** palette.

Figure 5-30.

Figure 5-31.

3. ***Check the existing image size.*** To see just how many pixels make up the image, do the following:

- Click the ▶ arrow in the bottom-right corner of the palette to display a menu of options. Then make sure that **Document Dimensions** is selected.

- Click the ✛ icon (indicated by the red arrow in Figure 5-31) to display a pop-up menu of measurements and choose the **Pixels** option.

Circled green in the figure, the Info palette now lists the image size in pixels: 2,250 pixels wide by 2,720 pixels tall, for a total of 2,250 × 2,720 = 6.12 million pixels. When printed at 300 ppi, the image will measure 7.5 inches wide by a little more than 9 inches tall.

4. ***Magnify the image to 100 percent.*** Double-click the zoom tool icon in the toolbox. Then scroll around until you can see the sign tacked to the front of the chair. Pictured in Figure 5-32, the text on the sign is perfectly legible, a testament to the high resolution of the photograph. But there's also a lot of noise (see Step 8 of "Correcting Camera Raw," Lesson 3, page 103). So even though we have scads of pixels, they aren't necessarily in great shape.

5. ***Decide whether you need all these pixels.*** This may seem like a cerebral step, but it's an important one. Resampling amounts to rewriting every pixel in your image, so weigh your options before you plow ahead.

Figure 5-32.

> **PEARL OF ⬤ WISDOM**
>
> In this case, the image contains 6.12 million pixels, just sufficient to convey crisp edges and fragile details such as the text on the sign. But these pixels come at a price. Lots of pixels consume lots of space in memory and on your hard drive, plus they take longer to transmit, whether to a printer or through email or to the Web.

Let's say you want to email this image to a couple of friends. If your friends want to print the photo, they can print it smaller or at a lower resolution. But chances are they won't print it at all; they'll just view it on screen. A typical high-resolution monitor can display at most 1,600 by 1,200 pixels, a mere 30 percent of the pixels in this photo.

Conclusion: Resampling is warranted. This is a job for the Image Size command.

6. ***Choose the Image Size command.*** Choose **Image→Resize→ Image Size**, or press Alt and type I-R-I. Photoshop Elements displays the **Image Size** dialog box (see Figure 5-33), which is divided into two parts:

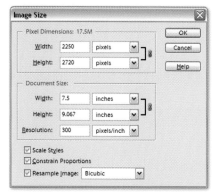

Figure 5-33.

- The Pixel Dimensions options let you change the width and height of the image in pixels. Lowering the number of pixels is called *downsampling*; increasing the pixel count is called *upsampling*. We'll be downsampling, which is by far the more common practice.

- The Document Size options control the size of the printed image. They have no effect on the size of the image on the screen or on the Web.

7. ***Turn on the Resample Image check box.*** Located at the bottom of the dialog box, this option permits you to change the number of pixels in an image.

8. ***Select an interpolation setting.*** To the right of the Resample Image check box is a pop-up menu of interpolation options, which determine how Photoshop Elements blends the existing pixels in your image to create new ones. When downsampling an image, only three options matter:

- When in doubt, select Bicubic, which calculates the color of every resampled pixel by averaging the original image in 16-pixel blocks. It is slower than either Nearest Neighbor or Bilinear (neither of which should be used when resampling photographs), but it does a far better job as well.

- Bicubic Smoother compounds the effects of the interpolation to soften color transitions between neighboring pixels. This helps suppress film grain and noise.

- Bicubic Sharper results in crisp edge transitions. Use it when the details in your image are impeccable and you want to preserve every nuance.

Because this particular image contains so much noise, **Bicubic Smoother** is the best choice.

As often as not, you'll have no desire to change the number of pixels in an image; you'll just want to change how it looks on the printed page. By focusing exclusively on the resolution, you can print an image larger or smaller without adding or subtracting so much as a single pixel.

For example, let's say you want to scale the original *Enormous chair.jpg* image so that it prints 10 inches wide by 12 inches tall. Would you upsample the image and thereby add pixels to it? Absolutely not. The Image Size command can't add detail to an image; it just averages existing pixels. So upsampling adds complexity without improving the quality. There are times when upsampling is helpful—when matching the resolution of one image to another, for example—but they are few and far between.

The better solution is to modify the print resolution. Try this: Open the original *Enormous chair.jpg*. (This assumes that you have completed the "Resizing an Image" exercise and saved the results of that exercise under a different filename, as directed by Step 15 on page 164.) Then choose Image→Resize→Image Size and turn off the Resample Image check box.

Notice that the Pixel Dimensions options are now dimmed and a link icon (⊕) joins the three Document Size values, as in the screen shot below. This icon tells you that it doesn't matter which value you edit or in what order. Any change you make to one value affects the other two, so you can't help but edit all three values at once. For example, change the Width value to 10 inches. As you do, Elements automatically updates the Height and Resolution values to 12.089 inches and 225 ppi, respectively. So there's no need to calculate the resolution value that will get you a desired set of dimensions; just enter one of the dimensions and Elements does the math for you.

Click OK to accept your changes. The image looks exactly the same as it did before you entered the Image Size dialog box. This is because you changed the way the image prints, which has nothing to do with the way it looks on-screen. If you like, feel free to save over the original file. You haven't changed the structure of the image; you just added a bit of sizing data.

To learn more about printing—including how you can further modify the print resolution from the Print Preview dialog box—read the first exercise in Lesson 11, "Printing to an Inkjet Printer."

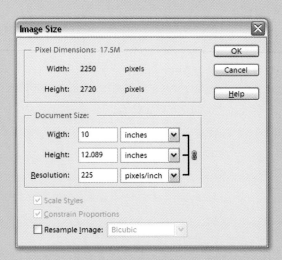

9. *Turn on the Constrain Proportions check box.* Unless you want to stretch or squish your image, leave this option turned on. That way, the relationship between the width and height of the image—known as the *aspect ratio*—will remain constant.

10. *Specify a Resolution value.* When Resample Image is checked (Step 7), any change made to the Resolution value affects the Pixel Dimensions values as well. So if you intend to print the image, it's a good idea to get the Resolution setting out of the way first. Given that we're emailing the image and we're not sure whether it'll ever see a printer, a **Resolution** of 200 ppi should work well enough.

11. *Adjust the Width value.* The Pixel Dimensions values have dropped to 1,500 by 1,813 pixels. But given that most screens top out at 1,600 by 1,200 pixels, that's still too big. Under **Pixel Dimensions**, reduce the **Width** value to 900 pixels, which changes the Height value to 1,088 pixels. This also reduces the Document Size to 4.5 by 5.44 inches (see Figure 5-34), plenty big for an email picture.

12. *Note the new file size.* The Pixel Dimensions header should now read *2.80M (was 17.5M)*, where the M stands for *megabytes*. This represents the size of the image in your computer's memory. The resampled image will measure $900 \times 1,088 = 979,200$ pixels, a mere 16 percent of its previous size. Not coincidentally, 2.8M is precisely 16 percent of 17.5M. The complexity of a file is directly related to its image size, so this downsampled version will load, save, print, and email much more quickly.

13. *Click OK.* Photoshop Elements reduces the size of the image on-screen and in memory. As verified by Figure 5-35, the result continues to look great when printed, but that's in part because it's printed so small. The real test is how it looks on your screen.

Figure 5-34.

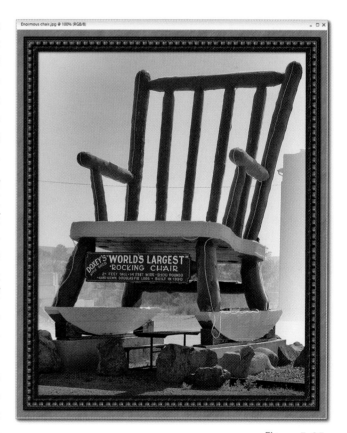

Figure 5-35.

14. *Magnify the image to the 300 percent zoom ratio.* Use the zoom tool to zoom in on the sign, as in Figure 5-36. The letters are rougher—no surprise given the lower number of pixels—but they remain legible. And the photo overall is less grainy. Downsampling with the Bicubic Smoother setting (see Step 8, page 161) goes a long way toward smoothing away the noise.

Figure 5-36.

15. *Choose the Save As command.* Choose **File→Save As**, or press Ctrl+Shift+S. Then give the file a new name or save it to a different location. Don't fret about the JPEG settings; just go ahead and accept the defaults. The reason I have you do this is to emphasize the following very important point.

PEARL OF WISDOM

At all costs, you want to avoid saving your downsampled version of the image over the original. *Always* keep that original in a safe place. I don't care how much better you think the downsampled image looks; the fact remains, it contains fewer pixels and therefore less information. The high-resolution original may contain some bit of detail you'll want to retrieve later, and that makes it worth preserving.

WHAT DID YOU LEARN?

Match the key concept in the numbered list below with the letter
of the phrase that best describes it. Answers appear upside-down
at the bottom of the page.

Key Concepts

1. Cropping

2. Whole-image transformations

3. Interpolation

4. Divide Scanned Photos

5. Gang scanning

6. Shield

7. Origin point

8. Reveal All

9. Print resolution

10. Downsampling

11. Bicubic Smoother

12. Resample Image

Descriptions

A. Operations such as Image Size and the Rotate commands that affect an entire image, including any and all layers.

B. The center of a rotation or another transformation.

C. Although designed to accommodate multiple images, this command is Elements' best method for cropping and straightening a single image.

D. The number of pixels that will print within a linear inch or millimeter of page space.

E. This command enlarges the size of a layered image to display any hidden pixels that lie outside the image boundaries.

F. Turning off this check box keeps the Image Size command from interpolating the pixels in an image.

G. The process of throwing away pixels and making up new ones by averaging the existing pixels in an image.

H. To change the physical dimensions of an image by reducing the number of pixels.

I. The translucent film of color that covers the portions of an image that will be deleted after you apply the crop tool.

J. A means of cutting away the extraneous portions of an image to focus the viewer's attention on the subject of the photo.

K. A quick-and-dirty method of capturing several images with a flatbed scanner to a single image file, which you then crop later.

L. An interpolation setting that makes a special effort to suppress film grain, noise, and other artifacts.

Answers

LESSON

6

PAINT, EDIT, AND HEAL

SO FAR, WE'VE seen a wealth of commands that correct the appearance of an image based on a few specifications and a bit of numerical input. On balance, there's nothing wrong with these commands, and many are extraordinarily useful. But all the automation in the world can't eliminate the need for some occasional old-fashioned, hard-fought, wrist-breaking, sometimes-toilsome-but-always-rewarding artistic labor.

Such is the case with painting and retouching in Photoshop Elements. Whether you want to augment a piece of artwork or adjust the details in a photograph, it's time to give the commands a slip and turn your attention to the toolbox. Elements devotes nearly half its tools—including all those pictured in Figure 6-1—to the tasks of applying and modifying colors in an image. The idea of learning so many tools and putting them to use may seem intimidating. And because they require you to paint directly in the image window, they respond directly to your talents and dexterity, not to mention your lack thereof. Fortunately, despite their numbers, the tools are a lot of fun. And even if your fine motor skills aren't everything you wish they were, there's no need to fret. I'll show you all kinds of ways to constrain and articulate your brushstrokes in the following exercises.

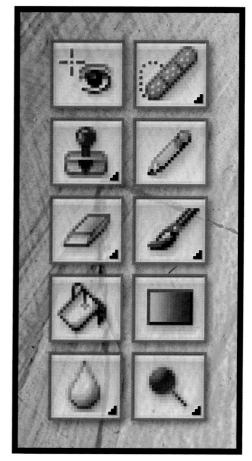

Figure 6-1.

The Essential Eight, Plus Two

Of the tools shown in Figure 6-1, six include flyout menus of additional tools. In all, these ten icons let you access 20 tools. Of those, 16 are *brush-based*. Select such a tool and drag in the image window to create a brushstroke of colored or modified pixels. The remaining four tools are modeled after the selection tools discussed in Lesson 4. You either click to replace a colored region, as with the magic wand, or drag to change a free-form area, as with the lasso.

ABOUT THIS LESSON

Project Files

Before beginning the exercises, make sure that you've installed the lesson files from the CD, as explained in Step 5 on page xv of the Preface. This should result in a folder called *Lesson Files-PE3 1on1* on your desktop. We'll be working with the files inside the *Lesson 06* subfolder.

The exercises in this lesson explain how to use Photoshop Elements' paint, edit, and healing tools to brush color and effects into an image. You'll learn how to:

- Hand paint the lines in a scanned piece of black-and-white artwork . . . . page 170
- Retouch a face using the dodge, burn, sponge, and smudge tools . . . . page 176
- Fix a trio of common color aberrations using the paintbrush, red-eye removal, and color replacement tools . . . . page 181
- Restore a damaged photo and its timeworn subject using the healing brushes . . . . page 186

Video Lesson 6: Brush Options

Many of the paint, edit, and heal tools rely on a common group of options and settings that Adobe calls the *brush engine.* These options dictate the thickness, fuzziness, and scatter pattern of a brushstroke. You can even assign tapered ends to a brushstroke, as shown on the right.

You can adjust brush engine settings from the options bar and keyboard, as well as from the Tablet Options and More Options palettes. To get a feel for how these settings work, watch the sixth video lesson on the CD. Insert the CD, click the **Start** button, click the Set **2** button in the top-right corner of your screen, and then select **6, Brush Options** from the Lessons list. Clocking in at 11 minutes and 21 seconds, this video introduces you to the following tools and shortcuts:

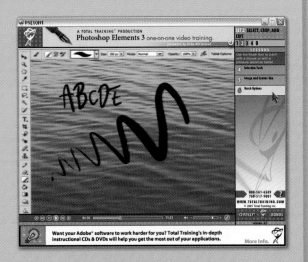

Tool or operation	Keyboard equivalent or shortcut
Brush tool	B
Incrementally enlarge the brush	⬚ (right bracket)
Incrementally shrink the brush	⬚ (left bracket)
Make the brush harder or softer	Shift+⬚ or Shift+⬚
Change the Opacity setting of the active brush	1, 2, 3, . . . , 0
Change the Flow setting of the active brush	Shift+1, 2, 3, . . . , 0
Display the More Options palette	Click the ✎ icon in the options bar

Brush-based or otherwise, you don't need to learn every one of these tools. As with everything in Photoshop Elements, some tools are good, some tools are bad. In this lesson we'll focus on what I consider to be the Essential Eight brush-based tools: the paintbrush (which Adobe calls the brush tool); the dodge, burn, sponge, smudge, and color replacement tools; and the spot and standard healing brushes. We'll also look at two selection-type tools, the paint bucket and the red-eye removal tool.

This emphasis on brushes may lead you to think that tools such as the paintbrush and sponge are best suited to creating original artwork. Although you *can* create artwork from scratch in Elements, it's not really what the program's designers had in mind. The real purpose of these tools is to help you edit photographic images or scanned artwork, and that's how we'll use them in this lesson.

The Three Editing Styles

Photoshop Elements lets you use tools—brush-based or otherwise—to apply and modify colors in three ways:

- The first group of tools, the *painting tools*, comprises the paintbrush, the paint bucket, and others. They permit you to paint lines and fill shapes with the foreground color. I drew the lines in Figure 6-2 with the paintbrush while switching the foreground color between black and white.

- *Editing tools* is a catch all category for any tool that modifies rather than replaces the existing color or luminosity of a pixel. The burn tool darkens pixels, the smudge tool smears them, and the color replacement tool swaps out hue and saturation values, as demonstrated in Figure 6-3.

Figure 6-2.

Figure 6-3.

Figure 6-4.

• The *healing tools* permit you to clone elements from one portion of an image to another. Using a sophisticated color-matching algorithm, the tools are capable of merging the cloned details with their new backgrounds to create seamless transitions, as illustrated in Figure 6-4.

Coloring Scanned Line Art

Photoshop Elements is great at manipulating digital photographs. But it's also a capable program for creating original art and coloring scanned artwork. This means you can exploit the best aspects of traditional and digital media:

• It's easier to draw on paper with a pencil and pen than it is to sketch on screen, if only because you can see the entire sheet of paper all at once without zooming or panning.

• Meanwhile, it's easier to add colors in Photoshop Elements than hassle with conventional paints.

Skeptical about that last point? Fair enough. In this exercise, you'll take a hand-drawn illustration and apply colors to it using just two tools: the paint bucket and paintbrush. Not only will you learn how to paint *precisely* inside the lines—and without exercising the least bit of care—but you'll also do so without harming so much as a single stroke in the original drawing. It really is the best of all worlds.

1. *Open the scanned artwork.* Starting in the Editor workspace, go to the *Lesson 06* folder inside *Lesson Files-PE3 1on1* and open *Butterfly.tif*. Pictured in Figure 6-5 on the facing page, this artwork is part traditional and part digital. It started as a sketch that I drew with a common, run-of-the-mill Sharpie on a piece of cheap copier paper. While these are admittedly low-tech art tools, I prefer them to anything Elements has to offer. But my original sketch included just the left half of the butterfly. To create the entire insect, I copied the sketch, flipped it, and joined the two halves together, all inside Photoshop Elements.

Your job is to color the butterfly. That means painting the black lines and leaving the white background alone. One way to approach this task is to select the lines using, say, the magic wand, and then paint inside the selection. But while the wand does a terrific job of selecting the blacks, it isn't so hot at capturing the transitions between blacks and whites around the edges. That's why we're going to take advantage of an easier technique that involves painting on an independent layer.

Figure 6-5.

2. *Make a new layer.* Choose **Layer→New→Layer** or press Ctrl+Shift+N to add a layer to your image. In the **New Layer** dialog box, name the layer "Color." Then click the word **Normal** and choose **Screen** from the **Mode** pop-up menu, as in Figure 6-6. Click the **OK** button to add the new layer to the top of the Layers palette.

3. *Change the foreground color to red.* Let's start by coloring the butterfly red. Choose **Window→Color Swatches** to display the **Color Swatches** palette, which contains a collection of predefined colors. Make sure the pop-up menu at the top of the palette is set to **Default**. Then click the very first color swatch, red, to make it the active foreground color, as in Figure 6-7.

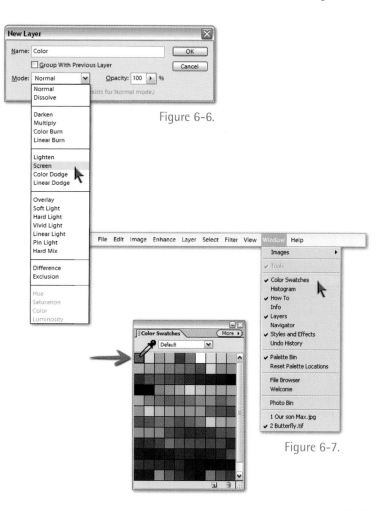

Figure 6-6.

Figure 6-7.

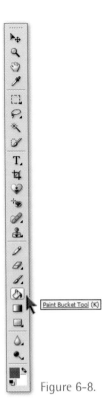

Figure 6-8.

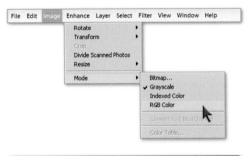

Figure 6-9.

4. *Select the paint bucket tool.* Click the paint bucket icon in the toolbox, as in Figure 6-8. Or press the K key.

5. *Click inside the image window.* To fill the entire butterfly with the foreground color, click anywhere inside the image window. The Screen mode that you assigned in Step 2 ensures that only the black lines are affected. But hey, what gives? Instead of filling lines with red, the paint bucket colors them gray. The problem: this is a grayscale image. Ideally suited to black-and-white line art, a grayscale file is simple and small. This is because each pixel is permitted a luminosity value and nothing more; hue and saturation are out of the picture. To add color to the image, you must first convert it.

6. *Convert the image to RGB.* To open up the color spectrum, choose **Image→Mode→RGB Color.** A highly misleading alert message prompts you to flatten your artwork and get rid of the layer you created in Step 2. This inane suggestion is intended to avoid the color shifts that sometimes result when recalculating blend modes. The problem is, these shifts are *not even possible* when converting from grayscale to RGB. In other words, there's no reason on Earth to flatten. Sadly, there is no Heck No! or Are You Crazy? button. So you'll have to satisfy yourself by clicking the **Don't Flatten** button, as in Figure 6-9.

To choose the RGB Color command from the keyboard, press and hold the Alt key and type I-M-R. Then press the D key to activate the Don't Flatten button.

---

7. *Fill the layer again.* Again click inside the image window with the paint bucket tool. Now that the image is set to accommodate color, the black lines of the butterfly turn red.

To color the butterfly from the keyboard, press Alt+Backspace. This handy shortcut fills the entire layer with the foreground color.

---

8. *Select the paintbrush tool.* Photoshop Elements supplies you with two painting tools, the paintbrush (AKA, the brush tool) and the pencil. The pencil paints jagged lines, making it most useful for changing individual pixels. The paintbrush is more versatile, permitting you to modify the sharpness of a line and tap into a wealth of controls that the pencil can't touch. (A third tool, the impressionist brush, doesn't count as a painting tool because it doesn't apply color to an image.

Instead, it randomly shuttles the colors that are already present in an image to create crude impressionistic effects.) Conclusion: when you want to paint, get the paintbrush. To do exactly that, click the paintbrush icon in the toolbox (see Figure 6-10) or press the B key.

9. *Change the foreground color to blue.* Click the fifth swatch in the top row of the Color Swatches palette (the swatch displays the hint *RGB Blue* when you hover over it) to change the foreground color to blue.

10. *Select the soft 300-pixel brush.* Go to the options bar at the top of the screen and click the ⏷ arrow to the right of the brush preview (just to the left of the word Size) to bring up a pop-up palette of predefined brush settings. Scroll down the list and click the brush labeled **300**. (When you hover over the brush setting, you should see the hint *Soft Round 300 pixels*, as in Figure 6-11.) This selects a circular brush with a diameter of 300 pixels and a hardness of 0. That is to say, the brush is big and fuzzy. To hide the pop-up palette and accept your changes, press the Enter key. Or just start painting in the image window. (The other way to hide the pop-up palette is to press the Esc key, but that also abandons your changes.)

Figure 6-10.

Figure 6-11.

To incrementally change the size of the brush, raise or lower the Size value in the options bar. You can also change the brush attributes from the keyboard using, of all things, the bracket keys. Press the ⟦ key to reduce the brush diameter; press ⟧ to raise it. Press Shift+⟦ to make the brush softer; press Shift+⟧ to make it harder. These shortcuts may seem weird, but once you come to terms with them, they're a heck of a lot easier than hunting around for the corresponding options.

---

11. *Paint inside the butterfly.* Paint as much of the butterfly as you like, wherever you like. As you do, Photoshop Elements confines your brushstrokes to the line art, as shown in Figure 6-12 on the next page.

Figure 6-12.

12. *Adjust the Scatter and Fade values.* If you're hungry for more brush options, click the ✍ icon to the right of More Options on the far right side of the options bar. This displays the pop-up palette pictured in Figure 6-13, which includes many of the options that I discussed in Video Lesson 6, "Brush Options." Then do the following:

- Increase the fifth value, **Scatter**, to 25 percent. This separates the spots of color laid down by the paintbrush, as you can see previewed on the left side of the options bar (labeled in Figure 6-13).

- Increase the **Fade** value to 150. This tells Photoshop Elements to gradually fade the brushstroke to transparent over the course of 150 spots of color. This ensures that you don't obliterate one color as you lay on another.

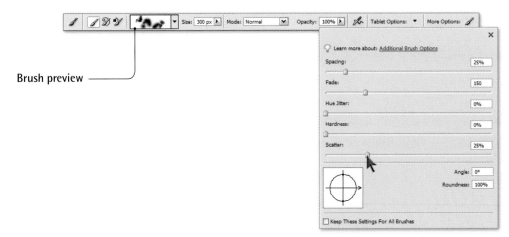

Brush preview

Figure 6-13.

When you finish, press the Enter key to accept your changes and hide the palette. If the palette remains visible, press Enter again.

13. *Switch colors and paint.* Select a color that strikes your fancy and paint inside the butterfly. When the paint runs out (according to the Fade value), switch colors and paint some more. To achieve the result pictured in

Figure 6-14, I painted one brushstroke in yellow, a second in green, and a third in a color called Pure Yellow Orange (which happens to be swatch number 67 in the Color Swatches palette). The colors go a long way toward offsetting the rigid symmetry of the insect. Naturally, I'm all for that. The only reason the butterfly is symmetrical in the first place is because I was too lazy to draw the other half.

14. *Enter 0 for the Fade and Scatter values.* Click the ✎ icon on the far right side of the options bar. Then restore the **Fade** and **Scatter** values to their default settings of 0 and press Enter.

15. *Switch to black and choose the Overlay mode.* Press the D key to restore black as the foreground color. Then choose **Overlay** from the **Mode** pop-up menu in the options bar. The Overlay mode will paint with black while maintaining some of the most vivid colors that you added in previous steps.

16. *Paint inside the bug's body.* Paint the body and the two antennae. If the effect is too light, paint a second brushstroke. Each stroke results in a progressively darker effect.

17. *Paint the tips of the wings.* Press the right bracket key (⬚) twice to increase the diameter of the brush to 500 pixels. Paint along the top and bottom edges to give the wings a bit of a toasting, as shown in Figure 6-15. Again, feel free to paint in multiple strokes.

18. *Save your artwork.* If you want to keep your artwork, choose **File→Save As** or press Ctrl+Shift+S. Inside the Save As dialog box, choose **Photoshop (*.PSD; *.PDD)** from the **Format** pop-up menu. Then click the **Save** button.

Figure 6-14.

Figure 6-15.

Dodge, Burn, Sponge, and Smudge

We now move from painting to editing. And by *editing*, I mean using Photoshop Elements' tools to modify the saturation values, brightness levels, and color transitions in a photographic image. We start with Elements' core editing tools:

- The dodge tool lightens pixels as you paint over them.

- The burn tool darkens pixels as you paint over them. If you're having problems keeping the dodge and burn tools straight, just think of toast—the more you burn it, the darker it gets.

- The sponge tool adjusts the saturation of colors, making them either duller or more vivid.

- The smudge tool smears colors. Used in moderation, it can be useful for smoothing out harsh transitions.

Elements provides other edit tools, but those above are the ones you'll most likely use. The following exercise explains how to use these four edit tools to solve some common retouching problems.

Figure 6-16.

1. *Open the photo of some poor sap who requires an emergency makeover.* Open the image titled *My apologies in advance.jpg* in the *Lesson 06* folder inside *Lesson Files-PE3 1on1*. The file features an all too accurate head shot of me, your gruesome-looking author, pictured in horrifying detail in Figure 6-16. In his *Maxims for the Use of the Overeducated*, Oscar Wilde wrote, "A subject that is beautiful in itself gives no suggestion to the artist. It lacks imperfection." That said, my face is extremely suggestive. In that same volume, Wilde wrote, "Those whom the gods love grow young." Well, the gods may not love me in real life, but they're going to fawn all over me in Photoshop Elements. *The Picture of Dorian Gray* has nothing on this program.

If you don't want to use my face—and really, who can blame you?—use a picture of yourself, a loved one, or a dire enemy. The specific concerns may be different, but the general approach will be the same. One potential difference: Because my flesh tones trend toward glow-in-the-dark white boy, my face needs a little dodging and a whole lot of burning. If the face you're working on is rich in melanin, it may require just the opposite.

---

2. *Click the dodge tool in the toolbox.* At the end of the toolbox (see Figure 6-17), the dodge tool is the first of the *toning tools*. To get the dodge tool from the keyboard, press the O key. (That's the letter, not zero.) If another tool appears at the bottom of the toolbox, keep pressing O until you get the dodge tool.

3. *Reduce the Exposure value to 30 percent.* Located in the options bar, the **Exposure** value controls the intensity of edits applied by the dodge tool. In my experience, the default value of 50 percent is too extreme for most editing work. Just press the 3 key. Or select the value and change it to 30 percent.

4. *Drag over the image details you want to lighten.* In my case, I started with my nose—my big old splotchy, freckly nose. I reduced the brush diameter a few notches (to, say, 40 pixels) and dragged inside the eyes, teeth, and eyelids. I also dragged over the smile lines trailing away from my nose. In Figure 6-18, the areas that received my attentions appear in color. (Unaffected areas are overlaid in blue-gray stripes.) Feel free to follow my lead or go your own way.

Figure 6-17.

Figure 6-18.

The biggest mistake people make when working with the edit tools is to push things too far. For example, it's tempting to take my coffee-stained teeth (positive note: no spinach stuck inside them) and scrub them until they're pearly white. But if you do that, my newly brilliant smile will look ridiculous compared with the rest of me. Better to make small adjustments—one or two passes at most—so that you leave the shadows intact. We'll get rid of the yellow in Step 10.

5. *Select the burn tool in the toolbox.* Click and hold the dodge tool icon to display a flyout menu and then choose the little hand icon that represents the burn tool, as in Figure 6-19. Or if you prefer, press the Alt key and click the dodge icon to advance to the next tool. Or just press the O key.

6. *Reduce the Exposure value to 20 percent.* Again, the default Exposure value is 50 percent, far too radical for burning. Press the 2 key to permit yourself more subtlety and flexibility.

Figure 6-19.

Figure 6-20.

7. *Drag over the image details that you want to darken.* The burn tool adds shadows, and shadows give an image volume, depth, and form. I started by increasing the brush diameter several notches (to something in the 250- to 300-pixel range) and dragging up and down both sides of my face, including over the ears. Then I reduced the brush to around 80 pixels and painted under my eyebrows, nose, cheekbones, and chin; along the sides of my nose; and over my thinning hair, as indicated by the full-color areas in Figure 6-20. Basically, use the burn tool anywhere you would apply makeup—assuming of course that you feel comfortable applying makeup to a manly, he-man bucko of virile potency like myself.

Don't worry about dragging over the same spots with the burn tool as you did with the dodge tool. If they require burning, edit away. About the worst that can happen is you under-saturate color values, but that's something you can remedy later with the sponge tool.

Attention Caucasians: The burn tool can serve as a nifty tanning aid, but don't overdo it. A few brushstrokes are all that stand between plausibly augmented skin tones and surreal George Hamilton territory, as in **Figure 6-21**.

Healthy glow — Not even remotely possible

Figure 6-21.

8. *Select the sponge tool in the toolbox.* Now to modify the saturation levels. Press Alt and click the burn tool icon in the toolbox to advance to the next toning tool, the sponge. Or press the O key.

9. *Reduce the Flow value to 30 percent.* Although it's calculated differently, the **Flow** value in the options bar serves the same purpose as the dodge and burn tools' Exposure value—it modifies the intensity of your brushstrokes. In my experience, the default value of 50 percent is too much. Press the 3 key to knock it down to 30 percent.

10. *Drag in the image to leech away aberrant colors.* Make sure the **Mode** option in the options bar is set to **Desaturate**. Then drag inside the teeth. A couple of passes gets rid of most of the yellow and leaves the teeth a more neutral white. (Be sure to leave behind some yellow. Gray teeth won't look right.) I also dragged over some of the more lurid pinks in the eyelids, ears, and lips, as well as some unusually orange patches in the fore-head, as indicated by the colored areas in Figure 6-22.

11. *Switch the Mode setting to Saturate.* You can also increase the saturation of colors using the sponge tool. After choosing **Saturate** from the **Mode** pop-up menu in the options bar, click a few times inside each iris. This brings out both the olive-green of the iris and the red-eye. We'll remedy the latter in the next exercise.

Oh, the humanity.jpg @ 50% (RGB/8)

Figure 6-22.

Figure 6-23.

12. *Select the smudge tool in the toolbox.* Click and hold the blur tool icon—the one that looks like a drop of water—to display a flyout menu of *focus tools*. Then choose the smudge tool, as in Figure 6-23. Or press the R key one or more times to cycle between the focus tools until you see the smudge tool icon.

13. *Reduce the Strength value and change the Mode setting.* The smudge tool's default settings are designed to create painterly effects. If you want to use it to edit an image, you need to rein the tool in a bit. Press the 2 key to reduce the **Strength** value in the options bar to 20 percent. Then choose **Lighten** from the **Mode** pop-up menu (see Figure 6-24). Now the tool will smear light colors into dark ones and not the other way around.

Figure 6-24.

Figure 6-25.

14. *Drag in the image to smear colors.* Press the] key a couple of times to increase the brush diameter to 30 pixels. (If nothing happens, press the Esc key to deactivate the Mode option, and then press the bracket key again.) Drag across my bottom lip to smooth over the grooves and make the skin look more hydrated. Be sure to trace along the lip, as demonstrated by the area highlighted in color in Figure 6-25. (Dragging across recruits colors from the teeth and whiskers.) In all, you may have to paint the lip three or four times to give it that "Just ChapStick'ed" look. I also painted over some of the more pitted portions of my skin. I realize that doesn't narrow it down too much, so again look to the highlighted areas in Figure 6-25 for the specifics.

To limit the area affected by the smudge tool, draw a selection outline. For example, if you lasso the lower lip, you can drag anywhere you please inside the image but affect only the lower lip. This technique works for all the paint and edit tools, including the paintbrush. But it's especially useful when using the smudge tool, which is unique in that it can smear colors from deselected pixels even as it modifies selected ones.

15. *Save your image.* The photo suffers a few remaining problems, which we'll do our utmost to resolve in the next exercise. As a precaution, choose **File→Save As** or press Ctrl+Shift+S and rename the image "Partially fixed.jpg" or words to that effect. In the JPEG Options dialog box, leave the **Quality** set to 10 and click **OK**. And leave the image open.

Red-Eye and Other Color Errors

Red-eye is a common by-product of consumer cameras. Because the strobe is mounted so close to the lens element on a point-and-shoot camera, the flash has a tendency to pass through a moderately dilated iris and bounce off the back of the retina, as illustrated in Figure 6-26. And when you view the well-lit interior of an eye from a few feet away, it looks red.

Although red-eye can occur in real life—when you catch a pedestrian in the beams of your car headlights, for example—the effect is fleeting and rare. As a result, red-eye in a photograph looks weird—so weird, in fact, that Photoshop Elements 3 provides two tools to eliminate it:

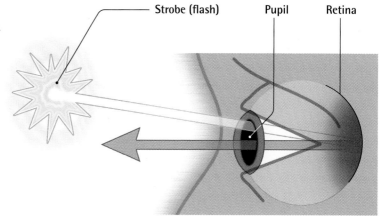

Figure 6-26.

- The first, the red-eye removal tool, is the most expedient and can correct red pupils with a single click.

- The second, the color replacement tool, is the more versatile. Although designed to fix red-eye (its predecessor in Photoshop Elements 2 was called the red-eye brush tool), it can correct all varieties of color problems, including pet eyes and otherwise.

We'll use these tools to fix the red of my pupils and the splotchy colors in my uniquely imperfect face. But first, we'll fix my thinning hair with a more familiar tool, the paintbrush.

1. *Open my face.* If your *Partially fixed.jpg* photograph remains on screen, you're ready to go. Otherwise, please locate and open it now. If you can't find it, or you'd prefer to work from my version of the photo, open the file called *Pupil problems.jpg* contained in the *Lesson 06* folder inside *Lesson Files-PE3 1on1*.

2. *Click the paintbrush in the toolbox.* Or press B. We'll use this tool to fill in my fine hair.

3. *Eyedrop a representative hair color.* With the paintbrush active, press the Alt key to temporarily access the eyedropper, and then click a shade of brown in one of the rare full portions of my hair. To see what color you lifted, click the brown foreground color swatch at the bottom of the toolbox to bring up the **Color Picker** dialog box. My color was in the neighborhood of **R**: 100, **G**: 90, **B**: 80. You may end up with something different because my hair has a lot of variation, especially depending on how much you burned it back in Step 7. Feel free to use the color you eyedropped or dial in the number suggested above—either should work fine.

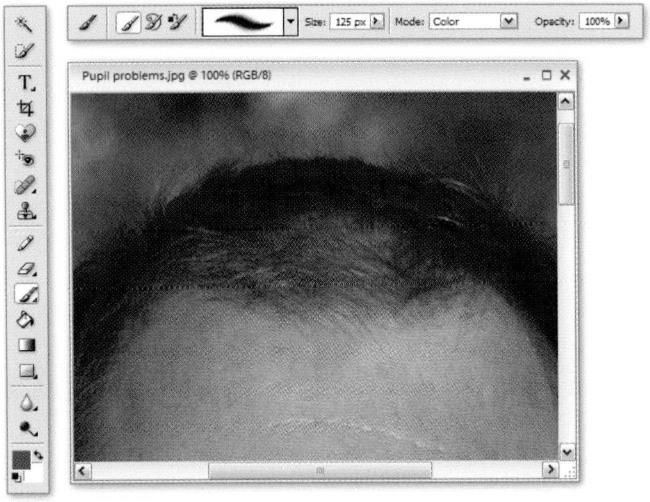

4. *Paint the scalp using the Color mode.* Change the **Mode** setting in the options bar to **Color**. Or press the keyboard shortcut, Shift+Alt+C. Change the brush diameter to 125 pixels. Then paint the top of my scalp to get the effect shown in Figure 6-27.

5. *Paint some more using the Multiply mode.* Choose **Multiply** from the **Mode** menu, or press Shift+Alt+M. Press 2 to lower the **Opacity** value to 20 percent. (If Elements ignores you, press Esc to deactivate the blend mode option and then press 2 again.) Then paint short strokes in the light areas of the scalp to darken them, as in Figure 6-28.

6. *Select the red-eye removal tool in the toolbox.* Your next task is to remove the red-eye caused by the camera's flash. Click the eyeball icon in the toolbox, as in Figure 6-29. Or press the Y key.

7. *Click near one of the pupils.* Just so we're on the same page, zoom in on the left pupil (my right). Then click up and to the left of the eye, at the approximate position indicated by the yellow arrow in Figure 6-30. So long as you click on or even *near* the pupil, Elements replaces the red-eye with black.

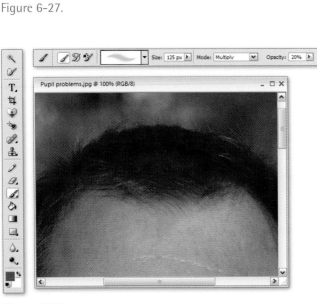

Figure 6-27.

Figure 6-28.

PEARL OF WISDOM

What makes the red-eye removal tool so smart that it can find a pupil in the vicinity of your click point? First, it finds the nearest area of red or pink in the image. Second, it confirms that an ellipse will fit inside that area and paints the ellipse black, making sure to preserve all highlights. To get a sense of what the tool does when there's no pupil to be seen, click in my mouth. True to form, Elements draws a black oval inside the pink of the tongue or lips.

If you have a sharp eye—the one in your head, not in the image—you may notice that the red-eye removal tool darkens a bit more than the pupil. In my case, the tool ever-so-slightly darkened my upper eyelid and eyelashes. If you find that bothersome, you can modify the behavior of the tool using a couple of values in the options bar:

- Use the first option, **Pupil Size**, to expand or reduce the area affected by the tool. Virtually any value results in the pupil getting colored. But a lower value—such as 20 percent—prevents the eyelashes from being affected.

- If the pupil ends up looking gray instead of black, undo the operation, raise the **Darken Amount** value, and try again. If you discover that you're losing highlights, lower the value.

Well, that's how the options are supposed to work anyway. In my experience, even radical adjustments—a Pupil Size of 1 percent and a Darken Amount of 100 percent, for example—produce such subtle changes that you can barely see the difference. If you really want to control the red-eye removal process, try the next step instead.

8. *Drag around the other pupil.* Draw a rectangular marquee around the right pupil. For the best results, your marquee should completely enclose the pupil but not extend much outside the iris, as demonstrated in Figure 6-31. (If you don't get it right the first time, press Ctrl+Z to undo the operation and try again.) Assuming everything goes according to plan, Elements blackens the pupil without harming so much as a neighboring follicle.

9. *Select the color replacement tool.* Straightforward and fast, the red-eye removal tool is one of the shining stars of the Elements toolbox. But it is also the program's most narrowly focused tool—it fixes red-eye and nothing else. If you want to remove other kinds of color aberrations—like the ruddy patches in my skin—it's time to take up the more sophisticated color replacement tool. To get it, click and hold the paintbrush icon in the toolbox. Then choose the color replacement tool from the flyout menu, as in Figure 6-32 on the following page.

Figure 6-29.

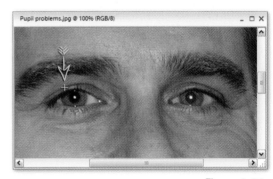

Figure 6-30.

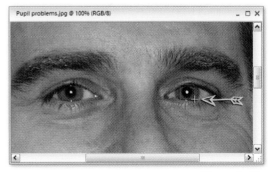

Figure 6-31.

Figure 6-32.

If you start right in painting, you'll make my face and everything else with which you come in contact gray. This is because the foreground color is set to a grayish brown and the options bar settings are too aggressive. In other words, a few preliminary adjustments are in order.

10. *Eyedrop a flesh tone.* Press the Alt key and click one of the areas of my skin that trends toward orange as opposed to pink. A good color to match is **R**: 205, **G**: 165, **B**: 150 (which you can confirm from the Info palette, if it's open, or by clicking the tan foreground color icon at the bottom of the toolbox).

11. *Change the Mode, Sampling, and Tolerance settings.* Now to adjust the options bar settings. Increase the **Size** value to 60 pixels and reduce the **Hardness** setting in the **More Options** area to 0 percent. (Remember, that's ⬚ and Shift+⬚ from the keyboard.) Then do the following:

   • Set the **Mode** option to **Hue**, which replaces the core hues while leaving the saturation values intact.

   • Change the **Sampling** option from Continuous to **Once**, as in Figure 6-33. The Once setting tells Elements to replace only colors that match the pixel at which you began to drag. It's a way of constraining the tool so it replaces fewer colors at a time.

Figure 6-33.

   • Reduce the **Tolerance** value to 20 percent by pressing 2. (As usual, if nothing happens, press Esc and press 2 again.) This setting limits the number of colors affected at a time.

12. *Paint away the pinks in the skin.* Paint over the pink areas in the eyelids, cheeks, and nose, as well as the more understated pinks of the neck, ears, and forehead, all outlined in Figure 6-34 on the facing page. As you do, these areas will turn a uniform fleshy peach color, as if my face were coated in a subtle but forgiving layer of foundation.

13. *Continue to adjust details as needed.* Don't expect to be able to retouch an image in 30 or so tidy steps over the course of two exercises. After all, a change made with the color replacement tool might beg you to make another with the burn tool, which in turn requires you to take up the sponge tool, and so on. In short, expect to revisit all these tools as you create that near-perfect image.

As you switch between the various tools, here are a few techniques and words of advice:

- The dodge and burn tools affect specific color ranges. By default, the **Range** menu in the options bar is set to **Midtones**, which changes the midtones and protects the highlights and shadows. If you prefer to adjust the lightest or darkest colors, choose **Highlights** or **Shadows** instead. In Figure 6-35 on the next page, I set the burn tool to Highlights and dragged around the perimeter of the background to create a slight vignette effect.

- The dodge and burn tools are interchangeable. Just press the Alt key to darken with the dodge tool or lighten with the burn tool. Pressing Alt is a great way to take the settings assigned to one tool—such as a brush diameter and Range setting—and apply them to the opposite function.

- The dodge, burn, sponge, and smudge tools work best when used with a soft brush (typically, a **Hardness** value of 50 percent or lower). The color replacement tool can go either way, hard or soft.

- Feel free to cheat. Just because you have all these edit tools doesn't mean you have to use them. For example, my lower lip was resolutely determined to remain a bright crimson despite my best efforts. So I selected the lip with the lasso tool. Then I used Enhance→Adjust Color→Adjust Hue/Saturation to nudge it more toward red and bring down the saturation. As long as you get results, it doesn't matter how you get there.

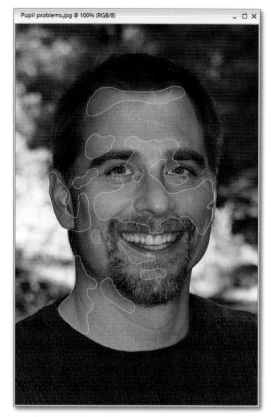

Figure 6-34.

Figure 6-35 compares the original photograph to the edited version. Now you know why I never let a picture of me (or anyone else I care about) leave the house without a proper retouching.

Figure 6-35.

Healing a Damaged Image

The edit tools are well suited to a variety of retouching scenarios. But they can't create detail where none exists. To fix dust and scratches or cover up scars and wrinkles, you need tools that can paint imagery on top of imagery. Tools like the healing brushes:

- The spot healing brush paints one section of an image onto another, a process called *cloning*. After you paint, the tool mixes the cloned pixels with the color and lighting that surrounds the brushstroke to create a seamless *patch*.

- The standard healing brush clones like the spot healing brush. But instead of Elements deciding which section of the image to clone, you decide for yourself. As usual, that means more work in return for improved results.

This next exercise shows you how to use these powerful tools to fix a variety of photographic woes, ranging from rips and tears to blemishes and age spots.

1. *Open a broken image.* Open the file *PhotoSpin bluebeard.jpg* located in the *Lesson 06* folder inside *Lesson Files-PE3 1on1*. Available in perfect condition from PhotoSpin's Ed Simpson International People collection, this version of the photo appears so tragically scratched because, well, I scratched it. I printed the image to a continuous-tone Olympus P-400 image printer. Then I folded the output once vertically and again horizontally, scored the crease with a pair of scissors, pressed it flat, and scanned it. The result appears in Figure 6-36. The image is representative of the worst sorts of photographic wounds, directed both at the subject of the photo and the medium.

2. *Click the healing brush in the toolbox.* As witnessed in Figure 6-37, the spot healing brush looks like a band-aid with a handful of dots to the left of it (✐). Click the band-aid or press the J key. (If you don't see the dots, press J again.)

3. *Confirm the default settings.* In the options bar, make sure **Type** is set to **Proximity Match**. This setting uses the pixels around the perimeter of a brush-stroke to determine how the painted area is healed. (The other setting, Create Texture, averages the colors inside the brushstroke. While this may sound okay, it usually results in an unacceptably blurry patch.) Also confirm that the brush preview on the left side of the options bar has a hard edge. If in doubt, press Shift+[a few times just to be sure.

4. *Click the lesser mole below the giant mole.* Increase the brush diameter a couple of notches, to 30 pixels. Then click on the little mole below the great mole on the left cheek (his right), which appears circled in yellow in Figure 6-38. In one operation, Elements selects the area you clicked, looks for a close equivalent elsewhere in the image, clones from the equivalent area, and blends it with the surrounding image data. Upshot: the mole disappears, as witnessed in the right half of the figure.

If Elements replaces the unsightly mole with some other unsightly defect, don't fret. Press Ctrl+Z and try again.

Figure 6-36.

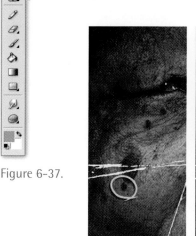

Figure 6-37.

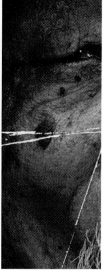

Figure 6-38.

5. *Heal the giant mole.* Now for something a bit more challenging—and less predictable. Drag over the giant mole on the left cheek. As you drag, Elements draws what looks like a selection marquee. Which is hardly surprising because that's exactly what it is—a temporary selection. When you release, the program hunts down what it regards as an equivalent section of the image and merges it with the area around the mole.

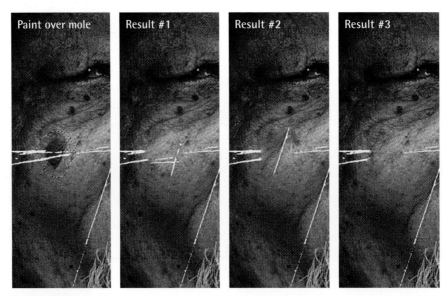

Figure 6-39.

At this point you may wonder, what good is an automated tool if it requires this much effort to make it function properly? My answer: not much. In my none-too-humble opinion, the spot healing brush is one of Elements' failed experiments. It was designed to simplify the performance of the standard healing brush, which hails from the full version of Photoshop (Version 7, to be exact). But what Adobe regards as the more complex tool, I see as more capable, more expedient, and thus easier to use. And use it we shall in the remaining steps.

6. *Select the standard healing brush.* Click and hold the band-aid icon in the toolbox and then choose the second tool, which is the standard variety of the healing brush, as in Figure 6-40. Alternatively, you can Alt-click the band-aid icon or press the J key.

7. *Confirm the default settings.* Again consult the options bar and confirm that the default settings are in play. Specifically, check that **Source** is set to **Sampled** and the **Aligned** check box is off. The Sampled setting tells Elements to clone pixels from a spot inside an image (as you'll specify in the next step); turning off Aligned lets you clone several times from that one pristine spot.

If these options are not set properly, you can restore all default settings in one operation by clicking the band-aid (🖉) icon on the far left side of the options bar and choosing the **Reset Tool** command.

---

8. *Set the source point for the healing.* The healing brush uses a source point to identify which portion of the image you want to clone. To set the source point, press the Alt key and click at the spot below the left cheek indicated by the crosshairs in Figure 6-41.

9. *Heal the left part of the scratch.* Check the options bar to make sure the brush diameter is set to 19 pixels. Then do the following:

   • Drag over the top-right fragment of the left-hand scratch, indicated by the yellow brushstroke in the top image in Figure 6-42. (Note that the brushstroke colors in this figure are for illustration purposes only; your brushstrokes will appear normal.)

   • Press the ⬚ key to reduce the brush diameter to 10 pixels. Then drag along the bottom fragment, as indicated in cyan in the figure.

   • In a separate brushstroke, drag along the remaining portion of the left scratch, indicated in purple.

   • Finally, paint the area pictured in green.

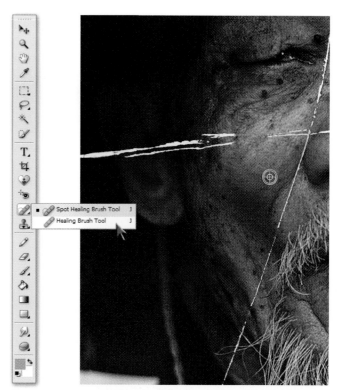

Figure 6-40.

Figure 6-41.

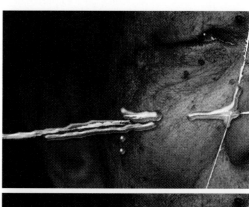

Figure 6-42.

In each case, I started my brushstroke on the right and dragged to the left. If you're right handed, this may seem backward. But it's important to follow my lead in this case; if you drag from left to right, you will clone the vertical scratch and mar your image.

 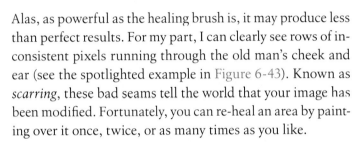
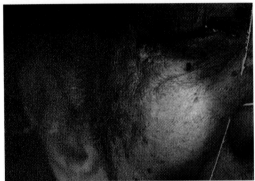

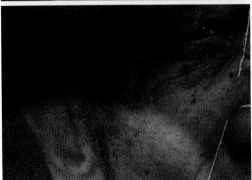

Figure 6-43.

Alas, as powerful as the healing brush is, it may produce less than perfect results. For my part, I can clearly see rows of inconsistent pixels running through the old man's cheek and ear (see the spotlighted example in Figure 6-43). Known as *scarring*, these bad seams tell the world that your image has been modified. Fortunately, you can re-heal an area by painting over it once, twice, or as many times as you like.

10. *Move the source and paint short strokes.* Using the healing brush effectively is all about selecting a good source point. The previous source worked well across the forward portion of the cheek, but then we ran into a bad spot. Thankfully, when one source fails, you can switch to another. Sources generally work best when set in an area that closely resembles the *destination* (the area you want to heal).

   • To heal inside the ear, for example, Alt-click in the top part of the ear and then drag over the scarred section.

   • To heal in the face, set the source point in the lower area of the cheek, where the flesh is relatively smooth.

   • To heal the black background, Alt-click somewhere in the black background. If you get some haloing along the edge of the ear—a function of Elements recruiting ear colors into its healing algorithm—Alt-click along the edge of the ear and paint again.

Keep your brushstrokes short. When using larger brushes, individual clicks can be very effective. I finally arrived at the revised cheek and ear shown in the bottom image in Figure 6-43.

11. *Set a new source.* Now to fix the nearly vertical scratch in the bottom half of the image. Scroll down. Then press Alt (or Option) and click just to the left of the scratch along the red hat strap, as shown on the left side of Figure 6-44.

12. *Click and Shift-click to draw straight lines.* Set the brush diameter to 20 pixels. Click at the point where the scratch intersects the red strap, indicated by the yellow target in the right half of Figure 6-44. Then press the Shift key and click midway up the scratch, at the point indicated by the cyan target in the figure. Photoshop Elements connects the two points with a straight line of healing, which I've colorized in orange. Finish off the scratch by Shift-clicking just to the left of the nose, indicated by the purple target.

13. *Heal the bottom of the scratch.* That still leaves an inch or so of scratch at the bottom of the image. Once again, click where the strap intersects the scratch (the yellow target in Figure 6-44) to reset the relationship between the source and destination points. Then press Shift and click down and to the left to heal away the scratch.

14. *Fix scars and repeated details.* If you look closely enough, you can make out repeated details around the nose and mouth. But the bigger problems occur near the collar and among the whiskers, as highlighted on the left side of Figure 6-45. To fix these, you'll need to source very similar areas—meaning collar-to-neck transitions and whiskers at similar angles—and paint them in using very small brushes, as small as 6 or 7 pixels in diameter. To build up the two horizontal whiskers, I sourced what little remained intact of one, clicked to double its width, sourced that, clicked again, and so on. It takes a little patience, but in the end, you can build something out of almost nothing (shown in the right half of the figure).

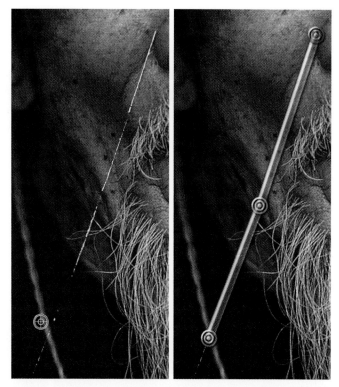

Figure 6-44.

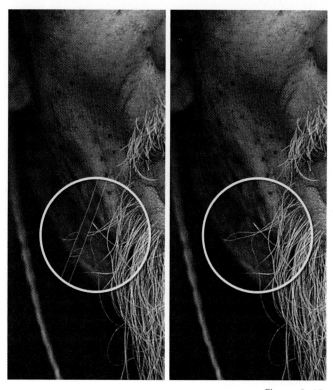

Figure 6-45.

15. *Clean up the remaining scratches.* From here on out, it's more of the same. You can fix the remaining scratches—those in the top and right-hand portions of the image—by setting new source points and using the Shift-clicking technique laid out in Step 12. If you're looking for additional practice, the healing brush is an excellent tool for cleaning up blemishes. For my part, I went ahead and painted over most of the moles and age spots. But I left the wrinkles. Wrinkles add character, and this particular gentleman wears them well.

Figure 6-46 compares the original version of the image—that is, the one I purposely damaged—to the document as it appears after I healed it inside Photoshop Elements. If you search hard enough, you can find a few scars and flaws. But I suspect most folks would have no idea this image has been tampered with at all.

Figure 6-46.

WHAT DID YOU LEARN?

Match the key concept in the numbered list below with the letter
of the phrase that best describes it. Answers appear upside-down
at the bottom of the page.

Key Concepts

1. Painting tools
2. Editing tools
3. Healing tools
4. Screen
5. Bracket keys ([and])
6. Scatter
7. Fade
8. Dodge tool
9. Burn tool
10. Sponge tool
11. Exposure
12. Cloning

Descriptions

A. This tool lightens pixels as you paint over them.

B. If you paint on a layer that has this blend mode applied to it, your painting will lighten everything beneath it.

C. Available from the More Options pop-up palette, this slider bar separates the spots of color laid down by the paintbrush.

D. The process of painting one section of an image onto another.

E. These tools permit you to clone photographic details from one portion of an image to another.

F. This tool adjusts the saturation of colors, making them either duller or more vivid.

G. These tools permit you to create lines and to fill shapes with the foreground color; the brush and pencil tools belong to this category.

H. This tool darkens pixels as you paint over them.

I. Available from the options bar, this value controls the intensity of the edits applied with the dodge and burn tools.

J. These tools modify (rather than replace) the existing color or luminosity of a pixel; examples include the burn and smudge tools.

K. These are the most convenient way to change the diameter of a brush; adding Shift changes the hardness of the brush.

L. This brush option tells Elements to gradually reduce the opacity of the brushstroke to transparency.

Answers

1G, 2J, 3E, 4B, 5K, 6C, 7L, 8A, 9H, 10F, 11I, 12D

FILTERS AND DISTORTIONS

PHOTOSHOP ELEMENTS offers more than a hundred *filters*. Named for the interchangeable camera lenses once commonly used to adjust and tint a scene before it was captured on film, Elements' filters permit you to modify the focus, color, and overall appearance of an image long after it is captured.

But while this group of commands derives its moniker from traditional filters, one bears little if any resemblance to the other. In fact, comparing Elements' filters to *anything* is an exercise in futility. Some filters modify the contrast of neighboring pixels, others trace the contours of a photograph, still others deform an image by moving pixels to new locations. (See Figure 7-1 for examples.) And that's just to name a few. If I had to come up with a definition for filters, I would call them a loosely associated collection of commands—some easy to use, others

Original image Filter→Blur→Motion Blur Filter→Artistic→Colored Pencil Filter→Distort→Wave

Figure 7-1.

ABOUT THIS LESSON

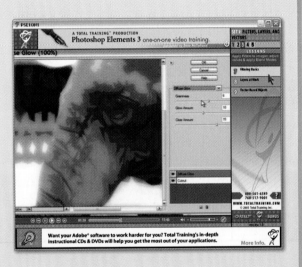

Project Files

Before beginning the exercises, make sure that you've installed the lesson files from the CD, as explained in Step 5 on page xv of the Preface. This should result in a folder called *Lesson Files-PE3 1on1* on your desktop. We'll be working with the files inside the *Lesson 07* subfolder.

In this lesson, I explain how to modify the perceived focus of a photograph, apply effects filters, and apply free-form distortions. You'll learn how to:

Video Lesson 7: Filtering Basics

The Filter menu offers access to just over 100 commands. Known generically as *filters*, these commands range from extremely practical to wonderfully frivolous. This lesson is about some of the best of the filters, including those that let you sharpen an image, add special effects, and apply complex, transformative distortions.

To get a sense for how these filters work—as well as how to repeat a filter and adjust its results after applying it—watch the seventh video lesson on the CD. Insert the CD, click the Start button, click Set 3 in the top-right corner of your screen, and then select **7, Filtering Basics** from the Lessons list. The 11-minute, 43-second movie contains information about the following commands and shortcuts:

Command or operation	Keyboard equivalent or shortcut
Hide or display the Styles and Effects palette	F7
Hide or show the thumbnails in the Filter Gallery	click ⊗ or ⊗ button
Zoom image behind a filter's dialog box in or out	Ctrl+⊡ (plus), Ctrl+⊡ (minus)
Adjust selected value incrementally	↑ or ↓
Adjust selected value by 10x increment	Shift+↑ or ↓
Advance to next (or previous) value	Tab (or Shift+Tab)
Duplicate (jump) image to independent layer	Ctrl+J
Reapply last-applied filter (with different settings)	Ctrl+F (Ctrl+Alt+F)
Change the Opacity setting of active layer	1, 2, 3, . . . , 0

quite complex—that apply effects to an image and reside in both the Filter menu and the Filters section of the Styles and Effects palette. Otherwise, filters are as varied as they are abundant.

This lesson makes no attempt to introduce you to all the filters in Photoshop Elements, or even a broad cross-section of them. Either task would consume an entire book, and not a particularly helpful one at that. For one thing, filters are too unpredictable in approach, implementation, and quality to warrant that sort of attention. More to the point, you can learn most of what you need to learn through personal experimentation. Choose a command, adjust a few slider bars, apply the filter, see how it looks.

Filter→Distort→Pinch, Amount: 50%   Undo, Pinch again: −30%

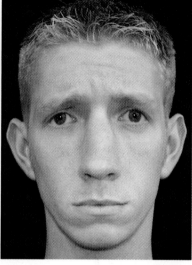

For example, try this: Open a picture of a person's face. Choose Filter→Distort→Pinch. Set the Amount value to 50 percent and click OK. Admire the goofy effect for a moment or two. Then press Ctrl+Z to undo the filter. Suddenly, the original face (which once looked fine) appears downright swollen. For extra fun, reapply Pinch with a negative value to bulge the face further (see Figure 7-2).

As parlor tricks, filters rate high marks. But as a rule, they tend to be better time-wasters than tools. So for the sake of expediency, I'll spend this lesson honing in on a small handful of representative

Figure 7-2.

filters that serve a practical or creative purpose. Before you read on, take a moment to watch Video Lesson 7, "Filtering Basics" (as explained on the facing page). It'll give you a sense for how filters work, as well as how to make the most of your experimentation.

The Subterfuge of Sharpness

The most useful filters in Photoshop Elements are devoted to the task of adjusting focus. If you think that sounds a bit far fetched, you're right. After all, the focus of an image is defined when it is formed by the camera lens. The moment you press the shutter release, you accept that focus and store it as a permanent attribute of the photograph. If the photograph is slightly out of focus, it stays out of focus. No post-processing solution can build more clearly defined edges than what the camera actually captured, or fill in missing or murky detail.

So how does Elements adjust focus? It fakes it. Although the program can't reach back into your camera and modify the lens element for a better shot, it can *simulate* the appearance of worse or better focus. It can compare neighboring pixels to enhance or impair what edges exist inside an image. Your eyes think they see a differently focused image, but really they see an exaggerated version of the focus that was already there.

Consider the photos in Figure 7-3. The first is a detail from a high-resolution image that was shot to film and then scanned. The focus is impeccable, but even so, you can make out film grain in the magnified inset. The second and third images show variations imposed by Photoshop Elements. Softening blurs the pixels together; sharpening exaggerates the edges. Softening bears a strong resemblance to what happens when an image is out of focus. Sharpening is a contrast trick that exploits the way our brains perceive definition, particularly with respect to distant or otherwise vague objects. A highly defined edge with sharp transitions between light and dark tells us where an object begins and ends.

This is not to impugn Elements' sharpening capabilities. Photography itself is a trick that simulates reality, very specifically geared to the human eye and brain. If Elements' sharpening augments that trick, more power to it. I just want you to know what you're doing. After all, the magician who knows his bag of tricks is better equipped to perform magic.

Real focus   Elements-imposed softening   Elements-imposed sharpening

Figure 7-3.

Sharpening an Image

The job of the filters in the Filter→Sharpen submenu is to sharpen the perceived focus of a photograph. I say "perceived" because, they can't *really* modify the focus—only a camera lens can do that. But filters can (and do) detect the edges in an image and trace dark and light pixels around those edges to accentuate the contrast. Our eyes read the enhanced edges as sharply defined details.

Of the four Sharpen filters, only one, Unsharp Mask, lets you control the amount of sharpening you apply to an image. As a result, it does everything the other three filters do—which isn't much, frankly—plus a whole lot more. Unsharp Mask derives its name from an old and largely abandoned traditional darkroom technique in which a photographic negative was sandwiched with a blurred, low-contrast positive of itself and printed to photographic paper. Ironically, this blurred positive (the "unsharp" mask) accentuated the edges in the original, resulting in the perception of sharpness.

To learn how Unsharp Mask's arcane origins translate to the way the function works in Photoshop Elements, read the sidebar "Using Blur to Sharpen," which begins on page 204.

In the meantime, the goal of this exercise is to learn how to put the Unsharp Mask command to everyday use.

1. *Open a couple of soft images.* Go to the *Lesson 07* folder inside *Lesson Files-PE3 1on1* and you'll find two photos of an unconscious young tabby, *Sleepy kitten.jpg* and *Sloppy kitten.jpg* (see Figure 7-4). I shot both pictures at a nearby farm. The kitten slept in a pen, so I had to position the camera lens between links in the surrounding fence. Unfortunately, my companions included an army of enthusiastic preschoolers who would, without warning, grab the fence and shake it until their mothers made them stop. When I captured the first photo, *Sleepy kitten.jpg*, the fence was in between shakes. Not so lucky on the second photo—I got smacked.

Figure 7-4.

The results: The first image is soft, meaning that it's a little off from its ideal focus, most likely a function of me moving the camera after focusing it. The second image, however, looks blurred because the camera was moving when I took the shot. This makes a big difference in how we approach the images and just how much good we can do.

2. *Bring the soft image to the front.* We'll start with the soft, cuddly *Sleepy kitten.jpg*, so click its title bar to make sure the image is active and ready for edits.

3. *Choose the Unsharp Mask command.* Elements gives you three ways to access the Unsharp Mask dialog box. The method you employ is up to you:

• Choose **Filter→Sharpen→Unsharp Mask**.

• Press Alt+T to bring up the **Filter** menu. Then release Alt and type S, Enter, U in sequence (not at the same time).

• Display the **Styles and Effects** palette, which appears bottom-left in Figure 7-5. Set the first pop up menu in the palette to **Filters**. Then scroll to the bottom of the list and double-click the item labeled **Unsharp Mask**.

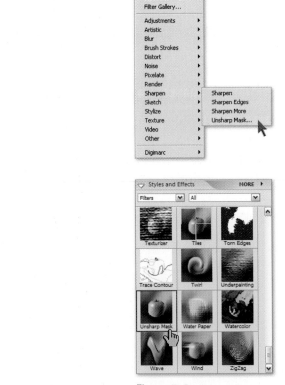

Figure 7-5.

4. *Turn on the Preview check box.* Pictured in Figure 7-5, the **Unsharp Mask** dialog box supports all the previewing options that I demonstrated in the video. It includes a cropped preview of the effect inside the dialog box. When the **Preview** check box is on, Elements applies the effect in real time to the larger image window as well.

5. *Click in the image window.* Click the cat's forward-facing paw to center the preview inside the dialog box. In any case, you want to center on some detail that you'd like to bring into sharper focus. Drag inside the preview box to further adjust the view.

6. *Set the previews to different zoom ratios.* Press Ctrl+Alt+⓪ to set the image window to the 100 percent view size and the preview to 50 percent, or vice versa. This way, you have two views into the results of your changes.

Why 100 and 50 percent? Because the first shows you every pixel in the image, and the other more closely represents the image as it appears when printed (which packs more pixels into a smaller space). Also worth noting, 50 percent is an interpolated zoom, meaning that Elements properly smooths over pixel transitions. By comparison, odd zooms such as 67 and 33 percent are jagged and misleading.

7. *Raise the Amount value to 200 percent.* This is a temporary value that merely exaggerates the effect and permits us to see what we're doing.

8. *Specify a Radius value of 2.5 pixels.* Even though **Radius** is the second value, I recommend you start with it because it's the hinge pin of the sharpening operation. Unsharp Mask simulates sharper edges by drawing halos around the edges (see "Using Blur to Sharpen," page 204). The Radius value defines the thickness of those halos. Thin halos result in a precise edge; thick halos result in a more generalized high-contrast effect. Figure 7-6 shows some examples.

Amount: 200%, Radius: 1 pixel

Radius: 2.5 pixels

Radius: 10 pixels

Figure 7-6.

For everyday sharpening, the best Radius value is the one you can just barely see. Naturally, this varies depending on how your final image will be viewed:

- If you intend to display the image on screen (say, for a Web page), enter a very small value, such as 0.5 pixel.

- For medium-resolution printing, a Radius of 1.0 to 2.0 pixels tends to work best.

- For high-resolution printing, a Radius of 2.0 or higher results in sharp edges.

The examples in Figure 7-6 were printed at 280 pixels per inch, so the 2.5-pixel Radius delivers the best edges. A smaller Radius value most likely looks better on your screen, but for now, I'd like you to pretend you're going to print, so enter 2.5.

Amount: 150%

Amount: 125%

Amount: 100%

Figure 7-7.

Use the ↑ and ↓ keys to nudge the value by its smallest increment, 0.1 in the case of Radius, 1 in the case of Amount and Threshold. Add Shift to nudge 10 times that increment.

9. *Lower the Amount value to 100 percent.* The **Amount** value controls the degree to which the image gets sharpened. Higher Amount values result in more crisply defined edges. The effects of the Amount value become more pronounced at higher Radius values as well. So where 200 percent may look dandy with a Radius of 1 pixel, the image may appear jagged and noisy at a Radius of 2.5. An image set to too high an Amount value is said to be *oversharpened*, as is presently the case for our tabby.

Press Shift+Tab to highlight the Amount value. Then press Shift+↓ a few times in a row to nudge the value down in increments of 10 percent. Figure 7-7 shows a few examples. For my money, the final setting is the best fit.

10. *Leave the Threshold value set to 0.* The final value, **Threshold**, decides whether or not neighboring pixels are factored into the sharpening equation. Threshold is measured in luminosity levels; the default, 0, means that neighboring pixels have to be at least 0 levels different from each other to be considered a potential

edge. In other words, all pixels are sharpened uniformly. Higher Threshold values rule out more and more pixels. For those of you who enjoy symmetry in your software, the Threshold value measures colors just like the magic wand's Tolerance setting (see Step 5, page 114). Only instead of including pixels, as Tolerance does, Threshold rules them out.

In theory, the Threshold value helps avoid sharpening grain and other artifacts. In practice, it just doesn't work. Because Threshold is an on or off proposition—pixels get sharpened or they don't—any value large enough to produce a visible effect does as much to create grain as defeat it. For example, a Threshold of 40 calls out random flecks in the kitten's fur, shown in **Figure 7-8** at 100 and 200 percent. That's why I prefer to leave this value set to 0 under all circumstances.

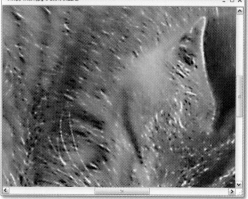

Figure 7-8.

11. *Click the OK button.* Confirm that your values match those in Figure 7-9. Turn on and off the **Preview** check box to see how far you've come. And then click **OK** to apply the filter.

12. *Bring the blurry image to the front.* That pretty well fixes the first photograph. Now what can we do about the second? Well, sad to say, not a whole lot. To see for yourself, bring the *Sloppy kitten.jpg* image up front by clicking its title bar or choosing its name from the bottom of the **Window** menu.

13. *Again display the Unsharp Mask dialog box.* But don't choose Filter→Sharpen→Unsharp Mask. Instead, click the **Filter** menu and notice that the first command now reads Unsharp Mask, as in Figure 7-10. As I explained back in Video Lesson 7, "Filtering Basics" (see page 196), choosing this command would reapply the filter with the same settings as before. However, don't do that. Instead, press and hold the Alt key and then choose **Filter→Unsharp Mask**. Or better yet, press the keyboard shortcut Ctrl+Alt+F. Elements revisits the dialog box, permitting you to apply the filter with different settings.

Figure 7-9.

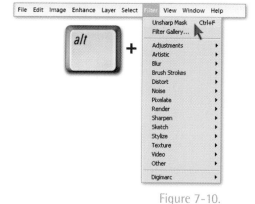

Figure 7-10.

Using Blur to Sharpen

The "unsharp" in Unsharp Mask is a function of the softly tapering halo applied by the Radius value. Understand this and you can master the art of focus in Photoshop Elements.

Consider the line art in the figure below. The top-left example features dark lines against a light background. The other three images are sharpened with increasingly higher Radius values. (Throughout, the Amount value is set to 200 percent.) In each case, the Unsharp Mask filter traces the dark areas inside the lines (the brown areas) with a blurry dark halo and the light areas outside the lines (the green areas) with a blurry light halo. The thickness of these halos conforms to the Radius value. So all Unsharp Mask does is increase the contrast by tracing halos around edges.

Given that the Radius value is all about blurring, it's no surprise that this option also appears in the Gaussian Blur dialog box (Filter→Blur→Gaussian Blur), where it once again generates halos around edges. In fact, if we were to trace the lineage of these filters, Gaussian Blur is Unsharp Mask's grandparent. The missing family member in between is an obscure command called High Pass.

Why should you care? Because Unsharp Mask's parent, High Pass, is a more flexible sharpening agent than its progeny.

Try this: Go ahead and open *Sleepy kitten.jpg*. (If it's still open from the "Sharpening an Image" exercise, choose Edit→ Revert to Saved to revert the image to its original appearance.)

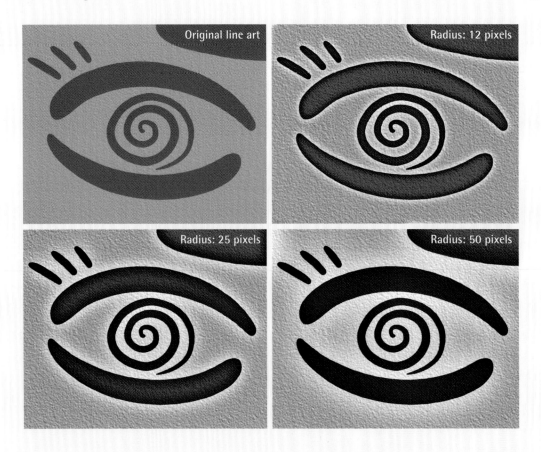

Original line art

Radius: 12 pixels

Radius: 25 pixels

Radius: 50 pixels

Now press Ctrl+J to copy the image to an independent layer. Next, choose Filter→Other→High Pass. Pictured below, the High Pass dialog box contains a single option, Radius. Change this value to 2.5 pixels, the same Radius you applied in the exercise using Unsharp Mask. Then click OK.

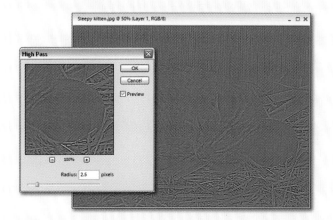

Looks like a big mess of gray, right? But there are tenuous edges in there. To bring them out, press Ctrl+L or choose Enhance→Adjust Lighting→Levels to display the Levels dialog box. Change the first and third Input Levels values to 75 and 180, respectively, as in the figure below. Then click OK.

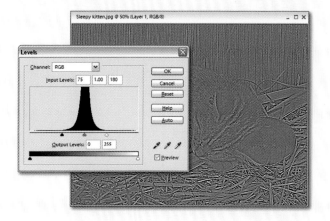

Still looks terrible. But what you're looking at are the very same light and dark halos that Unsharp Mask creates. To apply those halos to the original photograph, go to the Layers palette and choose Overlay from the top left pop-up menu. Just like that, Photoshop Elements drops out the grays, blends in the edges, and makes it all better, as shown below. The result is almost exactly what you'd get if you applied Unsharp Mask with a Radius of 2.5 and an Amount of 200 percent. (In other words, the current High Pass layer is twice as strong as the equivalent Unsharp Mask.) This means that the photograph is oversharpened just as it was at the outset of Step 9 on page 202. To match the more pleasing Amount value of 100 percent that we eventually settled on in the exercise, reduce the layer's Opacity setting to 50 percent.

Why go through all this just to get the same effect we achieved in the exercise? Because now you have a floating layer of sharpness whose Amount you can change at any time just by modifying the layer's Opacity setting. This means you can change your mind well into the future, as opposed to being locked into the static result of Unsharp Mask. Sure, it's an unusual approach, and it takes a bit of experience to get it down pat. But the additional flexibility you gain is well worth the effort.

Figure 7 11.

14. *Raise the Amount value.* This image requires more sharpening than the first one. So click in the **Amount** option in the Unsharp Mask dialog box and press Shift+↑ several times to increase the value in 10 percent increments. This increases the sharpness of the image, but it also brings out more of the diagonal lines of noise associated with the motion blur, as shown in Figure 7-11.

For my money, an Amount of 200 percent gets things as close to focused as they're going to get. What about raising the Radius value? Doesn't really help. Might not Threshold reduce the noise? As I said, that option doesn't work under the best of conditions, and it doesn't stand a chance against the directional noise produced by a motion blur. My experience: This is as good as it gets.

PEARL OF WISDOM

Just imagine if this was your *only* picture of this cute little kitten sleeping on a pumpkin—what in the heck do you do?! Well, I have good news and bad news. The good news is, this is the only place I'm going to share the following bad news in the entire book. The bad news is, your only option is to give up. Oh sure, there are all kinds of ways to tweak this image, make it look all artsy, gussy it up. But it won't look sharper. I know of no program, including Photoshop Sr., that can take a blurred image and somehow clarify such fuzzy details. It would require a degree of intelligence that current technology does not possess. Maybe someday, but not today.

15. *Wipe away the tears and get on with your life.* Click **OK** to accept your revised Amount value of 200 percent. It's not so bad, right? In fact it looks kind of cool.

Not satisfied? Then grab your camera, go back to that farm, and try your best to talk the kitten into sleeping on that pumpkin just one more time. And be quick about it because, I swear, when those preschoolers land they move fast.

Playing with the Filter Gallery

The Filter Gallery is a cluster of special effects filters that you can mix and match inside a single dialog box before applying them. Less than half of the 100 or so filters in Photoshop Elements qualify for inclusion in the Filter Gallery. These special filters hail from an ancient collection called Gallery Effects that Adobe inherited when the company purchased the core technology for its layout application, InDesign.

Many of the Filter Gallery effects are so-called *media filters*, meaning they try to make your digital photos look like drawings and paintings created with traditional tools such as chalk, charcoal, and watercolor. Needless to say, some are more successful than others. But the best thing about the Filter Gallery is that it lets you apply multiple filters in sequence, and you can even juggle the order in which the filters are applied, all from a central location. The order in which you apply filters can make a big difference in the final result, and with the Filter Gallery, it's easy to experiment until you're satisfied.

In this exercise, you're going to work on another photo of an orange kitty cat—this one a ferocious Bengal tiger. We'll maneuver through the Filter Gallery and combine its media filters to construct a unique and foreboding effect.

1. *Open an image.* Go to the *Lesson 07* folder inside *Lesson Files-PE3 1on1* and open the file *Tiger.jpg*,  an iStockPhoto.com image captured by Kitch Bain. Figure 7-12 shows a screen shot of the majestic feline.

Figure 7-12.

2. *Prepare the interface.* Many of the filters in the Filter Gallery draw on the active foreground and background colors to work their magic. Press the D key to set the former to black and the latter to white. If your colors were previously set to something other than black and white, you'll see the change at the bottom of the toolbox.

Hide/show thumbnails

3. *Open the Filter Gallery.* There are lots of ways to open the Filter Gallery. For example, you can choose any of the 47 filters that are members of the Gallery from either the Filter menu or the Styles and Effects palette. But the most straightforward method is to invoke the command with clear intent: Choose **Filter→Filter Gallery** to display a window like the one in Figure 7-13.

4. *Zoom in on the image.* The left side of the Filter Gallery features a generous image preview that you can navigate by clicking the ⊟ or ⊞ button in the lower-left corner or by using familiar keyboard equivalents.

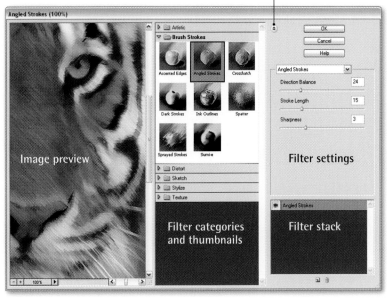

Figure 7-13.

Ctrl-click in the preview to zoom in; Alt-click to zoom out. Alternatively, you can press Ctrl+☐ or Ctrl+☐. To scroll the image, just drag inside it.

I want you to zoom the preview to 100 percent. So press the shortcut Ctrl+Alt+☐. Then drag the image so you can see the tiger's face, as in Figure 7 13 on the previous page.

5. *Tuck away the thumbnails.* The middle section of the Filter Gallery houses filter thumbnails, arranged in folders that correspond to the submenus found in the Filter menu and the Styles and Effects palette. To give yourself more room to preview your edits, collapse this section by clicking the ⊗ button to the left of the OK button.

6. *Apply a filter.* We want to begin by applying an etched-line effect to the tiger. And the best way to start things off is with a filter that traces edges. Click the pop-up menu below the Help button and choose the **Glowing Edges** filter. You should see light edges against a black background, as in Figure 7-14.

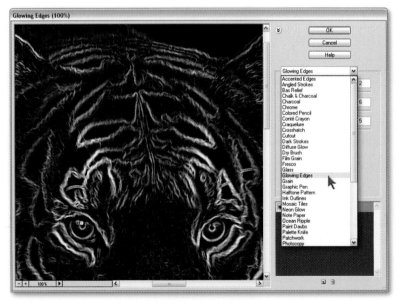

Figure 7-14.

7. *Add a second filter.* Glowing Edges does a fine job of finding edges, but the result is more intricate than what I have in mind. I want to add another filter to simplify the edges. And that filter is Cutout. Problem is, if I were to select Cutout from the pop-up menu, I'd replace the Glowing Edges filter. I want to combine the effects of the two filters, so I need to add a filter to the stack. So click the ▣ icon in the bottom-right corner of the dialog box to add a new effect.

8. *Switch to the Cutout filter.* By default, the Filter Gallery adds another layer of Glowing Edges. Obviously, we don't need that. Click **Glowing Edges** in the pop-up menu up top and choose the **Cutout** filter in its place. The result is a dim series of chiselled polygons, interesting, I suppose, but not what I'm looking for. I want the Cutout filter to simpifly the behavior of the Glowing Edges filter, so I need to reverse the order of the commands.

9. *Reorder the filters.* To hide the effects of a filter, click the ◉ icon beside its name in the lower-right region of the dialog box. For example, if you click the ◉ in front of Glowing Edges, you can observe the effect of the Cutout filter on its own. Cutout reduces an image to a few distinct fields of color, making it look like the image is clipped from construction paper. If this filter is to simplify the effects of Glowing Edges, it needs to be behind it. So turn the **Glowing Edges** filter back on. And then drag the word **Cutout** below Glowing Edges. When you see a heavy horizontal line below Glowing Edges, release your mouse button. Figure 7-15 shows the result.

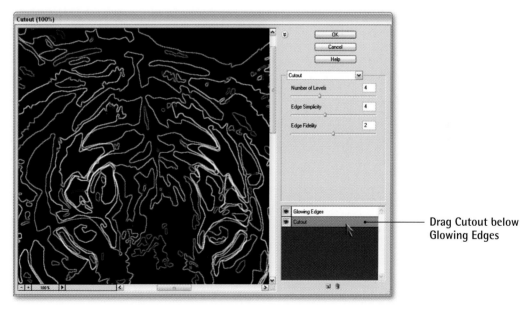

Drag Cutout below Glowing Edges

Figure 7-15.

10. *Add a third filter.* Click the ▣ icon again to add another filter to the top of the stack, this time a copy of Cutout. Click **Cutout** in the pop-up menu and swap it for **Plaster**. The Filter Gallery converts the colors to grayscale and carves the lines into deep grooves against the black background. Now we're talking.

Tiger.jpg @ 40% (RGB/8)

Figure 7-16.

11. *Adjust the filter settings.* Now we have the correct filters in place—and in the desired order, no less—we just need to do a little noodling with the settings:

- Select the **Cutout** filter at the bottom of the stack to display its settings. The line effect is currently a little busy, so raise the **Edge Simplicity** value to 5 to have the filter ignore some of the more complex details.

- The result is still too complex, so let's take a more drastic plan of attack: Shift+Tab to select the **Number of Levels** value and press ↓ to lower the value to 3.

- Click the **Glowing Edges** item in the middle of the filter stack. I think the edges could be thicker in general, so raise the **Edge Brightness** value to 8. This gives the Plaster filter a better opportunity to carve into the edges.

We could spend all day goofing around with these settings. But let's not. Click **OK** to close the Filter Gallery and accept your changes. Figure 7-16 shows the etched-line effect.

PEARL OF WISDOM

As you play away inside the Filter Gallery, make sure you take a moment to appreciate what's happening. For example, when you updated the settings of the Cutout filter, you saw the changes refracted through the two subsequent filters, Glowing Edges and Plaster. Had you applied a similar command outside the Filter Gallery, you would have no such option to tweak one and preview its effect on the other two. The Filter Gallery gives you an extra dimension of creative flexibility; the shame is that so many of Elements' filters—particularly the really great ones like Unsharp Mask—aren't included.

12. *Undo and layer.* Let's say that I'm happy with the chiseled appearance of the image. But I'd like to retrieve the rich array of colors from the original. To do that, I need to restore my original image and add a layer. But if I undo the current effect, I lose it, right? Not quite. Here's what I want you to do:

- Click the ↩ icon in the shortcuts bar or press Ctrl+Z to undo the effects of the Filter Gallery.

- Press Ctrl+J to create a duplicate of the Background layer named Layer 1.

- Click the **Background** layer in the **Layers** palette or press Alt+⌷ to make the rear version of the tiger active.

Go to the **Filter** menu and notice that it now begins with two variations of the Filter Gallery command, the second with an ellipse (...) and the first without. The first command applies the most recent filter—or in our case, filters—subject to the same settings. The second one brings up the Filter Gallery dialog box so you can apply new settings.

13. *Reapply the three filters.* Choose the first **Filter→Filter Gallery** or press Ctrl+F to reapply the Cutout, Glowing Edges, and Plaster filters to the Background layer. You won't see any changes in the image window because Layer 1 is covering them. But you can see the filter combo applied to the Background thumbnail in the Layers palette. In other words, take heart—the filter worked and everything is going according to plan.

14. *Apply a new filter.* Click **Layer 1** in the Layers palette or press Alt+[to make the top layer active. Then choose the second **Filter→Filter Gallery**, or press the shortcut for invoking the last-used filter with new settings, Ctrl+Alt+F. Once again, Photoshop Elements displays the Filter Gallery dialog box. Most likely, you'll see the same trio of filters—Cutout, Glowing Edges, and Plaster—in the stack at the bottom. If so, click the trashcan icon in the bottom-right corner of the dialog box twice in a row to delete the Plaster and Glowing Edges filters. You should be left with a single application of Cutout.

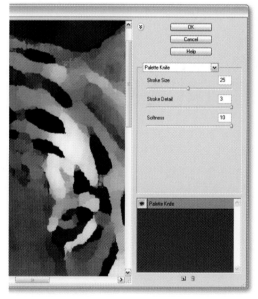

Figure 7-17.

The Filter Gallery offers another technique that lets you wipe out all filters in one fell swoop. Hold down the Ctrl key and notice that the Cancel button changes to Default. With Ctrl still down, click that button. Elements removes all the filters and leaves you with nothing. Then click the ⬓ icon in the bottom-right corner of the dialog box to add a brand-new filter to the stack.

---

15. *Apply the Palette Knife filter.* Click the pop-up menu below the Help button and choose the **Palette Knife** filter. Palette Knife tries to simulate the blotchy effect of oil paint applied to canvas with a knife, but a close inspection reveals that it leaves jagged edges. So raise the **Softness** slider all the way up to 10, as in Figure 7-17.

16. *Add one last filter.* Click the ⬓ icon to add another filter to the stack. The Filter Gallery creates a copy of the Palette Knife filter. Click the pop-up menu at the top of the dialog box and choose the **Craquelure** filter instead. Named for the cracking that occurs in very old paintings (and which is often imitated

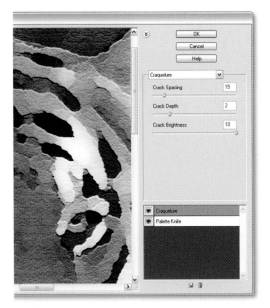

Figure 7-18.

by art forgers to simulate age), Craquelure adds a cracked plaster surface to the face of the tiger. The problem is, the cracks go a little too deep. To soften things up a bit, reduce the **Crack Depth** value to 2. Then boost the **Crack Brightness** to 10 to take that last bit of edge off, as in Figure 7-18.

17. *Click the OK button.* Photoshop Elements applies the Palette Knife and Craquelure filters to Layer 1.

18. *Apply a blend mode.* We have an etched-line effect on one layer and a digital fresco effect on another. All that's left is to combine the two. See that option in the top-left corner of the **Layers** palette that says **Normal**? Click it to bring up a list of *blend modes* that let you mix the active layer with the ones below it using a variety of mathematical calculations. Choose the **Screen** option, which marries the painted tiger on Layer 1 with the black areas of the Background layer below. The result is a kind of deliciously retro textile art riddled with deeply etched seams, suitable for printing and display under black light. As witnessed in Figure 7-19, this particular cat looks infinitely more ominous after his trip through the Filter Gallery.

Figure 7-19.

Applying Free-Form Distortions

If Unsharp Mask is the most practical filter and Filter Gallery is the most fun, the award for the most powerful filter in Photoshop Elements 3 goes to Liquify. Less a filter, it's more an independent program that happens to run in the Editor workspace. Liquify lets you distort an image by painting inside it using a collection of tools. One tool stretches pixels, another twists them into a spiral, and a third pinches them. These and other tools make Liquify ideally suited to cosmetic surgery. Whether you're looking to tuck a tummy, slim a limb, or nip a nose, Liquify gives you everything you need to get the job done.

In this exercise, we'll do something more radical. We'll take a photo of my mild-mannered 2-year-old Sammy and morph him into a teenage superhero, complete with square chin, rugged jaw, cocky sneer, and eyes bright with righteous anger. In all Gotham City, only one filter can aid us in this goal, and that filter is Liquify.

PEARL OF 〇 WISDOM

Be forewarned: Unlike other exercises, in which my instructions are concrete and easy to replicate, these next steps are subject to more interpretation. I'll be asking you to paint—not inside lines, as in Lesson 6, but completely free-form. You don't necessarily need heaps of artistic talent, but a little doesn't hurt. And regardless of how talented you are, your results and mine will be different. Don't sweat it. Even when all you're doing is making a big mess, this is one entertaining function. In fact, I have never once demonstrated the Liquify filter—whether to a few family members or an audience of 500 professionals—that it doesn't inspire giddy laughter. So don't be frustrated; be amused.

1. *Open an image that you want to distort.* After capturing the very cute picture of Sammy dressed up for Halloween that appears at the top of Figure 7-20, it struck me that it might be fun to make him appear every bit the caped crusader that his outfit suggests. A couple of hours of dodging, burning, sponging, healing, and finally painting the snapshot eventually produced the bottom image in the figure. Although it possesses an undeniably graphic, surreal quality, my fair-haired boy continues to exude cuteness, the kind one associates less with a guardian angel and more with an excitable cherub. Few superheroes list "cute" or "cherubic" on their resumés, and so these attributes, however laudable, must be eradicated. To join me in my quest to convert child into champion, open the image titled *Gold hero.jpg*, included in the *Lesson 07* folder inside *Lesson Files-PE3 1on1*.

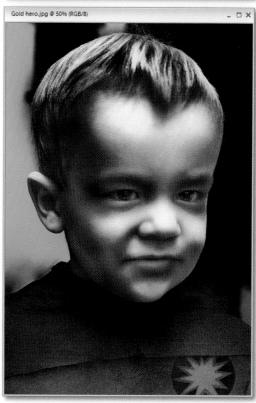

Figure 7-20.

2. *Choose the Liquify command.* Go to the **Filter** menu and choose **Distort→Liquify**. Or press Alt+T and then type the following keys in sequence: D, Enter, L. Photoshop Elements displays the **Liquify** window, which appears in Figure 7-21. The window sports 11 tools on its left edge and a few options on the right. The rest of the window is devoted to the image itself.

The same navigation techniques that work outside the Liquify window work inside it as well. You can zoom in or out by pressing Ctrl+⌐ or Ctrl+⌐, respectively. Press the spacebar and drag to pan the image.

Figure 7-21.

3. *Select the warp tool.* Click the topmost tool in the Liquify window or press the W key to select the warp tool, which lets you stretch or squish details in an image by dragging them. Of all Liquify's tools, this one is the most consistently useful.

4. *Increase the Brush Size value to 100 pixels.* Select the **Brush Size** value (or press Alt+S) and enter 100 in its stead.

As elsewhere in the Standard Edit mode, you can change the brush size by pressing a bracket key. But the shortcut behaves a bit differently. Press the ⬚ or ⬚ key to scale the brush by 1 pixel. Press and hold the key to scale more quickly. Press Shift+⬚ or ⬚ to scale the brush in 10-pixel increments. (In Liquify, there is no such thing as brush hardness.)

5. *Arch the eyebrows.* Using the warp tool, drag the eyebrows to make them appear arched, as in Figure 7-22. This is an exaggerated effect, so if you try to pull it off in one or two brushstrokes, you'll smear the colors and wind up with digital stretch marks. Here's how to achieve more photo-realistic results:

- Keep your strokes very short—just a few pixels at a time.

- Because you're keeping your brushstroke short, you'll need a lot of them. I reckon I laid down about 20 strokes in all.

- Drag *on* the detail you want to move. For example, to move an eyebrow, center your brush cursor on the eyebrow and then drag. If you drag next to the eyebrow (which, though it may sound weird, is the more natural tendency), you'll pinch the eyebrow and slim it down to a thin line.

Warp tool —

Adjust brush size

Drag directly on eyebrows

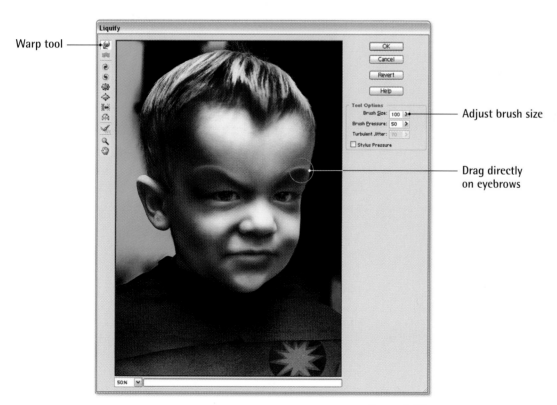

Figure 7-22.

If you make a mistake, you'll be glad to learn that Liquify offers multiple undos. But how they work is weird. Pressing Ctrl+Z undoes or redoes a single brushstroke only. To revert further, press Ctrl+Alt+Z. To redo brushstrokes, press Ctrl+Shift+Z. It's a sloppy holdover from the senior version of Photoshop, which handles all undos this way.

For the present, be careful to avoid painting the eyes. We'll edit them in the next steps with a different tool.

6. *Switch to the pucker tool.* Click the fifth tool down or press the P key. This selects the pucker tool, which lets you pinch portions of an image, in much the same way as the Pinch filter, which I mentioned at the beginning of this lesson (see Figure 7-2 on page 197).

7. *Reduce each of the eyes.* Toddlers have lots of physical characteristics that distinguish them from adults. They're short, they have pudgy cheeks, and their skin is really smooth except for occasional patches of dried snot and spaghetti sauce. But if I had to choose their most unique feature, it'd be their eyes. Kids have adult-sized eyeballs packed inside pint-sized heads, which makes them look enormous. Outside Japan, superheroes don't have big old baby eyes, and so Sammy's must be reduced.

Raise the **Brush Size** value to 200 pixels. Then click on each of Sammy's eyes. Click quickly and do not drag. If one click doesn't do the trick, give it another one. The finished eyes should look like those shown in Figure 7-23 on the facing page.

8. *Switch to the twirl clockwise tool.* To give Sam a menacing appearance—so that he can more easily intimidate criminals and thwart their evil plans—I want to slant his eyes very slightly. Click the third tool on the left side of the window or press the R key to select the twirl clockwise tool.

9. *Slant the eyes.* Center the brush cursor on the iris of the left eye (his right). Then click. Again, click briefly; do not hold or drag. The eye spins a degree or two clockwise, raising the outside edge and lowering the inside.

To slant the right eye (his left) in the opposite direction, you could switch to the twirl counterclockwise tool. But as it turns out, both tools do double duty. To twirl a detail opposite to the direction in which the tool usually works, press the Alt key and click. The results of both twirls appears in **Figure 7-24**.

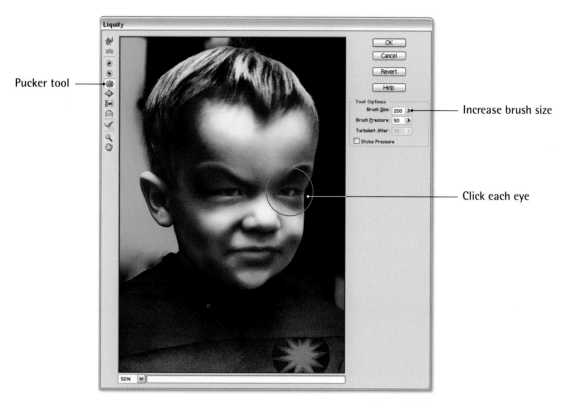

Pucker tool

Increase brush size

Click each eye

Figure 7-23.

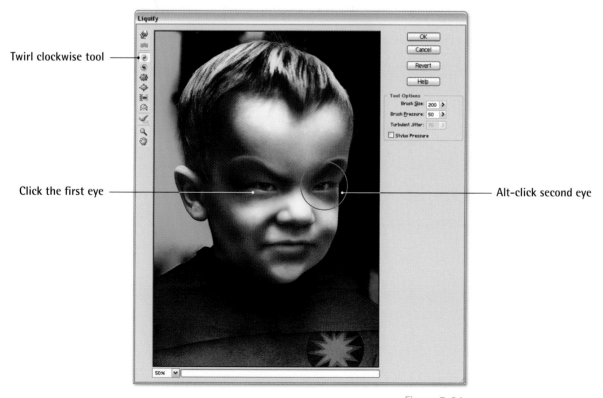

Twirl clockwise tool

Click the first eye

Alt-click second eye

Figure 7-24.

10. *Return to the warp tool.* I imagine Sammy to be the sort of edgy, cynical, postmodern superhero who openly sneers at his archenemies and lesser opponents. And there's no better tool for constructing sneers than the warp tool. Get it now by pressing the W key.

11. *Work the nose and mouth into a sneer.* Reduce the **Brush Size** to 120 pixels. Then drag downward on the nose, up on the nostrils, up on the left side of the mouth, and down on the right. You'll also want to drag that crease that connects the nose and mouth on the left side of the image. The results of my 30 or so brushstrokes appear in Figure 7-25.

12. *Switch to the bloat tool.* Okay, we've managed to outfit Sam with smaller eyes, arching eyebrows, and a tough-guy sneer. But he's still a little kid. It's time to bulk him out. Click the sixth tool on the left side of the window or press the B key to select the bloat tool.

13. *Bloat the chin and jaw.* Start by increasing the **Brush Size** value to 400 pixels. Then test the waters by clicking and holding for a brief moment on Sammy's chin. Also click a few times along the left and right sides of the jaw. I want you to really exaggerate the jaw line (see Figure 7-26), so feel free to hold the mouse button down for, say, a half second or so at a time. However, as when using the pinch and twirl tools, I recommend you refrain from dragging. (In other words, hold the mouse button down but keep the mouse still.)

14. *Pucker the forehead.* In real life, Sammy doesn't have much hair, but he has an ample forehead. That gives him a sort of Poindexter look that superheroes shun. Best way to get rid of it? Pinch it down to a more reasonable size. Best tool for the job? The one you already have, the bloat tool.

Center your brush cursor somewhere along the hairline. Then press the Alt key and click for a half second or more. Pressing Alt reverses the behavior of the tool, swelling with the pucker tool or, in our case, pinching with the bloat tool.

Continue to Alt-click along the hairline until you get an effect similar to the one pictured in Figure 7-26. For the best results, move the mouse at least slightly *between* (not during) clicks. This varies the center of the distortion and keeps your pinches from resulting in sharp points of converging color.

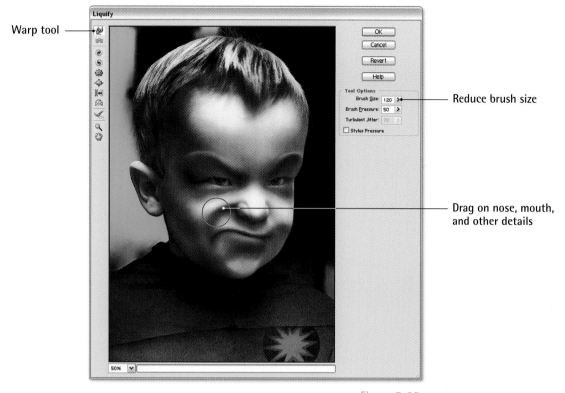

Warp tool

Reduce brush size

Drag on nose, mouth, and other details

Figure 7-25.

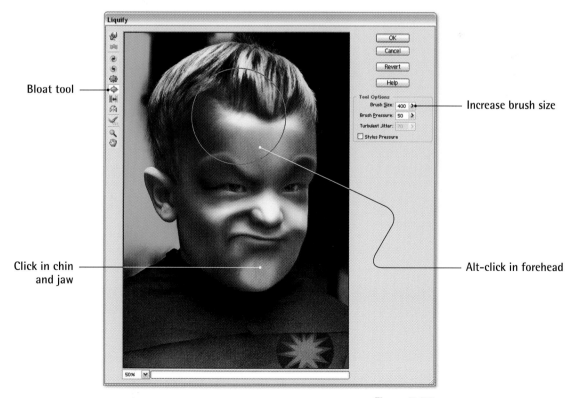

Bloat tool

Increase brush size

Alt-click in forehead

Click in chin and jaw

Figure 7-26.

15. *Apply your finishing touches.* Continue distorting my son's face as you see fit. (Naturally, I rely on you to apply your adjustments in good taste—he is my beloved progeny, after all.) For my part, I smoothed out the eyebrows, lifted the cheeks, tugged down the hairline, lifted the shoulders, and increased the size of the chest, all using the warp tool. When you arrive at an effect you like, click the **OK** button to accept your changes and return to the Standard Edit mode. Just for the sheer joy of it, Figure 7-27 shows my final effect incorporated into an elaborate poster treatment. Note that I used Image→Resize→Image Size to stretch the image vertically. This gives the head a less squat appearance. I also dodged and burned the chin to lend it more volume.

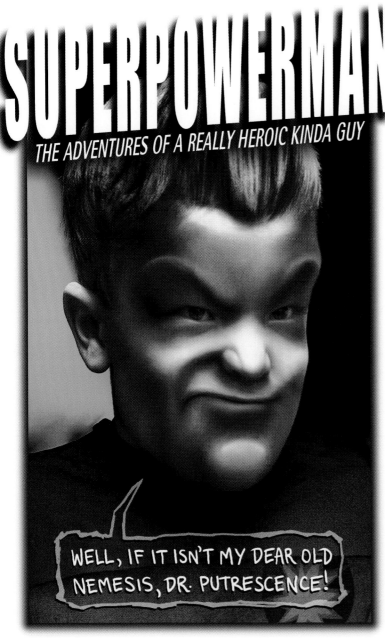

Figure 7-27.

WHAT DID YOU LEARN?

Match the key concept in the numbered list below with the letter of the phrase that best describes it. Answers appear upside-down at the bottom of the page.

Key Concepts

1. Focus
2. Filters
3. Edge
4. Unsharp Mask
5. Radius
6. Threshold
7. High Pass
8. Media filters
9. Blend modes
10. Warp tool
11. Pucker tool
12. Bloat tool

Descriptions

A. This Unsharp Mask option decides whether or not neighboring pixels are factored into the sharpening equation, and is best left set to 0.

B. When applied to layers, these let you mix a layer with the layers beneath it using a variety of mathematical calculations.

C. Bulging and enlarging are the speciality of this funciton, available exclusively inside the Liquify dialog box.

D. This Liquify function lets you pinch selective portions of an image.

E. A filter that mimics the functionality of Unsharp Mask (or, more accurately, Unsharp Mask mimics it) by retaining areas of high contrast and sending low-contrast areas to gray.

F. A ridge formed by areas of extreme contrast between adjacent pixels.

G. The most consistently useful of the Liquify functions, this lets you stretch or squish details in an image by dragging them.

H. The clarity of the image formed by the lens element and captured by the camera.

I. The thickness of the effect applied by a filter, often expressed as a softly tapering halo.

J. These are designed to make your digital photos look like drawings and paintings created with traditional tools.

K. A filter named for a traditional technique in which a photographic negative is combined with a blurred version of itself.

L. Named for camera lenses once commonly used to adjust and tint a scene before it was captured on film, these permit you to modify the focus, color, and overall appearance of an image after it is captured.

Answers

1H, 2L, 3F, 4K, 5I, 6A, 7E, 8J, 9B, 10G, 11D, 12C

LESSON

8

BUILDING LAYERED
COMPOSITIONS

EVERY IMAGE begins life as a few panes of primary color—
most commonly, one each for red, green, and blue—fused into a
single, continuous image (see Figure 8-1). Whether it comes from
the least expensive digital camera or the most expensive drum scanner, the image exists entirely on one layer. One and only one
full-color value exists for each and every pixel, and there
is no such thing as transparency. Such an image is
said to be *flat*.

But as soon as you begin combining images, you add
layers. Each layer serves as an independent image,
which you can stack, transform, or blend with other
layers.

A document that contains two or more layers is called
a *layered composition*. There's no need to wait until
a certain point in the editing cycle to build such a
composition—you can add layers to a document any
old time you like, as we have several times in previous lessons. But layers have a way of becoming even
more useful after some of the basic editing work is
out of the way. That's why I've waited until now to
show you the many ways to create and manage layers
in Photoshop Elements.

Three channels combine to make one layer

Figure 8-1.

The Benefits and
Penalties of Layers

Photoshop Elements' reliance on layers makes for an exceedingly
flexible (if sometimes confusing) working environment. As long as
an image remains on a layer, you can move or edit it independently of
other layers in the composition. Moreover, you can create relationships
between neighboring layers using a wide variety of blending options,

ABOUT THIS LESSON

Project Files

Before beginning the exercises, make sure that you've installed the lesson files from the CD, as explained in Step 5 on page xv of the Preface. This should result in a folder called *Lesson Files-PE3 1on1* on your desktop. We'll be working with the files inside the *Lesson 08* subfolder.

In this lesson, we'll explore the many facets of building a layered composition in Photoshop Elements, from creation to navigation, from stroking to stacking order, from free-form transformations to four-point distortions, from applying blend modes to erasing backgrounds. You'll learn how to:

Video Lesson 8: Layers at Work

Layers are nothing more than independent images that you can set to interact with each other from the Layers palette. But what a difference they make. By relegating image elements and effects to independent layers, you give yourself the flexibility to adjust your artwork well into the future.

To get a sense of how layers work in Elements, as well as see a brief sampling of the benefits they can provide, watch the eighth video lesson on the CD. Insert the CD, click the **Start Training** button, click the Set ③ button in the top-right corner of your screen, and then select 8, Layers at Work from the Lessons list. The movie lasts 9 minutes and 55 seconds, during which time you'll learn about the following operations and shortcuts:

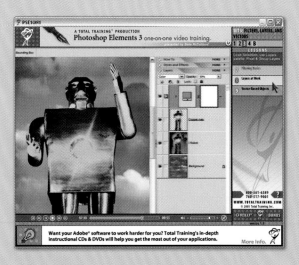

Operation	Keyboard equivalent or shortcut
Show or hide Layers palette	F11
Load selection outline previously saved with image	Alt+S, L
Convert selection to independent layer	Ctrl+J
Reduce layer opacity to 50 percent	5*
Deactivate highlighted option (such as blend mode)	Esc
Group active layer with layer below it	Ctrl+G
Create and name new layer	Ctrl+Shift+N

* Works only if selection or move tool is active.

all of which work without changing the contents of the layers in the slightest.

But layers come at a price. Because they are actually independent images, each layer consumes space both in memory and on your hard drive. Consider the following example:

- I start with the image on the right, which measures 2,100 by 2,100 pixels, or 7 by 7 inches at 300 pixels per inch (see Figure 8-2). Each pixel takes up 3 bytes of data. The result is a total of 4.41 million pixels, which add up to 12.6MB in memory. Because the image is flat, I can save it to the JPEG format, which compresses the file down to 3.7MB at the highest quality setting.

- I introduce another image that measures the very same 2,100 by 2,100 pixels. Photoshop Elements puts the image on its own layer. I apply the Multiply blend mode to get the effect shown in Figure 8-3. The image size doubles to 25.2MB in memory. I can no longer save the layered composition in the JPEG format because JPEG doesn't permit layers. Thus, I save it in Photoshop's native PSD format instead. Although PSD is versatile, it lacks JPEG's exceptional compression capabilities, and so the file on disk balloons to 25.7MB.

- I then add a series of image and text layers to fill out the composition, as pictured in Figure 8-4 on the next page. Because the layers are smaller, and the text layers are defined as more efficient vectors (see Lesson 9, "Text and Shapes"), the size of the image grows only moderately in memory (34.4MB) and barely at all on disk (26.2MB).

So as you add layers, your composition gets bigger. And as your composition gets bigger, Photoshop Elements requires more space in memory and on disk to manage the file. Generally speaking, you can let Elements worry about these sorts of nitty-gritty details. But bear in mind, no matter how sophisticated your computer, its memory and hard disk are ultimately finite. And if either the memory or (worse) the hard disk fills up, your ability to edit your marvelous multilayer creations may come to a skidding halt.

Flat image, 2100 × 2100 pixels
12.6MB in memory, 3.7MB on disk (saved in JPEG format, Quality 12)

Figure 8-2.

Second layer, full 2100 × 2100 pixels
25.2MB in memory, 25.7MB on disk (saved in native PSD format)

Figure 8-3.

How to Manage Layers

Fortunately, a few precautions are all it takes to keep layered compositions on a diet and Photoshop Elements running in top form:

- First, don't let your hard disk get anywhere close to full. I recommend keeping at least 1GB available at all times, and more than that is always welcome. (Consult your computer's documentation to find out how to check this—or just hope and pray you're okay, like everyone else does.)

- Back up your Elements projects regularly to CD, DVD, or some other storage medium (which you can do by choosing File→Backup inside the Organizer workspace). This not only preserves your images, but also permits you to delete files from your hard disk if you start running out of room.

- As you work in Photoshop Elements, you can keep an eye on the size of your image in memory by observing the Doc: values at the bottom of the Info palette. (Choose Window→Info or press F8 to display the palette. If you don't see the Doc: values, click the ▶ arrow in the lower-right corner of the palette and choose Document Sizes.) The value before the slash tells you the size of the image if flattened; the value after the slash tells you the size of the layered composition.

- You can reduce the size of an image on disk by *merging* two layers into one by choosing Layer→Merge Down or pressing Ctrl+E.

- To merge all layers and return to a flat image, choose Layer→Flatten Image. But be aware, this is a radical step. I usually flatten an image only as a preamble to printing it or placing it into another program. And even then, I make sure I save the flattened image under a different name in order to maintain my original layered file.

Additional layers, various sizes
34.4MB in memory, 26.2MB on disk (saved in native PSD format)

Figure 8-4.

Finally, when in doubt, err on the side of too many layers as opposed to too few. This may sound like strange advice, but it's better to push the limits and occasionally top out than unnecessarily constrain yourself and hobble your file. After all, you can always upgrade your computer to better accommodate your massive compositions. But you can never recover an unsaved layer (that is, one that you merged or flattened before saving and closing the file).

Arranging and Modifying Layers

The most basic use for layers is to keep objects separated from each other so you can modify their horizontal and vertical position as well as their front-to-back arrangement. Elements also permits you to transform layers by scaling, rotating, or even distorting them, as you'll see in the second of the upcoming exercises.

By way of demonstration, we'll take a cue from the classical artist I believe would have benefited most from layers, 16th-century imperial court painter Giuseppe Arcimboldo. Celebrated in his time as a master of the "composite portrait," Arcimboldo rendered his subjects as fanciful collections of fruits, vegetables, flowers, trees, animals, meats—he even famously represented one fellow upside-down (right image, Figure 8-5). Naturally, we'll embark on something infinitely simpler—Giuseppe had to thrill and delight Emperor Maximilian II; happily, we do not. But even so, you'll get an ample sense of just how much pure imaging flexibility layers afford.

In the following exercise, you'll begin the process of assembling a layered piece of artwork. You'll establish the content and order of the key layers in the composition, and in the process, learn how to select layers, modify their contents, change their order, and even rotate them.

Figure 8-5.

1. *Open a layered composition and some images to add to it.* We'll be looking at three files altogether, *Composite cowboy.psd*, *Cowboy hat.tif*, and *Eight ball.tif*, all included in the *Lesson 08* folder inside *Lesson Files-PE3 1on1*. At first glance, the layered image (shown on the in Figure 8-6) looks like a football with flippers standing on a pile of towels. But as we'll see, there's so much more.

Figure 8-6.

2. *Bring up the Layers palette.* If it's already on-screen, fabulous. If not, choose **Window→Layers** or press the F11 key. The **Layers** palette shows thumbnails of every layer in the document, from the front layer at the top of the palette to the rearmost layer at the bottom. This arrangement of layers from front to back is called the *stacking order*.

3. *Make the multilayer file active.* Click the *Composite cowboy.psd* title bar to make that image active. If you take a peek at the Layers palette, you'll see that the file contains ten layers in all. And yet we can see just four items in the image window—football, flippers, towels, and background. (In case you're curious, the flippers are found on the Collar layer. More on that topic shortly.) The other layers are turned off or hidden by the football.

4. *Send the Football layer backward.* Click the **Football** layer in the Layers palette to make it active. Then drag it down the stack in this same palette to just between the **Teeth** and **Collar** layers. You should now see all visible layers from the Teeth upward, as illustrated in Figure 8-7 on the facing page. Things don't look at all right, but they will soon.

5. *Load a selection outline.* The next step is to carve the football into the shape of a face, which we'll accomplish using a selection outline that I defined in advance and saved with this image. To access this selection, choose **Select→Load Selection**. Make sure the **Selection** pop-up menu is set to **face outline**, as in Figure 8-8. Then click **OK**.

6. *Reverse the selection.* Choose **Select→Inverse** or press the short-cut Ctrl+Shift+I to reverse the selection and select the area outside the cowboy's face.

7. *Delete the selected pixels.* Make sure the Football layer is active (confirmed in the title bar by the word *Football* in parentheses). Then press the Backspace or Delete key to erase the selected pixels. Only the cowboy's silhouette remains, as shown in Figure 8-9.

8. *Restore the face selection.* Now let's add a cartoon outline around the cowboy's face. To restore the face outline from Step 5, again choose **Select→Inverse** or press Ctrl+Shift+I.

9. *Create a new layer.* Choose **Layer→ New→Layer** or press Ctrl+Shift+N to display the **New Layer** dialog box. (Or you can press the Alt key and click the ⬚ icon at the top of the Layers palette.) Name the layer "Cowboy Outline" and click **OK**.

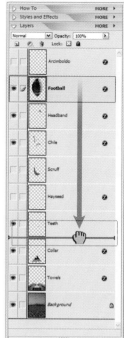

Figure 8-7.

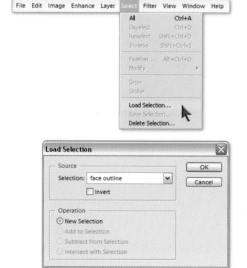

Figure 8-8.

Figure 8-9.

10. *Stroke the selection.* Choose **Edit→Stroke (Outline) Selection** to bring up the **Stroke** dialog box, which allows you to trace a colored outline around the contours of a selection outline. There is no shortcut for this command, but you can get to it from the keyboard by holding the Alt key and then typing E and S.

11. *Specify the stroke settings.* Let's say you want to create a yellow outline that's 13 pixels thick. You do so by changing the numbered settings in Figure 8-10 as follows:

    • Change the **Width** value to 13 pixels (❶ in the figure).

    • Click the **Color** swatch (labeled ❷ in Figure 8-10) to display the **Color Picker** dialog box.

    • Change the **R**, **G**, and **B** values to 255, 240, and 180, respectively (see ❸ in the figure). The result is a pale yellow. Click the **OK** button to accept the new color.

Check that the other options in the Stroke dialog box are set to their defaults (as they are in Figure 8-10). Then click the **OK** button to apply the stroke. Elements traces a 13-pixel yellow brushstroke around the perimeter of the face, as in Figure 8-11.

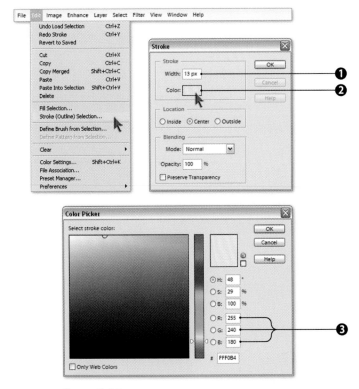

Figure 8-10.

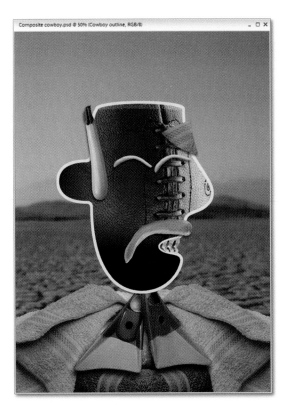

Figure 8-11.

12. *Deselect the image.* We're finished with the selection outline. So choose **Select→Deselect** or press Ctrl+D to get rid of it.

13. *Click the Scruff layer.* Again in the Layers palette, click the item called **Scruff**. As always, you might need to scroll up or down the layer list to find it. It looks like badly rendered sandpaper, but it's actually our fellow's stubbly beard.

14. *Set the blend mode to Multiply.* Click the word **Normal** at the top of the Layers palette to display a list of blend modes. Then choose **Multiply** from the list. Or press the keyboard shortcut Shift+Alt+M. Multiply drops out the whites and preserves the dark colors, thus burning the stubble into the cowboy's football flesh, as in Figure 8-12.

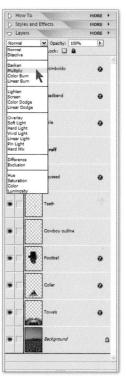

Figure 8-12.

15. *Turn on the Hayseed layer.* This time, I want you to click not directly on the **Hayseed** layer but rather in front of it, in the column of 👁 icons. This shows the layer without activating it. The layer in question turns out to be a sliver of barley clasped tightly in the cowboy's teeth (the latter of which are actually seams in a baseball, for what it's worth). Shown in Figure 8-12, the look is interesting but inconsistent. The face outline should be in front of the teeth, hayseed, and scruff. The football flesh needs to be nudged up a couple of notches as well.

16. *Select the Cowboy Outline layer.* You may find it simplest to just click the layer name. But I would be remiss in my duties if I didn't tell you how to do it from the keyboard.

You can cycle from one layer to the next by pressing Alt with a bracket key. First, press Esc to make sure no options are active. Then press Alt+[to select down the layer stack; press Alt+] to select up. In this case, pressing Alt+[three times cycles from the Scruff layer down to Cowboy Outline.

17. *Bring the Cowboy Outline layer in front of Scruff.* You can accomplish this by choosing **Layer→Arrange→Bring Forward** three times in a row. But isn't life short enough without choosing inconveniently located commands multiple times in a row? Yes it is. Better to learn the shortcut.

To move a selected layer up or down the stack, press Ctrl with a bracket key. Ctrl+[moves the layer back one notch; Ctrl+] moves it forward. To properly arrange the Cowboy Outline layer, press Ctrl+] three times in a row.

18. *Select the Football layer.* Again, you can just click the layer name in the palette. But I have another technique for you to try. Press the V key to select the move tool. Then click an unobstructed portion of the hayseed in the image window. Elements automatically switches to the Hayseed layer. (If it doesn't, try clicking some other portion of the weed.) Then click inside the football to select that layer. The move tool's ability to switch layers is a function of the Auto Select Layer check box, which is active by default in the options bar.

PEARL OF WISDOM

In some cases, clicking with the move tool may grab the wrong layer. For example, if you click the lower portion of the fellow's face, you will most likely select the Scruff layer instead of the Football layer. Both layers share pixels at the click location and Scruff is in front. When beset by such troubles, try right-clicking instead, which displays a shortcut menu of possible layers. For example, if you right-click the bottom left tip of the hombre's mustache, the shortcut menu lists four layers—Chile, Scruff, Football, and Background (see **Figure 8-13**)—each of which contains an opaque pixel at the click point. Choose Football to go to that layer.

19. *Bring the Football layer in front of Hayseed.* To make it happen, press Ctrl+] twice to make it happen. The properly arranged layer elements appear in Figure 8-13.

Composite cowboy.psd @ 50% (Football, RGB/8)

Chile
Scruff
Football
Background

Figure 8-13.

20. *Switch to the Collar layer.* Click the reddish snorkeling fins with the move tool to select the Collar layer. You may reckon those flippers look more like a dandy kerchief than a rugged collar, but that's just because they're upside-down. Let's remedy that, shall we?

21. *Rotate the flippers 180 degrees.* The best way to flip a layer upside-down—assuming that you don't want to create a mirror image of it—is to rotate it 180 degrees. To do so, choose **Image→Rotate→Layer 180°**. This command spins the fins so they look like a collar. To perform the operation from the keyboard, press Alt+I and then type E, 1 (⏎).

22. *Nudge the flippers upward.* Press Shift+↑ seven times in a row. Assuming the move tool is still active, each press of Shift+↑ nudges the layer up 10 pixels; so in all, you will have moved it 70 pixels. If you prefer to move the layer manually, just drag it into the approximate location pictured in Figure 8-14.

23. *Save your changes thus far.* Choose **File→Save** to update the existing *Composite cowboy.psd* document on disk. Or if you prefer to save versions as you go along—always a splendid idea because it means you can come back and recover elements from your original image later—choose **File→Save As** and give your file a new name. Make sure the **Layers** check box is on and the **Format** option is set to **Photoshop (*.PSD; *.PDD)**. After you click **Save**, an alert message appears to warn you of Elements' fervent but ill-advised desire to maximize the compatibility of the saved file. Unless you plan on using the file with Adobe's companion video product, Premiere Elements, turn off the **Maximize compatibility** check box and click **OK**.

Figure 8-14.

Importing and Transforming Layers

Now that you've successfully arranged the layers in the composition, it's time to bring into the mix the rest of the elements, namely the eyes and the hat. In this exercise, you'll introduce portions of the *Cowboy hat.tif* and *Eight ball.tif* images into the composition that you've created so far (and saved in Step 23 of the previous exercise). Then you'll scale and otherwise transform the layers so they fit into place. The result will be a fanciful cowboy face made of objects that you don't often see on cowboys—especially that hat.

1. *Bring the eight ball image to the front.* If you did not complete the previous exercise, you need to do so now. Then make sure all the documents from the previous exercise remain open—namely *Cowboy hat.tif*, *Eight ball.tif*, and the updated *Composite cowboy.psd*. Click the title bar for *Eight ball.tif* to make the pool ball active.

2. *Select a central portion of the pool ball.* Use the elliptical marquee tool to select the circular area shown in Figure 8-15. Or, to guarantee that your circle exactly matches mine, load the one that I included in the image. How, you ask? Choose **Select→Load Selection**, confirm that the **Selection** option is set to **circle**, and click the **OK** button.

3. *Drag the eight ball into the cowboy composition.* Press the V key to make sure the move tool is active. Then drag the selection from *Eight ball.tif* into the *Composite cowboy.psd* image window. Drop it near where one of the eyes should go. In all likelihood, you'll see the pool ball land in an undesirable position, behind the head, as in Figure 8-16. Photoshop Elements places the object in front of the previously selected layer, Collar. Looks like we'll need to rearrange.

Figure 8-15.

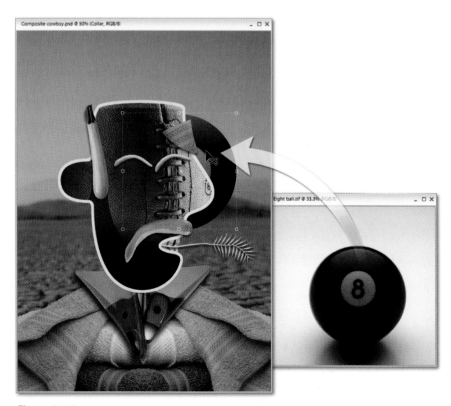

Figure 8-16.

4. *Rename the new layer.* In the **Layers** palette, double-click the current layer name, **Layer 1**, to highlight the letters. Then change the name to the more descriptive "Eyes."

5. *Bring the Eyes layer in front of Cowboy Outline.* Either drag the layer up the stack or press Ctrl+⬜ five times in a row.

6. *Choose the Auto Contrast command.* The eight ball is dimly lit with respect to its new surroundings. So choose **Enhance**→ **Auto Contrast** or press Ctrl+Shift+Alt+L to correct the brightness without upsetting the color balance.

7. *Scale the pool ball to 32 percent of its original size.* The pool ball is too big, so you need to scale it. To be precise, you need to reduce it to 32 percent of its current size. Armed with the move tool, you can pull this off in one of two ways:

   - Notice the dotted marquee with square handles that surrounds the pool ball. This is the *bounding box*, which allows you to scale, rotate, or otherwise transform a layer. (If you do not see the marquee, turn on the Show Bounding Box check box in the options bar.) To scale a layer uniformly— so that the width and height are affected equally—press the Shift key and drag a corner handle to constrain the proportions of the ball. As you drag, keep an eye on the scale values that appear in the options bar. When they reach 32 percent (or thereabouts), release the mouse button, and then release Shift.

   - For more precision, scale by the numbers. Move your cursor over the edge of the bounding box until it looks like ↕ or ↔, and then click to make the bounding box active and enter the *free transform mode.* Click the ⅌ between the W and H scale values in the options bar (which I circled in Figure 8-17) to constrain the proportions of the layer. Change either the **W** or **H** value to 32 (thanks to ⅌, both will update) and press Enter.

Figure 8-17.

To accept the scaled image and exit the free transform mode, press the Enter key (yes, again) or click the ✔ to the right of the numbers in the options bar.

8. *Move the eye into position.* For the sake of convenience, let's imagine that this pool ball is the left eye (which, to be fair to this fictitious person, is the cowboy's right). Drag the eye into the position shown in Figure 8-18.

Figure 8-18.

9. *Add a drop shadow.* The interior of the layer exhibits the interplay of highlight and shadow that one typically associates with a real-world object. (Or as Giuseppe himself might have said, the pool ball possesses *chiaroscuro.*) But it fails to interact with its environment. Most obviously, it lacks a shadow. To remedy this gross oversight, do like so:

• Bring up the **Styles and Effects** palette. (If the palette is not open by default, choose **Window→Styles and Effects**.)

- Choose **Layer Styles** from the pop-up menu in the top-left corner of the palette. Then choose **Drop Shadows** from the top-right pop-up menu.

- Click the thumbnail labeled **Soft Edge**. This adds a fuzzy drop shadow positioned close to the object itself.

Elements casts a fuzzy black shadow behind the active layer.

10. *Add an inner shadow.* Now for some shadow along the inside edge of the layer. Choose **Inner Shadows** from the top-right pop-up menu in the Styles and Effects palette. Then click the first thumbnail, which goes by the name **Low**.

11. *Set the blend mode to Screen.* Return to the **Layers** palette and change the blend mode from **Normal** to **Screen**. You can also use the keyboard shortcut Shift+Alt+S. (If the shortcut doesn't work, press the Esc key and try again.) The opposite of the Multiply mode, Screen drops out the blacks and preserves the light colors, creating the appearance of a glass eyeball against the football background.

12. *Scale the shadows to 50 percent.* The transparent portions of the eye reveal the drop and inner shadows we applied in Steps 9 and 10. Only problem: the shadows are too big. To shrink them, choose **Layer→Layer Style→Scale Effects**. Change the **Scale** value to 50 percent and click **OK**. The glass eye and its more acceptable shadows appear in Figure 8-19.

13. *Select the eye and clone it.* Even a guy with a football for a head deserves depth perception. Therefore, I suggest we add a second eye. Of all the ways you can duplicate the eye, here's the easiest:

   - Press the Ctrl key and click the **Eyes** layer in the Layers palette. This traces a selection outline around the exact perimeter of the layer.

Figure 8-19.

• Check that the move tool is still active. Then hold down both the Shift and Alt keys, and drag the eye to the right. Pressing the Shift key constrains the movement along a horizontal axis. Pressing Alt creates a clone of the eye. After you get the pool ball into more or less the location pictured in Figure 8-20, release the mouse button and then release the Shift and Alt keys.

Figure 8-20.

PEARL OF WISDOM

The result of these steps is pretty impressive. It may even appear more impressive than it really is. For example, the right eye looks as if it's distorting the laces of the football just as a piece of rounded glass really would. But that's an illusion—Elements is doing no such thing. The fact that the effect reads like a glass distortion is pure bonus.

14. *Deselect the image.* Press Ctrl+D to abandon the selection, which has now served us to its utmost capacity.

15. *Bring the cowboy hat image to the front.* The only thing missing in our strange and amazing composition is the hat. Let's go get it. Click the title bar for *Cowboy hat.tif.*

16. *Select the hat.* The hat is a little more difficult to select than the eight ball. So wouldn't you know it, this image contains a predefined selection outline to help you on your way. Choose **Select→Load Selection**. Make sure the **hat outline** selection is active and click **OK**. The selected hat appears in Figure 8-21.

PEARL OF 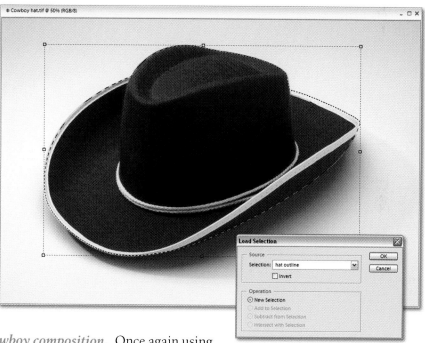 WISDOM

An interesting thing to note: I did not create this particular selection outline. The image vendor, PhotoSpin, included it as part of the photograph. PhotoSpin provides selections with many of its "object" photographs, as do other full-service stock agencies.

17. *Drag the hat into the cowboy composition.* Once again using the move tool, drag the selection from *Cowboy hat.tif* into the *Composite cowboy.psd* image window. Drop the hat near the top of the head. Naturally, it comes in all wrong. The hat is too low on the head, too far down the stack, and *way* too big, as in Figure 8-22 on the next page. Such are the ways of the layered composition, and the reasons for the remaining steps.

Figure 8-21.

18. *Rename the new layer.* Double-click the current layer name (as always, **Layer 1**) and change its name to "Hat."

19. *Bring the hat to the front of the composition.* Choose **Layer→Arrange→Bring to Front** or press Ctrl+Shift+]. The layer pops all the way to the top of the stack, where it rightly belongs.

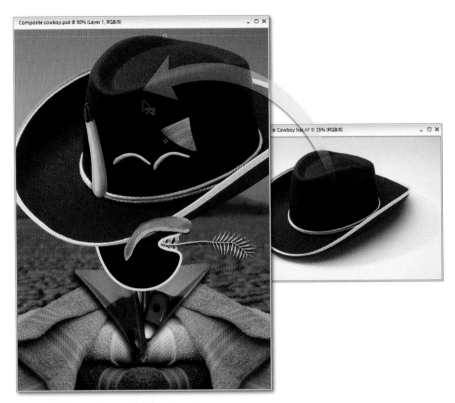

Figure 8-22.

20. *Lower the Opacity value to 50 percent.* Change the **Opacity** value in the Layers palette. Or with the move tool active, you can bypass the option and just press the 5 key.

We'll want the final hat to be fully opaque. So why lower its opacity? By making the hat translucent in the short term, you can more easily align it with elements underneath. Note that it's essential that you perform this step now; you cannot modify the opacity or the blend mode when inside the free transform mode.

---

21. *Scale and rotate the layer.* Because the bounding box handles extend off-screen, I recommend that you start things off by scaling the hat numerically. Here's the wisest approach:

    • Click any side of the bounding box with the ↕ or ↔ cursor to enter the free transform mode.

- Click the 🌐 icon between the W and H values in the options bar. Then change either **W** or **H** to 62 percent (see the circled values in Figure 8-23).

- Having reduced the size of the hat so the bounding box fits inside the image window, you can rotate the image in one of two ways. Move the cursor outside the bounding box and drag to spin the hat around its center until the rotate value in the options bar (△, to the right of H) reads 3.5 degrees. Or enter 3.5 into the △ option box and press Enter.

- Drag inside the boundary to move the hat as needed. You can also nudge the layer from the keyboard by pressing one or more arrow keys.

Don't press the Enter key yet—you want to remain in the free transform mode for the next step.

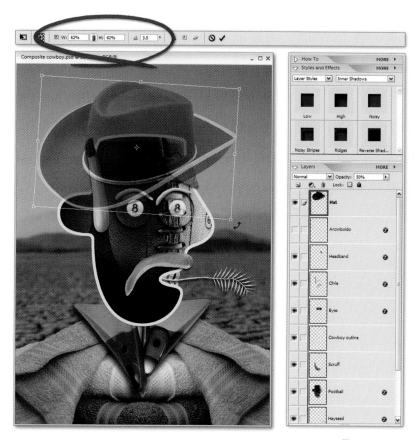

Figure 8-23.

22. *Distort the hat.* The one variety of transformation that you can't express entirely with numbers is the *four-point distortion*, which permits you to scale or slant one portion of a layer independently of another. To distort a layer in Elements, press the

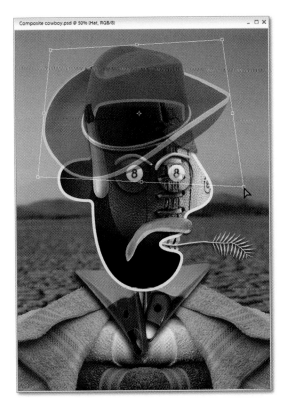

Composite cowboy.psd @ 50% (Hat, RGB/8)

Figure 8-24.

Ctrl key and drag a corner handle. The handle moves independently of the other handles, stretching the hat in that one direction. I ended up Ctrl-dragging all four corner handles to taper the top of the hat as shown in Figure 8-24. (Note that your scale and rotate values in the options bar will change as you perform the distortion. The values only partially track the transformation, so feel free to ignore them.)

23. *Accept the transformation.* Click the ✔ in the options bar or press the Enter key. Photoshop Elements applies the various transformations and exits the free transform mode.

PEARL OF WISDOM

You may notice that you just finished applying several operations inside one free transform session. I recommend that you work this way when creating your own projects as well. Each session rewrites the pixels in the image, so each is potentially destructive. By applying all changes inside a single session, you rewrite pixels just once, minimizing the damage caused by multiple interpolations.

24. *Restore the opacity to 100 percent.* Press the 0 key (that's zero, not the letter) or change the **Opacity** value in the Layers palette. The hat becomes opaque again.

EXTRA CREDIT

Everything looks pretty good. But in my opinion, the Hat and Cowboy Outline layers are just begging for drop shadows. If you don't share that opinion, skip ahead to the next exercise, "Erasing a Background," on the facing page. But then you'll miss yet another new technique. For rather than define the shadows manually, as you did back in Steps 9 and 10 (see pages 236 and 237), we'll repurpose them from other layers.

25. *Copy the Collar layer's drop shadow.* Click the **Collar** layer in the Layers palette to make it active. Then choose **Layer→Layer Style→Copy Layer Style**. This tells Elements to tag the layer and make a mental note of the shadows and other effects assigned to it.

26. *Paste the drop shadow on the Hat layer.* Click the **Hat** layer to make it active. Then choose **Layer→Layer Style→Paste Layer Style**. The cowboy hat receives a drop shadow that exactly matches the one applied to the flippers.

27. *Add a scaled drop shadow to the Cowboy Outline layer.* Click the **Cowboy Outline** layer and choose the **Paste Layer Style** command again. The shadow is way too big for the yellow

outline, so let's scale it. Choose **Layer→ Layer Style→Scale Effects**. Change the **Scale** value to a mere 20 percent and click the **OK** button to accept your changes. The shadow slims down to a more reasonable size, as in Figure 8-25.

28. *Turn on the Arcimboldo layer.* Click the eyeball in front of the one hidden layer to display a line of frivolous text I drew by hand with a Wacom tablet.

29. *Save your composition.* So ends another jam-packed exercise. Choose **File→Save** to update the file on disk or choose **File→ Save As** to save an independent version.

Erasing a Background

So far we've been talking about creating and managing the contents of layers. Now let's talk about ways to delete from layers and, paradoxically, create layers as we delete from them.

How is this possible? The answer resides with the Editor's trio of eraser tools. When used on any layer other than the Background, each of the eraser tools does just what you think it would do—it wipes away pixels from the layer, leaving transparency in its wake. However, when working on the Background layer, transparency is not an option. So the first of the three erasers, known simply as the eraser tool, paints with the background color, which is white by default. But the other two erasers—the background eraser and the magic eraser—do something extraordinary. They convert the Background layer to an independent layer and then set about erasing to transparency. When the eraser can't go to the mountain, Photoshop Elements brings the mountain to the eraser.

In this exercise, you'll use each of the erasers to eliminate the background from an image, thereby permitting you to combine the extracted foreground with an entirely different background and still maintain a photorealistic effect. You'll see that each eraser tool resembles one of Elements' selection tools. Indeed, you'll discover that erasing and selecting are closely related tasks.

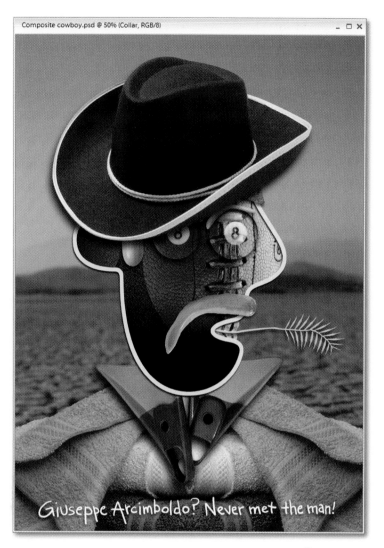

Figure 8-25.

Figure 8-26.

1. *Open a couple of flat images.* Open *Ruins.jpg* and *Zephyr.jpg*, both conveniently located within the *Lesson 08* folder inside *Lesson Files-PE3 1on1*. Make *Zephyr.jpg* the active image. And note that like all JPEG's, this photograph is flat, possessing a single Background layer and nothing more. This piece of sculpture happens to be Zephyr, the god of wind, which seems only appropriate to the topic of erasing. We're going to blow his background away.

2. *Select the magic eraser in the toolbox.* The first eraser we'll explore is the enticingly named magic eraser. Like its mentor, the magic wand, the magic eraser identifies an area of homogeneous color. Unlike the wand, it then deletes that area. Click and hold the eraser tool to display a flyout menu of erasers; then select the magic eraser as in Figure 8-27. Alternatively, you can press the E key (or Shift+E) to switch between erasers until you get the one with the sparkle.

3. *Set the eraser tools back to their defaults.* To make sure your eraser tools work like mine, click the pink eraser icon on the far left side of the options bar and choose **Reset All Tools** from the pop-up menu. Click **OK** to restore the default settings for all tools, erasers and otherwise.

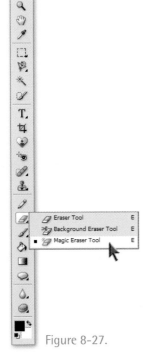

Figure 8-27.

PEARL OF WISDOM

The options bar settings are mostly identical to those that accompany the magic wand (see "Selecting Colored Areas with the Magic Wand," Step 3, page 113). The one addition is Opacity, which permits the tool to create translucent pixels. This option should be called Transparency because the default setting of 100 percent makes erased pixels 100 percent transparent.

---

4. *Magically erase part of the sky.* Click the wedge of cloudy sky to the right of Zephyr, as circled in Figure 8-28. In a heartbeat, the magic eraser blasts away the patch of sky that falls inside the Tolerance range, just as if you had clicked with the magic wand and then pressed Backspace. The difference is that the magic eraser has automatically turned the Background layer into a floating layer, giving it the name Layer 0. The gray checkerboard represents transparency, or nothingness.

Figure 8-28.

5. *Switch out the checkerboard pattern.* The checkerboard isn't ideal for judging the outline of this particular layer. The checkers are too busy and too light. So let's change them:

   • Choose **Edit→Preferences→Transparency**, or press the shortcut Ctrl+K and then Ctrl+4.

   • Click each of the color swatches under the Grid Colors option and enter the **H**, **S**, and **B** values listed in Figure 8-29. The result is a vivid red pattern with little variation between one square and the next.

   • Click the **OK** button.

   Now zoom in on the image. Examine the outline along the back of the Zephyr's head and you'll see a thin but sharp line of light aqua fringe. Unacceptable; let's try again.

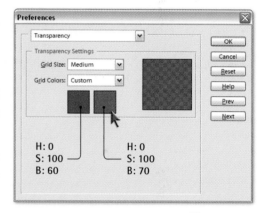

Figure 8-29.

6. *Raise the Tolerance value.* Apparently, the magic eraser didn't erase enough pixels. So we need to incorporate more colors into the erasing equation. Click the word **Tolerance** in the options bar, raise the value to 75, and press Enter.

7. *Undo the magic eraser.* As was the case with the magic wand, the Tolerance value is static, affecting the next erased area, not the current one. So we have to run the operation again. Click the ⟲ icon in the shortcuts bar or press Ctrl+Z. Happily, Elements undoes Step 4, not Step 5 or 6. Because the Undo command ignores the changing of preferences and other settings, the last thing it remembers is the magic eraser.

8. *Click again with the magic eraser tool.* Click again where you clicked before, behind the droopy-looking Zephyr's head. Thanks to the more liberal Tolerance setting, the magic eraser leaves only the slimmest hint of a gossamer fringe around the sculpted head. Indeed, as a bonus, the generous Tolerance value has permitted the tool to erase most of the blue area at the top of the sky as well. The much improved results appear in Figure 8-30.

Figure 8-30.

9. *Select the background eraser.* The remainder of the background is too complex for the simple but ultimately remedial magic eraser. So let's switch to a more powerful eraser. Click the background eraser tool in the options bar (as in Figure 8-31) or choose it from the flyout menu in the toolbox.

Figure 8-31.

Strictly speaking, the background eraser is a brush-based tool. Even so, it works a little like the magnetic lasso tool; you trace loosely around the perimeter of an object and the tool does its best to accurately identify the edges (see "The Magnetic Lasso," page 131). But in my experience, the background eraser has a tendency to produce more desirable effects. In addition to evaluating edges, much as the magnetic lasso does, the background eraser reads which colors you want to erase as you drag over them. The trick is to keep the *sampling point*—identified by + in the center of the cursor—in the background, and move the outside of the brush over the object's edge and slightly into the foreground. It's tricky, but you'll soon get a sense of it.

10. *Adjust the option bar settings.* As seen in Figure 8-31, the background eraser offers three settings in the options bar. Modify them as follows:

- Click the **Brush** preview to see a pop-up palette of options that control the size and shape of the brush. For this exercise, I suggest you press the ⬜ key several times to increase the brush diameter to 60 or 70 pixels.

- The **Limits** option determines which colors get erased inside the brush diameter. The default setting, Contiguous, erases only those colors that fall inside the Tolerance range *and* are adjacent to the sampling point; Discontiguous leaps over colors, sometimes into the foreground object. For most work, **Contiguous** is the better choice.

- The Tolerance (now measured as a percentage) defines how close a color has to be to the pixel under the + to be erased. We can't really evaluate this option until we try it, so leave the **Tolerance** set to 50 percent for now.

11. *Give the background eraser a try.* Position the background eraser as shown in the first example in Figure 8-32, with the cursor's central + inside the thin fringe of blue sky visible between the green of the tree and the red of the checkerboard. Drag around the perimeter of Zephyr until you are about level with his nose, as in the second example in the figure.

Multiple brushstrokes are okay. For the best results, paint slowly so Elements has time to sample colors along the way. Keep the + outside the Zephyr but overlap the outer edge of the brush into the sculpture.

Figure 8-32.

The results are uneven. The tool did a pretty good job distinguishing the foliage from the sculpture when the + passed through the green of the trees. But when the + hit a blue patch of sky, the background eraser erased some of the sculpture as well.

12. *Adjust the tolerance and undo.* Reduce the **Tolerance** value to 30 percent, a little more than half its default setting. After all, it was working okay; no sense in being *too* conservative. Then press Ctrl+Z one or more times to undo the background eraser brushstrokes. (If you back up too far and undo the magic eraser operation, click the ↻ icon in the shortcuts bar or press Ctrl+Y to redo the operation.)

13. *Try painting again.* But with a few changes:

- Position the brush just after the little patch of sky at the top of the Zephyr's head, as indicated by the circled cursor in the first example in Figure 8-33. The sky is too complex for the background eraser to handle; we'll clean it up in a moment with the standard eraser tool.

Figure 8-33.

- Click to set the initial spot that you want to erase. Then Shift-click at brief intervals along the perimeter of the Zephyr's head, down to the fellow's chin. Take care to Shift-click often; each click samples colors, and it's important to have lots of them.

- You'll have the best luck dragging in the neck region. If you see red creep into the Zephyr's face, undo the brushstroke and try again. Keep dragging until you come up with something resembling the right image in Figure 8-33.

Figure 8-34.

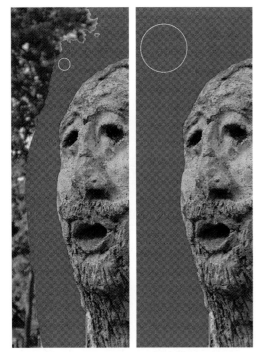

Figure 8-35.

14. *Select the eraser tool.* We'll finish things off with the ordinary eraser tool, which is nothing more than a brush that paints transparency. Click the first of the three eraser icons in the options bar, labeled in Figure 8-34. Or press the E key (or Shift+E) a couple of times. Then press the] key four times to increase the brush size to 50 pixels.

15. *Finish erasing around Zephyr.* Use the eraser to complete the selection. You'll have to undo every once in a while, so minimize your pain by keeping your brushstrokes short. Note that the vertical aquamarine bar along the neck is the edge of a tile and belongs to the sculpture rather than the background; you can click at the top of the outside edge and then Shift-click at the bottom to erase in a straight line. Otherwise, reduce the brush diameter as you need to, and best of luck. Eventually, you should get a nice edge, as in the left example in Figure 8-35. Finally, switch to a huge 200-pixel brush and erase the last of the background, leaving Zephyr awash in a red checkered sea, as in the right example in the figure.

16. *Relocate Zephyr to a new image.* Press the V key to get the move tool. Then drag the Zephyr and drop it into the *Ruins.jpg* image. Move the Zephyr to the lower-right corner of the ruins until it snaps into place. In Figure 8-36, I also switched to the **Background** layer and applied **Filter→Blur→Gaussian Blur** with a **Radius** of 8 pixels to create a quick depth-of-field effect. With a little help from the eraser tools, the god of wind has blown himself all the way from his original home of Nashville, Tennessee to the crumbled ruins in Antigua, Guatemala.

Figure 8-36.

WHAT DID YOU LEARN?

Match the key concept in the numbered list below with the letter
of the phrase that best describes it. Answers appear upside-down
at the bottom of the page.

Key Concepts

1. Flat
2. Layered composition
3. Stacking order
4. Free Transform
5. Photoshop (PSD) format
6. Merge Down
7. Bring Forward
8. Four-point distortion
9. Magic eraser
10. Background eraser
11. Sampling point
12. Eraser tool

Descriptions

A. The one command that enables you to scale, rotate, flip, skew, or distort one or more linked layers.

B. This type of transformation permits you to scale or slant one portion of a layer independently of another.

C. When you trace loosely around the perimeter of an object with this tool, Elements tries to identify the edges and delete just those pixels that fall outside the edges.

D. Nothing more than a "dumb" brush, this tool paints in the background color (by default, white) on the Background layer, or with transparency on any other layer.

E. The arrangement of layers in a composition, from front to back, which you can adjust by pressing Ctrl with the bracket keys, ⌷ and ⌷.

F. This command moves a layer upwards in the stacking order.

G. The ideal file format for saving all layers, blend modes, selections, layer styles, and anything else you can create in Photoshop Elements.

H. The original single-layer state of a digital photograph or scanned image.

I. Identified by +, this component of the background eraser cursor samples reads colors from the image and decides which pixels to delete.

J. A Photoshop Elements document that contains two or more images on independent layers.

K. Choose this command to combine the contents of the active layer with the layer beneath it.

L. When you click with this tool, it identifies an area of homogeneous color and then deletes that area.

Answers

1H, 2J, 3E, 4A, 5G, 6K, 7F, 8B, 9L, 10C, 11I, 12D

TEXT AND SHAPES

AS YOU'VE NO doubt discerned by now, the primary mission of Photoshop Elements is to manipulate pixel-based digital images. But there are two exceptions. The culprits are text and shapes, two features that have nothing whatsoever to do with correcting or manipulating digital photographs, scanned artwork, or pixels in general.

Where text and shapes are concerned, Photoshop Elements is more illustration program than image editor. You can create single lines of type or set longer passages. You can select text you created long ago and edit typos. You have access to a variety of common formatting attributes, including typeface, size, and style. You can even distort type along a curve. In addition to type, you can augment your designs with rectangles, polygons, and custom predrawn symbols—the kinds of geometric shapes that you take for granted in a drawing program but rarely see in an image editor.

All this may seem like overkill, the sort of off-topic falderal that tends to burden every piece of consumer software these days. But while you may not need text and shapes for *all* your work, they're incredibly useful on those occasions when you do. Whether you want to prepare a bit of specialty type, mock up a commercial message (see Figure 9-1), or design a Web page, Elements' text and shape functions are precisely the tools you need.

This text acts as a label to the above graphic. Alas, if only I had something to say.

Figure 9-1.

ABOUT THIS LESSON

Project Files

Before beginning the exercises, make sure that you've installed the lesson files from the CD, as explained in Step 5 on page xv the Preface. This should result in a folder called *Lesson Files-PE3 1on1* on your desktop. We'll be working with the files inside the *Lesson 09* subfolder.

In this lesson, I show you how to use Photoshop Elements' text and shape tools, as well as ways to edit text and shapes by applying formatting attributes and transformations. You'll learn how to:

- Create a text layer and modify its appearance using typeface, size, and other formatting attributes. . . . . .page 254

- Apply transformations and filters to produce special text effects . . . . .page 260

- Draw, combine, transform, and duplicate scalable vector-based shapes . . . . .page 267

- Edit text on a path as well as warp text by bending and distorting it . . . . .page 275

Video Lesson 9: Vector-Based Objects

Photoshop Elements treats text and shapes as special kinds of layers. As long as you don't merge or flatten the layers, you can edit them to your heart's content. And because they're vector-based layers, you can scale or otherwise transform them without degrading their quality in the slightest.

To learn more about the incredible world of scalable vector art inside Photoshop Elements, watch the ninth video lesson that I've included on the CD. Insert the CD, click the **Start** button, click the Set **3** button in the top-right corner of your screen, and then select **9, Vector-Based Objects** from the Lessons list. Lasting 9 minutes and 16 seconds, this video introduces you to the following tools and shortcuts:

Tool or operation	Keyboard equivalent or shortcut
Select the type tool	T
Update text layer and return to the Standard Edit mode	Enter on keypad (or Ctrl+Enter)
Escape the text edit mode and abandon changes	Esc
Fill text or shape layer with background color	Ctrl+Backspace
Select a shape tool	U
Position a shape on the fly as you draw it	spacebar
Cycle through custom shapes	[or] (left or right bracket)
Constrain proportions of the custom shape	Shift-drag

The Vector-Based Duo

Generally speaking, Photoshop Elements brokers in pixels, or so-called *raster art*. But the subjects of this lesson are something altogether different. Elements treats both text and shapes as *vector-based objects* (or just plain *vectors*), meaning that they rely on mathematically defined outlines that can be scaled or otherwise transformed without degradation in quality.

For a demonstration of how vectors work in Elements, consider the composition shown in Figure 9-2. The Q is a text layer with a drop shadow. The black crown and the orange fire are shapes. The background is a pixel-based gradient. The reason the artwork appears so jagged is because it contains very few pixels. The image measures a scant 50 by 55 pixels (less than 2,800 pixels in all) and is printed at just 15 pixels per inch!

Clearly, you'd never create such low-resolution artwork in real life. I do it here to demonstrate a point: If this were an entirely pixel-based image, we'd be stuck forevermore with jagged, indistinct artwork. But because the Q, crown, and fire are vectors, they are scalable. And unlike pixel art, vectors grow smoother as you make them bigger.

The best way to scale vectors is to apply the Image Size command. To achieve the result pictured in Figure 9-3, I chose Image→Resize→Image Size and turned on the Resample Image check box. (Scale Styles and Constrain Proportions were also turned on.) Then I increased the Resolution value to a whopping 480 pixels per inch and clicked the OK button. The result is an amazing transformation, with vectors and drop shadow growing in picture-perfect form to fit the enhanced resolution. Only the pixel-based gradient remains jagged.

The upshot is that vectors are a world apart from anything else inside Photoshop Elements, always rendering at the full resolution of the image. To see more on this topic, watch Video Lesson 9, "Vector-Based Objects" (introduced on page 252).

An incredibly low-res composition
(50 x 55 pixels), rendered at 15 ppi

Figure 9-2.

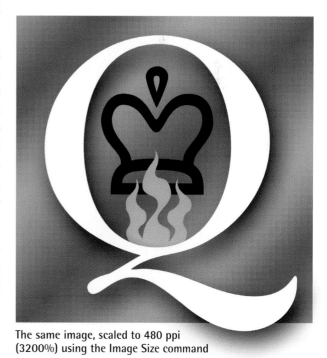

The same image, scaled to 480 ppi
(3200%) using the Image Size command

Figure 9-3.

Creating and Formatting Text

Text inside Photoshop Elements works like it does inside your everyday average publishing application. You can apply typefaces, scale characters, adjust line spacing, and so on. However, because Elements isn't well suited to routine typesetting, we won't spend much time on the routine functions. Instead, we'll take a look at some text treatments to which Photoshop Elements is well suited, as well as a few functions that are exceptional or even unique to the program.

In this exercise, we'll add text to an image and format the text to fit its background. In the next, we'll apply a few special effects.

1. *Open an image.* Not every image welcomes the addition of text. After all, text needs room to breathe. So your image should have ample dead space, the kind of empty background you might normally crop away. Such is the case with *Pumpkin light.psd* (see Figure 9-4). Found in the *Lesson 09* folder inside *Lesson Files-PE3 1on1*, this digital photo includes two strong foreground elements with lots of empty space below and above. These are perfect places for some relevant text.

PEARL OF WISDOM

When you open this document, you may see the following alert message: "Some text layers might need to be updated before they can be used for vector based output." Hopefully you won't, but if you do, click the **Update** button. This ensures that the one live text layer remains editable.

Figure 9-4.

2. *Click the type tool in the toolbox.* Or press the T key. Elements provides four type tools, but the horizontal type tool—the one that looks like an unadorned T (see Figure 9-5)—is the only one you need. So press T until you get it.

3. *Establish a few formatting attributes in the options bar.* When the type tool is active, the options bar provides access to *formatting attributes*, which are ways to modify the appearance of live text. Labeled in Figure 9-6, they include the following:

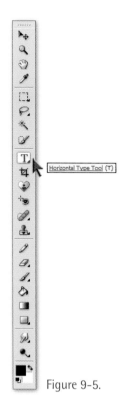

Figure 9-5.

- Click the first ⊡ arrow to see a list of typefaces available to your system. I prefer the term *font families* (or just plain *font*) because, technically speaking, most typefaces include multiple styles, such as bold, italic, and so on.

  To make the figures in this book look their best, I'll be using **Adobe Caslon Pro**. (If it happens to be installed on your computer, you'll find it alphabetized under the C's.) Most likely, you don't have Caslon, in which case select **Times**, **Times New Roman**, or a similar font.

- The type style pop-up menu lists all stylistic alternatives available for the selected font. Set the style to read **Regular** or **Roman**. (All style icons toward the middle of the options bar should be off.)

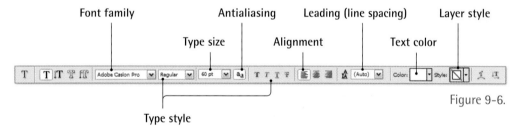

Figure 9-6.

- If using Caslon Pro, set the type size to 60 points. If using Times or Times New Roman, set the value to 68 points. Be sure to press the Enter key after setting a Size value.

- The ⓐⓐ icon determines whether Elements applies antialiasing (edge softening) to the text. Leave it turned on.

- The alignment icons let you align rows of type to the left, center, or right of the point at which you click with the type tool. Leave the first icon set to ▤ for *flush left* text.

- The distance between one line of type and another is called *leading*. By default, Elements' leading is set to Auto, which is 120 percent of the prevailing type size. This text will include just one line, so the leading is inconsequential.

- The color swatch determines the color of the type. By default, it matches the foreground color. For the moment, press Esc to deactive the Size option. Now press the D key followed by the X key to make the swatch white.

- The final option lets you apply a layer style to the text. For now, this option should be set to none, as in ⬚.

You can change every single one of these formatting attributes after you create your text. Getting a few settings established up front merely saves a little time later.

4. *Click in the image window.* Click below the pumpkins in the lower-left portion of the image. Don't worry about the exact location. Better to get the text on the page and align it later.

5. *Enter a line of text.* Tap the Caps Lock key on your keyboard. Then type "fright lights." Be sure to turn off Caps Lock when you're finished. You should see white capital letters across the bottom of your image, as in Figure 9-7. If the **Layers** palette is visible, you'll also notice the appearance of a new layer marked by a **T** icon. This **T** indicates that the layer contains live text.

Figure 9-7.

If you see a weird red pattern in the thumbnails in your Layers palette, it's because you changed the transparency pattern (albeit, per my instructions) in the preceding lesson. To restore the default gray, press Ctrl+K, press Ctrl+4, change Grid Colors to Light, and click OK.

6. *Accept your changes.* Press Enter on the keypad (not the Enter key above Shift) to exit the type mode and accept the new text layer. You can also press Ctrl+Enter. But don't press the standard Enter key on its own—doing so will add a carriage return.

At this point, Elements changes the name of the new text layer in the Layers palette to **FRIGHT LIGHTS**. The program will even update the name if you make changes to the type. You can also rename the layer, but doing so prevents Elements from updating the layer name later.

7. *Drag the text to the lower-left portion of the image.* Press the Ctrl key and drag the text into the position illustrated in Figure 9-8. The text should be positioned slightly to the left of the large pumpkin and slightly below the little one.

Figure 9-8.

8. *Click the Body Copy layer in the Layers palette.* This activates the Body Copy layer, which contains a paragraph of type set in the world's ugliest font, Courier New. (For you, it may appear in some other Courier derivative, but rest assured, they're all dreadful.) The only reason the layer is here is to spare you the tedium of having to enter the type from scratch on your own. But that doesn't mean there's nothing for you to do. Much formatting is in order.

9. ***Assign a better font.*** As long as a text layer is active, you can format the entire layer by adjusting settings in the options bar. For starters, click the word **Courier**. This highlights the font name and provides you with a couple of options:

- Press the ↑ or ↓ key to cycle to a previous or subsequent font in alphabetical order. This permits you to preview the various fonts installed on your system, handy if you have no idea what fonts like **CRITTER** or **CUTOUT** look like. (Those are just examples; your strange fonts will vary.)

- Enter the first few letters of the name of a font you'd like to use.

For example, type V-e-r, which should switch you to the commonly available Verdana (included on all personal computer systems). Then press the Enter key to apply the font and see how it looks. Figure 9-9 shows the text in Verdana.

Figure 9-9.

10. ***Make the first two words of the paragraph bold.*** Zoom in on the words *Happy Jacks* at the beginning of the paragraph to better see what you're doing, either by pressing Ctrl+⊞ (plus) or by switching to the zoom tool. Then select the type tool again, if necessary, and follow these instructions:

- Select both words by double-clicking *Happy* and dragging over *Jacks*.

- Choose **Bold** from the type style menu in the options bar, as shown in Figure 9-10. You can do the same from the keyboard by pressing Ctrl+Shift+B.

11. **Make the word clowns italic.** Find the third-to-last word in the paragraph, *clowns*, and double-click it. Then choose **Italic** from the type style menu in the options bar or press the keyboard equivalent Ctrl+Shift+I.

Even if a font doesn't offer a bold or an italic style, the keyboard shortcuts still function. In place of the missing designer style, press Ctrl+Shift+B to thicken the letters for a *faux bold*; press Ctrl+Shift+I to slant them for a *faux italic*. Beware: Faux styles don't always look right or even good.

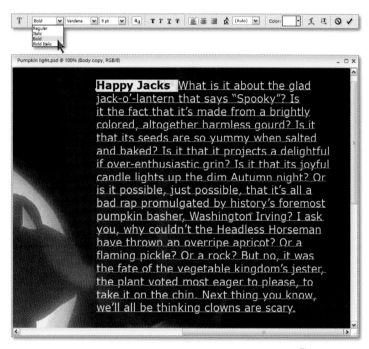

Figure 9-10.

12. **Select the entire paragraph, except the first two words.** Let's next change all but the first two words, *Happy Jacks*, to a yellowish orange to match the pumpkin. Start by double-clicking the third word, *What*. Then press the Shift key and click just after the period at the end of the paragraph.

13. **Change the color to a yellowish orange.** Click the white color swatch in the options bar to display the **Color Picker** dialog box. Then move the cursor into the image window and click in one of the fleshy areas inside the big pumpkin's nose, as shown in Figure 9-11 on the next page. You should end up with a color in the approximate vicinity of **H**: 40, **S**: 50, **B**: 90. (If you can't get a good match, go ahead and enter the values manually.) When you do, click the **OK** button to recolor the text. (Note that the text will appear blue on white because it's highlighted.)

14. *Accept your changes.* Press Enter on the keypad or press Ctrl+Enter to exit the type mode and accept the changes to the Body Copy layer. Then press Ctrl+⊟ to zoom back out a bit.

15. *Save your composition.* You're going to need this file to complete the next exercise. So choose **File→Save As**. Name your updated file "My pumpkin type.psd" and save it in the same *Lesson 09* folder inside *Lesson Files-PE3 1on1*. An alert message will ask you whether you want to maximize the compatibility of the file. Click **OK** to move on. If you plan on moving on to the next exercise immediately, go ahead and leave the file open and skip to Step 2 on the facing page.

Figure 9-11.

Applying a Special Text Effect

All this editing and formatting is fine and dandy, but it's the kind of thing that you could accomplish in a layout program such as Adobe InDesign, which is better designed for composing and printing high-resolution text. In this exercise, however, you'll do something that's possible only in an image editor like Photoshop Elements: apply some photographic depth and shadow treatments.

1. *Open the file you saved in the last exercise.* If the jack-o'-lanterns remain open, skip to the next step. Otherwise, find the file called *My pumpkin type.psd* in the *Lesson 09* folder inside *Lesson Files-PE3 1on1*. (Note that this is the file you created and saved in the preceding exercise. If you can't locate the file, you can create it by following the steps in the preceding section.)

2. *Turn on the Color Holder layer in the Layers palette.* A tiny brown pumpkin appears above the big pumpkin's head. This layer holds some of the attributes we'll be applying to the large Fright Lights text.

3. *Eyedrop the brown pumpkin.* Press the I key to select the eyedropper tool and then click the little pumpkin to make its brown the foreground color.

4. *Fill the Fright Lights layer with the sampled brown.* Click the **Fright Lights** layer in the **Layers** palette to make it active. Then press Alt+Backspace to fill the text with brown, as shown in Figure 9-12. When filling an entire text layer, this handy shortcut lets you recolor text without having to visit the Color Picker dialog box.

5. *Expand the image window.* The next trick is to add a *cast shadow*—that is, a shadow cast by the letters in the direction opposite the light source. In this case, the light source is the pumpkin, so a cast shadow would extend toward the viewer in the area below the letters. To do this, you'll need a bit of extra room at the bottom of the image. Drag the bottom edge of the image window downward to enlarge the window and reveal a half inch or so of empty gray pasteboard both above and below your image.

Figure 9-12.

6. *Transform and duplicate the text layer.* Press Ctrl+Alt+T. This does two things: It duplicates the layer and enters the free transform mode. But for the moment, you'll have to take this on faith; the Layers palette doesn't show you the new layer until you begin editing it.

Ten More Ways to Edit Text

I couldn't begin to convey in one or two exercises all the wonderful ways Photoshop Elements permits you to edit and format text. So here are a few truly terrific tips and techniques to bear in mind when working on your own projects:

- Double-click a T thumbnail in the Layers palette to switch to the type tool and select all the text in the corresponding layer.

- Armed with the type tool, you can double-click a word to select it. Drag on the second click to select multiple words. Triple-click to select an entire line.

- To underline some type, press Ctrl+Shift+U. To draw a line through the type, press Ctrl+Shift+🔲. To restore the Regular or Roman style of a font, as well as turn off any underline or strikethrough style, press Ctrl+Shift+Y.

- To increase the size of selected characters in 2-point increments, press Ctrl+Shift+🔲. To reduce the type size, press Ctrl+Shift+🔲. To change the type size by 10 points, press Ctrl+Shift+Alt+🔲 or Ctrl+Shift+Alt+🔲.

- To override the default leading, click the 🄰 icon in the options bar to highlight the word (Auto) and then type a number. In the figure below, I changed the leading to 16 points. Note that the new leading value affects the distance between a selected letter and the line above it.

- To right-justify a layer of type so the right edges are aligned and all text appears to the left of the alignment point, press Ctrl+Shift+R. To center the text, press Ctrl+Shift+C. To return the text to flush left (preferable for long passages), press Ctrl+Shift+L.

- To move text when it's active, press the Ctrl key and drag inside the text.

- The foreground color icon at the bottom of the toolbox does not always reflect the color of highlighted text. But if you change the foreground color, any highlighted text changes as well.

- To change the formatting of multiple text layers at a time, select or link the layers. Then press the Shift key and choose a font, style, size, or other formatting setting. Thanks to Shift, all linked text layers change at once.

- When editing text, Edit→Undo is dimmed and Ctrl+Z is ineffective. Your only option for undoing a text edit or formatting adjustment is to press the Esc key. Problem is, this abandons *all* changes made since you entered the text-editing mode. Furthermore, if you press the Esc key in the midst of creating a new text layer, you forfeit the entire layer. And because Esc can't be undone, there's no way to retrieve the layer.

Happy Jacks What is it about the glad jack-o'-lantern that says "Spooky"? Is it the fact that it's made from a brightly colored, altogether harmless gourd? Is it that its seeds are so yummy when salted and baked? Is it that it projects a delightful if over-enthusiastic grin? Is it that its joyful candle lights up the dim Autumn night? Or is it possible, just possible, that it's all a

7. *Flip and scale the duplicate layer.* I have a couple of instructions for you here:

- Drag the top handle of the transform boundary downward, beyond the bottom of the canvas and into the gray pasteboard. The text will flip upside down, hinging at its base, much like a reflection. Keep dragging until the **H** value in the options bar reads –116 percent or thereabouts. The negative value tells you that the height of the layer has been reversed—in the words, the layer is flipped vertically.

- Press Shift+↓ to scoot the text 10 pixels down from the bottom of the original, upright text.

The final position is illustrated in Figure 9-13. When you get it more or less right, press Enter to accept the transformation.

Figure 9-13.

A couple of special benefits when transforming a text layer: The type remains live and editable, so you can add text or fix typos. And because Photoshop Elements is working from vectors, the transformation does not stretch pixels or otherwise reduce the quality of the graphic. This means you can transform the text in multiple sessions without fear of degrading the quality.

8. *Rename the layer.* Double-click the name of the new layer in the **Layers** palette and change it to "Cast Shadow." Press Enter twice to accept the new name and deactivate the font option. Then press Ctrl+⊔ to move the renamed layer behind the original Fright Lights letters, as you can see in the Layers palette.

9. *Set the blend mode to Multiply and reduce the opacity.* This layer is a shadow, so it must darken its background. Choose **Multiply** from the blend mode menu at the top of the Layers palette, or press Shift+Alt+M. Also press the 9 key to reduce the **Opacity** to 90 percent.

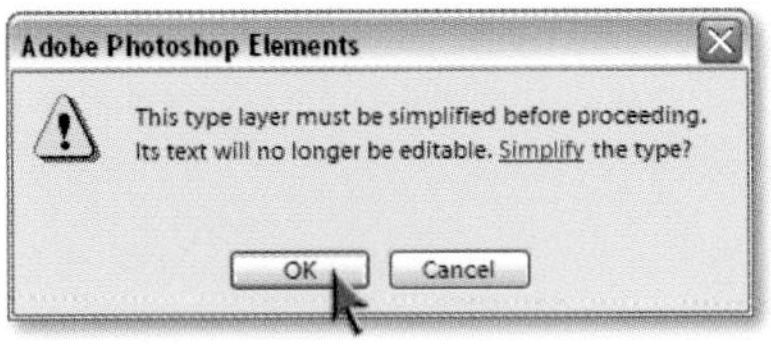

Figure 9-14.

10. *Choose the Gaussian Blur filter.* To create a soft shadow, you need to apply one of the filters from the Filter→Blur submenu. But Elements' filters are applicable only to pixels; none of them can change live type. So when you choose **Filter→Blur→Gaussian Blur**, the program alerts you that continuing requires you to "simplify" the type (see Figure 9-14), which is Elements' euphemism for converting the type to pixels. (After 250 pages of arduous lessons, you have to wonder what's so *simple* about pixels?) Click **OK** to confirm. From here on, you can no longer edit this particular layer with the type tool.

11. *Enter a Radius value of 6 pixels.* Then click the **OK** button. The blurred shadow type appears in Figure 9-15.

Figure 9-15.

12. ***Again enter the free transform mode.*** Now let's give the shadow some directional perspective so it looks like it extends out toward the viewer. Press Ctrl+T to enter the free transform mode, this time without creating a duplicate.

13. ***Distort the shadow type.*** The image in Figure 9-16 illustrates the two distortions I want you to apply, the first highlighted in red and the second in blue:

   • Once again, you need more room to work. So expand the width of the image window by dragging the right edge farther to the right.

   • Click the skew icon (⬜) in the options bar, which I've labeled in the figure.

   • Drag the handle in the lower-right corner of the transform boundary directly to the right. Keep dragging until the **W:** value in the options bar reads 115 percent (as indicated by the red circle and cursor in Figure 9-16).

   • Drag the lower-left handle of the transform boundary to the left, this time until the **W:** value reads 121.5 percent (blue in the figure).

Skew icon

Figure 9-16.

When you're satisfied that your shadow looks like mine—or, if you prefer, more to your liking than mine—press the Enter key to apply the perspective distortion.

It may occur to you to wonder why two fundamentally opposite distortions are tracked by a single scale value. Although I'm confident that some deep recess of Elements' code provides a reason, I know of none that sheds light on its performance. It is, simply put, a byproduct of the program's fundamental inability to track distortions numerically.

PEARL OF WISDOM

You may also wonder why I had you wait until now to apply this distortion. Why didn't we do it when we were flipping and stretching the text back in Step 7? Because while Elements lets you scale, rotate, and slant live type, you can't distort it. Therefore, this step had to wait until after the pixel conversion that took place in Step 10.

14. *Turn on the Style Holder layer in the Layers palette.* Click **Style holder** to turn it on. The layer is empty of pixels, so you won't see any change to the image window. But our empty layer includes a bevel style that will help sell the type effect.

15. *Move Style holder behind Fright Lights.* Either drag the **Style holder** layer down the stack, or press Ctrl+⬜ three times to move the layer backward incrementally from the keyboard.

16. *Merge the Fright Lights and Style Holder layers.* Click the **Fright Lights** layer to make it active. Then choose **Layer→ Merge Down** or press the keyboard shortcut Ctrl+E. Either way, Elements merges the two layers together, converts the text to pixels, and applies the beveled edges associated to the Style Holder layer with the Fright Lights letters.

17. *Delete the Color Holder layer.* Drag the **Color Holder** layer (the one that contains the brown pumpkin face) to the trash icon at the top of the Layers palette. The finished artwork appears in Figure 9-17.

18. *Save the file.* Choose File→Save As, and give the file a different filename, such as "Happy Jacks.psd," and click **Save**. As always, you'll get a message asking you to maximize the compatibility of your file. Leave the option on and click the **OK** button. If you decide to revisit this file in the future, the Body Copy layer will remain editable with the type tool. You can modify the other layers as pixels.

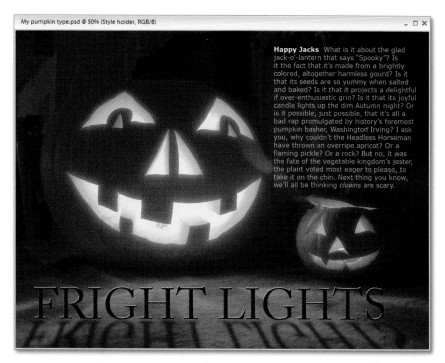

My pumpkin type.psd @ 50% (Style holder, RGB/8)

Happy Jacks What is it about the glad jack-o'-lantern that says "Spooky"? Is it the fact that it's made from a brightly colored, altogether harmless gourd? Is it that its seeds are so yummy when salted and baked? Is it that it projects a delightful if over-enthusiastic grin? Is it that its joyful candle lights up the dim Autumn night? Or is it possible, just possible, that it's all a bad rap promulgated by history's foremost pumpkin basher, Washington Irving? I ask you, why couldn't the Headless Horseman have thrown an overripe apricot? Or a flaming pickle? Or a rock? But no, it was the fate of the vegetable kingdom's jester, the plant voted most eager to please, to take it on the chin. Next thing you know, we'll all be thinking *clowns* are scary.

FRIGHT LIGHTS

Figure 9-17.

Drawing and Editing Shapes

Elements' shape tools allow you to draw rectangles, ellipses, polygons, and an assortment of prefab dingbats and symbols. On the surface, they're a pretty straightforward bunch. But when you delve into them a little more deeply, you quickly discover that the applications for shapes are every bit as wide-ranging and diverse as those for text.

You got a sense of how to draw rectangles and ellipses back in "Using the Marquee Tools" (page 119). And you experimented with custom shapes in "Cropping with the Cookie Cutter" (page 153). The techniques you learned on those exercises apply to the rectangle, ellipse, and custom shape tools as well. So in the following exercise, we'll focus on shapes you haven't yet seen, namely polygons, stars, and lines.

1. *Open an image.* Open the file *Election.psd* located in the *Lesson 09* folder inside *Lesson Files-PE3 1on1*. You'll be greeted by what appears to be a couple of text layers set against a fabric background, as shown in Figure 9-18 on the next page. But in fact, the word *Election* is a shape layer. I originally set the text in Copperplate, a well-regarded typeface that you probably don't have on your system. To avoid

having the letters change to a different font on your machine, I converted them to shapes using the more expensive Photoshop CS2. This prevents you from editing the type, but you can scale or otherwise transform the vector-based shapes without any degradation in quality.

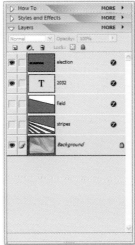

Figure 9-18.

2. *Convert the 2032 layer to pixels.* Let's say we want to similarly prevent the text 2032 from changing on another system. Unlike the senior Photoshop CS2, Photoshop Elements doesn't let you convert text to shapes. But you can convert it to pixels. Right-click the word **2032** in the **Layers** palette and then choose the **Simplify Layer** command (see Figure 9-19). Or select the type layer and choose **Layer→Simplify Layer**. Either way, Elements converts the characters to pixels, which will easily survive the journey from one system to another.

3. *Select the polygon tool in the toolbox.* Click and hold the shape tool icon near the bottom of the toolbox to display the flyout menu pictured in Figure 9-20. Then choose the polygon tool, which lets you draw regular polygons—things like pentagons and hexagons—as well as stars.

4. *Change the foreground color to white.* Press the D key followed by X. Elements now knows to draw the shape in white.

5. *Select the Election layer.* Click the **Election** layer in the Layers palette. This tells Elements to assign the drop shadow from this layer to the next shape it creates.

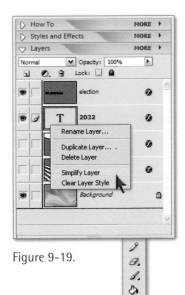

Figure 9-19.

Figure 9-20.

6. **Set the Polygon Options to Star.** Our image is a States-side election graphic, so naturally one feels compelled to wrap the composition in stars and stripes. Click the ⏷ arrow to the left of the **Sides** value in the options bar. This displays the **Polygon Options** pop-up menu pictured in Figure 9-21:

   - Turn on the **Star** check box to have the tool draw stars.

   - Make sure both **Smooth** check boxes are off so the corners are nice and sharp.

   - Set the **Indent Sides By** value to 50 percent. This ensures that opposite points align with each other, as is the rule for a 5-pointed star.

Figure 9-21.

7. **Set the Sides value to 5.** You can either select the **Sides** value and change it to 5, or you might try the following trick:

To raise the Sides value in increments of 1, press the ⎡⎤ key. To lower the value, press the ⎡⎤ key. Add the Shift key to raise or lower the value by 10. This tip holds true for any other value that may occupy this space in the options bar.

---

8. **Draw the first star.** The polygon tool draws shapes from the center out. To draw the star shown in Figure 9-22, drag from the location highlighted by the yellow ⊕ to the one highlighted by the dark green ⦿. The new star receives a white fill and a gray drop shadow.

Figure 9-22.

9. *Carve a second star out of the first.* Press the Alt key and draw another star from the same starting point (marked by the yellow ⊕ in Figure 9-23) to just inside the first star point (marked dark green ✚ in Figure 9-23). Because the Alt key is down, Elements subtracts the new shape from the previous one. The result is a star-shaped white stroke.

Figure 9-23.

As you draw the inner star, you may find that your alignment is a wee bit off. If so, bear in mind that you can adjust the placement of a shape on-the-fly by pressing and holding the spacebar. When you get the star in the right position, release the spacebar and keep drawing.

10. *Click the arrow tool in the toolbox.* Or press the U key three times to advance to the black arrow, which Elements calls the shape selection tool (see Figure 9-24). As we'll see, it permits you to select and modify path outlines in a shape layer.

11. *Select both inner and outer star paths.* Click the inner star to select it. Then press the Shift key and click one of the outer points of the outside star. Elements selects both paths. This can be tricky; if you have problems, a few of words of advice:

    • Keep an eye on the cursor. It should look like a black arrow, with a stem (▶) during both the click and the Shift-click.

    • If the bounding box gets in the way, get rid of it by turning off **Show Bounding Box** in the options bar.

12. *Transform and duplicate the star.* Press Ctrl+Alt+T to duplicate the selected star paths and enter the free transform mode. As usual, you have to take on faith that you've duplicated the star because the cloned paths overlap the originals.

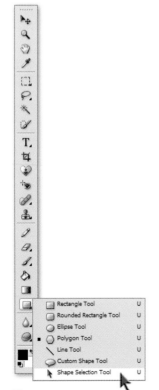

Figure 9-24.

13. *Scale, rotate, and move the duplicate star.* At this point, I need you to make some rather precise adjustments:

- Click the 🎗 icon between the W and H values to scale the star paths proportionally. Then change either the **W** or **H** value to 80 percent.

- Tab to the rotate (△) value, change it to –16 degrees, and press the Enter key. This tilts the star counterclockwise.

- Drag the shape until the smaller star is offset above and to the left of the larger one, as in Figure 9-25.

When the new star appears in the proper position, press the Enter key to confirm the transformation.

 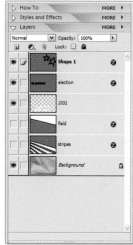

Figure 9-25.

14. *Repeat the last transformation three more times.* This means pressing Ctrl+Alt+T to duplicate the latest star and enter the transform mode. Again scale the star proportionally to 80 percent, rotate it –16 degrees, move it to the left, and then press Enter twice. Repeat the process twice more. It's a bit tedious, but the result—the arcing sequence of five stars shown in Figure 9-26 on the next page—is well worth the effort. I mean, really, how often are you rewarded with five stars?

15. *Name the new layer.* By default, the layer full of stars is called Shape 1. Double-click the layer name in the **Layers** palette and enter the new name "Stars."

16. *Turn on the Field layer.* Click the **Field** layer in the Layers palette to display a slanted blue shape layer. I created this layer by drawing a plain old rectangle with the rectangle tool and then distorting it in the free transform mode.

17. *Set the Field layer to Hard Light.* Choose the **Hard Light** mode or press Shift+Alt+H. Press the Esc key to deactivate the blend mode setting. Then press 8 to lower the **Opacity** value to 80 percent. Even though Field is a vector shape layer, it's subject to the same blend modes and transparency options that are available to all layers throughout Photoshop Elements.

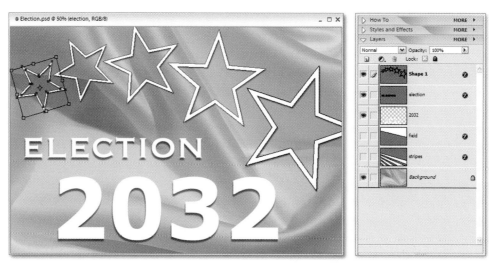

Figure 9-26.

18. *Turn on the Stripes layer.* Click the **Stripes** layer to turn on a sequence of red stripes. I created the top stripe by distorting a rectangle. Then I duplicated and transformed the other four.

19. *Set the Stripes layer to Multiply.* Press Shift+Alt+M to burn the stripes into the background image. The resulting effect appears in Figure 9-27.

Figure 9-27.

20. *Select the line tool.* The next step is to draw a rule under the word *Election*. The best tool for this job is the line tool. You can select it in any of the following ways:

   • Select the line tool from the shape tool flyout menu, just as you chose the polygon tool back in Step 3.

   • Assuming a shape tool is active (most likely the arrow tool), click the line tool icon in the options bar, as shown in Figure 9-28.

   • Alt-click the shape tool icon in the toolbox or press the U key as many times as it takes to advance to the line tool.

Figure 9-28.

21. *Increase the Weight value to 12 pixels.* The Weight value determines the thickness of lines drawn with the line tool. You can modify the value directly in the options bar, or press Shift+⬚ to raise the value by 10 and ⬚ to raise it another 1.

22. *Click the Stars layer in the Layers palette.* This tells Elements to create the next shape layer in front of the Stars layer and pick up the Stars layer's attributes.

23. *Draw a line under the word* Election. I want the rule to extend beyond the left edge of the canvas, so it's easiest to draw from right to left. Begin your drag just to the right of the last letter in *Election* and slightly below the letters, as illustrated in Figure 9-29. *After* you begin dragging, press and hold the Shift key to constrain the rule to precisely horizontal. (If you press

Figure 9-29.

Shift before you start to drag, you run the risk of adding the line to the existing Stars layer.) Drag beyond the edge of the canvas before releasing the mouse and then release Shift.

If you don't like the position of your line, change it. To move the line as you draw it, press and hold the spacebar. To nudge the line after you draw it, Ctrl-click the shape outline to select it and then press Ctrl along with the appropriate arrow key (↑, ↓, ←, or →).

---

24. *Name the new layer.* Again, the layer is called Shape 1. Double-click the layer name and enter the new name "Underscore." Then click the **2032** layer to accept the name and hide the vector outlines around all the shape layers. The final artwork appears in Figure 9-30.

Figure 9-30.

The beauty of this design is that most of it is scalable. For example, to turn this into a piece of tabloid-sized poster art, choose **Image→Resize→Image Size**, turn on the **Resample Image** check box, and change the **Width** value in the **Document Size** area to 17 inches. Make sure all three check boxes at the bottom of the dialog box are selected. To heighten the effect, change the Bicubic setting to **Nearest Neighbor** and then click **OK**. The background image and the pixel-based 2032 become jagged. But as witnessed in Figure 9-31 on the facing page, everything else remains super smooth, a testament to the power of vector-based shapes in Photoshop Elements.

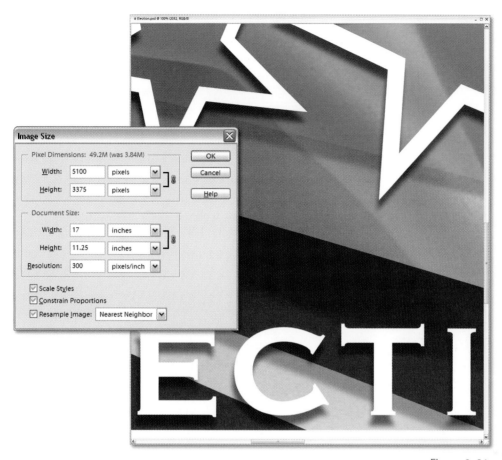

Figure 9-31.

Bending and Warping Type

The nimble-minded reader will recall that back in Step 13 of the "Applying a Special Text Effect" exercise (see page 265), I mentioned that you can't distort live type in the free transform mode. But that doesn't mean distortions are entirely out of the question. Elements offers a text-specific distortion function called Warp Text. And it's so fantastic and easy to use, I very much lament that it can't be applied to shapes and images.

This exercise shows you how to work with distorted type in Photoshop Elements. We'll start things off by editing text wrapped around the perimeter of a circle. Then we'll stretch and distort letters inside the contours of a predefined free-form shape. All the while, our text layers will remain live and fully editable.

1. *Open a layered image.* This time around, the file in question is *Radio-free space.psd*, which you'll find in the *Lesson 09* folder inside *Lesson Files-PE3 1on1*. If the program complains that some layers need to be updated, click the **Update** button. Pictured in Figure 9-32, the composition contains several layers of shapes and live type. We'll modify a couple of the text layers in the upcoming steps.

Figure 9-32.

Figure 9-33.

2. *Select the text in the Bottom Type layer.* Among the text layers are two—Top Type and Bottom Type—that I aligned to a circle inside Photoshop CS2. As the fates would have it, Photoshop Elements lacks any means for creating text on a circle, but it does let you edit it. For example, let's say we want to reverse the order of the words *utter & complete* along the bottom of the circle. To select this type, double-click the T thumbnail to the left of **Bottom Type** in the **Layers** palette. Elements switches to the type tool and highlights the text.

3. *Edit the text.* While a versatile tool, the type tool is not very adept at selecting type along a curve. Better to select the text from the keyboard as follows:

   • Press the ← key to move the insertion marker to the beginning of the text.

   • Press Ctrl+→ three times in a row to advance to the word *utter*.

   • Press Ctrl+Shift+→ three times to highlight *utter & complete*, as shown in Figure 9-33.

   Now replace the type with "complete & utter," which I believe is the more conventional word order—here on Earth, at any rate. Feel free to enter the words as lowercase characters; Elements will automatically change them to uppercase thanks to a special formatting attribute that I assigned in Photoshop CS2. When you finish, press the Enter key on the keypad to accept your changes.

4. *Select the Radio-Free Space! layer.* Press Alt+⊡ to drop down to the layer. Right now, the text treatment at the top of the page is almost comically bad. Cyan letters, wide leading, big thick red strokes, Verdana—how much worse could it get? We'll start by spicing up the text with a blend mode, and then we'll warp the text for a classic pulp fiction look.

5. *Change the blend mode to Overlay.* Select **Overlay** from the pop-up menu at the top of the Layers palette. Or press Shift+Alt+O. The already much improved result appears in Figure 9-34.

6. *Click the warp icon in the options bar.* Press T to reselect the type tool. Then look to the far right side of the options bar for an icon that looks like 𝐓 (labeled in Figure 9-35). Click this icon to bring up the **Warp Text** dialog box.

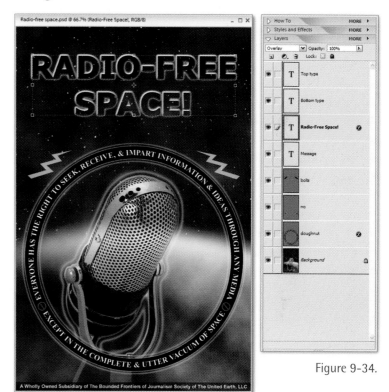

Figure 9-34.

7. *Apply the Arc Lower style.* The Warp Text dialog box features these options:

- The **Style** pop-up menu defines the shape inside which the text bends. The icons provide hints as to what the effect will look like. But if in doubt, choose an option and watch the preview in the image window.

- Change the angle of the warp by selecting the **Horizontal** or **Vertical** radio button. With Western-world text like the stuff we're working with here, Horizontal bends lines of type and Vertical warps the individual letters.

Figure 9-35.

- Use the **Bend** value to change the amount of warp and the direction in which the active text layer bends. You can enter any value from –100 to 100 percent.

- The two **Distortion** sliders add a hint of perspective to the warp effect.

For example, Figure 9-36 shows four variations on the Arc Lower style. The icon next to the style name represents the effect as flat on top and bent at the bottom. Assuming Horizontal is active, this means the warp is applied exclusively to the bottom of the text. A positive Bend value tugs the bottom of the text downward (first image); a negative value pushes it upward (second image).

To achieve a strict perspective-style distortion, choose any Style option and set the Bend value to 0 percent. Examples of purely horizontal and vertical distortions appear in the last two images in Figure 9-36.

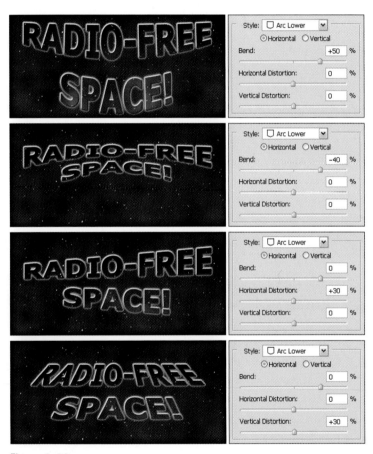

Figure 9-36.

For this exercise, choose **Arc Lower** from the **Style** pop-up menu. Then set the **Bend** value to −40 percent. The resulting effect looks awful—easily the worst of those shown in Figure 9-36—but that's temporary. Have faith that we'll fix things in future steps and click **OK**.

8. *Increase the size of the word* Space! Triple-click the word *Space!* with the type tool to select both it and its exclamation point. Press Ctrl+Shift+⊡ to increase the type size incrementally until the width of the selected text matches that of the text above it. (To resize faster, press Ctrl+Shift+Alt+⊡.) Or just change the type size value in the options bar to 88 points, as in Figure 9-37.

9. *Increase the leading.* Although the selected word better fits the horizontal dimensions of its layer, it overlaps the line above it. Click the $\overset{A}{\text{I}\kern-1pt\text{A}}$ icon in the options bar to highlight the leading value. Change it to 76 points and press Enter (see Figure 9-38).

10. *Accept your changes.* Press the Enter key on the keypad to exit the text edit mode and accept the formatting adjustments.

11. *Scale the text vertically.* One of the byproducts of warping is that it stretches or squishes characters, thus requiring you to scale them back to more visually appealing proportions. In our case, the text is *really* squished, so some vertical scaling is in order. Choose **Image→Transform→Free Transform** or press Ctrl+T. Then change the **H** value to 167 percent and press the Enter key twice in a row to make the letters taller without making them wider, as in Figure 9-39.

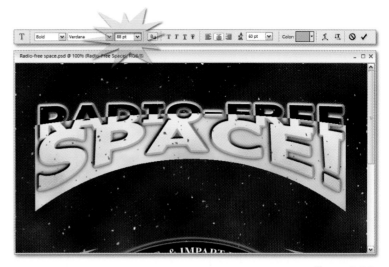

Figure 9-37.

Figure 9-38.

Figure 9-39.

Figure 9-40.

12. **Nudge the text down.** The text now rides too high on the canvas. Press Ctrl+Shift+↓ three times in a row to nudge the text down 30 pixels. The final composition appears in Figure 9-40.

It's important to note that throughout all these adjustments, every single text layer remains fully editable. For example, to change the text from *Radio-Free Space!* (indicating a space completely free of radio) to *Radio Free Space!* (which implies that the radio in space is free to all), simply replace the hyphen with a space character. The layer effects are likewise live. To change the style of warp, simply select the text layer and click the text warp icon in the options bar. I ask you, what in the world could be more flexible?

WHAT DID YOU LEARN?

Match the key concept in the numbered list below with the letter
of the phrase that best describes it. Answers appear upside-down
at the bottom of the page.

Key Concepts

1. Raster art
2. Vector-based objects
3. Formatting attributes
4. Font family
5. Flush left
6. Leading
7. Faux styles
8. Point text
9. Simplify
10. Live type
11. Weight
12. Warp Text

Descriptions

A. Mathematically defined text and shapes that can be scaled or otherwise transformed without any degradation in quality.

B. Digital images composed exclusively of colored pixels.

C. Text that has no maximum column width and aligns to the place at which you clicked with the type tool.

D. The distance between lines of type.

E. A typeface and its multiple related styles.

F. This dialog box bends and distorts live text to create wavy, bulging, and perspective effects.

G. Lines of text that are aligned along the left side.

H. To convert live type into noneditable, rasterized type.

I. This value determines the thickness of lines drawn with the line tool.

J. These can be used when a font doesn't come with bold or italic versions.

K. Text that remains editable.

L. Font family, type style, size, leading, alignment, and a wealth of other options for modifying the appearance of live text.

Answers

STYLES AND ADJUSTMENT LAYERS

I LONG FOR the day when everything in Photoshop Elements is a live effect. Imagine if hours after applying the Unsharp Mask command, you elected to revisit the filter and tweak its settings. But instead of applying the new settings on top of the old ones, as happens now, you were able to apply them *in place of* the old ones. In other words, imagine if the filter were dynamic. And not just Unsharp Mask, but every single function throughout the program. Photoshop Elements would transform overnight from amateur photo editor to the most flexible imaging application on the planet.

Alas, that glad day continues to elude us. But that's not to say the present is bleak. Today's Photoshop Elements provides us with occasional glimpses into the world of dynamic image editing in the form of layer styles and adjustment layers. If all of Elements were this forgiving, it would be impossible to make a permanent mistake.

Figure 10-1.

The Amazing World of Live Effects

Layer styles are collections of predefined color and contour attributes that let you add dimension, lighting, and texture to otherwise flat objects. *Adjustment layers* are collections of settings that correct or modify the colors of the layers behind them. As their names imply, both layer styles and adjustment layers depend on layers to work their magic. So I've assembled a simple layered document to show you how both features work:

- Figure 10-1 shows a composition with two floating layers—an image and a strip of torn paper—set against a teal background. To each layer, I applied one of the most common kinds of layer styles: a *drop shadow*, which is nothing more than a silhouette of the layer that is offset and blurred. The shadow implies a gap in

ABOUT THIS LESSON

Project Files

Before beginning the exercises, make sure that you've installed the lesson files from the CD, as explained in Step 5 on page xv of the Preface. This should result in a folder called *Lesson Files-PE31on1* on your desktop. We'll be working with the files inside the *Lesson 10* subfolder.

In this lesson, you'll explore the worlds of layer styles and adjustment layers, both of which enable you to modify an image composition without harming a single pixel in the original photographs. Specifically, you'll learn how to:

- Apply and modify a few of the more than 80 custom-designed layer styles included with this book. . . . . page 287
- Use adjustment layers and gradients to colorize and correct the brightness values in a black-and-white photograph . . . . page 291
- Try your hand at using adjustment layers to both generate artwork and apply special effects in a layered composition . . . . page 297

Video Lesson 10: Introducing Styles

Many folks regard layer styles as little more than a means for adding drop shadows. But drop shadows are only the beginning. Used properly, layer styles are automated painting tools that let you not only enhance photographic layers, but also turn hand-drawn elements, text layers, or vector shapes into fully realized objects with dimension and depth.

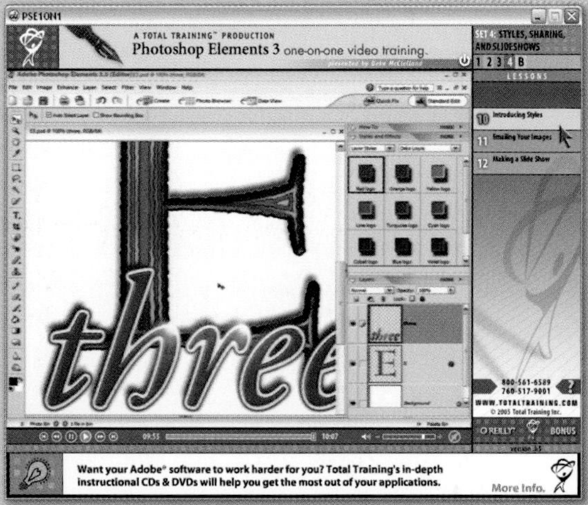

For a firsthand introduction to layer styles, as well as the predefined styles that both I and Adobe have included in the Styles and Effects palette, watch the tenth video lesson on the CD. Insert the CD, click the **Start** button, click the Set 4 button, and then select **10, Introducing Styles** from the Lessons list. In this 10-minute 7-second movie, I tell you about the following operations and shortcuts:

Operation	Keyboard equivalent or shortcut
Show or hide the layer styles thumbnails	F7, then choose Layer Styles from pop-up menu
Append one layer style to another	Click thumbnail in Styles and Effects palette
Replace one layer style with another	Shift-click thumbnail in Styles and Effects palette
Deactivate style library name in pop-up menu	Esc
Display the Style Settings dialog box	Double-click icon to the right of layer name
Change the direction of one or more effects	Drag in image when Style Settings dialog box is open
Render out or delete a layer style	Right-click layer name and choose desired command

depth between the layers. And because the shadows drop downward, they suggest a light source that shines from above.

- Drop shadows are handy, but they are just one of several different kinds of layer styles. In Figure 10-2, I created a new layer. Using two separate layer styles, I traced a dark outline around the outside of the layer and a light outline around the inside. This results in a slight "toasting" effect, which helps separate the layer from its environment even more.

- The lower-right corner of Figure 10-3 sports an adjustment layer. Based on the Gradient Map command (see the "Colorizing an Image with Adjustment Layers" exercise, page 291), this adjustment layer inverts and colorizes the paper, the photograph, and the background layers beneath it.

- Figure 10-4 illustrates another Gradient Map adjustment layer. But this one doesn't invert colors; it just changes them, including the layer of yellow from the preceding figure. I even managed to assign a style to the adjustment layer, one that sculpts the perimeter of the layer.

Figure 10-2.

Figure 10-3.

Figure 10-4.

The upshot is that layer styles and adjustment layers possess an amazing capacity for interaction. One layer style can mix with another, one adjustment layer can modify another, and layer styles can be applied directly to adjustment layers. You'll see examples of these interactions—and get a sense of just how useful they can be—in the upcoming exercises.

Layer Attributes Versus Layers

Layer styles and adjustment layers share many things in common. Both are *parametric*, which means that they're based on adjustable numerical settings. Additionally, both take up very little room in memory, are accessible from the Layers palette, and remain editable as long as you save them in the native Photoshop PSD format.

But layer styles and adjustment layers are ultimately unique functions, implemented in different ways:

- You assign a layer style to an existing layer. An adjustment layer exists as a layer all its own. Figure 10-5 shows examples of each as they appear in the Layers palette.

- A layer style controls the appearance of just one layer at a time. An adjustment layer affects the color and luminosity of all layers beneath it (according to your specifications, as we'll see).

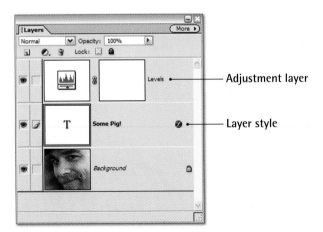

Figure 10-5.

The first exercise in this lesson covers the topic of layer styles. The remaining two are devoted to adjustment layers. We'll see one highly practical use for adjustment layers and another that might be best expressed as wildly creative. Whether you intend to put them to practical or creative use, these are two tools you'll want to spend more time with.

Applying and Modifying Layer Styles

Layer styles serve two opposing purposes: to set layers apart and to bring them together. For example, a layer style that casts a shadow suggests that the layer is raised above the surface of its surroundings. This calls attention to the perimeter of the layer and adds depth to the image, both of which help to distinguish the layered element from a busy composition. Meanwhile, a layer style can also blend the interior or perimeter of a layer with its background. The independent layers appear not as disparate elements of a composition, but as seamless portions of a cohesive whole.

The following exercise demonstrates both capacities of layer styles. We'll take a very plain composition and embellish it using a trio of predefined styles that I created in Photoshop CS2. (Photoshop Elements can only modify styles not create them.) Before beginning this exercise, make sure that you've installed my style libraries onto your computer (see Step 5 on page xv of the Preface). In all, these libraries contain more than 80 styles that you can apply, mix, and modify as you please.

1. *Open a layered composition.* Go to the *Lesson 10* folder inside *Lesson Files-PE3 1on1* and open the file called 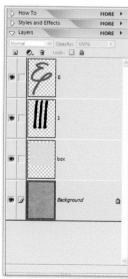 *Paper letters.psd*. Pictured in Figure 10-6, this image features a total of four layers. The background was scanned from a brown paper bag. The other layers are filled with various shades of gray. How drab can you get? But as it just so happens, it is precisely this kind of drab art that benefits most from layer styles.

2. *Select the E layer.* Click the top layer in the **Layers** palette or press the keyboard shortcut Shift+Alt+⟩.

3. *Open the layer styles.* First make sure the **Styles and Effects** palette is available on screen. (If necessary, press the F7 key.) Then choose **Layer Styles** from the top-left pop-up menu. Most likely, you'll see a series of none-too-exciting thumbnails that represent various kinds of drop shadows. Don't let that dissuade you; there's plenty of exciting stuff here—you just have to know where to look.

Figure 10-6.

Figure 10-7.

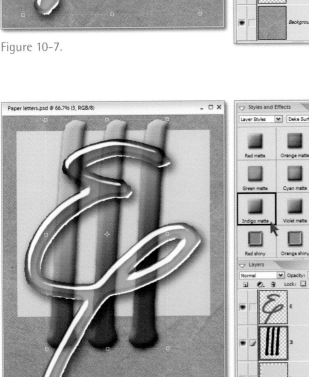

Figure 10-8.

4. *Apply the Green Glass style.* The upper-right pop-up menu lets you select a library of styles that Elements loaded automatically when you started the program. Click the pop-up menu and choose a library midway down titled **Deke Glass**. (If you don't see this option, refer to the preface for installation instructions.) You should see a total of 12 candy-colored thumbnails. Click the one called **Green Glass** to apply the shimmering, translucent effect shown in Figure 10-7.

5. *Apply the Indigo Matte style to the 3 layer.* Sometimes a style works as is, right out of the box. Such is the case with the almost liquid Green Glass effect. Other times, a style needs some help, as we'll see in this next example. Let's start by applying a base style to another layer:

   • Click the **3** layer in the Layers palette to make it active. Or press Alt+☐ to move backward. (If the shortcut doesn't work, press the Esc key to deactivate the style library name and then press Alt+☐.)

   • Choose **Deke Surfaces** from the upper-right pop-up menu in the Styles and Effects palette.

   • Click the style marked **Indigo Matte**. The result appears in Figure 10-8.

6. *Edit the style settings.* I like the color and drop shadow associated with this style, but I don't care for the beveled edges. They're just too much. To modify the style, double-click the ✿ icon that now appears to the right of the 3 layer in the Layers palette. This brings up the **Style Settings** dialog box, which lets you modify the attributes

associated with the active style. Here's a quick rundown of the options that currently confront you, along with the settings I want you to enter:

- Set the **Lighting Angle** value to 100 degrees, which shifts the light source more directly above the layer. This casts a shadow in the opposite direction, almost straight down.

- Notice that the **Use Global Light** check box is turned on. This locks in the light source at 100 degrees for all other directional layer styles for which Use Global Light is similarly turned on. At the present, no other layer is affected, so don't worry about it.

- Press Tab a couple of times to advance to the **Shadow Distance** option. Enter a value of 20 pixels to move the shadow 20 pixels away from the layered objects.

- Next tab to the **Bevel Size** option, which controls the thickness of the beveled edges. Reduce the value to 5 pixels to make the edges thin indeed.

- The **Bevel Direction** should be set to **Up**, which makes the layer appear raised as opposed to recessed.

- If it isn't already on, go ahead and check the **Preview** box so you can see the results of your edits.

Click the **OK** button to accept your changes. Both the settings and the modified result appear in the resplendent Figure 10-9.

Figure 10-9.

7. *Group the 3 layer with the square below it.* I want the vertical lines of the 3 layer to fit inside the gray square. And I can do that using a special function called a *clipping mask*, in which one layer fits inside the layer below it. So choose **Layer→Group with Previous** or press Ctrl+G to combine the two layers into a clipping mask, as in Figure 10-10.

8. *Apply Orange Glass to the box layer.* Now to turn our attention to the final layer, the light gray square:

- Click the word **Box** in the **Layers** palette or press the handy shortcut Alt+⬚ to make the layer active.

- Again choose **Deke Glass** from the upper-right pop-up menu in the Styles and Effects palette.

- Click the **Orange Glass** layer.

Figure 10-10.

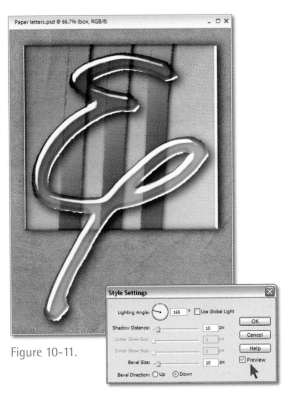

Figure 10-11.

9. *Edit the style settings.* The result is nice, but again it needs work. Double-click ❼ and change the settings like so:

- Set the **Angle** value to 165 degrees. The Use Global Light check box is off, so adjusting the Angle value won't affect the other layers.

- Lower the **Shadow Distance** to 10 pixels.

- Likewise lower the **Bevel Size** value to 10 pixels. Then change the **Bevel Direction** option to **Down** to create the effect of a slight depression in the background.

When your settings—and the altered effect—look like those in Figure 10-11, click the **OK** button.

10. *Change the fill opacity to 30 percent.* Photoshop Elements offers a remarkable hidden feature that lets you adjust the transparency of the pixels in a layer independently of the layer style. Termed *fill opacity*, this function is represented neither by command nor option. You can get to it only from the keyboard.

Try this: Press the V key to confirm that the move tool is active. Then press Shift+1. Notice how the layer becomes more transparent but the drop shadow and bevel remain unchanged. You just changed the fill opacity to 10 percent. Now press Shift+0. The light gray of the square returns, because you restored the fill opacity to 100 percent. Do you feel the rare satisfaction of discovering a top secret, ultrahidden feature? You should, because that's precisely what you have just done.

Now that you've had a chance to experiment, press Shift+3 to change the fill opacity to 30 percent.

11. *Nix the Indigo Matte style on the 3 layer.* Having had time to reflect, I'm not terribly impressed by the layer style I applied to the 3 layer. So let's get rid of it. Right-click to the right of the **3** in the Layers palette. Then choose **Clear Layer Style** from the shortcut menu. The style and its associated fill opacity setting go away, leaving behind fully opaque black stripes.

12. *Change the standard opacity to 30 percent.* Press the 3 key without Shift to reduce the standard opacity of the 3 layer to 30 percent. Or you can adjust the **Opacity** value in the Layers palette directly. The final composition appears on the facing page in Figure 10-12.

Colorizing an Image with Adjustment Layers

We now move from layer styles to adjustment layers. These insanely practical functions permit you to apply popular color adjustments such as Hue/Saturation and Levels as well as most of the commands under the Filter→Adjustments submenu. What's more, an adjustment layer works just like its command counterpart. The Levels adjustment layer shows you the same dialog box—complete with Input Levels values and histogram—as does Enhance→Adjust Lighting→Levels. However, unlike commands, an adjustment layer affects all layers beneath it and remains editable far into the future.

Adjustment layers are so flexible that many designers use them to correct flat photographs. This way, if they later decide to tweak the colors in an image to meet the demands of a different screen or printing environment, they always have their original photograph on hand, with the last-applied color correction ready and waiting in the wings.

In this exercise, we'll use an adjustment layer to colorize a grayscale image. We could use the Hue/Saturation command for this purpose, but it limits you to one Hue value and one Saturation value per operation. My preferred approach involves a little-known function called Gradient Map, which allows you to substitute luminosity values with as many hue and saturation values as you like. Problem is, Gradient Map is fairly obscure and I haven't introduced you to it yet. Meanwhile, Hue/Saturation is familiar and commonly employed for colorizing. Hence I feel compelled to do something I don't normally do in an exercise—compare and contrast. In the following steps, we'll make use of both Hue/Saturation and Gradient Map, and you can decide for yourself which is better.

1. *Open an image.* Open the grayscale image titled *Woman in hood.jpg*, contained in the *Lesson 10* folder inside *Lesson Files-PE3 1on1*. Pictured in Figure 10-13 on the next page, this photo was captured by Ramsey Blacklock and hails from iStockPhoto.com. It's a swell pic, but it'll look livelier after we add some color.

Figure 10-12.

2. *Convert the image to RGB color.* A grayscale image doesn't merely lack color; it lacks all capacity for color. This means an image that lists *Gray* in its title bar (as this one does) cannot be colorized without first undergoing a subtle but very important transformation. Choose **Image→Mode→RGB Color**, as in Figure 10-14. Or press the Alt key and type I-M-R. The photo won't look any different, but take my word for it: It's now ready for color to blossom.

Figure 10-13.

3. *Create a Hue/Saturation adjustment layer.* Click the half-black, half-white ◑ icon at the top of the **Layers** palette to display a menu of 11 specialty layers (3 fills followed by 8 color adjustments). Then choose **Hue/Saturation**, as in Figure 10-15. Photoshop Elements adds a layer called Hue/Saturation 1 and displays the **Hue/Saturation** dialog box.

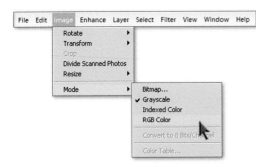

Figure 10-14.

Figure 10-15.

4. *Turn on the Colorize check box.* Located in the lower-right corner of the dialog box, the **Colorize** check box applies the Hue and Saturation settings as absolute values. By this, I mean that all pixels are assigned one uniform Hue value and one uniform Saturation value. The moment you turn on Colorize, Photoshop Elements changes the Hue to 0 degrees (or possibly 360 degrees, same diff) and the Saturation to 25 percent, which turns the entire image a low-saturation red, as shown in Figure 10-16.

Figure 10-16.

5. *Adjust the Hue and Saturation values.* At this point, I encourage you to experiment. Enter any **Hue** value documented in the sidebar "The Visible-Color Spectrum Wheel" (Lesson 3, page 85), and you will see that very color come to life before your very eyes. Meanwhile, a **Saturation** of 0 percent invariably results in gray; 100 percent delivers the most vivid color Photoshop Elements can achieve.

For my part—and you're welcome to follow along with me if you like—I entered a **Hue** of 40 degrees and a **Saturation** of 30 percent. The result is an orange-amber *duotone*, so called because it contains two tones, black and the 40-degree amber (see Figure 10-17).

Figure 10-17.

6. *Click the OK button.* The result is a pleasant enough effect. But frankly, it's not good enough. The moment you turned on the Colorize check box, you lost all selective control. The Edit pop-up menu dimmed, and thus you lost the ability to adjust the hue and saturation of individual colors. Why sacrifice that kind of control when you don't have to?

7. *Swap Hue/Saturation for Gradient Map.* To change the Hue/Saturation layer to a Gradient Map adjustment, first make sure the Hue/Saturation 1 layer is active and then choose **Layer→Change Layer Content→Gradient Map**. Photoshop Elements displays the **Gradient Map** dialog box, which substitutes (or *maps*) the luminosity values in the image with the colors in a gradient. If the program initially inverts the photo, as in Figure 10-18, fear not. You have my word, things will improve dramatically over the course of the next few steps.

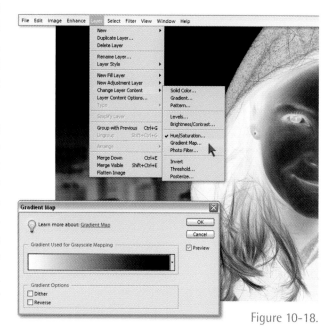

Figure 10-18.

Figure 10-19.

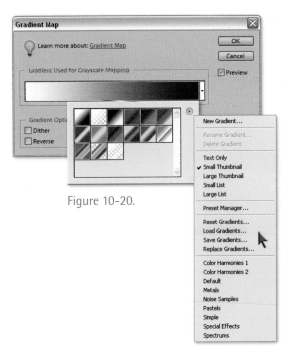

Figure 10-20.

For those who may be wondering, a *gradient* is a continuous fountain of colors. The gradient may transition from black to white, from one color to another, or between a whole slew of colors, as illustrated by the examples in **Figure 10-19**.

The great thing about Gradient Map is that it gives you so much control. You can map every single gray value, from black to white, to a specific color. And all you need to make this happen is an easy-to-create, easy-to-edit gradient.

8. *Load the custom gradients.* The predefined gradients that ship with Photoshop Elements don't work very well for colorization. So I've created a handful of colorization gradients for you to play with. Here's how to get to them:

   • In the Gradient Map dialog box, click the ▾ arrow to the right of the main gradient bar. This displays a panel of small gradient swatches.

   • Click the ⊙ arrow to the right of the swatches and choose **Load Gradients** from the menu, as in Figure 10-20.

   • After the **Load** dialog box appears, find the *Lesson 10* folder inside the *Lesson Files-PE3 1on1* folder and open the file called *Four gradients.grd*. Four new gradient swatches will appear in the Gradient Map dialog box.

9. *Select the Quadtone supreme swatch.* Hover your cursor over the first of the four new swatches. You should see the hint *Quadtone supreme*. When you do, click to select the swatch. Assuming the **Preview** check box is on (as by default), Photoshop Elements will apply the colors in this gradient to the luminosity values in the image. The gradient progresses from black to very dark magenta followed by a dull red, orange, and finally white, each of which finds a home over the course of the gray values in the photograph, as in Figure 10-21. That's a total of four colors plus white, hence a *quadtone*.

If your image still appears black and white, it's because you didn't convert the image from grayscale to RGB using **Image→Mode→RGB Color**, as explained in Step 2.

10. *Open the Gradient Editor.* A gradient map behaves a lot like the Levels command (see "Adjusting Brightness Levels," on page 90 of Lesson 3) because it lets you lighten or darken luminosity values. To make brightness adjustments, click inside the gradient bar above the swatches panel to display the **Gradient Editor** dialog box.

Although the dialog box is brimming with options, most of the action centers on the gradient bar. Labeled in Figure 10-22, the gradient bar is festooned with tiny box icons above and below. The boxes above the bar (▣) control the opacity of the gradient, and have no effect on the outcome of the Gradient Map command. The boxes below the bar (▣) let you add key colors to the gradient. Because they determine the position of the colors, they are known as *color stops.*

11. *Edit the gradient.* Click the second color stop from the left—the dark magenta one—to select it. (I know, the swatch looks purplish, but if you go by the Hue value, it's magenta. I guess I'm a stickler.) Two options, Color and Location, become available at the bottom of the dialog box. Click the Color swatch if you want to change the color; modify the Location value or drag the color stop to move the color in the gradient. Increasing the Location value darkens the colors in the image; reducing the value lightens them. (This isn't always the case—it depends on the colors in your gradient—but that's how it works in this gradient.)

I want you to do the following:

- With the dark magenta color stop selected, reduce the **Location** value for the dark magenta color stop to 15 percent. This helps to lighten the shadows and bring out details in the hair.

- Click the next color stop over—the dull red one—and change its **Location** to 50 percent. Elements darkens the midtones in the face.

Figure 10-21.

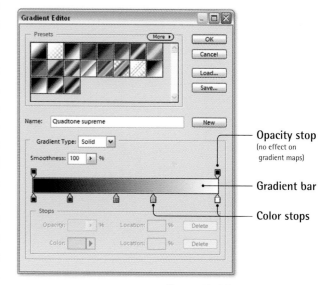

Opacity stop
(no effect on gradient maps)

Gradient bar

Color stops

Figure 10-22.

- Click the final, white color stop. This time I want you to try something a little different: Press the Alt key and drag the swatch to the left until the **Location** value reads 80 percent. This duplicates the color stop and draws out the highlights in the woman's face.

- Select the orange color stop, the one with a Location value of 65 percent. Alt-drag this stop to the right until **Location** reads 95 percent. Elements deepens clouds from the overly bright background of the sky, as in Figure 10-23.

Figure 10-23.

12. *Save your revised gradient.* Enter "Quadtone Modified" into the **Name** option box and click the **New** button to add a swatch to the end of the Presets list.

13. *Click OK.* Click **OK** to accept your changes and return to the **Gradient Map** dialog box.

14. *Try out the other gradients.* To see what other gradients look like when applied to *Woman in hood.jpg*, click the ▾ arrow to the right of the gradient bar and select a different gradient swatch. The images in Figure 10-24 illustrate three additional gradients that I provided—Cool palette, Deep sky, and Vivid contrast—as well as one of Photoshop Elements' default gradients, Copper. In the last case, I turned on the **Reverse** check box, which reverses the order of the colors in the gradient and inverts the colors in the image.

15. *Click OK.* Once you arrive at a favorite gradient map, click the **OK** button or press the Enter key to accept the colorized image. (If the gradient swatch panel is visible, you may have to press Enter twice.)

You can, of course, apply more colorful gradients to an image. But the more you vary the colors, the more psychedelic and convoluted your colorized image becomes. I advise subtle changes. Even small shifts in color can make a big difference.

Using Adjustment Layers to Create Special Effects

Because adjustment layers are fully functioning layers, you can mix and match them, as well as combine them with blend modes, layer masks, shapes, layer styles, and even clipping masks. Simply put, they permit you to venture into creative territories that static commands simply can't accommodate.

In this exercise, your assignment is to build a book cover for a dime-store novel using a couple of digital photos and a petroglyph silhouette that I saved for you as a selection outline. Your publisher has asked for something "dark, brooding, and suspenseful." Given that this is all the instruction you've received, it seems imprudent to make any permanent changes to the images. So you wisely decide to do everything with adjustment layers.

1. *Open a layered image.* This time we're going to work from a single file, *End of Road.psd*, which you'll find in the *Lesson 10* folder inside *Lesson Files-PE3 1on1*. (If the program asks to update the text layers, click the **Update** button.) Pictured in Figure 10-25 on the next page, this composition contains a text layer sandwiched between two photographic layers, both of which I shot nearly a decade ago using a 1.5-megapixel Kodak DC265. I set the layer that contains my shadow to the Multiply blend mode, thus toasting it into the orange type and drive-in movie screen.

Cool palette

Deep sky

Vivid contrast

Copper, Reverse

Figure 10-24.

Figure 10-25.

2. *Add an Invert adjustment layer.* What's the easiest, most brain-dead way to make an image look scary? Invert it, of course. And that's exactly what we're going to do with the drive-in screen. Check that the **Background** layer is active in the **Layers** palette. Click the ◐ icon at the top of the palette and choose the **Invert** command. Elements adds a layer called Invert 1 that creates a negative version of the drive-in movie screen behind it.

3. *Change the blend mode to Luminosity.* Currently, the Invert 1 layer reverses both the luminosity values and the colors in the drive-in. This means that the blue of the sky turns to orange, and the orange of the ground turns to blue. Fine, but suppose you don't want that; suppose you want to invert only the luminosity values. Then choose **Luminosity** from the blend mode pop-up menu in the top-left corner of the Layers palette, or press the keyboard shortcut Shift+Alt+Y. Elements restores the blue sky and orange ground, as in Figure 10-26.

Figure 10-26.

4. *Add a Levels adjustment layer.* Inverting the background made the image overly dark, and the best way to lighten it is with the Levels command. But you can't apply Levels to the Invert 1 layer, and if you lighten the Background layer directly, you'll darken the inverted image because the luminosity values are reversed. Solution: Click the ⊘ icon at the top of the Layers palette and choose **Levels**. Inside the **Levels** dialog box, advance to the second **Input Levels** value and change the gamma to 2.00, as demonstrated in Figure 10-27. Then click the **OK** button to apply the adjustment.

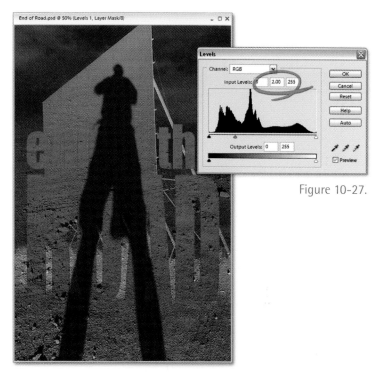

Figure 10-27.

5. *Turn on the top three text layers.* In the **Layers** palette, click the blank boxes to the far left of each of the top three text layers to display the ◉ icons. Imagine that the publisher provided these layers to you with the directive, "Keep the quote and author's name in blue, and make them leap off the page." But because blue is one of the most pervasive colors in the image, the text gets a little lost (see Figure 10-28). Obviously, another adjustment layer is warranted.

6. *Add a Hue/Saturation adjustment layer.* Click the **Levels 1** layer in the Layers palette to specify where you want to insert the next layer. Then press the Alt key as you choose **Hue/Saturation** from the ⊘ icon at the top of the palette. This allows you to name the new layer as you create it. Call it "Color Spin" and click the **OK** button to display the **Hue/Saturation** dialog box.

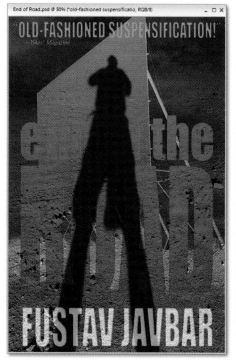
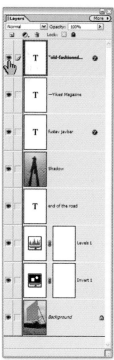

Figure 10-28.

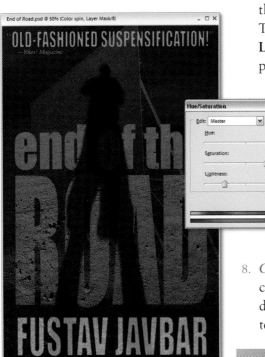

Figure 10-29.

7. *Rotate all hues throughout the image 180 degrees.* Change the **Hue** value to 180 degrees to invert all colors in the image. Then boost the **Saturation** value to +50 percent and reduce the **Lightness** value to –50 percent. Click **OK** to accept the changes, pictured in Figure 10-29.

At this point, you might quite naturally wonder why in the world we just inverted the colors when we were so careful *not* to invert the colors in Step 3. The reason is that for the moment, all we're concerned about is making the blue text "leap off the page." Once that's accomplished, we'll restore the appearance of the central portion of the image using a layer mask (see Step 9). But first . . .

8. *Change the blend mode to Multiply.* As far as the blue text is concerned, the background art remains too light. To make it darker, choose **Multiply** from the blend mode pop-up menu in the top-left corner of the **Layers** palette, or press Shift+Alt+M.

PEARL OF WISDOM

It's worth noting that so far, despite the fact that you've added three layers and applied blend modes to two of them, the size of the file has grown by just a few K, or a little more than 0.03 percent. Happily, adjustment layers are not only flexible but also models of efficiency.

Figure 10-30.

9. *Click the gradient tool in the toolbox.* If you look at the Layers palette, you'll see that each one of the three adjustment layers that you've created so far includes a white thumbnail to the right of it. Each white thumbnail indicates a *layer mask*, which permits you to limit the portion of an image that's affected by an adjustment layer. Strange as it sounds, painting black inside the layer mask hides that portion of the color adjustment; painting white reveals the adjustment. We'll create a soft transition between adjusted and unadjusted areas of the image by painting inside the Color Spin layer mask with the gradient tool. Click the tool's icon (see Figure 10-30) or press the G key to select it.

10. *Paint gradients at the top and bottom of the image.* The aim is to relegate the effects of the Color Spin layer to the areas immediately behind the blue text at the top and the bottom of the image. That means painting the central portion of the layer mask black. It's a tricky proposition, so I'll break it into pieces:

- Press the D key to make the foreground color white and the background color black, as is the default when working in a layer mask.

- Press Shift+⌐ (Shift+comma) to set the gradient tool to draw gradients from the foreground color to the background color, or white to black.

- Press the Shift key and drag from directly below the top text to the chest in the shadow, as indicated by the yellow arrow at the top of Figure 10-31. This should lighten all but the topmost portion of the image.

- Now to reinstate some darkness at the bottom of the image. Start by pressing the ⌐ key (period), which changes the style of gradient to Foreground-to-Transparent.

- In the image window, Shift-drag from directly above the author name (the esteemed Fustav Javbar) to about an inch or so up, as indicated by the orange arrow at the bottom of Figure 10-31. Both the top and bottom of the image should now appear dark.

11. *Invert the* End of the Road *text.* Now we're ready to address the book's title. The publisher has informed us that as long as we make Fustav Javbar's name prominent, we can do anything we want with the title. So let's have some fun. I want to use the letters to invert the portion of the image below them. The only problem is that Elements doesn't let you fill live text with an adjustment layer. So we first have to convert the text to a layer mask filled with an Invert adjustment layer. Here's how:

- Press the Ctrl key and click the **End of the Road** item in the **Layers** palette. This selects the outlines of the letters.

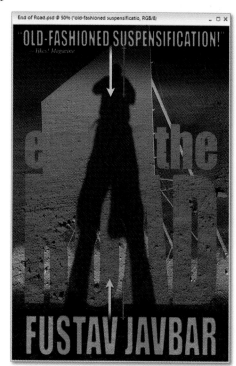
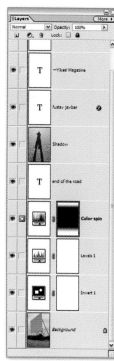

Figure 10-31.

- Click the ⬤ icon at the top of the Layers palette and choose the **Invert** command. Elements creates a new layer, called Invert 2, in front of the Color Spin layer. The selection outline disappears, replaced by a layer mask that traces the exact outlines of the book title.

- Click the **End of the Road** layer or press Alt+⬜ to make the text layer active.

- Press Ctrl+Shift+⬜ (or choose **Layer→Arrange→Bring to Front**) to pop the layer to the top of the stack.

- Click the 👁 in front of the **End of the Road** layer to hide the layer.

If the last few steps seem like a lot of busy work, take heart: They prepare you for the upcoming steps and get a few important housekeeping chores out of the way.

Figure 10-32.

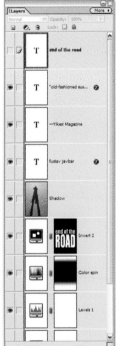

Shown in Figure 10-32, the effect is high in drama but low in legibility, particularly if we were to turn off the non-printing path outlines. One solution is to increase the contrast of the inversion effect, as in the next step.

12. *Add a Threshold adjustment layer.* Click the **Invert 2** layer to make it active. Press the Alt key and choose **Threshold** from the ⬤ icon at the bottom of the Layers palette. This displays the **New Layer** dialog box. Enter the name "Black or White" because the Threshold command changes all colors to either black or white. Then turn on the check box **Group with Previous Layer** (see Figure 10-33) to clip the new adjustment layer inside the letters of the Invert 2 shape layer.

Figure 10-33.

13. *Accept the default Threshold value.* Click the **OK** button to display the **Threshold** dialog box. Shown in Figure 10-34, this dialog box changes all luminosity values darker than the Threshold Level to black and all values lighter to white. A **Threshold Level** of 128 splits the colors right down the middle. Click **OK** to apply this setting.

Notice that rather than making the text layer black and white, the Threshold adjustment seems to have made it black and gravelly. The text is actually black and white; the Shadow layer above it is responsible for burning the gravel into the white areas.

14. *Apply an Inner Glow style to the Invert 2 layer.* Let's say you want to make the black portions of the text lighter. Click the **Invert 2** layer to make it active. Then apply an inner glow effect as follows:

   - Make sure the **Styles and Effects** palette is visible on screen. If it ain't, press the F7 key until it is.

   - Choose **Layer Styles** from the upper-left pop-up menu in the Styles and Effects palette. Then choose **Inner Glows** from the upper-right pop-up menu.

   - Click the **Heavy** thumbnail inside the palette. Elements fills the letters with a glow—well, almost.

   - Double-click the **𝒇** icon to the right of the Invert 2 layer in the **Layers** palette to display the **Style Settings** dialog box. Raise the **Inner Glow Size** value to 100 pixels, and then click the **OK** button. The glow now fills the letters in their entirety, as in Figure 10-35.

Figure 10-34.

Figure 10-35.

15. *Add a Drop Shadow layer style.* The text could use a little extra definition in the form of a drop shadow. Go to the Styles and Effects palette and do like so:

    - Choose **Drop Shadows** from the upper-right pop-up menu to display a list of predefined shadow styles.

    - Click the **Low** thumbnail to add a soft, subtle shadow to the existing Inner Glow style.

    - Double-click the ❼ to the right of the **Invert 2** layer in the Layers palette to display the **Style Settings** dialog box.

    - Change the **Lighting Angle** value to –90 degrees so that Photoshop Elements shines the light source from below and casts the shadow straight up.

    - Change the **Shadow Distance** value to 10 pixels.

    - Click the **OK** button to accept your spine-tingling drop shadow, shown in Figure 10-36.

Figure 10-36.

16. *Turn on the top layer and set the blend mode to Screen.* Click the **End of the Road** layer at the top of the **Layers** palette to make it active. Then choose **Screen** from the blend mode pop-up menu. In one simple operation, we manage to maintain the texture and detail from the Invert 2 layer and increase its legibility several times over, as witnessed in Figure 10-37 on the facing page.

The final task is to add a ghost to the book cover. The publisher has supplied the ghost in the form of a saved selection. (In case you're curious, the selection hails from a several hundred-year-old Navajo petroglyph. Seriously, those guys rocked.) We'll use this selection to create one last adjustment layer.

17. *Click the Color Spin layer in the Layers palette.* The ghost needs to rest between the various title layers and any adjustment layers that might otherwise modify it. In other words, it belongs behind the Invert 2 layer and in front of Color Spin.

18. *Load the Petroglyph selection outline.* Choose **Select→Load Selection**. In the Load Selection dialog box, select **Petroglyph** from the **Selection** pop-up menu (see Figure 10-38). Finally, click the **OK** button to invoke the ghostly selection outline.

19. *Add a Hue/Saturation adjustment layer.* To name the layer as you make it, press Alt as you choose **Hue/Saturation** from the ⊘ icon at the top of the Layers palette. Name the layer "Blue Man" and click the **OK** button. Then adjust the settings in the **Hue/Saturation** dialog box as follows (see Figure 10-39):

   • Turn on the **Colorize** check box.

   • Change the **Hue** to 220 degrees, a cobalt-blue that matches the color of the text.

   • Increase the **Saturation** to 100 percent.

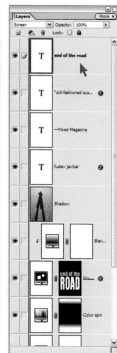

Figure 10-37.

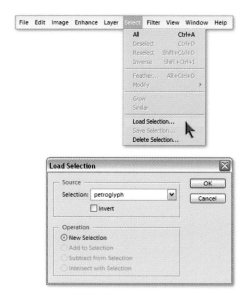

Figure 10-38.

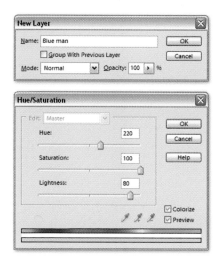

Figure 10-39.

- Raise the **Lightness** value to 80 percent. Usually, I recommend you steer clear of this clumsy option. But in this case, we're using Lightness not to correct colors but to create an effect. And in that regard, it works fine.

- Click the **OK** button to apply your settings.

20. ***Save your composition.*** Choose **File→Save As** and name the file "Best seller in Blue.psd." If you see the **Maximize Compatibility** check box, click **OK**. Notice that the Hue/Saturation adjustment subscribes to the confines of the Petroglyph selection outline. Elements manages this by converting the selection into a layer mask, as evident in the Layers palette in Figure 10-40.

From here on, all adjustment layers in this composition remain editable. If you decide you want to modify the settings for an adjustment layer, double-click the layer's thumbnail in the Layers palette. The appropriate dialog box will appear, complete with the settings currently in force. (The only exceptions are the two Invert layers, which have no settings.) You can also turn adjustment layers on and off, change their stacking order, and edit their masks.

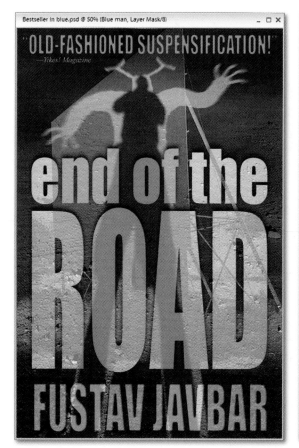

Figure 10-40.

WHAT DID YOU LEARN?

Match the key concept in the numbered list below with the letter of the phrase that best describes it. Answers appear upside-down at the bottom of the page.

Key Concepts

1. Layer style
2. Adjustment layer
3. Drop shadow
4. Parametric
5. Bevel Direction
6. Use Global Light
7. Group with Previous
8. Fill opacity
9. Gradient map
10. Color stop
11. Layer mask
12. Threshold

Descriptions

A. Available inside the Gradient Editor, this feature determines the placement of a color within the gradient.

B. This check box locks down the light source so that all directional layer styles in the composition cast highlights and shadows according to a consistent angle.

C. This powerful function lets you paint inside an adjustment layer to limit the portions of an image that are affected by that adjustment.

D. An adjustment layer that substitutes the luminosity values in the image with the colors in a gradient.

E. This layer style option makes a layer appear to rise toward you as opposed to recede.

F. Based on adjustable numerical settings and named options; layer styles and adjustment layers are examples.

G. A series of dynamic color and contour attributes that let you assign dimension, lighting, and texture to a layer.

H. This layer style offsets and blurs a silhouette of the active layer.

I. This command clips a layer so that it is only visible within the confines of the layer beneath it.

J. This feature lets you adjust the transparency of the pixels in a layer independently of the layer style.

K. This adjustment layer allows you to specify a luminosity level beyond which darker values are changed to black and lighter values are changed to white.

L. A collection of color adjustment settings that correct or modify the colors of the layers beneath them.

Answers

1G, 2L, 3H, 4F, 5E, 6B, 7I, 8J, 9D, 10A, 11C, 12K

SHARING YOUR PHOTOS

UNTIL FAIRLY RECENTLY, "sharing" photos meant bundling them into a 45-minute slide show and inflicting them on an innocent and undeserving audience of future ex-friends. The more merciful photo enthusiast might collect his or her prints into a photo album so that guests could tour them at their leisure. But the ancient conventions illustrated in Figure 11-1 are becoming increasingly uncommon and even unrealistic. Thanks to the proliferation of digital cameras, desktop scanners, and other varieties of capture devices, we create ten images for every one amassed by our parents. Many of us have too many photos to fit them into albums, and if we did, what casual visitor in his or her right mind would want to sift through them all?

Thankfully, today's notion of photo-sharing has expanded to keep up with our increasingly frenzied and eclectic habits. Certainly, we *can* print our photos; and under many circumstances, the printed snapshot remains our best and most practical image-sharing medium. (Which is why I devote the first exercise to the printing of single photographs.) But you can likewise group photos onto a page, email images to friends and colleagues, and collect the photos in an online gallery. Happily, photo-sharing is one of Photoshop Elements 3 for Windows' strongest and best developed features. Ecstatically, photo-sharing also happens to be the topic of the pages and video included with this lesson.

The old ways of sharing photos were quaint

Figure 11-1.

ABOUT THIS LESSON

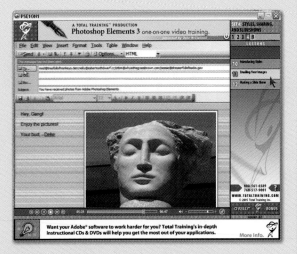

Project Files

Before beginning the exercises, make sure that you've installed the lesson files from the CD, as explained in Step 5 on page xv of the Preface. This should result in a folder called *Lesson Files-PE3 1on1* on your desktop. We'll be working with the files inside the *Lesson 11* subfolder.

This lesson explains ways to share your images with other people, whether by printing or distributing the electronic files online. You'll learn how to:

- Print an image from your PC to an inkjet printer and ensure both high quality output and accurate color. . . . . page 312

- Use photo-grade paper to produce film-quality output from an inexpensive inkjet printer . . . . . . page 318

- Combine multiple images onto a single page using the Organizer's Print command . . . . page 321

- Share pictures online for free using the Kodak EasyShare Gallery service . . . . page 329

Video Lesson 11: Emailing Your Images

Of all the ways Elements lets you share images with others, emailing is the most convenient. All you need is an email account and an Internet connection. No supplies, no mysterious printer settings, no new subscription fees. Your only concern is to fire off the photos to your various friends and associates; if they want to print them, that's their business.

Elements 3 prepares an email-friendly document with such aplomb that I devote an entire video lesson to the topic. Insert the CD, click the **Start** button, click Set 4 in the top-right corner of your screen, and select **11, Emailing Your Images** from the Lessons list. Even if you've never emailed an attachment before, this brief movie will have you sending out images in no time. During your 6-minute and 47-second journey, you'll learn about the following operations:

Operation	Keyboard equivalent or shortcut
Switch between one image and the next in the Editor workspace	Ctrl+Tab
Return to the Organizer workspace	Click the Photo Browser button
Display the Properties palette (for entering captions)	Alt+Enter
Zoom an image in the Organizer workspace	Double-click image thumbnail
Select multiple non-adjacent images	Ctrl-click image thumbnails
Email selected images in the Organizer	Ctrl+Shift+E
Send off your email to the recipients list	Alt+S

21st-Century Sharing

Don't get me wrong, nothing says you *have* to share your images. (In fact, you may prefer to keep your initial attempts at image editing to yourself.) But once you gain a sufficient degree of confidence, you'll want to let loved ones and just plain acquaintances see what you're up to. And no program—not even the professional-grade Photoshop CS2—lets you share with the ease and proficiency of Photoshop Elements. Figure 11-2 is an illustration of a supernova, but it gives you a rough sense of the approximately infinite ways in which Elements lets you share images. And besides, after spending two hours painting a supernova—in Elements, no less—there's no way I'm not using it in my book, however flimsy its relevance.

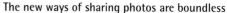

The new ways of sharing photos are boundless

Figure 11-2.

You and I will begin this lesson by printing an image directly from the well-worn and beloved Editor workspace. But to truly exploit sharing, we must return to the workspace that launched us on this journey, the Organizer. As I show you in Video Lesson 11, "Emailing Your Images," the Organizer can assemble pages of photos and transfer them directly to your favorite email program. The Organizer is also capable of packaging photos onto pages like those you get from a professional photo studio, as well as posting images online using Kodak's EasyShare Gallery. And if that's not enough, stay tuned for Lesson 12, where I show you how to make slide shows, postcards, video CDs, and a host of other creations. It's corny to say Elements gives you a universe of image-sharing options. But on a page that features a supernova, how could I resist?

Printing to an Inkjet Printer

When it comes to printing full-color photographic images, your best, most affordable solution is an inkjet printer. Available from Epson, Hewlett-Packard, and a cadre of others, a typical inkjet printer costs just a few hundred dollars. In return, you get printed images with outstanding color and definition (see the sidebar "Quality Comes at a Price" on page 318), better than you can achieve from your local commercial print house. However, you can't reproduce artwork for mass distribution from a color inkjet printout. Inkjet printers are strictly for personal use.

In the following exercise, you'll learn how to get the best results from your inkjet device. If you don't have a color inkjet printer, don't fret. You won't be able to follow along with every step of the exercise, but you'll get an idea of how the process works.

Assuming you have an inkjet device at your disposal, please load it with the best paper you have on hand, ideally a few sheets of glossy or matte-finish photo paper, readily available at any office supply store (again see "Quality Comes at a Price" for more information). If you don't have such paper, or if you simply don't feel like parting with the good stuff for this exercise, go ahead and load what you have. Just remember what kind of paper you loaded so you can address it properly in Steps 14 and 15 on page 316.

PEARL OF WISDOM

Obviously, I have no idea what printer you're using, so your experience may diverge from mine starting at Step 14, as I explain in the exercise. And I must leave it up to you to make sure your printer is set up properly and in working order. This means that the power is turned on, the printer is connected to your computer, print drivers and other software are installed, the printer is loaded with plenty of paper and ink, and the print head nozzles are clean. For more information on any of these issues, see the documentation that came with your printer.

1. *Open the test image.* Look in the *Lesson 11* folder inside *Lesson Files-PE3 1on1* and you'll find a file called *Y2K+10 invite.psd*. Pictured in Figure 11-3 on the facing page, this file hails from a wildly successful Y2K party some friends and I threw a few years back. In addition to making some adjustments for time—who knows what Y2010 has in store?—I expanded the range of hues and luminosity values to make it easier to judge the accuracy of our color prints. The image is sized at 4 by 5 inches with a resolution of 300 pixels per inch. But as you'll see, that can be changed to fit the medium.

2. *Choose the Flatten Image command.*
This file contains a photographic background composition as well as some text layers that I converted to pixels using Layer→Simplify Layer. While great for editability, layers require more computation and thus slow down the print process. Best solution: Get rid of them by choosing **Layer→Flatten Image**.

3. *Save the file under a different name.*
Naturally, you don't want to run the risk of harming the original layered image, so choose **File→Save As** or press the shortcut Ctrl+Shift+S. As long as you save the image under a different name, you're safe. But here are the settings that I recommend:

- In the Save As dialog box, select the option **TIFF (*.TIF; *.TIFF)** from the **Format** pop-up menu.

- Make sure the **ICC Profile: Adobe RGB (1998)** check box is on.

- Click the **Save** button.

- In the **TIFF Options** dialog box, click **LZW** to minimize the file size without harming the image.

- From **Byte Order**, select the platform you're using, presumably **IBM PC**.

- Click **OK** to save the file.

The original layered file is safe as houses and the flat file is ready to print.

4. *Choose the Print command.* Choose **File→Print** or press Ctrl+P. Elements displays the **Print with Preview** dialog box, which shows you how the image sits on the page, as in Figure 11-4.

Figure 11-3.

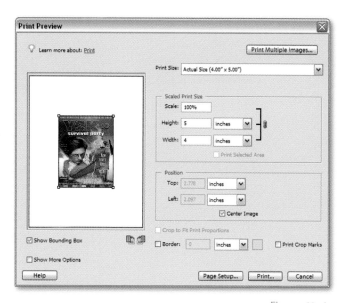

Figure 11-4.

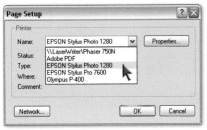

Figure 11-5.

5. *Click the Page Setup button.* Before going any further, it's important to specify the size and orientation of the paper that you'll be printing to. Click the **Page Setup** button to display the **Page Setup** dialog box.

6. *Select your printer model.* Next click the **Printer** button to display a second dialog box that still goes by the name of **Page Setup**, as shown in Figure 11-5. Choose the model of printer you want to use from the **Name** pop-up menu and click the **OK** button to return to the first Page Setup dialog box.

7. *Choose the desired paper size.* If you're using special photo paper, consult the paper's packaging to find out the physical page dimensions. In the case of my so-called Premium Glossy Photo Paper, for example, each piece of paper measures 8 by 10 inches, slightly smaller than the letter-size format. Whatever the paper size, choose it from the **Size** pop-up menu in the **Paper** section of the Page Setup dialog box. Then click the **OK** button to close the Page Setup dialog box and return to the **Print with Preview** window.

8. *Select the Fit On Page option.* The **Print Size** option at the top of the dialog box is probably set to Actual Size (4.00" × 5.00"). Click the pop-up menu and change it to **Fit On Page** to expand the image to fill the maximum printable portion of the page. Note that Elements does not resample the image; it merely lowers the resolution value so that the pixels print larger. This way, you don't waste any of your expensive paper by, say, printing a tiny image smack dab in the middle of the page.

PEARL OF WISDOM

You may notice a warning that tells you that the image will now print at less than 220 pixels per inch. This might lead you to believe that 220 ppi is a resolution threshold, above which the image looks good and below which it looks bad. Not so. It's a ballpark figure, and a rough one at that. Assuming you follow my advice in the remaining steps, your image will look fine.

The Editor workspace's Print command prints a single image file per piece of paper. If you want to print multiple images at a time, you can click the Print Multiple Images button, which switches you to the Organizer and chooses that workspace's more versatile Print command, as discussed in the "Printing Multiple Pictures" exercise on page 321.

9. *Turn on the Show More Options check box.* The bulk of the options in the Print with Preview dialog box are devoted to helping you position and scale the image on the page. But even more important are a pair of options that can be displayed only by selecting **Show More Options** below the image preview. (If the check box is already on, all the merrier.)

10. *Confirm the source and printer spaces.* Direct your attention to the **Color Management** options, which I've circled in Figure 11-6. These options control how Photoshop Elements converts the colors in the image from your screen to your printer. To print the colors as accurately as possible, you must identify the *source space*—the color space used by the image itself—and the *destination space* employed by the printer software.

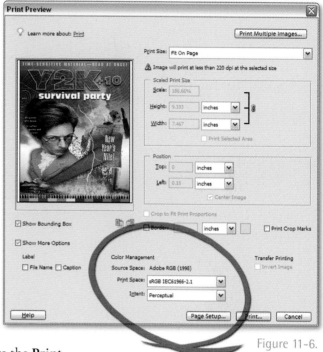

Figure 11-6.

- Below Color Management you will see the words **Source Space: Adobe RGB (1998)**. This correctly identifies the variety of RGB employed by the *Y2K+10 invite* image file.

- I have yet to encounter an inkjet printer that is calibrated to use a color space other than *sRGB*, the standard RGB space embraced by all varieties of consumer-level hardware. To accommodate this popular trend, make sure the **Print Space** option is set to **sRGB IEC61966-2.1**. Do *not* change this setting to Same As Source or Printer Color Management. Although both of these options may sound like better choices, sRGB is the universal standard and is more likely to ensure agreement with your printer.

- Change the **Intent** option to **Perceptual**, which maintains the smoothest transitions when converting colors—the best solution for photographic images.

Figure 11-6 shows the dialog box as it should appear up to this point. Only the dimmed Scaled Print Size values may read differently, to reflect the different dimensions of your paper.

11. *Click the Print button.* This closes the print preview window and sends you on to the main **Print** dialog box.

12. *Verify that the right printer is selected.* It's unlikely that anything has changed since Step 6, but as long as we're here, it's worth a glance just to be sure.

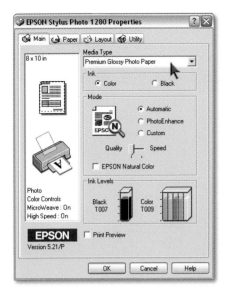

Figure 11-7.

13. *Display the specific properties for your printer.* Click the **Properties** button to display the options defined by your specific printer's driver software. From here on, things vary fairly significantly from one model of printer to another, but I'll do my best to make sure everything makes sense.

14. *Indicate the kind of paper loaded into your printer.* Look for an option called **Media Type** or the like. In my case, I changed Media Type to **Premium Glossy Photo Paper** (see the arrow cursor in Figure 11-7), which happens to be a literal match of the name listed on the paper's original packaging (see the second figure on page 318). If possible, try to find a literal match for your brand of paper as well.

15. *Select the highest print quality for your printer.* This assumes you're printing to photo-grade paper. If not, choose a lower setting. The quality setting can be hard to find, so you may have to do a bit of digging. I had to forage through the following options, illustrated by the numbered items in Figure 11-8:

- I first selected **Custom** from the **Mode** options (labeled ❶ in Figure 11-8). This gave me access to a more sophisticated set of options.

- Then I clicked the **Advanced** button (❷) to enter yet another dialog box, pictured on the right side of the figure.

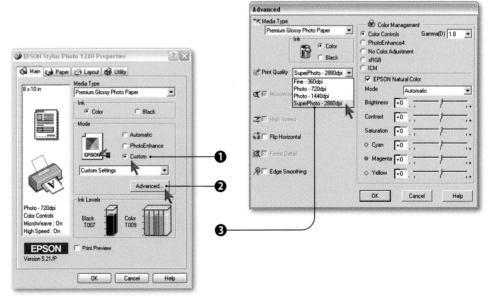

Figure 11-8.

- There, I found the option I was looking for, **Print Quality**. I set it to the printer's maximum, **SuperPhoto–2880dpi** (labeled ❸ in the figure).

Once you've selected the right paper and the correct print resolution, all that's left is to select the most accurate means of reproducing the colors.

16. *Select the best color management method.* In Step 10, you told Elements how to convert the RGB colors in the image to the color space used by the printer. Now you're presented with the trickier proposition of explaining to the printer's software how it should convert colors from the RGB space to CMYK.

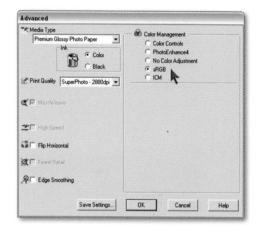

Figure 11-9.

Not all printer manufacturers permit you to modify the color management method. And those that do often offer paltry controls. As it turns out, Epson's printer drivers do about the best job of it, as illustrated in Figure 11-9. Still inside the **Advanced** dialog box, I found a series of **Color Management** radio buttons. Most required me to mess with imprecise slider bars and image comparisons. But by selecting **sRGB**, I was able to identify sRGB as the source space for the color after it leaves Photoshop Elements. From there, it was up to the printing software to do the work. (As a second-best solution, I could have selected ICM, which would have used the color matching software built into the Windows operating system.)

Quality Comes at a Price

Inkjet printers are cheap, often sold at or below cost. But the *consumables*—the paper and the ink—are expensive, easily outpacing the cost of the hardware after a few hundred prints. Unfortunately, this is one area where it doesn't pay to pinch pennies. Simply put, the consumables dictate the quality of your inkjet output. Throwing money at consumables doesn't necessarily ensure great output, but scrimping guarantees bad output.

Consider the following scenario:

- Of the handful of inkjet devices I own, my current favorite is my Epson Stylus Photo 1280. A modern equivalent retails for about $400. Given that it can print as many as 2880 dots per inch, that's a heck of a deal.

- The Stylus Photo 1280 requires two ink cartridges, pictured below. The first cartridge holds black ink; the second contains five colors, including two shades of cyan, two shades of magenta, and yellow. (As the reasoning goes, the lighter cyan and magenta better accommodate deep blues, greens, and flesh tones.) Together, the cartridges cost about $60 and last for 45 to 120 letter-sized prints, depending on the quality setting you choose. The higher the setting, the more ink the printer consumes. So the ink alone costs 50¢ to $1.33 per page.

- You can print to regular photocopier-grade paper. But while such paper is inexpensive, it's also porous, sopping up ink like a paper towel. To avoid over-inking, you have to print at low resolutions, so the output tends to look substandard—about as good as a color photo printed in a newspaper.

- To achieve true photo-quality prints that rival those from a commercial film processor, you need to use *photo-grade paper* (or simply *photo paper*), which increases your costs even further. For example, 20 sheets of the stuff in the packet below costs $13.50, or about 67¢ a sheet.

The upshot: a low-quality plain-paper print costs about 50 cents; a high-quality photo-paper print costs about 2 bucks. Although the latter is roughly four times as expensive, the difference in quality is staggering. The figure below compares details from the two kinds of output magnified to 6 times their printed size. The plain-paper image is coarse, riddled with thick printer dots and occasional horizontal scrapes where the paper couldn't hold the ink. Meanwhile, the photo-paper image is so smooth, you can clearly make out the image pixels. Where inkjet printing is concerned, paper quality and ink expenditure are the great determining factors.

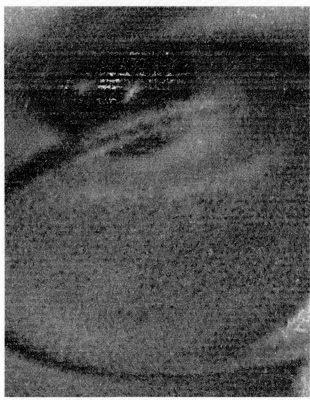

360 dots per inch, plain paper, 50¢

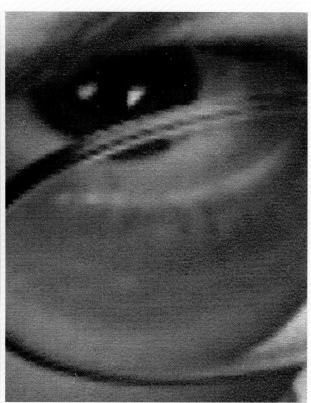

2880 dpi, glossy photo paper, $2⁰⁰

17. *Save your settings.* Whether you can save a collection of print settings depends on the software provided by your printer. In the case of my Epson device, I clicked the **Save Settings** button in the Advanced dialog box and assigned the settings a name, such as "Premium hi-res."

18. *Send the print job on its way.* You may have to exit a few dialog boxes to apply your changes. I had to click two **OK** buttons to navigate my way back up to the **Print** dialog box, and then click **OK** again to start the job printing.

19. *Wait and compare.* It takes a long time (usually several minutes) to print a high-quality image from an inkjet printer. But thanks to the miracle of background printing, you can continue to use Photoshop Elements and even get a head start on the next exercise. When the print job finishes, compare it to the image on screen. Assuming that your printer is functioning properly (no jams, no paper flaws, all inks intact, no missing lines in the output), the colors in the printout should bear a healthy resemblance to those in the image that you see on your computer monitor.

But there are always variations. On the facing page, Figure 11-10 shows two versions of the same image printed to photo-grade paper from my Stylus Photo 1280. The only difference is the color management that I used to print the image.

- The image printed using the sRGB setting is darker and bluer than the other one. But it also happens to be a very close match to what I saw on my screen. Therefore, the result is a rousing success.

- I printed the second image using Microsoft's ICM color matching. Although this version more closely matches the previous figures in this book, it strays from the image's appearance on my monitor. So I would call it the less successful print.

PEARL OF WISDOM

If the output doesn't match the screen image to your satisfaction, try experimenting with your printer-specific options (those covered in Steps 14 through 16) until you arrive at a better result. When you do, write the settings down for future reference.

sRGB (dark, a bit blue)

ICM (lighter, slightly cyan)

Figure 11-10.

Printing Multiple Pictures

Now that you've successfully printed a single image to your inkjet printer, it's time to learn how to print multiple photos at a time. Turns out, this is nothing short of a minor miracle. Adobe limits the senior and more expensive Photoshop CS2 to printing a single image to a single page, and yet it blesses the supposedly lesser Photoshop Elements 3 with the ability to group multiple images at a time and even print a sequence of images, all without preparing a special file in advance (which is Photoshop's way). Does that make Photoshop Elements better than Photoshop CS2? In this particular regard, yes it does.

Multiple photo printing is the exclusive domain of the Organizer. Even if you begin your work in the Editor, Elements transfers you to the Organizer. So whether you want to assemble quick-and-dirty proof sheets or make the most of your expensive inkjet paper, Elements does a superb job of fitting different sized images onto a page—which is precisely what we'll do in this next exercise.

1. *Open the PE3 1on1 catalog in the Organizer.* Most likely, the *PE3 1on1* catalog that you created at the outset of Lesson 1 (see "Getting Photos into Elements," Step 2, page 6) remains the active catalog in the Organizer workspace. If not, please open it now by going to the Organizer, choosing **File→Catalog**, clicking the **Open** button, and locating the *PE3 1on1.psa* file.

2. *Open a few images in the Editor.* To ensure that this exercise appears on your screen just as it does in this book, I need you to follow these directions exactly:

   • First, make sure the Editor workspace is up on screen. (If you're still in the Organizer, press Ctrl+I to switch; there's no need to select a thumbnail in the photo browser.)

   • Close any images open in the Editor workspace.

   • Choose **File→Open** or press Ctrl+O. Go to the *Lesson 11* folder. Then click the *Burton bugs.jpg* file (it's important you click this one first) and Ctrl+click *Puppet puppet.jpg*.

   • Click the **Open** button to make the two images appear on screen. If one overlaps the other, don't worry about it.

3. *Choose the Print Multiple Photos command.* Choose **File→ Print Multiple Photos** or press Ctrl+Alt+P. Photoshop Elements launches the Organizer (assuming it wasn't running already) and displays the **Print Photos** dialog box shown in Figure 11-11. The two images from the Editor appear in a column on the left side

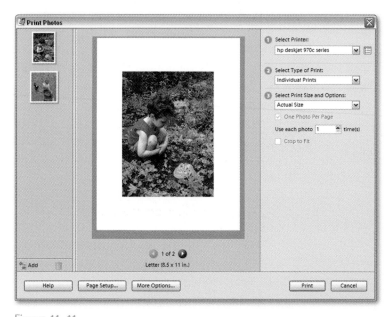

Figure 11-11.

of the dialog box. You'll also see one or both of the images positioned inside the large preview window in the middle of the dialog box. To the right, you'll find the Organizer's three-step printing method. But don't rush right into step 1; the actual first step is to make sure you've successfully amassed all the photos you want to print.

4. *Add an image from the catalog.* Click the **Add** button in the lower-left corner of the dialog box to display the dialog box in Figure 11-12. The left-hand column of options lets you specify the images you want to add to the print queue. By default, Elements selects Photo Bin because the two photos that we've chosen thus far are open inside the Editor workspace's photo bin. The four other options work as follows:

Figure 11-12.

- Photo Browser lets you add a photo from those currently displayed in the Organizer's browser window. If you're viewing the results of a tag search, not all the photos in the catalog will be available.

- The Entire Catalog option gives you access to all the photos in the catalog, whether they appear in the photo browser or not.

- If you created any collections, the Collection radio button gives you access to them.

- If you want to add an image and you remember assigning a tag to it, select the Tag option to specify a tag and find the associated images.

For our purposes, I want you to select **Entire Catalog**. The contents of the *PE3 1on1* catalog appear on the right side of the dialog box. Click the check box next to the first thumbnail, the saber-toothed tiger skull, as in Figure 11-13. Then click **Add Selected Photos** at the bottom of the dialog box. The check mark for the skull goes away and the dialog box remains open, so naturally you think Elements is ignoring you. But not so; the photo has been added to the queue.

Figure 11-13.

Figure 11-14.

5. *Add a tagged photo.* Select the **Tag** option from the left side of the dialog box. Next choose **Max** from the associated menu to limit your view to those images that include the Max tag. Click to place a check by the thirteenth thumbnail, which shows Max wearing a crown (see Figure 11-14), and then click **OK**. Elements adds the two photos to the left column of the Print Photos dialog box (see Figure 11-15).

If you add a photo to the print queue by mistake, simply select the photo in the Print Photos dialog box and click the little trashcan icon in the bottom-left corner of the dialog box. To add more photos, click the Add button and repeat Steps 4 and 5 as the mood hits you.

6. *Choose your printer.* Choose the printer you'll be using from the **Select Printer** pop-up menu on the right side of the dialog box (identified by a gray ❶). Click the 📑 icon to the right of the menu (circled red in Figure 11-15) to display your printer's Properties dialog box, which lets you specify the print quality, paper type, and color management settings. See Steps 14 through 16 on pages 316 and 317 for more information.

Figure 11-15.

7. *Specify the printing layout.* By a remarkable twist of logic, Elements lets you print multiple images in multiple ways. To pick a way, choose an option from the **Select Type of Print** pop-up menu (labeled ❷ in the dialog box). Here are your choices:

- Choose the Individual Prints option to print your many images to many pieces of paper. You can specify the size of the photos, how many to print per page, and how many copies of each image you want to print. Use the ◐ and ◑ buttons under the large preview area in the middle of the dialog box to navigate from page to page.

- The Contact Sheet option prints small thumbnail images of the selected files, which is helpful if you want to check colors before committing to larger prints, add pages to a printed catalog, or make a hard copy of a recent photo session. You specify the number of columns you want on a page, and the Organizer adjusts the size of the thumbnails and the number of pages to make everything fit.

- Choose Picture Package to print multiple copies of one or more images onto your printed pages. Designed to accommodate portrait photographers who routinely need to print common picture sizes onto cut sheets that they can sell to their clients, I for one use it anytime I want to print multiple images at a time.

- Labels gives you access to several layouts designed to perfectly align your images to Avery-brand label sheets.

If for no other reason than that I regard it to be the most flexible of the multi-image printing functions, choose the **Picture Package** option.

8. *Dismiss the warning.* If this is your first time visiting the Picture Package option, Elements warns you that the images will print at resolutions of "less than 220 dpi at the requested print size." This extremely misleading message implies that your images don't contains enough pixels; in fact, they have plenty of pixels. Meanwhile, the Organizer tends to downsample images to 220 pixels per inch to accelerate the printing process no matter what. So what is the sense of this warning? Rhetorical, for there's nothing you can do about it. Click **OK**, as you see me doing with some small aggression in Figure 11-16.

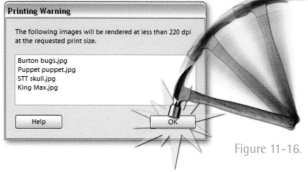

Figure 11-16.

9. *Choose your desired layout grid.* Pop-up menu ❸, **Select a Layout**, lets you choose from 15 ways of organizing photos on the page. Choose the first option, **Letter (1) 5×7 (2) 2.5×3.5 (4) 2×2.5**, to see the layout pictured in Figure 11-17. The Organizer takes a stab at placing each of the selected photos inside the layout. *Burton bugs.jpg* fills the one 5×7 slot; the puppet and skull fill the two 2½×3½ slots; and *King Max.jpg* fills one of the four 2×2½ slots, leaving the other three empty.

If you don't like the placement of the photos within the layout grid—maybe you wanted the 5×7 to be *Puppet puppet.jpg*—you can adjust this later. Choosing your layout grid simply tells the Organizer how many of what sized photos you want, whether it's two 5×7's or twenty 2×2's.

Figure 11-17.

10. *Set the remaining options.* Set the **Select a Frame** option to **None**. Leave **One Photo Per Page** turned off. And turn on **Crop to Fit**. For those of you who want to know what the heck you're doing, I provide the following details:

- The Select a Frame option allows you to choose a frame for the perimeter of each photo in your picture package. These frames run from fairly stylish (Painted Edge) to downright kitschy (Strawberry Patch). Just keep in mind that the frame encircles every photo you print, so make sure you choose a frame that works well for all photos, not just one. Also note that the frame takes up some amount of space, resulting in a cropped image.

PEARL OF WISDOM

Don't count on being able to maintain a white border around each photo, whether you add frames or not. Some layouts force the Organizer to print photographs with the edges flush against each other.

- When turned on, the One Photo Per Page check box generates a separate page for each selected photo and fills each page with multiple copies of that single photo, great for creating various sizes of a single photo. Remarkably, it's still possible to swap out different photos within each page's layout, as we'll see shortly. But as I say, for this exercise, leave the check box off.

- Finally, turn on Crop to Fit to shave away the height or width of a photo so that it conforms to the aspect ratio of the slot it occupies. The best way to understand this is to turn the Crop to Fit check box on and off and watch the effect this has on the preview. The difference is most obvious in the case of *Puppet puppet.jpg.* When Crop to Fit is on, the image appears larger on the page and the nearly square aspect of the original photo is cropped on the sides (see Figure 11-18). This option makes quick work of fitting photos to the dimensions of a real-life store-bought frame, so turn it on.

Figure 11-18.

11. *Arrange the photos within the layout grid.* Now that all the other decisions have been made, it's time to place our photos the way we want them within the layout grid:

- Let's say we want our picture package to contain one 5 by 7-inch print of *Puppet puppet.jpg* and one 2½ by 3½-inch print of *Burton bugs.jpg*. To accomplish this, drag one of these two photos in the central preview window and drop it onto the other. The images switch places.

- I want the other 2½×3½ slot to contain *King Max.jpg*. So drag Max and drop him onto the skull photo to switch these two images.

- Now I want to fill the four 2×2½ slots with two skull images and two of the curly-haired Burton. Drag the skull from the left column and drop it to the right of the skull thumbnail in the preview window; a green outline shows you where the photo will appear. Then drag Burton a couple of times from the left column into each of the remaining 2×2½ slots. Confused? Then just drag around thumbnails until your layout looks the one in Figure 11-19.

1 of 1
Letter (8.5 x 11 in.)

Figure 11-19.

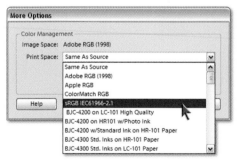

Figure 11-20.

12. *Set your color management preferences.* Click the **More Options** button at the bottom of the dialog box to display another dialog box, as shown in Figure 11-20. As you learned in the preceding exercise, sRGB is the standard color space for the vast majority of inkjet printers. (If there's an exception that's been manufactured in the last three years, I'd like to know about it. I know, I know, I'm repeating myself. But broken records aren't the only ones with repeating choruses.) So choose **sRGB IEC61966-2.1** from the **Print Space** pop-up menu and click **OK**.

13. *Print the images.* All that's left is to click the **Print** button in the bottom-right corner of the dialog box. A few moments later, you'll have hard copy. Or if you don't want to waste paper, click Cancel instead. Who knows, maybe you don't want to waste ink and paper printing pictures of children and puppets you don't even know. Some people are weird that way.

PEARL OF WISDOM

When you click the Print button, the Print Photos dialog box closes and you lose your layout. So be sure to select the correct number of copies in your printer options before you send the photographs on their merry way.

Sharing Pictures Online

Printing is a local sharing solution. Someone visits your home or office, you have some extra photos of the young and dear ones, and you offer them with the gladdest of tidings. So what about the remote relations? In the old days, you could toss a few snapshots in an envelope and mail them. But that was when a postage stamp cost a fifth what it costs today (see Figure 11-21) and the Postal Service accounted for the transmission of most of the country's personal missives. These days, 37 cents and slow delivery just can't compete with the alternatives.

Online is the cheaper, speedier alternative. And wouldn't you know it, Photoshop Elements 3 for Windows helps you take advantage of this trend. Thanks to an online partnership between Adobe and Kodak, you can post photos from an Organizer catalog to an online album. At the time of this writing, there was no subscription fee to join the EasyShare Gallery. You just add your name to a list, and away you go. And your loved ones don't even have to do that. All they need to view your latest snapshots are a computer, an Internet connection, and a bit of curiosity.

In 1969, love was free and postage was cheap

Nowadays, love is priceless and stamps cost more

Figure 11-21.

The name of Kodak's service is the EasyShare Gallery (formerly called Ofoto, as you'll see in the figures). It lets you initiate an account, create an online album, notify friends about your pictures via email, and edit your album at a later date. In this exercise, we'll create an online album from three of the Victoria and Albert museum photos already contained in the *PE3 1on1* catalog. If you decide to email an announcement to a friend, feel free to lie and say that you shot the pictures on a recent weekend getaway to London. With all that money you saved not buying stamps, you can afford it.

PEARL OF WISDOM

Although Adobe for the present endorses EasyShare Gallery, and Kodak offers reasonably priced print services, you can find—and may even have accounts with—a large number of similar online photo-sharing operations. This exercise is intended as an introduction to the general topic of online photo sharing, pure and simple. Also note that unlike the relatively immutable and enduring Elements software on your hard drive, an online service is fluid, so EasyShare Gallery might change by the time you try out the steps. Fortunately, it behooves Kodak to keep the process easy (as the name implies), so you should be able to navigate around the differences.

1. *Select three photos in the Organizer.* Make sure the PE3 1on1 catalog that you used in the last exercise remains active in the Organizer. (Again, if it isn't, open it using File→Catalog.) Then click and Shift-click to select the three statue photos that I've circled in Figure 11-22.

Figure 11-22.

2. *Start the online-sharing process.* Click the **Share** button in the shortcuts bar and choose **Share Online**. After a moment, the screen shown in Figure 11-23 appears. In case you hadn't guessed it already, you're online.

PEARL OF WISDOM

Notice the ad on the left telling you that you can order Kodak prints. This is how Kodak makes money from its EasyShare Gallery, so this won't be the last time you see the ad. Also notice that my screen bears the Ofoto logo. Kodak was in the process of changing the service name at the same time this book hit the press. You'll see the EasyShare Gallery logo instead.

3. *Fill out the form.* To share your photos, Kodak requires you to create a free account.

   • For a **First Name**, enter whatever you want to be called, whether it's your actual name or a nickname like Scooter. But be warned that your email announcements will trumpet a new "Photo Album from Scooter," so choose your name carefully. (Case in point, here—look what my folks called me.)

- Next enter your **Email Address**. If you use America Online, note that you have to place "@aol.com" at the end of your screen name.

- Enter a **Password** at least six characters in length. The password is case-sensitive, so avoid capital letters unless you want to type them each time you enter the password.

- After confirming your password, you have a series of check boxes to contend with. Check **Remember my password** if you don't want to reenter it each time you go online. The only drawback to this option is that anyone with access to your computer could go online and order a zillion dollars' worth of photos in your name. If that doesn't seem likely in your case, select the check box.

- The next couple of check boxes reflect how much you want to be bothered—oops, make that *contacted*—by email from Kodak and Adobe. If you don't want the junk mail—er, *offers* and *promotions*—turn off those check boxes, but know that there's always the possibility you might miss out on a sales coupon or some similar promotion.

- Finally, you have to agree to the terms of service by selecting the final check box. Click the blue **Terms of Service** link if you want to actually read the rules and regulations you're agreeing to. Without this option selected, things will grind to a total halt. And we don't want that.

When you've set everything up the way you want it, click the **Next** button in the lower-right corner of the screen to advance to the **Share Online** screen, shown in Figure 11-24.

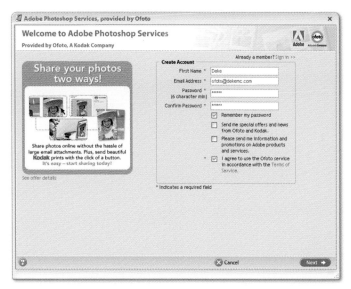

Figure 11-23.

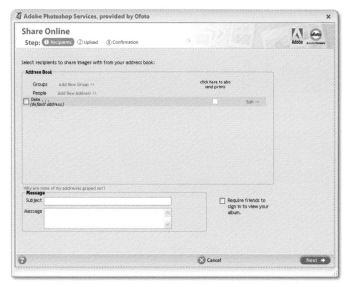

Figure 11-24.

4. *Specify the recipients of your email announcement.* Your next task is to input the contact information for the people you want to notify about your album. If you watched Video Lesson 11, "Emailing Your Images" (see page 310), you may recall that Elements maintains an email address book. Wouldn't it be great if you had access to that same address book here online? Yes, it would, but unfortunately you don't. You have to build a new address book to share photos via Kodak. A bummer to be sure, but let's get down to it.

   • Click the blue **Add New Address** link and you're taken to the screen in Figure 11-25. Fill in the first name and email address of your friend. As the red asterisks indicate, these are the only two bits of info you're required to enter. (You need to fill in the other fields only if you want to send prints to your friend.) We're not going to create any groups, so skip everything else and click **Next**.

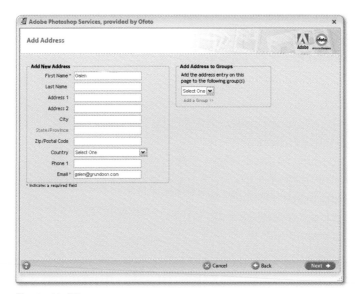

Figure 11-25.

   • Your new contact now appears in the Address Book section, just below your name. Click both check boxes in front of the names to indicate that you want to email notifications of your new album to you and your friend. (You'll want an email for closure—just so you know, you know?)

   Note that both names include an Edit link so you can edit the name and address information. Your friend's info includes a trash icon in case you guys split up or your friend issues a restraining order.

If you're feeling ambitious, enter a few more email addresses and add them to a group. An email group enables you to email photo links to an entire collection of people at once. To do this, click the Add New Group link. Then click Add New Group again, enter the name of your group, and click OK. You can then select the check boxes next to the names of the people you want to add to the group, click the Add to Group button, and the job is done. Just remember to click Back at the bottom of the screen to return to the Share Online window.

5. *Enter a subject and a message.* The **Message** section at the bottom of the Share Online screen lets you enter a subject and message for your email. Type whatever you like here. For my part, I set the Subject to "My trip to London" and the Message to "Snapped these at the Victoria and Albert Museum. Pip pip! Cheerio!" But that's just me.

6. *Activate the security feature, if you like.* Turning on the **Require friends to sign in to view your album** check box requires your friends to log into the EasyShare Gallery service to view your photos. This may sound like nothing more than a bonus for Kodak, but it's actually a security function that keeps the uninvited from crashing in on your album. Then again, how's anyone going to know the address for your album unless they get your email? So it's up to you. For the present, leave it off and click **Next**.

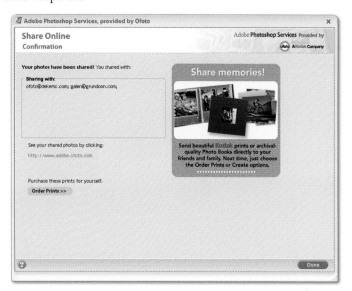

A progress bar appears to show that Elements is uploading the photos, one by one, from your computer to Kodak's remote servers. This screen is most noteworthy because it fails to provide you with any way to order prints.

Finally, you'll see the confirmation screen shown in Figure 11-26. Note that you can click an Order Prints button to order prints. I myself have problems seeing brightly colored buttons and ads, so I was worried you'd miss it.

Figure 11-26.

7. *View your online album.* Click the blue **http://www** link to launch your Web browser and view your online album.

- The EasyShare Gallery might ask you to log in. If so, click the appropriate button and cheerfully enter the requested email address and password.

- EasyShare should then greet you with a screen that shows the photo album you created, like the one in Figure 11-27. You may also see a photo album created by Kodak employees that shows how attractive their children are. (I mean, what is with these folks who want to show you pictures of their kids all the time? The nerve of some people.)

- Click the album you created, and thumbnails for the three photos in the album appear as in Figure 11-28 on the facing page. Clicking one of these thumbnails takes you to a new page with a larger view of that image. But for the present, forgo that action so we can examine the right-hand column of links in the next step.

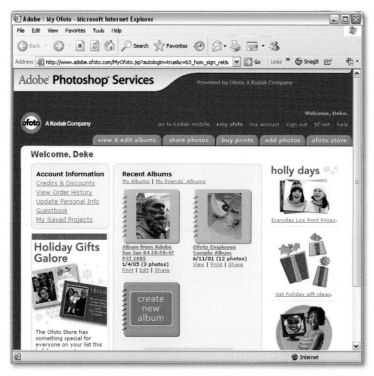

Figure 11-27.

8. *Experiment with the links on the right.* Because Kodak's site is in a state of transition, the links along the right edge of your browser window may change in name and order. But just so you have an idea of what you can do, here's a rundown of the links I encountered:

- You probably think we've all had enough fun with the Buy Prints link for one book. You'd be wrong.

- Share This Album takes you to a screen of more or less the same options that we saw back in Step 4. The upshot is that you can send notifications to people even after your album is created and online, great for adding folks whom you may have missed.

- The Add Photos link takes you to a page featuring a large window where it's possible to drag and drop photos straight from the Organizer (or anywhere on your hard drive) into the album. You might need to do a bit of software downloading and plug-in canoodling, but once you do, you have yourself an amazingly convenient way to add photos to an album.

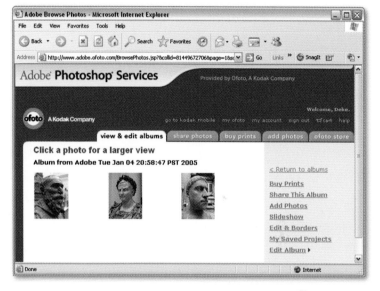

Figure 11-28.

- Slideshow opens a new window that plays a simple slide show of the album's images. Why, yes, you can order printed photos from this window. Thanks for asking.

- The Edit & Borders link allows you to apply simple image editing commands, effects, and borders to your image. Hopefully, you've learned enough ways to accomplish these tasks using Photoshop Elements' infinitely more powerful tools that you're not tempted to select this link.

- The My Saved Projects link allows you to view any saved creations that you made in the Organizer and uploaded for printing. We'll learn all about creations in Lesson 12, "Slide Shows and Other Creations."

Feel free to experiment with these options until you've exhausted your enthusiasm for them. Then click the **Edit Album** link to display an additional list of links that allow you to edit your album in detail.

9. *Edit the order of the images.* Clicking the Edit Album link twirls open a list of six additional links, which work as follows:

- Update Album Details opens a floating window where you can rename the album, provide a description, and change the creation date (even to a date the future).

- Add Photo Titles lets you enter a name that will appear under each photo when you click its thumbnail to see the larger view.

- Copy Photos allows you to add copies of pictures to other albums you may have created, or to create a new album on the spot that contains the copied photos.

- Use the Rearrange Photos link to determine the order in which the images appear in your album. The first photo also gets the honored cover spot when you view all your albums, as we saw back in Figure 11-27. We'll rearrange our photos in just a moment.

- The Delete Photos and Delete Album links are your friends when it comes time to pare your online contributions. As with everything, you have to keep it fresh.

Figure 11-29.

Now that you have the rundown, click the **Rearrange Photos** link to display the window pictured in Figure 11-29. As the instructions explain, you can drag the thumbnails to rearrange the images. Let's promote the last image to the first slot. To do so, drag the last thumbnail—the one of the guy with the stitched face—and drop it on the first one. The stitched fellow assumes the first position and the other two scoot over. Now click the **save** button. Finally, click the white **view & edit albums** tab to see how the stitched guy has made the cover of our album, as in Figure 11-30. Kinda makes you want to order a print of it, doesn't it?

Oh, by the way. Don't forget to check your email to see the announcement you sent yourself. And be ready to regale your friends with a few stories when they ask you all about your trip to London.

Album from Adobe
Tue Jan 04 20:58:47
PST 2005
1/4/05 (3 photos)

Figure 11-30.

WHAT DID YOU LEARN?

Match the key concept in the numbered list below with the letter
of the phrase that best describes it. Answers appear upside-down
at the bottom of the page.

Key Concepts

1. Print with Preview
2. Page Setup
3. Fit on Page
4. Source space
5. Destination space
6. sRGB
7. Perceptual
8. Contact Sheet
9. Picture Package
10. Crop to Fit
11. Ordering prints
12. Album

Descriptions

A. A standardized color space embraced by most consumer-level hardware, including nearly all brands of inkjet printers.

B. When printing from the Organizer, choose this option from the Select Type of Print list to combine multiple copies of one or more images onto your printed pages.

C. This Picture Package option crops the height or width of a photo to make it conform to the aspect ratio of the slot that it occupies.

D. With the Kodak EasyShare Gallery, you can create an online version of one of these to share your photos with distant friends and relatives.

E. This Intent option in the Print with Preview dialog box maintains the smoothest transitions when converting colors and is the best choice for photographic images.

F. When printing, this signifies the color space used by the image.

G. This Print with Preview option expands the image to fill the maximum printable portion of the paper.

H. The color space employed by the printer software.

I. This dialog box allows you to specify the desired printer, as well as the paper size and orientation.

J. This exciting online service is the Kodak EasyShare Gallery's worst-kept secret.

K. When printing from the Organizer, this Select Type of Print option prints small thumbnail images of the selected files.

L. When printing from the Editor, this dialog box shows you how the image will sit on the page.

Answers

1L, 2I, 3G, 4F, 5H, 6A, 7E, 8K, 9B, 10C, 11J, 12D

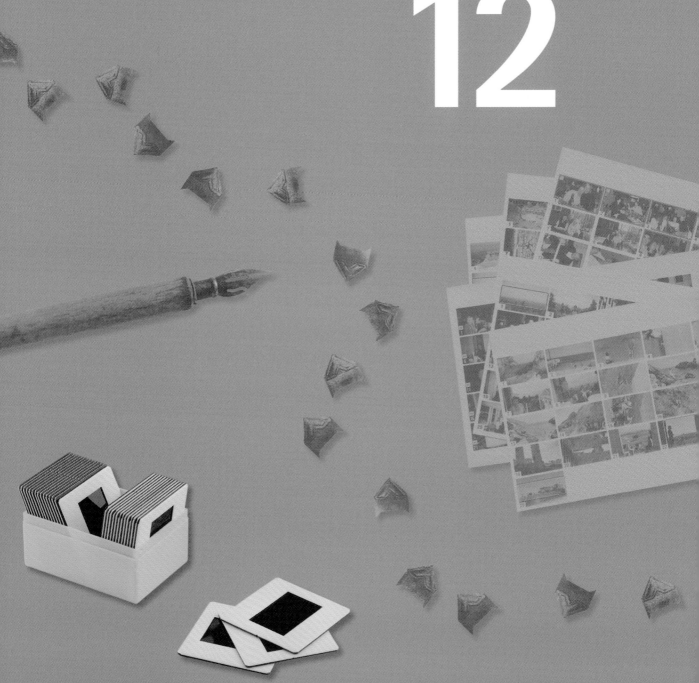

SLIDE SHOWS
AND OTHER CREATIONS

AFTER 20 YEARS in the computer graphics business, I've grown accustomed to the miracles of technology. So every once in a while, I may come off as a bit jaded in my views. Just the same, I remain captivated by Photoshop Elements, especially the features of the program that are absent from the senior Photoshop CS2. Given that the latter costs so much more, it almost defies belief that Elements offers so much as a single function that's missing from Photoshop CS2, let alone an entire group of functions, particularly a group of functions as useful and just plain fun as creations. But bleach my jade and color me amazed, it's true. Across the wide range of Adobe graphics applications, creations are unique to Photoshop Elements 3 for Windows.

Creation is Adobe's catch-all term for any media project that includes one or more images. It might be an on-screen slide show, a photo album, a Web site, or even something as essential as a wall calendar (see Figure 12-1). Elements provides the templates, you provide the photos, and together you and Elements assemble the finished projects.

My guess is, Adobe is loathe to build creations or the like into Photoshop CS2 for fear that professionals will write off the application as pandering to consumers and enthusiasts. But as a professional, I need at least one wall calendar every year. And I'd rather see images that have meaning to me than swimwear models, Dilbert cartoons, or Thomas Kinkade paintings. Thankfully I have Elements.

Figure 12-1.

ABOUT THIS LESSON

Project Files

Before beginning the exercises, make sure that you've installed the lesson files from the CD, as explained in Step 5 on page xv of the Preface. This should result in a folder called *Lesson Files-PE3 1on1* on your desktop. We'll be working with the files inside the *Lesson 12* subfolder.

In this lesson, you'll use the both the Organizer and Editor workspaces to assemble each of six kinds of creations. Along the way, you'll learn how to:

Video Lesson 12: Making a Slide Show

Of Photoshop Elements 3's many and various creations, the most essential is the common slide show. This simple function permits you to peruse a day's photo shoot, present a group of images to friends or clients, and even export the finished piece as a Windows Media movie, complete with music and fades.

To learn all about slide shows—as well as introduce yourself to the world of creations—watch the twelfth and final movie. Insert the CD, click **Start**, click Set **4** in the top-right corner of your screen, and then select **12, Making a Slide Show** from the Lessons list. The 8-minute, 23-second movie (which includes a closing message from yours truly) explains the following functions, which include these shortcuts:

Operation	Keyboard equivalent or shortcut
Open the Creation Setup wizard	Alt+F, N, C
Switch from one kind of creation to another	↑ or ↓
Advance from one slide to the next (or previous)	→ (or ←)
Add music from the Organizer workspace	Ctrl+M
Full-screen slide show preview	F11

How Creations Work

You make creations in a kind of mini-workspace called the Creation Setup window, accessible from both the Welcome screen and the Organizer. There, Elements walks you through the process of creating any of several kinds of creations using a hand-holding wizard. So you may wonder why I've elected to further hold your hand with a lesson full of step-by-step exercises. Three reasons:

- Things are never as easy as they seem. I have the luxury of spending hours talking to Adobe programmers and other support personnel, so I have insights to share.

- Some of the wizards deposit you into interfaces that are as complex as other parts of Elements. You're smart; you can figure it out. But so long as I'm here, I reckon I might as well be of service.

- The Creation Setup wizard suffers some odd limitations, sometimes preventing you from modifying an option, sometimes only appearing to do so. Oftentimes, there are workarounds.

To enter the Creation Setup wizard, click the **Make Photo Creation** button in the Welcome screen (see Figure 12-2), or click the **Create** button in the Organizer. Either way, you'll see a list of projects on the left and as many as four icons in the lower-right area of the dialog box. These are not clickable icons; they're merely informative, as follows:

- This icon means you can preview your creation on screen. It appears when creating slide shows and Web galleries.

- You can save most creations to the Portable Document Format (PDF). You can open the PDF file with Adobe Reader, available for free from *www.acrobat.com*.

- This icon tells you that you can email the finished project.

- You can burn slide shows to a VCD (Video CD), which you can play on many set-top DVD players.

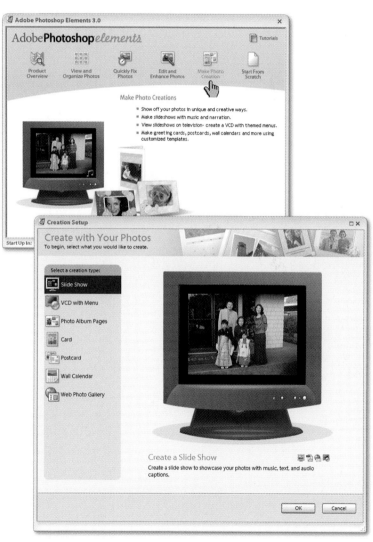

Figure 12-2.

When you complete a creation, Photoshop Elements usually adds it to the active Organizer catalog. You can then email, print, or export the project, depending on its type. I explain Elements' first and foremost creation in Video Lesson 12, "Making a Slide Show" (see page 340). I cover the others—including the Photomerge function, which is the one creation that Elements makes available from the Editor workspace—in the upcoming exercises.

Creating a Video CD

Photoshop Elements lets you save a slide show to the Video CD format so that you can play the slide show back on a television or computer screen. To understand how VCD works, and whether or not you might find it useful, a little technical background is in order.

PEARL OF WISDOM

A CD is just a "dumb" disc that can contain any form of digital media. The way a disc is formatted determines how it can be used. If a CD is formatted as an audio CD, you can play it in a stereo or other CD player. If you format the disc as a data CD, you can put it in your computer and back up photographs and other files to it. A CD can even contain a movie. The VCD format lets you create movies that play at the full 30 frames per second employed by U.S. television, complete with stereo sound. The downside is the resolution, a scant 352 by 240 pixels (352 by 288 pixels in Europe), which is about one fourth the pixels you get from your TV. In other words, VCD is the poor man's DVD. (Only if you have Premiere Elements installed do you have the option of burning a higher resolution DVD.)

Many DVD players support VCD. (Check your player's manual for Video CD, VCD, or SVCD support. You may also find a statement of Video CD support on the front of the machine.) If your DVD player does not support the VCD format (neither of my editors could make it work), you can play the movie on your computer using special software. I recommend visiting *www.download.com* and searching for "vcd player." I had the best luck with a compact little freeware program called Lalim VCD Player from Lalim Software (*www.angelfire.com/mb/lalim*).

In this exercise, we'll take a couple of slide shows that have already been rendered as Windows Media Video (WMV) files and burn them onto a Video CD. To complete the exercise, you'll need an active Internet connection, a CD-R or CD-RW drive that lets you record CDs, and a blank CD inserted into the drive. You also need to know whether your country subscribes to the NTSC or PAL video standard. As a general rule, North America, Central America, and Japan rely on NTSC; Europe and China use PAL.

1. *Create a new catalog.* The first thing you need to do is create a new catalog to hold the batch of files we're going to use for this lesson. Launch the Organizer if it isn't open already. Then choose **File→ Catalog** or press Ctrl+Shift+C. In the *Catalog* dialog box, click **New**. In the resulting *New Catalog* dialog box, type "PE3 1on1 Lesson 12" in the **File name** option, and click **Save**. A new empty catalog appears on screen.

2. *Import the files.* Click the camera icon in the shortcuts bar and choose **From Files and Folders**, or press Ctrl+Shift+G. Then do like so:

   • Navigate to the *Lesson 12* folder inside the *Lesson Files-PhE3 1on1* folder. The folder contains 19 photographs and 4 movie files. I want you to import all the photos and 2 of the movies, depending on your prevailing video standard.

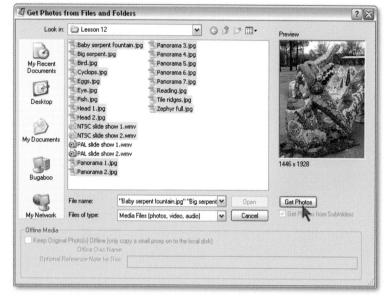

Figure 12-3.

   • Press Ctrl+A to select all the files in the folder. Then Ctrl-click the 2 movie files that you want to deselect. In NTSC countries such as the U.S., Ctrl-click the two files with *PAL* in their titles. In Europe and China, Ctrl-click the two *NTSC* files. Figure 12-3 shows the files I selected.

   • With 21 files selected, click the **Get Photos** button.

After a moment, the 21 files fill your browser window. If you see a warning, click the **OK** button to dismiss it. Then click the **Back to All Photos** button at the top of the screen. If you can't see all 21 files, drag the thumbnail size slider so that all files fit on screen at the same time, as in Figure 12-4.

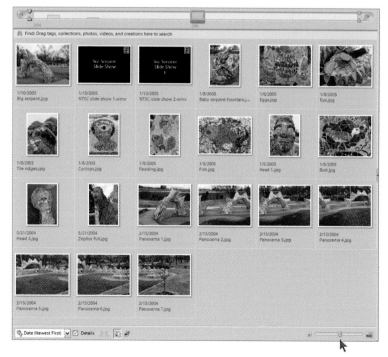

Figure 12-4.

The photographs explore details of the Sea Serpents sculpture in Fannie Mae Dees park in Nashville. This amazing, climbable sculpture is the result of a community project led by Chilean mosaic artist Pedro Silva. I created the WMV movie files from slide shows, much like the one in Video Lesson 12, "Making a Slide Show."

3. *Make sure your Creations are up-to-date.* From time to time, Adobe releases updates to Elements, as well as subsets of Elements like creations. These updates may affect the performance of the software, as well as your ability to follow along with these steps. To make sure your software is up-to-date, Choose **Edit→ Preferences→Services**. Click the **Update Creations** button, as in Figure 12-5. Assuming that you have an active Internet connection, Photoshop Elements will go online and check for updates. If you see directions, follow them. When you see a message telling you that the creations are now up-to-date, click **OK** twice to accept the message and close the dialog box.

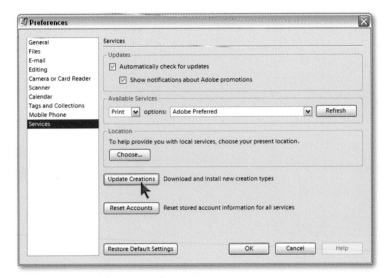

Figure 12-5.

4. *Click the Create button.* Press Ctrl+Shift+A to confirm that all the files are deselected. Then click the **Create** button in the shortcuts bar. Elements displays the **Creation Setup** wizard that we saw back in Figure 12-2.

5. *Initiate the Video CD.* Click the **VCD with Menu** on the left side of the wizard window to see the picture of the kid in the floppy blue hat on TV. Then click **OK**, or just double-click the VCD with Menu button.

6. *Add the two slide show movies.* Elements displays the **Create a VCD with Menu** dialog box, which complains that you neglected to select any slide show files or movies. To remedy this cataclysmic oversight, click the **Add Slide Shows** button. Photoshop Elements shows you the two movies in your catalog. Turn on the check boxes next to each of the movie files and click **OK**. The movies now appear inside the Create a VCD with Menu dialog box, as in Figure 12-6.

7. *Burn the Video CD.* Click the **Burn** button. A moment later, you should see the dialog box pictured in Figure 12-7.

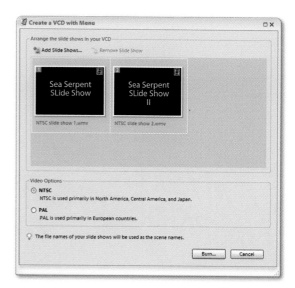

Figure 12-6.

- If your computer includes more than one CD or DVD drive, select the one you want to use from the **Select Destination Drive** list.

- Leave the **Select Drive Speed** option set to its default, which Elements supposes to be the fastest speed your drive can handle.

- Then click the **OK** button.

Figure 12-7.

After several minutes of burning, Elements greets you with the window shown in Figure 12-8. (In the unlikely event that the operation fails, it's probably because the CD has a problem. Insert a new disc and try again.) Click **OK** to close the success message, and then click the **Cancel** button to close the Create a VCD with Menu dialog box.

Figure 12-8.

8. *View your Video CD.* Eject your CD from the drive. I recommend that you go ahead and label it now as well—perhaps not as elaborately as Figure 12-9, but enough so you don't mix it up with the blank CDs lying around your den, office, and rec room. Then place the CD in a VCD-compatible set-top DVD player. (Note that you may have to press a Play or ▶ button to get things started.) You should see a menu screen, which Elements generates automatically, as in Figure 12-10. Use the number keys on your DVD player's remote control to select the slide show you want to view, and then sit back and enjoy photos, soundtrack, and all. If you can't get the VCD to play from your set-top device, get yourself a free player utility and play it from your computer. Lalim VCD Player 2.2.1 (the version I used) does not support VCD menus, but it does allow you to play the slide shows, as in Figure 12-11.

Figure 12-9.

Figure 12-10.

Laying Out Photo Album Pages

Although photo albums are decidedly low-tech compared to digital slide shows, Elements still manages to give albums a modern twist. Rather than painstakingly affixing each individual photo onto album pages with glue or other messy materials, why not lay out the photos on your computer and print them exactly the way you want them on fully rendered album pages? Not only does the Organizer let you do exactly that, it gives you the options of printing the pages yourself, creating a PDF for someone else to print, emailing the pages to friends and family, or even uploading the pages to an online service where they can be professionally printed and bound.

In these steps, you'll take a dozen photographs from the catalog you created in the preceding exercise and lay them out onto picture-perfect album pages.

1. *Hide the slide show movies.* First, a little housekeeping: We don't need to see the two movie files any longer, so let's get them out of the way. Inside the Organizer workspace, choose **View→ Media Types** or press Ctrl+Alt+M. In the **Items Shown** dialog box, turn off the **Video** check box and click **OK**. The movies remain part of the catalog, but disappear from the browser window.

2. *Make a new creation.* Press Ctrl+Shift+A to ensure that no photo is selected in the browser window. Then click the **Create** button in the shortcuts bar to display the Creation Setup wizard. We're working down the Select a Creation Type list, so double-click the button called **Photo Books and Album Pages**. Elements takes you to the window shown in Figure 12-12.

3. *Select a page style.* Your first step is to choose a style of page or album from the **Select a style list** on the right side of the window. All styles can be printed from your inkjet printer, but styles ending in the word "Book" can also be ordered online as bound photo collections.

As a rule, when Elements lays out album pages it crops all photos to a 4-by-3 aspect ratio, whether horizontal or vertical. The exception: if you select a style from the Full Photo section at the top of the list, Elements prints the entire image on the page regardless of its proportions.

Figure 12-11.

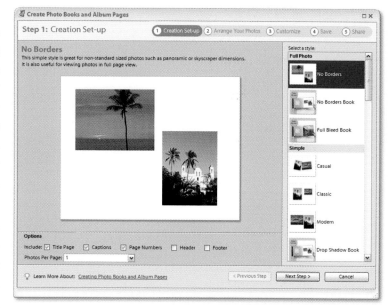

Figure 12-12.

Scroll down the list and click **Fun for Kids Book**, which is the second Fun for Kids style in the **Party** section. Because the Sea Serpent exists for the express purpose of letting kids climb on it, this seems an appropriate choice.

4. *Establish a few options.* The check boxes at the bottom of the window let you customize the appearance of your album:

- When you order a bound book online, it includes a window cut out of the front cover to reveal the photo on the first page. Select the **Title Page** check box to place a page at the beginning of your album especially designed to line up with the cover window.

- These photos include captions that I entered in the Properties palette in the Organizer workspace. Select the **Captions** check box to display these captions.

- Select the **Page Numbers** check box to add a page number to the lower-right corner of each album page.

- The Header and Footer check boxes add customizable text at the top and bottom, respectively, of every page except the title page. Select the **Footer** check box; leave the other unchecked.

- **Photos Per Page** presents you with several ways to distribute your photos in the album. You can choose to have the same number of photos appear on each page. Or you can select a Sequence option, which alternates the photo distribution. I'd like you to choose **Sequence: 1, 3, 2, repeat**. This means page 1 will have one photo, page 2 will have three, page 3 will have two photos, page 4 will again have one, and so on.

After you've made these choices, click the **Next Step** button at the bottom of the window.

5. *Import your photos.* Because no photos were selected when you entered the Creation Setup wizard, the Arrange Your Photos window is bare. Click the **Add Photos** button in the upper-left corner of the window to change this.

Elements displays the **Add Photos** dialog box. Select the **Photo Browser** option on the left to see all the images in the active catalog. Skip the first seven photos (which we'll save for the panorama exercise at the end of the lesson) and select the remaining twelve. Unfortunately, this dialog box lacks an efficient means for selecting a range of photos. For example, clicking the first image and Shift-clicking the last does not work here. But at least you don't have to click inside a check box to turn it on or off; clicking the thumbnail does the job just as well. When you have all 12 images pictured in Figure 12-13 selected, click **OK**.

6. *Acknowledge the warning.* The 12 thumbnails now appear inside the Arrange Your Photos window, but they are partially obscured by one of the Organizer's irritating resolution warnings. Apparently at least one of our images doesn't contain enough pixels to print smoothly. Turn on the **Don't Show Again** check box and click **OK**.

Figure 12-14 shows the culprit. The bluish and moustached Zephyr, the second image in the top row, sports a yellow ⚠ symbol, which I've gone ahead and circled in yellow. We'll fix the problem in the very next step.

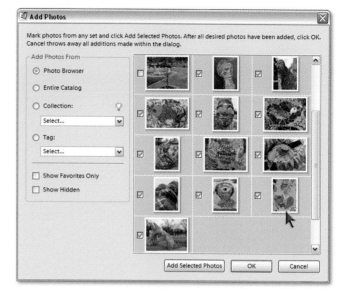

Figure 12-13.

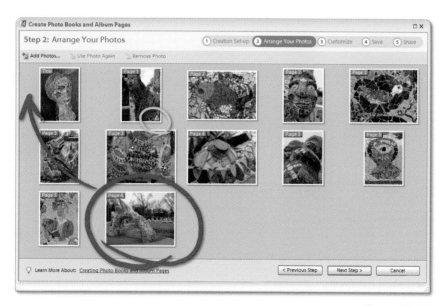

Figure 12-14.

7. *Arrange your photos.* Notice the text that appears in the upper-left corner of each thumbnail. This tells you the page number for each image. First comes the Title page and then the 1-3-2 sequence starts. This means our old friend Zephyr will appear alone on the first page. That's a problem, because the Zephyr contains the fewest pixels of any in the catalog, and a lone image prints big. Few pixels mean low resolution—hence the ⚠.

Turns out, I really want the last image in the group to appear on the title page. Drag the last image and drop it to the left of the current title page as indicated by the red arrow in Figure 12-14 on the preceding page. A vertical yellow line shows where the image will appear when you release the mouse. The image should now assume the title page spot, scooting all the other images over one slot. Zephyr now shares page 2 with two other images, thus reducing its print size and increasing its resolution. Unfortunately, the warning remains visible.

To force an update, click the **Next Step** button at the bottom of the window, and then immediately click the **Previous Step** button to return to the Arrange Your Photos screen. Zephyr's ⚠ icon disappears.

8. *Duplicate the title.* I want the title page image to also appear within the actual pages of the album. With the title image selected, click the **Use Photo Again** button at the top of the window. Drag the copy of the image (currently filling the page 1 slot) down to the right of the last image to place it at the end of the album. Then drag the seventh image (the second page 3 photo) between the first two images to promote that image to page 1. Finally, drag the page 4 image to the very end of the album. When your thumbnails appear in the order shown in Figure 12-15, click the **Next Step** button.

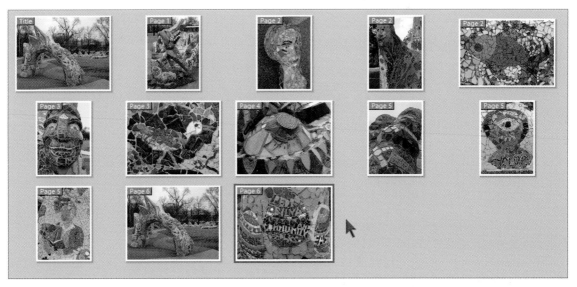

Figure 12-15.

9. *Browse the pages.* You should now see the **Customize** window. The title page appears in the middle of the window, flanked by navigational buttons (◑ and ◐) which take you from one page to another. Just to familiarize yourself with the layout, click the ◐ icon to view each of the pages in the album. Then choose **Title** from the **View Page** pop-up menu to return to the title page.

10. *Crop the title image.* Let's now make a few changes to the title page. The photo is selected, as indicated by the marching ants border. Notice that the photo appears cropped inside a rounded frame. Drag the image to the right so that the nose of the serpent is close to the right edge of the frame, as in Figure 12-16. Click again outside the image to deselect it. The right edge of the image is cropped away.

Figure 12-16.

11. *Edit the title page text.* Now to edit the text. Do as the **Double-Click to Insert Title** text bids—that is, double-click on it—to display the **Title** window. This window allows you to enter text that will appear on the page and provides you with basic formatting controls. Press Ctrl+A to select all the text and replace it with "Serpents." Set the type size to **36 pt**, confirm that the color is black, and click **Done**.

Next click the **Add Text** button in the upper-left corner of the **Customize** window. Again press Ctrl+A and type "Sea." Assuming the type size and color remain 36 point and black, respectively, click **Done**. Then drag the active text block down to position it as shown in Figure 12-17.

Figure 12-17.

12. *Edit page 1.* Click the ◐ icon to advance to the first page inside the album. The photograph appears at an angle with a caption to its right. Below the image is a line of faint text that reads *Double-Click to Insert Footer*. This is the footer you requested in Step 4.

Double-click the text to display the **Footer** dialog box. Press Ctrl+A to select all the placeholder type and replace it with the title of this album, "Sea Serpents."

Naturally, we want this same footer to appear at the bottom of all our pages. So turn on the **Apply to All Footers** check box. Then click the **Done** button to complete the first page, as in Figure 12-18.

Figure 12-18.

Figure 12-19.

13. *Edit page 2.* Click the ❍ icon to proceed to page 2, which has just one problem: The Zephyr image lacks a caption. Double-click the small placeholder caption in the top-center portion of the page. Then press Ctrl+A, type "Zephyr," and click **Done**.

14. *Edit page 3.* To switch to page 3, let's try something different. Press the Page Down key, which advances from one page to the next. (Hardly surprisingly, Page Up takes you to the previous page.) Now let's say that you surmise that the page would look better if the images were switched so that the bird was on the left, looking at the face. You might reasonably assume that you could drag and drop the images to swap their places. After all, that's how it works everywhere else. But if you give it a try, you'll see that dragging an image merely moves it inside its frame. Besides, the bird is a horizontal photo while the face is vertical. In other words, we need to switch the places of both the images and the frames, as follows:

- If you dragged a photo, click the **Reset Photos** button to restore both photos on the page to their default positions.

- Click the **Previous Step** button at the bottom of the screen (or press Alt+P) to retreat to the **Arrange Your Photos** window.

- Drag the bird thumbnail to the left of the face and drop it. This swaps the two images.

- Click the **Next Step** button to return to page 3. Lo and behold, the intelligent and ever-accommodating Elements has switched both photos and frames so that the bird is checking out the face, as in Figure 12-19.

15. *Edit page 4.* Press Page Down to move along to page 4, where we're met by a huge eye staring toward the heavens. Kind of has a creepy monster feel to it, don't you think? (As always, your blind agreement with the preceding question is gratefully appreciated.) This page adheres to the 1-3-2 sequence we requested in Step 4. Thankfully, we can override that if we want to. Notice the **Photos on This Page** pop-up menu in the upper-right corner of the window? Change it from Default to **2**. Elements creates a new image slot and fills it with a photo that was previous located on page 5, as illustrated in Figure 12-20.

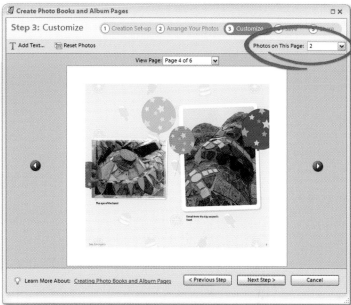

Figure 12-20.

16. *View the remaining pages.* Advance to page 5, and you'll see that it still contains its prescribed three images. Again, Elements has thoughtfully transferred one of the images from the succeeding page to fill the gap. But page 6 was slated to have two images; does that mean it will now have one photo and one blank frame? Press Page Down to find out. Wonder of wonders, Elements has automatically adjusted the layout so that page 6 includes a single large frame. Nice.

17. *Save your photo album.* Click the **Next Step** button to display the **Save** screen. Enter "Serpents Album" or words to that effect into the **Creations Name** option box. Then click the **Save** button to continue on to the final screen.

PEARL OF WISDOM

Even though you just clicked the Save button, this creation is not saved. If you now click the ✕ icon in the upper-right corner of the title bar, Elements would close the window and abandon your creation. In other words, the photo album would be lost forever. Only when you click the Done button can you rest assured that Elements has actually saved the creation. So whatever you do, *don't stop early.* It ain't done till you click Done.

18. *View your sharing options.* The Share screen shown in Figure 12-21 gives you four ways to share your album pages that you'll see repeated in future projects:

- Click the Create a PDF button to save a PDF version of your album pages that you can later open, view, and print using the free Adobe Reader software.

- The Print button permits you to print your pages from a connected inkjet or laser printer.

- Click the E-mail option to open a window where you can access your saved contacts and select recipients. Photoshop Elements then generates a PDF file and attaches the file to an outgoing email.

- The Order Online button likewise creates a PDF file. But this time, Elements submits the PDF file to an online service so that you can order a printed and bound photo book.

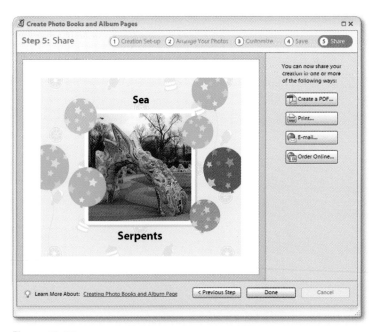

Figure 12-21.

After you have saved a creation, you can access these options at any time just by double-clicking the creation's thumbnail in the Organizer workspace. So for now, no need to export the album to PDF or print it. Just go ahead and click the **Done** button to exit the Creation Setup wizard and save your project. If you see a message telling you that your creation has been added to the Organizer's photo browser, read the pithy prose, turn on the **Don't Show Again** check box, and then click **OK**. Your photo album is complete, saved to disk, and safe as houses.

Creating a Greeting Card

The Organizer lets you choose between two kinds of greeting cards, which you initiate by clicking either the Card or Photo Greeting Card option. The first produces a folded card that includes a photo on the front and a place for a heartfelt, humorous, and/or derogatory message on the inside, much like a traditional greeting card that you buy at your local stationary store. You print the creation and fold the paper in quarters to create the finished project. Contrast that with the Photo Greeting Card option, which creates a large postcard that you can print at home or order online from Kodak, in boxed sets of 20 complete with envelopes.

In this exercise we'll look at creating a four-fold greeting card with the Card option. Many of the specific settings will be familiar from the preceding exercise, so we'll breeze through this one at a pretty brisk pace. Meanwhile, any new tips you encounter are easily adapted should you decide to try out the Photo Greeting Card option on your own.

1. *Select a photo in the Organizer.* Make sure that the *PE3 1on1 Lesson 12* catalog that you created in the first exercise is open in the Organizer workspace. Then click the thumbnail for the *Baby serpent fountain.jpg* image, which appears highlighted in the upper-right corner of Figure 12-22.

Figure 12-22.

2. *Start the creation process.* Click the **Create** button in the short-cuts bar to display the Creation Setup wizard. Double-click the yellow **Card** option on the left side of the screen to enter the **Create a Card** window.

3. *Select a greeting card style.* As when making a photo album, the next step is to choose a style of greeting card from the list on the right. Our selected photo is the baby serpent in the Sea Serpents sculpture, so choose the **Baby Stork (Pink)** style from the **Baby** category, as in Figure 12-23. Even hideous monsters deserve precious birth announcements, don't you think? Click the **Next Step** button to indicate that you do.

Figure 12-23.

Some styles, such as Casual Horizontal and Spring Vertical, are designed to best accommodate photos with the specified orientation. If a style doesn't mention an orientation, it most likely automatically adapts to a horizontal or vertical photo. One exception is the Heart style in the Valentine category, which works best with a horizontal photo. Also note that if you use the Snowglobe style in the Season's Greetings category, the snowglobe image will appear on the front of the card and your photo appears *inside* the card.

4. *Skip the next screen.* You are now presented with the Arrange Your Photos screen, which features your preselected photo. In the previous exercise this screen was handy for adding photos

to our album pages. But we already selected the photo we want, and one photo is all Elements' greeting card templates can accommodate. If you were to add more photos to this window, Elements would stamp each extra thumbnail as *Not Used*. So just click **Next Step** to move along.

5. *Edit the front of the card.* Elements presents you with the front of the greeting card. Obviously, a few changes are in order:

   • Double-click the text to open it, select it by pressing Ctrl+A, and replace it with "It's a Girl!" Then click **Done**.

   • Next, let's resize the photo to better display the baby serpent's winsome cuteness. Click the photo to make the selection border appear. Then drag the lower-right corner handle until the image appears more or less as shown in Figure 12-24.

   • Click outside the photo to deselect it and preview how it will look inside the frame. You can click the image again and make any further adjustments you like. When you're satisfied, click the ● icon to the right of the card or press the Page Down key to advance to the inside page.

Figure 12-24.

Figure 12-25.

Figure 12-26.

6. *Customize the inside of the card.* Double-click the main **Insert Greeting** text to open the **Greeting** window. Press Ctrl+A to select the placeholder text and enter: "At least, we think it's a girl." Then press the Enter key to start a new line and type "YOU check." Finally, click **Done** to return to the wizard.

While you might have preferred to italicize the word *You* as opposed to using all capital letters, the text input boxes available in the Creation Setup wizard don't let you mix fonts and type styles within the same text block. So all caps is our next best option.

Now, double-click the smaller **Insert Message** text. Select the placeholder text, type "Love, John and Marsha," and click **Done**. The inside of your card should now look like Figure 12-25. Now that the card is customized to serve our new and mostly unrecognizable bundle of joy, click **Next Step** to proceed.

7. *Save your twisted creation.* In the **Save** window, name the card "Sweet Serpent Girl" and click the **Save** button—bearing in mind that you aren't actually saving the card but rather preparing Elements to save it in the next step.

8. *Create a PDF of your card.* The **Share** window contains many of the same options we saw when creating a photo album. The only difference is that Kodak is unprepared to print our four-fold greeting card, so the Order Online button is dimmed.

Of the three remaining options, Print is the most viable choice. To find out why for yourself, try this interesting experiment:

- Click the **Create a PDF** button to display the **Save as PDF** dialog box, which presents you with three options.

- Go ahead and leave the default **Optimize for Viewing Onscreen** option selected, and then click **OK**.

- In the **Export PDF As** dialog box, navigate to a desired folder (or stay where you are, if you like). Accept the default filename, *Sweet Serpent Girl.pdf*, and click **Save**.

- After saving the PDF file, Photoshop Elements kindly asks whether you'd like to view the file you just finished creating. Click **Yes** to indicate, sure, what the hey. Depending on the software you have installed on your computer, Elements launches the free Adobe Reader or the commercial Acrobat application. Either way, the saved file appears on screen, as in Figure 12-26.

In the upper-left corner of the document is the front of your card, upside-down; in the lower-right corner is the customized message. While the baby serpent arguably looks better on its head, this birth announcement is strange enough already without proffering half of it upside-down. This, you must agree, does not make a satisfactory document when viewed online. You really have to print the card and fold it to make it work.

9. *Call it a day.* Click **Done** to close the **Share** window and to save your creation to the active catalog in the Organizer. You can close Adobe Reader (or Acrobat), too.

Making a Wall Calendar

As you learned when we explored the Date View function in Lesson 1 (see "Finding Photos by Date," page 31), the Organizer is very much concerned with knowing what day it is. So it should come as no surprise that one of the creations you can make with the Organizer is a calendar. Like photo album pages, you can either print a calendar yourself or order a professionally printed and bound calendar online. We'll look at the ins and outs of calendar creation in this exercise.

1. *Select a dozen photos.* Skipping the two saved creations, select the first twelve photos in the Organizer using the sure-fire technique illustrated in Figure 12-27. We'll use these photos to populate a 12-month calendar.

2. *Start the creation process.* Click the **Create** button in the shortcuts bar to display the Creation Setup wizard, with its by-now-familiar picture of dad, mom, grandma, and the poor unsmiling offspring forced to wear festive traditional garb, all posed in front of a hotel welcome mat that says *Beach.* (Yes, I've had far too much time to study this photo.) Double-click the **Wall Calendar** item on the left side of the dialog box to enter the **Create a Wall Calendar** window with its long list of calendar templates.

Figure 12-27.

3. *Select a style.* Selecting a style should be pretty familiar by now. Scroll down the list on the right side of the screen to the very bottom and select **Bright Spots Photo Calendar** from the **Playful** category. Elements recalls that kid in the floppy hat, this time surrounded by clown dots.

Some styles, such as Casual Horizontal under the Simple category, are designed to accommodate the month and calendar on a single sheet of paper. Others, such as our Bright Spots Photo Calendar style, are split across two pages. As with a traditional wall calendar, the photo appears on the top page and the calendar appears on the bottom. Styles such as these always end with the words Photo Calendar and can be ordered online, giving you the benefit of a spiral binding.

---

4. *Select the desired options.* At the bottom of the window you'll find a series of options that determine the appearance and duration of your calendar:

- Turn on the **Title Page** check box to add a front cover to your calendar, complete with photo.

- Select the **Captions** check box to display the captions that I assigned to each photo in the Properties palette. (When creating a calendar with photos that don't have captions, I recommend you turn this check box off.)

Figure 12-28.

- The date options define the span of the calendar. If you're going to order the calendar online, you're limited to twelve months. But there are no such restrictions when you print your own—heck, you might as well get a few years out of the way, if you like. In our case, we'll settle for a single year. Set the two **Starting** pop-up menus to **January** and **2006** and set the **Ending** options to **December** and **2006**, which, depending on the year you read this, may be the defaults. (If you've somehow come across this book in, say, 2017, feel free to use that year instead and populate the calendar with snapshots of your space car and servo robots.)

Your settings should look like those pictured in Figure 12-28. When they do, click the **Next Step** button.

5. *Arrange your photos.* Once again, it's time to arrange the photographs. Elements automatically assigns a month to each thumbnail. We have twelve images, but somehow December is missing. This is because the first photo is slotted for the title page. Easily remedied:

- Select the first thumbnail and click the **Use Photo Again** button. Elements copies the title photo and plunks it down in January, which nudges all the other images and fills out the calendar.

- No one wants to see the title image immediately duplicated in January. So click the **January** thumbnail and drag it to the end of the list. The serpent switches to December and the other photos shift forward a month.

Assuming that your thumbnails appear in the quantity and order pictured in the highly meticulous Figure 12-29, you are cleared to click the **Next Step** button.

Figure 12-29.

6. *Customize the title page.* The **Customize** screen appears, showing the title page for our calendar. Follow the advice of the tiny yellow **Double-Click to Insert Title** text. Press Ctrl+A and replace the placeholder text with "Sea Serpents 2006 Calendar." Click **Done** to see the new title below the cover photo.

7. *Add a holiday.* Click ❍ to the right of the title page preview or press Page Down to advance to the month of January. The top page shows the baby serpent with its caption below; the bottom page shows the calendar itself. Peer close and notice that

the calendar has no holidays—no New Year's Day, no Martin Luther King Day, no National Folic Acid Awareness Week, no nothing. But just because Elements is holiday-unaware doesn't mean you can't add a few holidays manually if you like. Here's how:

Figure 12-30.

- For the sake of example, let's advance to April. Either click the ◗ icon or press Page Down three times.

- Click the **Add Text** button in the upper-left corner of the window. Press Ctrl+A and type "April Fool's Day."

- Set the type size to **10 pt**.

- Click the color swatch, select a dark blue from the **Color** dialog box, and click **OK**.

- Click **Done** to exit the Text dialog box and create your custom holiday text.

- The text block appears centered above the photo on the top page. That's no good, so drag the text down until it appears fully inside the April 1 ccll, as in Figure 12-30. If you plan on adding other holidays to this month, it might be a good idea to reduce the text box size so it doesn't interfere with other dates. But for us, it's good as it is.

Admittedly, it's a royal pain in the neck to have to position tiny text like this for each and every holiday. And man, do I wish there was some way to zoom! But this method does at least afford you the option of jotting down a few personal events, such as birthdays, weddings, dental appointments, and other celebratory occasions.

If holidays are important to you, and you don't feel like entering them all manually, be aware that it's possible to bypass the Creation Setup wizard and order a calendar from Kodak using images from your online photo album (see Lesson 11, "Sharing Pictures Online," page 329). If you go this route, you can choose from U.S. and Canadian holidays. Sorry, no National Folic Acid Awareness Week, but you can always write that in.

8. *Fix November.* Choose **November 2006** from the **View Page** pop-up menu above the page preview. The top portion of this month features two problems: First, I forgot to include a caption with *Zephyr full.jpg.* Second, if you click the **Previous Step** button, you may notice that Zephyr sports a yellow ⚠. As we learned a couple of exercises ago, Elements considers the photo's resolution to be insufficient for high-quality printing.

Frankly, I've just about had enough of that Zephyr. But he does help to demonstrate the kinds of problems we may encounter during our creation adventures. And here's how we fix them:

- If you clicked Previous Step to see the ⚠ icon, please click the **Next Step** button to return to November.

- Double-click the teeny-weeny caption text, press Ctrl+A to highlight the placeholder text, and type "I curse thee, Zephyr!" Then click **Done**. The new caption is too small to read at this zoom size, but it was cathartic nonetheless.

- While we can't do anything about the number of pixels inside the Zephyr—not from the Creation Setup wizard, anyway—we can change the size at which the image prints. Click the image to select it. Then drag a corner handle inward to scale the image down. Drag the thumbnail to center it within the frame. You can also use the arrow keys to nudge the image if you prefer.

Figure 12-31.

When you finish, you should see something that resembles Figure 12-31. The image looks quite natural with a thick white border around it, and your resizing has increased the resolution. To see if Elements is happy, click the **Previous Step** button. With any luck, the warning icon has disappeared. If so, click **Next Step** to return to the Customize screen and breathe a sigh of relief. If not, click Next Step and scale the image smaller.

9. *Save the creation.* Click **Next Step** to advance to the **Save** screen. For once, just click the **Use Title for Name** check box, and let Elements automatically name the file *Sea Serpents 2006 Calendar*. Then click the **Save** button.

10. *View your sharing options.* The final screen presents you with the same four sharing options we encountered when creating a photo album (see Step 18, page 354). If you click the **Print** button to print the calendar from your inkjet printer, Elements will combine the top and bottom pages for each month onto a single upright sheet of paper. If you order a calendar online, you'll receive a standard spiral-bound booklet that measures approximately 10¼ by 15½ inches when open.

After you've shared the calendar to any and all extents you deem appropriate, click **Done** to save your latest creation to disk and post the file in the Organizer.

Designing a Photo Gallery for the Web

In the previous lesson you learned how to share your photos online using the Kodak EasyShare Gallery (see "Sharing Pictures Online," page 329). While Kodak quite generously provides you space on its servers for free, you don't have many options for customizing the appearance of your gallery and you're stuck with the random Web address that Kodak assigns you.

Happily, the Organizer gives you additional tools for creating an online photo gallery that you can post as a fully functioning Web site. The site starts off with a page of thumbnails that link to larger versions of the images. Elements currently offers more than 30 different Web site styles, as well as an assortment of options to customize your gallery. The only catch is that you have to locate your own Internet server space so that you can upload your gallery for public viewing.

In this exercise you'll learn how to create your own online photo gallery with the Organizer. And don't worry if you don't currently have a way to post the site to the Web; the Organizer lets you preview the finished gallery directly from your hard drive.

1. *Add a caption to the Zephyr.* We're going to use the same twelve photos in our online gallery that we used in the previous exercise. And as you've learned during this lesson, one of the twelve, *Zephyr full.jpg*, doesn't have a caption. You were able to add a caption while assembling the photo album and calendar, but you won't get the chance to do this while creating an online gallery. So let's add a caption now and avoid some heartache later.

   Select the Zephyr image in the Organizer workspace. Then double-click it to fill your screen with the strange Salvador Dali-headed creature, as in Figure 12-32 on the facing page. Make sure the **Properties** palette is visible in the lower-right portion of the screen. If it isn't, press Alt+Enter to make it so. If necessary, switch to the **General** panel of the palette and type "Cursed Zephyr" into the **Caption** field, as the figure shows.

2. *Start the creation process.* If you zoomed in on the creature like I did, press the Backspace key to zoom back out. Click the Zephyr to select him, and then Shift-click the first image in the photo browser to select the very same twelve photos we used in the calendar exercise. (If you forget which ones I'm talking

about, refer to Figure 12-27 on page 359.) Then click the **Create** button in the shortcuts bar to launch the Creation Setup wizard. Double-click the final option along the left side of the dialog box, **Web Photo Gallery**, to open the independent **Adobe Web Photo Gallery** interface. In Figure 12-33, I dragged the edge of the interface outward to expand it slightly and reveal thumbnails for all twelve images. I suggest you do this, too.

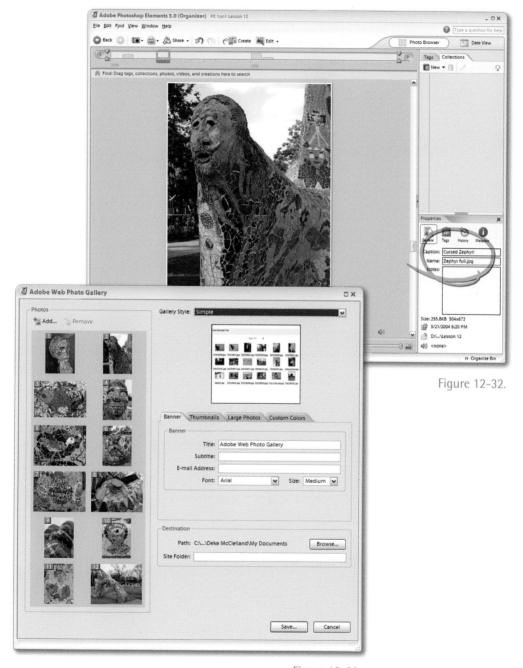

Figure 12-32.

Figure 12-33.

3. *Arrange the images.* As usual, I want to adjust the order of the photos. (In case you're wondering, "Why didn't you put these in the right order in the first place?" remember that you can reorder photos only inside a collection and we're working through these steps so *you* can get the experience.) The good news: I'm going to make you swap only one image. I want what is currently the final image, the wide view of the serpent, to be the first. Make sure that you can see all twelve images, as in Figure 12-33 on the preceding page. (Seeing the thumbnails in a single column makes it difficult to arrange them freely.) Then drag the serpent and drop it in front of the first thumbnail.

4. *Select a style.* The next step is to choose a Web gallery template from the pop-up menu at the top of the window. With a minimum of 33 styles to choose from (more may have been added since the writing of this book), the decision can be difficult. To preview the styles, try this:

   - Make sure the **Simple** option in the **Gallery Style** pop-up menu is highlighted in dark blue, as in Figure 12-33 on the preceding page. If it isn't, press the Tab key as many times as it takes to highlight the option.

   - Press the ↓ or ↑ key to switch from one style to another. As you do, keep an eye on the preview below the pop-up menu. It updates to show you a sample version of the first page in the active gallery.

Gallery styles fall into two categories: The first features an index page with thumbnails that link to different pages with larger images. Simple and Antique Lace are examples. The second features an ever-present row or column of thumbnails and displays the larger images within the same page. Fall and Horizontal Frame are examples of this category.

Worth singling out is the Horizontal Slide Show style, which is programmed to switch between large images automatically, creating a continuous parade of images in your Web browser.

Choose **Hello** from the **Gallery Style** menu. Or, with the Gallery Style option highlighted, just press the H key. The amber of the Hello template contrasts nicely with the mosaic serpents, plus it tosses in a bit of animation for good measure. As with most of the Gallery Style settings, this one makes available several options that, very confusingly, don't have any bearing on the final outcome of your site. We'll deal with these as they come.

5. *Choose your banner settings.* Below the amber gallery preview are four tabs, each of which takes you to a different panel of options. We'll start with the default panel, Banner. Most gallery styles, Hello included, don't actually include a banner. However, some of the information in the Banner panel will appear on your Web pages anyway.

- The Title text appears in the title bar of the Web browser and within the Web page itself. Note that Adobe includes a placeholder in the Title as a kind of free publicity missive, and it works: At press time, Google found over half a million pages on the Web entitled *Adobe Web Photo Gallery*. Don't let yours be one of them. Assuming that the Gallery Style option remains highlighted, press the Tab key thrice to select the **Title** text and change it to "Sea Serpents Shots."

- The Subtitle option lets you add a second line of text to your Web page. Our Hello style doesn't utilize this option, so leave Subtitle blank.

- If you enter an address into the E-mail Address field, it appears as a clickable link in the site. This is good and bad. When a person clicks the link, Outlook or another email program automatically launches and creates an outgoing piece of mail addressed to you. By the same token, professional spammers can harvest these links using industrious little "bot" programs that eternally rummage through the world's Web pages, thus leading to an increase in junk email. For now, go ahead and enter your address in the **E-mail Address** field, if only to see how it lands on the page.

- The **Font** option presents you with three fonts that reside on every computer sold in the last several years. Choosing the fourth option, Default, lets the Web browser determine the typeface. Leave this option set to **Arial**.

- The Hello template ignores the **Size** setting, so there's no sense even bothering with it. For reference, my suggested settings appear in Figure 12-34.

Figure 12-34.

6. *Adjust the settings for thumbnails.* Click the **Thumbnails** tab to advance to the next panel. The thumbnails in question appear on the first page of the gallery. When a person clicks a thumbnail, the browser goes to a page that features a larger version of that image.

Figure 12-35.

- First up is the Thumbnail Size menu, which determines how large the thumbnails will be. At one extreme, Small scales the image so that the larger of its height or width is a scant 64 pixels. At the other extreme, X-Large permits a maximum of 160 pixels. Turns out, using the largest thumbnails with the Hello gallery produces an interesting side effect. To see it for yourself (in a few steps, that is), choose **X-Large** from the **Thumbnail Size** menu.

- Next are a handful of options that add captions under the thumbnails. Keep the **Font** set to **Arial**; stylistically, it's probably best not to mix fonts within a gallery, especially fonts that don't go together like Arial, Times, and Courier. Again, the Hello template ignores the Size menu, so I invite you to ignore it, too.

- You can include the image's filename and caption with the thumbnail; the Hello style ignores the Date option. Turn on the **Filename** check box; leave Caption and Date off.

Figure 12-35 shows the settings.

7. *Set the large image options.* Click the **Large Photos** tab to display a panel of options that control the size of the full versions of your photos. The large images are the meat of a photo gallery site, the main attraction. You might wonder, then, why you would want to resize your images at all. Why not let your viewers enjoy every single pixel?

PEARL OF WISDOM

The reason is that when an image appears in a Web browser, there is a one-to-one correspondence between the pixels in the image and the pixels on the monitor. In other words, it's like viewing an image in the Editor at the 100-percent zoom factor. With the exception of the smallish Zephyr, the images we're using are (like most digital photos) far too large to display in their entirety at a one-to-one zoom factor. The standard solution is to shrink the image so that the whole thing fits on the screen.

Nevertheless, your first decision in the Large Photos panel is whether or not you want to resize the photos. If you deselect the Resize Photos check box, the Organizer won't downsample the images. They'll appear on the Web in all their hugeness, and folks will have to do a lot of scrolling to see every single pixel. Consider the cyclops image in Figure 12-36. On the printed page, I can scale it and retain all the pixels; on the Web, I cannot. At a one-to-one zoom ratio, the eye alone consumes the entire width of the page, as in the dimmed background behind this text. Not only that, consider that if you give your visitors the original photo, in all its glory, they'll have everything they need to print and otherwise repurpose high-resolution versions of your work. From a simple copyright perspective, this might not be something you want to encourage.

As tempting as preserving your enormous images may sound, I recommend that you leave the **Resize Photos** check box turned on. Then set the other options like so:

- The default Resize Photos setting of Large is, in truth, a little too large for portrait-oriented images to be fully displayed on most computer screens. So set the **Resize Photos** option to **Medium**. Elements will resize the images so that the larger proportion is 400 pixels.

- The Photo Quality slider determines the amount of JPEG compression that Elements applies to the large photos. A Low setting gives you very small file sizes (about 15K each) and fast loading times. But the image looks awful. A High setting gives you much larger file sizes (about 200K each) and more prodigious load times over slow Internet connections, but the images look great. I advocate that you leave the **Photo Quality** slider set to the halfway point, which is a swell compromise.

- Finally, Elements presents you with some more **Captions** settings. As always, leave the **Font** set to **Arial** and ignore the **Size** option. You have lots of room to display info beneath a large image, so make sure the **Caption** check box is selected. Ignore the Filename and Date check boxes; the Hello template pays them no nevermind whatsoever.

Between you and me, I've a special affinity for Figure 12-37. How come? It shows you my recommended settings.

8. *View (but don't change) the Custom Colors options.* Click the **Custom Colors** tab to move along to the final panel. These options are totally ignored by the Hello template—just as they are by most other gallery styles. Only the four

Figure 12-36.

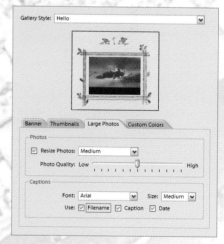

Figure 12-37.

Horizontal and two Table styles and the Simple and Vertical Frame styles fully utilize the options in the Custom Colors panel. A few others pick up the Text and Visited Link options, but that's about it. So leave all **Custom Colors** settings alone.

9. *Save your Web photo gallery.* When Elements creates your Web site, it stores the pages and images in a folder on your hard drive. The Destination options let you specify that folder's name and where it's placed.

- Click the **Browse** button, navigate to your computer's desktop, and click **OK**.

- Name the folder by entering "Sea Serpents Gallery" into the **Site Folder** option box.

- Click the **Save** button.

A Please Wait window momentarily appears while the Organizer creates your gallery. A moment later, you'll see the Web Photo Gallery Browser window, as in Figure 12-38. This window is the Organizer's built-in browser, made especially for viewing Web galleries.

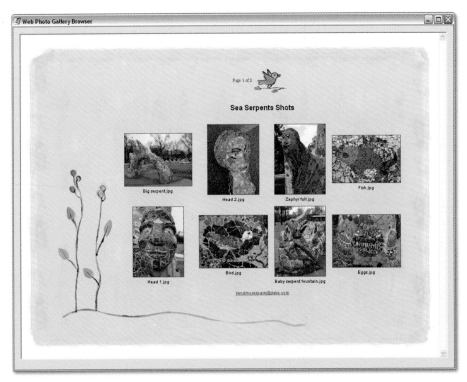

Figure 12-38.

10. *View the gallery.* Click the Maximize button (☐) on the far right side of the title bar to maximize the window. Notice the *Sea Serpents Shots* text above the thumbnails; if you were viewing this gallery in a browser such as Internet Explorer, this text would appear in the browser's title bar as well. Notice also the clickable email address below the thumbnails. Finally, notice that there are only eight thumbnails on this page. With the thumbnail size set to X-Large, the Organizer fits just 8 thumbnails on an index page, regardless of the size of your monitor.

  • To access the other four thumbnails, move your cursor over the little orange birdie at the top of the page. Just hover for a moment and watch. I'll let you enjoy his animated performance for yourself. Now click the bird to reveal the second index page with the remaining thumbnails.

  • Click the *Eye.jpg* thumbnail to display the full page pictured in Figure 12-39.

The left- and right-facing birdies above the photograph let you to navigate through the gallery. Click the plant between the birds to return to the index pages.

Figure 12-39.

Continue to explore the gallery at your leisure. When you're through, click the ✖ icon to close the Web Photo Gallery Browser window. Like the Video CD project at the beginning of this lesson, the Web site isn't saved as a creation document in the Organizer workspace. However, the next time you create a Web photo gallery, the last settings you used will remain in effect, making it easy to go back and tweak things if you're not entirely happy with your initial results. Not only that, the actual HTML files and accompanying image files are saved on the desktop level of your hard drive, permitting you to copy the site to an Internet server and post it for all to enjoy.

Creating a Panoramic Picture

And what about those seven photos that we imported in the first exercise and have neglected ever since? Fret not: In this, the final exercise of the book, the time for those photos has come at last. My coauthor, Galen Fott, shot these photos with the specific intention of stitching them together into a panoramic "big picture" view of the Sea Serpents sculpture. Naturally, the ready-for-anything Photoshop Elements has just the tool for the job.

The surprise is where this tool is located. Unlike the other creations we've explored in this lesson, panoramic pictures can't be created from the Organizer. For that task, you have to return that *yin* to the Organizer's *yang*, that *Chang* to the Organizer's *Eng*, that *Sid* to the Organizer's *Marty Krofft*—the Editor. In this last exercise, you'll learn how to create a panoramic picture using the Editor's Photomerge command, plus pick up a few tips on shooting suitable source pictures as well.

1. *Select the seven partial serpent photos.* Since we've spent the last five exercises in the Organizer, let's start there. Click to select the first photo that bears the date 2/15/2004. Then Shift-click on the last thumbnail dated 2/15/2004. The facing page's Figure 12-40 tells the whole story.

2. *Send the photos to the Editor.* Next, click the **Edit** button in the shortcuts bar and choose **Go to Standard Edit**. Or better yet, press the keyboard equivalent Ctrl+I. Elements launches the Editor workspace (if it isn't running already) and opens the seven photos.

3. *Begin the merge.* Creating a Photomerge panorama is one of the Editor's neatest tricks, but for some reason the good people at Adobe have chosen to bury the command in what seems to this humble author to be a remote location. Then again, who

cares? I know where it is, and my job is to pass along that info to you: Choose **File→New→Photomerge Panorama** to display the first **Photomerge** dialog box, shown in Figure 12-41, which gives you a place to gather photos that you want to merge. By default, any images open inside the Editor are added to the Source Files list, hence the inclusion of our seven serpent JPEGs. You can click the Browse button to add more photos. But we're full up, so click **OK**.

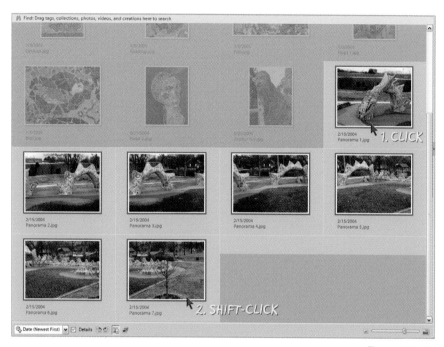

Figure 12-40.

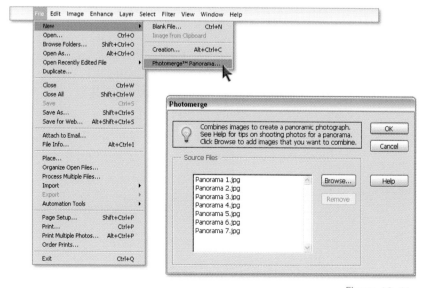

Figure 12-41.

Suddenly the Editor swings into action as if there were a ghost in the machine. A glance at the Layers palette reveals that the Editor is busy at work copying the seven images and pasting them together into a single document. Kind of mysterious and creepy, isn't it? Soon enough, the truly massive second Photomerge window appears. An alert message tells you that Elements tried valiantly to do all the work for you, but a slight problem occurred. What can you do? Some jobs you just have to do yourself. Click **OK** to cordially dismiss the message.

4. *Add the problematic photo.* Okay, obviously we have a small problem. But first, a very quick tour around the Photomerge window, depicted in Figure 12-42. The upper-left corner of the window features a smattering of tools helpful for merging images. The long thin strip across the top that currently houses a lone disenfranchised photo is known as the *light box*. If Photomerge can't automatically reckon how to merge an image with its brethren, to the light box it goes. You can also use the light box as a place to store photos that you decide to exclude from the merge; photos in the light box are excluded from the finally rendering.

Figure 12-42.

On the right side of the window, below the OK and Cancel buttons, are controls for manipulating your merge. The first of the controls is the Navigator panel, which behaves almost exactly like the Editor's Navigator palette, permitting you to move around the main work area.

Press the spacebar to temporarily access the hand tool, which lets you scroll the image inside the work area. Photomerge did a pretty good job fitting the photos together, but scroll to the left and notice an obvious problem: The big serpent is missing its head. Let's reattach it:

- If you still have the spacebar down, for heaven's sake, release it to reactivate the arrow tool. Then drag the lone photo from the thin light box into the larger work area.

- Notice that as you drag the head, the overlapping portions of the head and body appear translucent, helping you to see how the photographs merge.

- Drag the head to the far left side of the merged composition. Line up the images, but don't obsess over it. Because the Snap to Image check box is selected (see the right side of the window), the head image should snap easily into its proper place when you release the mouse button. You might have to try a few times to get it right, but with some experience, you'll know a snap when you see it.

5. *Adjust the blending.* Use the zoom tool to magnify the front of the serpent, as in Figure 12-43. You may see a diagonal shift in brightness as Photomerge tries to blend one image into another. Or you may see a sudden shift in detail, most evident in the blue and orange stripes in the ground. In the figure, I've highlighted the transitional area with a yellow circle.

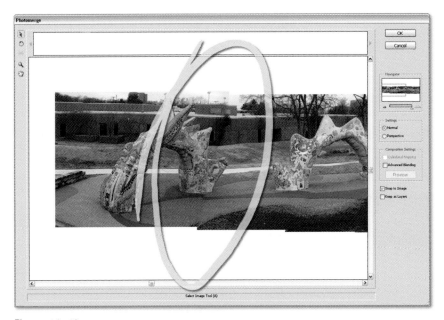

Figure 12-43.

To better blend between one image and the next, turn on the **Advanced Blending** check box in the Composition Settings along the right side of the window. Then click the **Preview** button and wait a few seconds to see the revised results. The transitions may not look perfect, but they should be better.

You can't continue to work in the Photomerge window while previewing the Advanced Blending function, so click the **Exit Preview** button to return to the Standard Edit mode. But leave Advanced Blending turned on; although it may not preview the effect, Elements will apply Advanced Blending to the final render.

---

6. *Apply some perspective to the merged scene.* Scroll a bit to the right and you'll notice a problem in the row of bricks next to the small tree in the foreground (circled in Figure 12-44 on the opposite page). Photomerge did a great job of merging the serpent and other background details, but it pretty well missed the mark with those bricks. By default, Photomerge positions and rotates images to help align them, but it doesn't distort them. Clearly some distortion is needed to fix the bricks.

Go to the **Settings** section of the controls and click the **Perspective** radio button. Photomerge takes a minute or so to calculate the perspective distortion and then displays the results in the work area. Alt-click with the zoom tool to take in the entire merge. As witnessed in Figure 12-45, the Photomerge function has distorted the images so that the bricks meet seamlessly. However, the perspective results in the dreaded "bow tie effect," where the ends flair outward as if the photo were projected on the inside of a cylindrical wall. That's great if you want to create the effect of an image projected onto a museum wall. But we're supposed to be outside, for heaven's sake. There must be a better way.

Figure 12-44.

7. *Fix the bow tie distortion.* Turn on the **Cylindrical Mapping** check box in the Composition Settings area. Again, this effect is too complex to preview automatically, so you'll have to click the **Preview** button to see it work. As shown in Figure 12-46 (see the next page), Photomerge avoids the inverted cylinder effect by wrapping each and every image around its own gradual cylinder. It may not be exactly right, but it's better—and better is as good as things get in Photomerge.

Figure 12-45.

8. *Merge the images.* All that's left to do is to click **OK**. After a couple minutes of calculation and tomfoolery, Photoshop Elements generates the nearly seamless panorama pictured in Figure 12-46. Okay, it's not perfect, but it is amazing.

If the Keep as Layers check box is activated when you exit the Photomerge dialog box, Elements will render each photo to a different layer. This can be helpful if you want to adjust a particular photo independently, but it comes at an expense. Keep as Layers cancels the Advanced Blending option, and therefore produces less satisfactory results. Unless you have a very particular reason for doing otherwise, leave the Keep as Layers check box turned off.

Figure 12-46.

Having arrived at a reasonably successful stitched panorama, you might be ready to call it a day, close this book for the last time, and get on with your life. (Life beyond this book—is there such a thing?) Or, possibly, you're wondering what you could ever do with the oddly curving image on your screen. If you want to see how to turn this image into something printable, read on.

9. *Rotate the image.* The Editor workspace offers a great function for reversing the curvature of an image. Unfortunately, it works vertically, not horizontally. So, to fix what ails this serpent, we first need to rotate it. Choose **Image→Rotate→90° Right** to turn the image onto its side.

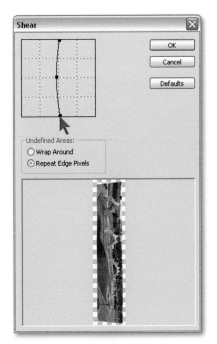

Figure 12-47.

10. *Apply the Shear filter.* Now it's time to apply one of the simplest, oldest, crudest, and most practical distortion functions available to Elements. Choose **Filter→Distort→Shear** to display the tiny dialog box with the squalid, entirely inadequate preview pictured in Figure 12-47.

Okay, enough bellyaching—here's the best way to approach our tricky but fetching serpent:

- Turn on **Repeat Edge Pixels**. This prevents the filter from wrapping pixels from one side of the image to the other.

- See that vertical line at the top of the dialog box? Adding and moving points along that line bends the image. The problem with our image is that its middle bends up—or to the right when on its side. So click in the middle of the line to add a point. Then drag that point three or four pixels to the left. That's right, *just three or four screen pixels*. The Shear filter is absurdly sensitive, so *very* slight changes produce big effects.

- Drag the top point one pixel to the right. Sounds crazy, but that's enough to add some lift to what will be the left side of the panorama.

- Drag the bottom point two pixels to the right.

If you're feeling ambitious (or merely fussy), you could try adding a few more points to the line. But given that single pixel movements equate to about 10 percent of bend in the image, you're not likely to achieve much more control. When your dialog box looks more or less like the one in Figure 12-47, go ahead and click the **OK** button.

11. *Un-rotate the image.* Choose **Image→Rotate→90° Left** to return the image to its original landscape orientation. Figure 12-48 shows the much more acceptable results.

Figure 12-48.

12. *Crop the image.* Press the C key to select the crop tool. Drag around the opaque portion of the image. The idea is to preserve as much of the image as possible, especially above the serpent where the space is tight. So feel free to press Ctrl+⊡ or Ctrl+Alt+⊡ to zoom in nice and tight. When you're confident that you've cropped the image with all the care of a mother burping her newborn, press the Enter key to accept the results.

Figure 12-49.

13. *Flatten the image.* The Photomerge command delivers a single layer against a transparent background. Frankly, that doesn't do us any good; it just prevents us from saving the panorama to some common file formats. So choose **Layer→Flatten** to fuse the layer into a flat image file.

14. *Save the panorama.* After all this work, you'll want to save the results. Choose **File→Save** or press Ctrl+S. Name the file "Serpentmerge" or something equally clever and trademarkable. Then set the **Format** option to **JPEG** (*.**JPG**; *.**JPEG**; *.**JPE**). Click the **Save** button, and then click **OK** in the JPEG Options dialog box.

The figures on this page show the merged, sheared, and cropped result. You might be able to make out some slight alignment problems in the close-up view (Figure 12-49), but seen from a distance (Figure 12-50), it looks great.

Congratulations! You've sewn up a sea serpent and polished off a book to boot. Time to give yourself a well-deserved break. But before you do, don't forget to take the last quiz. Otherwise, how will you know what you know?

Figure 12-50.

WHAT DID YOU LEARN?

Match the key concept in the numbered list below with the letter of the phrase that best describes it. Answers appear upside-down at the bottom of the page.

Key Concepts

1. Creation
2. Video CD
3. Update Creations
4. Header and footer
5. Done
6. Create a PDF
7. Add Text
8. Banner
9. Photomerge
10. Light box
11. Advanced Blending
12. Cylindrical Mapping

Descriptions

A. One of the sharing choices for several creations, this option generates a file that you can distribute online or output to a printer.

B. The "poor man's DVD," this low-resolution format offers stereo sound and the same frame rate as U.S. television.

C. The only Elements creation type that you access through the Editor, this function lets you stitch photos together into a continuous panorama.

D. If your Photomerge suffers from the "bow tie effect," this option can help unknot it.

E. This command in the Services panel of the Preferences dialog box ensures that all components of the Creation Setup wizard are up-to-date.

F. Adobe's catch-all term for any media project that includes one or more images.

G. This Web page feature doesn't appear in most Web photo gallery styles, but any information that you enter into it can be used elsewhere on the page.

H. Unused images are placed in this portion of the Photomerge interface.

I. These photo album options add customizable text to the top or bottom of every page except the title page.

J. With several creation types, clicking this button on the Share screen saves the creation to the photo browser.

K. This Photomerge feature helps smooth rough transitions in your final panorama.

L. Click this button to add holidays to a wall calendar.

Answers

1F, 2B, 3E, 4I, 5J, 6A, 7L, 8G, 9C, 10H, 11K, 12D

INDEX

UNLEASH YOUR POTENTIAL
Take your skills to the next level

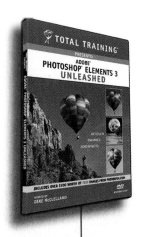

TOTAL TRAINING PRESENTS:
Adobe® Photoshop® Elements 3 Unleashed

Hosted by Deke McClelland • 6 hours on DVD-ROM • All project files included

PLUS–Over $100.00 worth of **FREE** images from PhotoSpin

Now that you know the basics, learn how to unleash the unbridled power of Photoshop Elements 3, for either the PC or the Mac! Learn advanced techniques, dramatic effects, and industry tips and secrets that will give your images that professional look you've always wanted. Work along with Deke on the installed project files. Take your skills, and your software, to the next level. (PC & Mac)

"Deke McClelland has the gift of talking clearly, teaching, and showing."
GARY MILLER
ALASKAN APPLE USERS GROUP

TOTAL TRAINING PRESENTS:
Digital Video & Adobe® Premiere® Elements

Hosted by Brian Maffitt • 3 hours on DVD-ROM • All project files included

PLUS–Over $100.00 worth of **FREE** footage from ArtBeats

Transform family memories into polished, professional quality DVDs and Web clips that you will treasure for a lifetime. Industry expert Brian Maffitt will open your eyes to the possibilities of this exciting new medium, starting with a quick review of the basics and ending with advanced techniques, including tips and secrets used by the pros. (PC only)

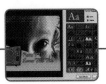

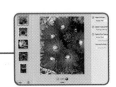

www.totaltraining.com/pse3/1on1 | 800-561-6589

SAVE 10%

 TOTAL TRAINING™

Adobe®
Solutions Network